D0596999

Alternatives to Growth—I:

A Search for Sustainable Futures

Contributors

Robert Allen
International Union for
Conservation of Nature
and Natural Resources
1110 Morges
Switzerland

Elise Boulding
Sociology Department
University of Colorado
Boulder, CO 80302

Herman Daly
Department of Economics
Louisiana State University
Baton Rouge, LA 70803

Joan Davis
Swiss Federal Institute for Water
Resources and Pollution Control
8600 Dubendorf
Switzerland

Earl Finkler
Planning Consultant
4452 E. Holmes
Tucson, AZ 85711

Jay W. Forrester
Sloan School of Management
M.I.T.
Cambridge, MA 02139

Edward Goldsmith, Editor
The Ecologist
73 Molesworth Street
Wadebridge, Cornwall
England

Bruce Hannon
Center for Advanced Computation
University of Illinois at Urbana
Urbana, IL 61801

Hazel Henderson, Co-Director
Princeton Center for Alternative Futures
60 Hodge Road
Princeton, NJ 08540

Jean Houston, Director
Foundation for Mind Research
Box 600
Pomona, NY 10970

Jacob Javits
U.S. Senator from New York
Senate Office Building
Washington, D.C. 20510

Maurice LaMontagne
The Senate, Centre Block
Ottawa, Canada

Amory Lovins
Friends of the Earth
9 Poland Street
London W1V 3DG

Samuel Mauch
INFRAS Consulting
Dreikönigstrasse 51
CH–8002 Zürich
Switzerland

Donella Meadows
Environmental Studies Department
Dartmouth College
Hanover, NH 03755

John Tanton, President
Zero Population Growth
Route 4, Box 272
Petoskey, MI 49770

John Todd, Director
The New Alchemy Institute
Woods Hole, MA 02543

Alternatives to Growth–I:

A Search for Sustainable Futures

edited by
Dennis L. Meadows

Papers adapted from entries to the 1975 George and Cynthia Mitchell Prize and from presentations before the 1975 Alternatives to Growth Conference, held at The Woodlands, Texas.

Ballinger Publishing Company • Cambridge, Massachusetts
A Subsidiary of J.B. Lippincott Company

International Standard Book Number: 0—88410—069—3 (Cloth)
0—88410—078—2 (Paper)

Library of Congress Catalog Card Number: 77–24148

Printed in the United States of America

Library of Congress Cataloging in Publication Data

Alternatives to Growth Conference, 1st, Houston, Tex., 1975.
Alternatives to growth.

Selection of papers presented at the conference, including 4 prize-winning essays submitted to the Mitchell Prize competition.
Bibliography: p.
1. Economic development—Congresses. 2. Economic policy—Congresses. 3. Social policy—Congresses.
I. Meadows, Dennis L.
HD82.A5496 1975 309.2'12 77–24148
ISBN 0—88410—069—3 (Cloth)
0—88410—078—2 (Paper)

To George and Cynthia Mitchell

Contents

*Mitchell Prize Winner

List of Figures

List of Tables

Preface

> The development of a steady-state economy will be the product of an unpredictable but conscious social evolution in which many ideas will be tried out. However, just as the auctioneer must begin by calling out some specific price, so it seems we must begin by calling out some specific notions about a steady-state economy, even though we know that they are no more likely to be the final solution than the auctioneer's initial price is [1].
>
> Herman Daly

A basic assumption underlying important decisions in all industrial societies is that sustained growth in material and energy consumption is possible, desirable, and even inevitable. There have always been dissenters who have questioned the notion of perpetual growth, and thus of a limitless improvement in personal welfare, on moral or ecological grounds. But their protests have been drowned out by those who have praised the progress achieved through the past two centuries of rapid expansion, and by those who have found growth more attractive than the prospect of redistribution. Whatever its merits, industrialization has been accompanied by environmental deterioration, social disintegration, and the depletion of resources. Growing awareness of these problems now lends great interest to the question, *how might a modern society be organized to provide a good life for its citizens without requiring ever-increasing population growth, energy resource use, and physical output?*

Each of the essays in this volume puts forth a partial answer to this question. In this book a diverse set of authors, representing a number of different nations and disciplines, deals with the varied human activities necessary to design a nongrowth society. These activities range from building solar energy systems, to implementing national planning, to extending human consciousness. Behind each essay is the conviction that designing a steady-state society is not only an intellectually fascinating endeavor, but also one of crucial practical importance.

The events that led to this book themselves indicate the rising public interest in designs for a sustainable society. In 1974 George Mitchell, a Texas businessman, resolved to encourage a more positive, rigorous, and comprehensive discussion of the constraints on and alternatives to growth. He brought together similarly-concerned businessmen, educators, and futurists, and challenged them to help design a ten-year program to define new social options.

Five guidelines were adopted for this effort:

1. The program should not attempt to prove or disprove the limits-to-growth thesis, but should search for the policy implications of a societal transition from growth of population, materials use, and energy consumption to steady state.
2. Directors of the effort should seek out and encourage the participation of the best minds from a large variety of cultural, disciplinary, and ideological perspectives.
3. The emphasis should be on long-term issues, those that will confront mankind over the next thirty years or more.
4. The investigation should emphasize the use of sound empirical data and rigorous analysis to provide viable images of the future.
5. The analysis must acknowledge global interdependencies. But the specific goal of the program should be to stimulate development of new information useful to decisionmakers in the industrialized West, as they work to decide what must be done *by them*, *now*, and *within their own countries*.

From this charter there emerged a plan for a set of international essay competitions to be conducted once every two years for a decade. Each of the best essays on the transition from growth to steady state was to receive an award, called the Mitchell Prize, at a series of five conferences, each held at the end of one competition. Over three hundred papers were submitted to the first contest, and the first four Mitchell Prize winners, along with more than 500 other participants from around the world, attended the first Alternatives to Growth conference in Houston in October 1975.

This book contains those four prize-winning essays by Robert

Allen, Joan Davis and Samuel Mauch, Bruce Hannon, and John Tanton. Also included is a selection of other papers submitted to the competition or presented at that conference. The text is organized into four broad subject areas: Nutrition and Energy in the Steady State, Economic Alternatives in an Age of Limits, The Politics of Equity and Social Progress in a Finite World, and Life-styles and Social Norms for a Sustainable State.

Because there are no disciplines, professional societies, institutes, or publications devoted to the analysis of steady-state options, the Mitchell program seeks to help in establishing a new field. It is thus designed to promote consensus on new research priorities, development of professional standards, and identification of the most creative individuals and the best clients for work on alternatives to growth. Because the growth ethic touches all aspects of life, the program and this book are deliberately broad in scope. Yet there is a unity of purpose and a set of common themes underlying the field and integrating the seventeen papers in this text. The following introduction summarizes those themes, and a brief summary before each of the four sections describes the focus of the papers that follow, their genesis and interrelationship. At the end of the volume are provided short biographies of each contributor, a schedule of reports presented at the 1975 conference, and a short bibliography of related publications by each author.

Organizing the prize competition, conducting the conference, and preparing the book required a great deal of work from my collaborators, and extraordinary patience from each of the authors. Of particular importance was the effort of John Naisbitt, who helped design and administer the first conference and Mitchell Prize competition, Coulson Tough and Joseph Kutchin, who managed the legal, financial, and promotional aspects of the conference; Robert Sweeney, Margery Boichel, and Marion McCollom, who helped me select the papers, edit the texts, and administer the publication process; and Jean Graf and Barbara Ferraro, who patiently retyped the several drafts of this manuscript.

I believe the resulting volume provides an exciting summary of current thought about the dimensions and imperatives of the steady state. Of course the chapters presented here do not offer total solutions to the social problems that motivate the Mitchell program, but they warrant optimism about the prospects for finding solutions. The papers suggest that the concept of zero material growth need not be the source of anxiety; instead it can be the stimulus leading to identification of new personal and social goals much more feasible and attractive than those that are currently pursued. The analyses presented here also justify hope that the paths to a sustainable society remain obscure, not because they are impossible to find, but because so little effort has been spent in searching them out.

Dennis Meadows

Plainfield, N.H.
April, 1977

Introduction

Dennis L. Meadows

> A stationary condition of capital and population implies no stationary state of human improvement. There would be as much scope as ever for all kinds of mental culture, and moral and social progress; as much room for improving the Art of Living and much more likelihood of its being improved, when minds cease to be engrossed by the art of getting on [1].
>
> John Stuart Mill

This book and the four volumes to follow are not intended to justify the notion of "limits to growth." Their purpose is to explore the implications of the limits thesis for decisionmakers at various levels in the Western world: teachers, family heads, leaders of nations, and directors of multinational organizations are among those influenced by declining physical growth rates. Many texts have put forth the case for developing a steady-state society, for example, John Stuart Mill's *Principles of Political Economy* [2], Harrison Brown's *The Challenge of Man's Future* [3], the *Ecologist's "Blueprint for Survival"* [4], Donella Meadows' *The Limits to Growth* [5], Dennis Pirages' and Paul Ehrlich's *Ark II* [6], and Herman Daly's *Toward a Steady State Economy* [7].

The limits thesis is by no means universally accepted; important debates still rage on issues ranging from the purpose of human life to the magnitude of the globe's ultimate carrying capacity. *However, the development of steady-state ethics, laws, institutions, and technologies is required today—it is not mandated only by the prospect of some distant, global, Malthusian collapse.* Many individuals, institutions, and even world regions are already confronted with essentially zero growth in their population, economic output, or use of specific energy, mineral, and land resources. In almost no instance are the resulting problems being dealt with effectively.

Some nations, accustomed to the growing use of oil imports to provide more energy, now face bankruptcy if they do not learn how to stabilize their use of fossil fuels. Rapidly falling population growth rates in some Western nations already pose daily problems. Industry in those countries must learn how to cope with a constant and aging work force. Schools must develop policies to remain solvent and innovative even though new student enrollments are now constant or declining. National social security schemes must find new ways to avoid bankruptcy while financing the support of a growing proportion of retired citizens. Whole sectors of the economy must develop appropriate responses to saturation in demand for the goods they are equipped to provide.

If these and many other contemporary problems associated with zero material and demographic growth are to be solved, new goals and procedures must be developed for decisionmakers who now consider their organization's annual rate of growth to be the preeminent index both of their own personal success and their potential for coping with future problems. While anthropologists give us some insights into the role of religion, economics, and population control in traditional, steady-state communities, those bucolic examples are of little obvious relevance to an industrialized, urbanized, mobile, energy-intensive society. Neither theoretical studies nor practical experience currently offer much assistance to those in Western nations forced to negotiate a transition from growth to steady state.

Herman Daly's book is one of the few important contributions to this dilemma, and it is from his introduction that I borrow a definition of the steady state:

> By "steady state" is meant a constant stock of physical wealth (capital), and a constant stock of people (population). Naturally these stocks do not remain constant by themselves. People die, and wealth is physically consumed—that is, worn out, depreciated. Therefore the stocks must be maintained by a rate of inflow (birth, production) equal to the rate of outflow (death, consumption). But this equality may obtain, and the stocks remain constant, with a high rate of throughput (equal to both the rate of inflow and the rate of outflow), or with a low rate [8].

This definition clearly states the necessary conditions for a *steady state*, but it does not specify the attributes of a *sustainable state*—that is, one consistent with global limits and also acceptable to the broad spectrum of individuals and institutions whose sustained compliance with diverse ethics, laws, and norms is required to make any social system viable. Reliance on continuous physical growth certainly makes any system unsustainable, but attainment of a steady state does not guarantee that a society is either intrinsically worthwhile or sustainable.

The goal of a sustainable steady state forces attention to ways of making zero material growth consistent with equity, personal liberty, cultural progress, and the satisfaction of basic physical and psychological needs. Even if levels of population and capital are constant, there are still many degrees of freedom in determining the appropriate magnitude of the flow through each physical stock, the degree of social equality, the rate of innovation, the form of the political system, the tradeoff between size of population and degree of material well-being, the nature of religion, art, science, recreation, education, commerce, and law.

At present it is easier to specify what attributes of society are *not* necessary to a steady state than to define what *is* required. For example, nothing in the definition of a global steady state implies either an equal or an unequal distribution of wealth or income across members of the population. Growth has increased equity in some regions and worsened it in others. It seems likely that zero growth will also be associated with a variety of distributional patterns. However, those who believe that a steady state is mandated by physical or institutional limits typically also believe that a modern society with great inequities cannot be politically stable over the long term. Thus they argue that the richer areas of the globe should begin now to end their period of material growth, while working internationally to raise consumption levels in the poorer regions.

Neither is there any reason to believe that a steady state must be technologically or culturally primitive. Historians traditionally recognize the Tokagawa period in Japan as witnessing several centuries of scientific and social sophistication within a nation that had little population or economic growth [9]. Indeed, greatly increased understanding of natural and social processes will be essential in bringing population and resource use into balance with the constraints of the planet.

Some demographers have correctly objected to the goal of a perfectly steady state, because natural fluctuations in biological and physical systems will always prevent attainment of absolutely constant levels in any population or material stock. But the idea of a steady state need not imply a perfectly static system. At the micro level, individuals and institutions will continue to pass through life cycles of growth and decline. At the macro level, it is only necessary that rates of change be significantly lower than those that persist today. Whether the overall growth in population and material stocks is slightly positive at some times and slightly negative at others is unimportant. It is only essential that the value system of the society direct activities toward attaining a *constant level* that is believed to be desirable and sustainable, rather than toward achieving a *positive growth rate*.

Other analysts have pointed out that a true steady state would be one that used no nonrenewable resources, since perfect recycling is impossible. Again, such a strict definition is neither intended nor useful. Any foreseeable steady state will include the use of nonrenewable resources, but at greatly reduced rates that leave virgin materials available to society over many generations, rather than just a few decades. Under these circumstances, technological advance and market forces will gradually shift to the use of those minerals economically available in greatest abundance. Compensation for lower consumption of finite resources will come from greatly increased reliance on renewable materials, from the design of products that are efficient and long lived, and from increased preferences for activities that require few materials and little energy.

There is also nothing inherent in the notion of a steady state that implies the necessity for a specific form of government. The type of political institutions most appropriate for each region depends much more on that region's cultural heritage than on the rate of change sustained by its population and capital stocks. It is clear that none of today's governments has the precise institutions required for it to attain a sustainable state. Material growth is still viewed as a panacea by communist, capitalist, socialist, totalitarian, and democratic states alike. Debate over the nature of changes to be introduced into each region's political institutions will be an enduring, difficult, and exciting part of the effort to conceive of sustainable societies.

It has been suggested that man's basic psychological processes require material growth and change. Of course, for most of man's existence on earth he has lived in steady-state societies. Today's dependence on material growth springs not from within the individual human psyche, but from the operations of current political and economic institutions. A sense of progress probably is essential to man's intrinsic well-being, but there are many dimensions of progress perfectly consistent with a material steady state. Indeed, it is these activities—music, art, learning, athletics, and spiritual development, for example—that most distinguish man from other species.

Finally, attainment of a steady-state system would not imply a loss of variety. To be sustainable over long periods, any social system must be consistent with local environmental conditions and with the ethics, norms, and institutions of its members. The challenge is not to conceive of *the* steady-state society, but of many steady-state options. It is unlikely and undesirable that all societies would choose the same goals or the same timing to guide their transition policies. There is no fundamental reason why an individual, family, corporation, community, or region could not begin shifting to a steady-state existence while it remains interdependent in important ways with others that continue to pursue growth.

While no specific social or technological trait must characterize all possible sustainable societies, the seventeen papers in this collection do reiterate a set of common themes. No paper contains reference to all of them, and some authors may even disagree with a few items on the following list. But a number of basic perspectives and beliefs permeate the thinking in most of these chapters.

1. Contact with the natural ecosystems is necessary to the physical and psychological well-being of man; it cannot be artificially reproduced by him. It is therefore important to preserve natural systems and to reestablish man's physical linkage with natural processes and cycles.

2. Social experimentation and learning are exciting processes to be encouraged, not avoided. Mankind has many cognitive capacities that have yet to be tapped. More human challenge, innovation, and satisfaction may come from trying to live within limits than from striving to transcend them.

3. In the richer countries, the accumulation of wealth is serving as an inferior surrogate for those environmental, psychological, and social amenities that are increasingly eroded in the process of producing more material goods. This vicious cycle can be broken not by producing more, but by redistribution and the substitution of more humane for materialistic goals.

4. The wealthy areas, particularly the United States, have a special potential, hence obligation, to develop steady-state policies within their own borders before promoting birth control, conservation, political reform, or value change for other countries.

5. The progressive centralization of economic power, political influence, and scientific expertise is detrimental to the global system's long-term viability. These trends deprive the individual of more and more power over the vital functions required to ensure his own humane and secure existence. They also rob the total society of its innovative potential and resilience. Smaller communities should resume more control over local norms and services and should strive

for greater self-reliance. Technological development should be redirected toward the production of machines and procedures that are diverse and matched to the needs of small communities rather than international markets.

6. A sustainable society requires economic and political decision-making processes capable of making significant short-term sacrifices in the pursuit of longer-term goals. Expressed in other terms, current decisions must be based much more on consideration for their distant consequences.

7. Few significant problems have purely technical solutions. Technologies must be designed in concert with changes in social values, goals, laws, and institutions. Because human institutions will always be prone to human error, society requires technical systems that can fail safely rather than those that must be fail-safe.

8. Market-determined prices and the desire for financial profit will remain important in the process of resource allocation in the Western economies. But the market system must be extended and augmented to accord intrinsic merit to the conservation of nonrenewable resources, and to ensure greater equity.

9. Changes in one component of society at a time, enacted on the margin, rarely solve important problems and often exacerbate them. There are no universal, quick, or easy solutions to the problems that make the current system unsustainable. A long, slow process of thorough revision lies ahead, guided by an image of a viable global system that can only be achieved in the distant future.

10. A sustainable state can only be attained by individual initiative and change. A large number of personal decisions, each influenced by shared, feasible images of the long-term future, though individually insignificant, can begin a process of change that will reinforce itself, gather momentum, and gradually produce a sustainable system that meets mankind's basic needs.

Of course the contributors to this book retain many areas of disagreement, including imperfect consensus about the precise policy implications of the guidelines above. But it is significant that individuals working in isolation from each other, within widely differing institutional and disciplinary contexts, should adopt a common set of themes so different from those implicit in most of current corporate and public sector policy.

It is easy to label these notions naive or utopian. But they seem less naive than proposals that global problems can be solved by intensifying those policies that produced the difficulties in the first place. They are also less utopian than the belief that current physical growth rates can be maintained for another generation. Since practically no resources have been invested in tracing the implications of the beliefs summarized above, it is premature to judge them. They are not offered as quick, easy, or unambiguous cures for the many problems that hold most of mankind in poverty and threaten the survival of the species. But they are fresh, challenging ideas, whose elaboration could provide some attractive alternatives to those that will result from the present preoccupation with material growth.

Part I

Nutrition and Energy in the Steady State

Introduction to Part I

Dennis L. Meadows

> Humanity's survival may ultimately depend upon a fundamental redesigning of the ways in which societies are sustained. A major reordering is called for—as dramatic in its own way as the societal changes brought about through industrialization and the massive use of petroleum. Beyond the need for limiting growth lies a need for a conceptual change in how planetary resources are regarded.
>
> *John Todd*—Chapter 2

No conception of a steady-state society will have wide-spread appeal unless it promises sufficient food, energy, and materials to meet basic needs. Much of mankind is today malnourished and materially impoverished; that fact is one source of strong political pressure to sustain growth. But if one hundred years of fabulous success in expanding production have still not eliminated material want even in all the richest countries, poverty clearly does not stem only from lack of growth. Indeed, current global energy, food, and material production would be adequate, if equally distributed, to provide all members of the human race with a decent standard of living. Poverty results from inefficient resource use, the production of wasteful goods and services, and unequal distribution of opportunities, wealth, and income. Analysts interested in developing a sustainable society must deal with material wants in those terms.

The Western nations began their development with relatively low populations and abundant nonrenewable resources. Under those circumstances, capital-intensive, large-scale industrial installations, efficient in using labor but wasteful of resources, were effective in raising living standards. But those technologies are hardly appropriate now, either for the rich countries during the mature, resource-scarce phase of their economic life cycle, or for the Third World with its enormous populations and limited resources. The example of China, the persuasive case made by E.F. Schumacher in his book *Small Is Beautiful* [1], and the growing bankruptcy of many nations have raised doubts about the necessity and even the possibility of meeting material want through indefinite growth in material and energy consumption by large, labor-saving, capital- and energy-intensive installations.

Intermediate technologies, conservation of nonrenewable resources, more sophisticated use of renewable resources, and redistribution offer an alternative path to material sufficiency that deserves exploration. That alternative is the focus of the four papers in this part. Each chapter examines some aspect of the relation between population and food or energy. Each suggests that society can satisfy its important goals with material production levels very much lower than those currently thought to be necessary. The first paper considers problems of global food availability; the latter three work out their analyses within the context of the United States. But all support the case that conservation, a shift in social demands, and a reorientation of technological objectives may be morally, physically, and economically preferable to simply increasing the scale of the current productive system.

In her chapter, Donella Meadows briefly summarizes the current basis for consensus on the magnitude and the determinants of the world food problem. She distinguishes four different ideological approaches to the design of food-aid policy: the Western ideal of free-market trade, the environmentalist concern for physical limits, the socialist pursuit of equality, and the approach based on faith in the positive effects of the industrialization process. She proposes a new, composite model that draws together the essential components of the first four to provide new insights into the nature and the implications of longer-term population-food interactions. From this model and an explicit statement of her own goals and ethics, she puts forward a comprehensive proposal for United States food policy, one designed to improve global nutrition levels and to bring an equitable steady state in population and food production.

She advocates programs to reverse the industrialization of agriculture and to distribute food more equally. She feels that zero population growth should be sought, with the United States taking the lead by announcing population stabilization as a domestic goal and then by linking foreign aid in health programs to the design and acceptance of effective, locally-defined birth control measures abroad.

Finally, the United States should strive to reduce consumption of food and resources and should be more humble about its ability to specify the precise development policies that will most effectively raise living standards in poorer parts of the world.

Beyond its substantial contribution to the food debate, Professor Meadows' paper illustrates a mode of causal analysis that cuts efficiently into a difficult socio-technical issue, so as to expose the basis for disagreement and to identify the grounds for consensus on policy initiatives.

John Todd describes the progress the New Alchemy Institute has made in developing integrated life-support systems for a decentralized society and summarizes the goals and values that lie behind its current work.

The Institute has developed a backyard fish farm-greenhouse, using solar-trapping structures to maintain a year-round growing environment for fish and vegetables. Careful experimentation has led to the development of a closed-loop aquatic system capable of sustaining a large fish population. Solar ponds, translucent pools above ground, have been proved capable of filling the dual role of heaters and algae producers for fish cultivation. Todd also describes a radical new wind-power technology based on sophisticated hydraulics and currently scheduled for testing on Canada's Prince Edward Island.

Todd's article ends with no forceful suggestions—his approach is rather to provide concrete demonstrations and then to let people come to their own conclusions. But the chapter is a strong challenge to several well-established views. It calls into question the necessity for large, uniform food-producing systems that require enormous amounts of external financing, expert management, fossil fuels, pesticides, and herbicides. Todd's work also belies the stereotype that decentralized, small-scale technologies must be unsophisticated, inefficient, or laborious to operate.

Finally he challenges the notion that the answer to want lies in the use of more resources. Instead, he shows that needs may be met by extracting more final value from physical inputs, by using renewable rather than nonrenewable resources, and by giving people the opportunity and the responsibility for achieving their own material sufficiency directly. Once a person has regained control over and some security in the basic requirements of life, Todd suggests, he or she may also develop a new consciousness about man's links to and constraints from the natural world.

Amory Lovins argues for an end to the preoccupation with declining oil and gas reserves as the principal limits to growth in energy consumption. He systematically traces out meteorological, economic, geopolitical, managerial, and ethical factors that will act to limit ultimate energy availability, even if infinite replacements are found for current fuels. He suggests that present efforts to develop large-scale, centralized electrical generating plants, principally fueled by uranium, may simply be infeasible even if all their technical problems were solvable. His fear is that continued focus on building larger and more centralized energy-supply systems may require so much time and so many resources that other, more attractive options are ruled out.

As an alternative approach, he sketches out the advantages of small-scale, coal-fired and solar-heated facilities, technologies much more tolerant of human failure than nuclear reactors. He concludes that the best policy is a deliberate move to zero energy growth in the United States by the mid-1980s.

Bruce Hannon's Mitchell Prize-winning paper is a nontechnical description of an energy input-output model developed to trace the flow of energy through each sector of the United States economy. He is motivated by his belief that little time can be lost in beginning the transition to a sustainable energy system based on renewable resources. Conservation is seen as the key to this transition, but his studies point to three difficulties inherent in the effort to achieve a voluntary reduction and stability in energy demand.

— Consumers tend to use more energy as their incomes rise.
— Industry has strong incentives to replace capital and labor inputs with cheap energy.
— Money saved through reduced direct purchases of energy tends to be spent on goods and services that embody energy indirectly.

Hannon describes two policy instruments available within the current economic system to ameliorate those forces: energy taxes and energy quotas or rationing. While each can be useful, he concludes that the ultimate solution will also require increased altruism by consumers, who must reduce their own material consumption to improve prospects for their disadvantaged contemporaries and for posterity.

Chapter 1

The World Food Problem: Growth Models and Nongrowth Solutions

Donella Meadows

INTRODUCTION

Two United Nations conferences in 1974, one in Rome and one in Bucharest, emphasized that most nations are aware of the interlocking nature of two major global problems: food shortages and rapid population growth. The World Food and Population Conferences dramatized the extreme difficulty of formulating effective policies for dealing with these problems on either a national or international level. The issues are complex, they involve areas of great political sensitivity, and "experts" and ordinary citizens alike express widely divergent viewpoints about the severity, causes, and possible cures of what is often called the "world food crisis."

If all those concerned with feeding the global population could agree upon any one thing, it would be that there is a problem, present or potential, that requires some action. No one seems to think that the food situation will get better if it is simply left alone. There is vast disagreement, however, about what food policies would be most effective and who should carry out those policies. Grain reserves, improved plant strains, increased aid, no aid, population control, market control, agribusiness control—all are seriously advocated. In the face of such disagreement, can any policy possibly be designed and implemented with sufficient diligence to produce

The original version of this paper appeared in *America in an Interdependent World*, David A. Baldwin, ed.; this version is included by permission of the University Press of New England, © 1976 by the Trustees of Dartmouth College.

a perceptible result? Is there any way to resolve the many interpretations of the world food problem, to understand and analyze the interrelationships between food consumption and population growth, and to develop somehow a comprehensive and effective food-population policy?

I believe the controversy about food policy arises from three major areas of difference: the boundaries of space and time within which the contenders view the problem, the theories by which they explain the causes of the problem, and the values underlying their respective choices of preferable costs and benefits. Each individual combines these three factors into a consistent mind-set or world view that influences not only his policy position, but also the facts he perceives as relevant and the questions he asks in order to elicit new information. Unfortunately, in debates about food or population policy the participants seldom state clearly which boundaries, theories, and values determine their positions. As a result, their arguments rarely address real disagreements, produce any mutual understanding, or lead to a basis for joint action.

In this paper, I will briefly review some statistics that describe the current rate and distribution of growth in food and population, and then make explicit the boundaries, theories, and values behind several different proposals for action the United States, as the world's largest grain exporter, might take to alleviate global hunger. Since I feel that no one can view this problem without some preestablished mind-set, I will not pretend to be an objective commentator on the various positions presented. Instead I will define my own position, which is based on an ecological and systems-theory world-view, within the same framework applied to the others. My hope is that this approach, simultaneously analytical and personal, may help future debates on this difficult issue proceed more constructively in two ways: by exposing some deep and implicit points of disagreement for further evaluation and discussion, and by recognizing in opposing arguments some points of consistency and agreement upon which an acceptable policy might be built.

THE POPULATION-FOOD SITUATION

Any summary of the "facts" of a controversial case must be considered suspect, since each participant in the controversy tends to notice and emphasize those aspects of the situation that seem to confirm his preferred conclusion. The problem is compounded when the subject is as difficult to quantify as the one under consideration here. Many nations do not take a regular census, very few have reliable vital statistics, and no uniform standards exist for measuring agricultural output, estimating the amount of product that bypasses the cash economy, or ascertaining the actual daily diets of most of the world's people. In other words, "facts" on the world food situation are scarce. Nevertheless, any policy discussion must proceed from some perception of the present state of the problem. The following summary is based on standard statistical sources, primarily from the United Nations and the United States government. All numbers cited should be assumed to reflect reality, but they are not necessarily accurate.

In mid-1975 the world population was estimated at about four billion persons. The global population was then growing at an average rate of about 1.9 percent per year (derived from an estimated average birth rate of about 3.2 percent per year, minus an average death rate of 1.3 percent per year) [1]. The total addition to the world population in 1975 numbered approximately seventy-eight million people. The rate of increase is estimated to have been 0.4 percent per year in 1800, 0.6 percent per year in 1900, and to have reached 1.9–2.0 percent per year only in the 1960s and 1970s [2]. This recent acceleration in the global population growth rate is due primarily to a decrease in the human death rate rather than an increase in the birth rate.

Population growth is not evenly distributed geographically or nationally. About 80 percent of the population increase in 1974 took place in the nonindustrialized countries of the world. Perhaps twelve million persons were added that year to the population of India, fourteen million to China, and a little over one million to the United States.[a] Population growth rates varied from 3.2 and 3.1 percent in Mexico and Pakistan to 0.3 percent in West Germany and Great Britain. The historic trends that have led to this widely varying set of birth, death, and growth rates will be discussed under the theory of the demographic transition later in this paper.

The average human being requires about 2,220 vegetable-equivalent kilocalories of food per day to survive [3]. In 1974 the total world grain production was approximately 1,200 million tons [4], or enough to supply about 2,900 vegetable-equivalent kilocalories per person per day. When nongrain foodstuffs are added to this total, it is clear that food production in that year would have been sufficient to support the world population at well above the subsistence level, if it had been distributed evenly.

[a]The natural increase (excess of births over deaths) in the United States population from February 1974 to February 1975 was 1.225 million. Added to that was a legal net inmigration of 395,000.

Total world food output has increased slightly faster than the population over the last decade. About half of this expanded output has come from extending cultivated land and half from better yields on land already cultivated [5]. Both area and yield increases required inputs of numerous other resources. For example, the 34 percent increase in world food production from 1951 to 1966 was accompanied by a 63 percent increase in yearly expenditures on tractors (in constant dollars), a 210 percent increase in use of fertilizers (by weight), and a 300 percent increase in expenditures on pesticides (in constant dollars) [6].

The figures quoted so far have been in terms of world totals and global averages. But food, like population, is by no means evenly distributed. In the late 1960s, the average Indonesian received 2,070 vegetable-equivalent calories per day, while the average Frenchman received 11,120. The typical American consumes more than five times the grain equivalent consumed by the typical Indian [7]. Over the last decade, total food output has grown at about the same rate in both the nonindustrialized and the industrialized regions of the world. In the industrialized regions this growth has amounted to a 15 percent increase in food per capita, while in the nonindustrialized regions, because of rapid population growth, average food output per capita has increased very slightly, if at all [8].

BOUNDARIES IN SPACE AND TIME

The differing emphases placed on growth in food production, as opposed to alternative policies, result in part from the conflicting time horizons by which different analysts delimit the problem. The solutions to malnutrition that appear feasible between now and the next harvest are obviously different from those that might be employed by the end of the century or beyond. A five-year policy view would center on measures such as grain buffer stocks, incentives to farmers, or organization of famine-relief efforts. A fifty-year view would encompass an entirely different set of factors: population stabilization, new technologies, and new ways of distributing land, labor, and food output.

Long or short time horizons can lead to differing assessments of the situation, and so can wide or narrow space horizons. Those who, by the mandates of their official duties, are concerned primarily with the United States agricultural system may be worried about a revisitation of unmarketable surpluses and falling prices. Those with a global view tend to be concerned about areas of periodic drought or about the effect of higher prices on families already spending 80 percent of their income on food.

Neither of the two extreme viewpoints, the short-term domestic or the long-term global, can be labeled incorrect, and any wise policy-maker must keep both in sight. However, in the case of food and population, I feel that the balance between the long and short term, and between domestic and international concerns, should be shifted more toward the long-term global view. The necessity for a global perspective is becoming more apparent daily. All the factors that contribute to greater international interdependence—proliferation of nuclear weapons, spreading communication and transportation networks, geographic concentration of energy and mineral resources, and the impossibility of isolating a starving nation—require a concern larger than any national boundary. The necessity of a long-term view arises from the very nature of food production and population growth processes. A global change in either food consumption habits or methods of food production would require shifts in capital stocks and in social attitudes that could be accomplished not in years but in decades. And the processes of population growth and stabilization are properly viewed not in decades, but in human generations. Furthermore, the problems of agricultural shortage and overpopulation are easier to prevent than to solve once they have actually appeared. Transporting improved seed strains by ship is cheaper than carrying famine relief supplies by helicopter. Overgrazing and erosion can be avoided rather easily, but can be reversed only at great cost. Thus a long-term perspective would be indicated not only by a moral concern for future generations, but also by the practical fact that some problems are inherently slow to develop and easier to prevent than to cure.

The rest of this paper and its final recommendations reflect my own preferences for wider time and space horizons in the consideration of food and population policies. This emphasis does not imply that short-term or domestic concerns should or will be ignored. However, since the balance of concern already leans so far in that direction, I will argue for the broader longer-term view, confident that no argument can make that view completely dominant, but hoping that the scale may be tipped in that direction.

THEORIES OF POPULATION-FOOD INTERACTION

Four distinct theories seem to underlie the most commonly recommended policies for dealing with the world food problem.

The Western Economic Model

Price and supply fluctuations are inevitable, as long as the forces of nature—weather and pests—prevail. Price changes are the only way necessary production adjustment, to meet supply and demand changes, will come in an incentive economy. . . . The whole question of food security finally comes down to the farmer and whether he will produce, whether he and his family benefit by producing, and whether he has the physical and financial tools available [9].

In the Western capitalist nations, classical microeconomic theory often forms the basis for policy. A model of the dynamics of this theory is shown schematically in Figure 1–1.[b] Food supply and food demand are assumed to be brought into balance by the operation of a free competitive market, where food price is the central variable. If supply of any commodity decreases relative to demand, the price will rise. Higher price has two effects—it decreases demand and provides both the funds and the incentive for increased investment in agricultural production. Both these effects automatically bring supply and demand back into equilibrium, with no need for regulation by any governmental authority.

On the supply side, investment can be allocated to any of three factors that increase production—development of new cultivated lands, increase in annual agricultural inputs (fertilizers, pesticides, energy), or increase in longer-lasting agricultural capital (tubewells, tractors, irrigation systems). Investment in research that produces new knowledge may be considered equivalent to investment in long-lasting capital. As land, agricultural inputs, and capital increase, so does food supply, eventually leading to a decrease in food price. Thus, if supply is low, price goes up, and new production is encouraged. The system is also self-correcting in the opposite situation. If

[b]The diagrammatic conventions used in Figure 1–1 and subsequent figures are as follows:

An *arrow* indicates a causal influence of one element on another.

A *plus sign* indicates that the influence is direct—as the element at the tail of the arrow increases, the element at the head of the arrow also increases (if the first element decreases, the second decreases). For example, as food demand goes up,food price also goes up.

A *minus sign* indicates an inverse relationship—as the first element increases, the second decreases; or if the first element decreases, the second increases. For example, as food supply goes up, food price goes down.

The diagrams do not specify the exact quantitative relationships between elements, nor the rate of response of one element to another (the response may be instantaneous or very much delayed). The diagrams represent only rough sketches of underlying models that may be very complicated.

Figure 1–1. The Western Economic Model

In the Western Economic Model, food supply and food demand are assumed to be brought into balance by the operation of a free competitive market, where food price is the central variable.

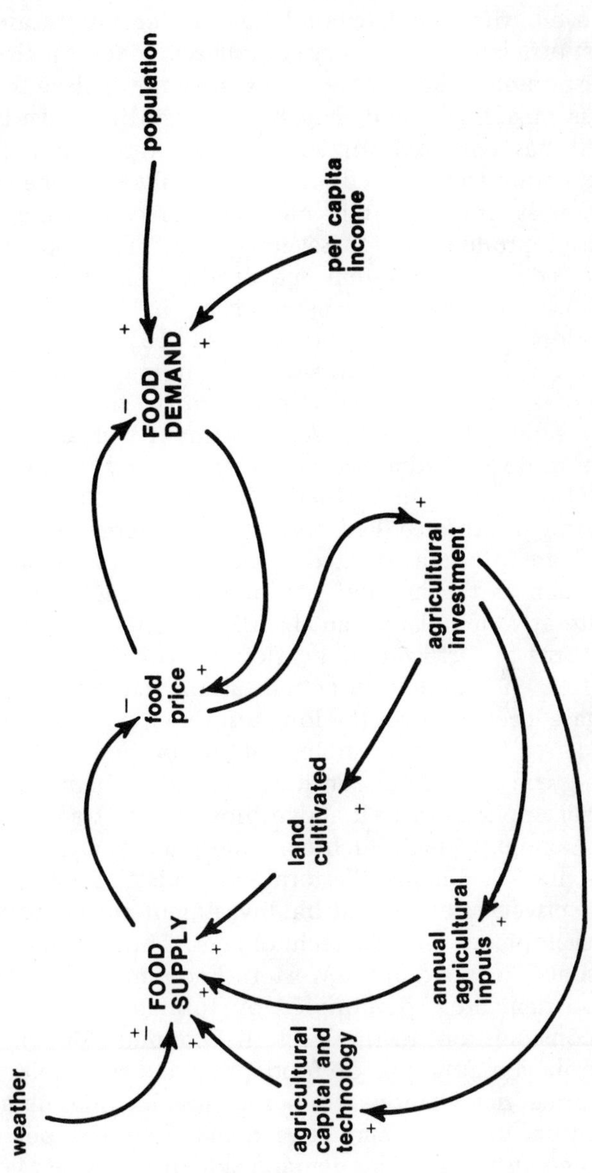

supply is high relative to demand, food price falls; then production is curtailed and new investment is postponed.

Several factors may interfere with regulation from the supply side of the market system. Weather adds uncertainty to the expected output, even when land, capital, and other inputs are utilized with utmost efficiency. The other complicating factor is the delay in farmers' response mechanisms. Farmers may not believe that a new higher price is meaningful and may not change their investment decisions until it has persisted for some time. Agricultural production can respond fully to increased investment only after one harvest cycle, at the soonest. Investment in new land or capital may not yield any increased production for several years. This response delay in the supply side of the system can produce alternate over- and undercompensation by suppliers, resulting in the well-known periodic oscillations in many commodity prices [10].

Those who favor the Western Economic Model are usually well aware of another potential impediment to the responsiveness of the supply side of the system. As investment increases, producing more and more output, diminishing returns to any of the three factors of production may be met—that is, a given amount of additional investment might produce less and less additional output. Diminishing returns are often associated with the approach to some physical limit, such as the amount of potentially arable land in a region, or the rate at which plants can absorb nutrients from the soil. Diminishing returns to fertilizer application, for example, are well understood and often encountered in actual farming situations. However, on an aggregate level and over the long term, diminishing returns have often been offset by new technological approaches. The "miracle grains" of the green revolution continue to produce higher yields at levels of fertilizer application well above those where traditional grains reach their maximum yield. Such examples, and analysis of actual historic trends, have led many Western economists to assume that limits to the effectiveness of agricultural investment are surmountable through the development of new technologies. Thus diminishing returns are not usually included in the Western Economic Model.

Food demand is determined by total population and per capita food consumption. In the Western Economic Model, per capita consumption is a function of food price and per capita income. When food price rises relative to per capita income, demand decreases. Population increase stimulates demand, unless per capita income simultaneously falls. The demand side of the system is not perturbed by unpredictable factors such as weather, but demand may shift to reflect variation in population, per capita income, or consumer tastes.

Response on the demand side is relatively rapid, since it depends on consumer decisions, not on biological or physical processes such as crop growth or construction of capital equipment.

Since it is more rapid, demand adjustment usually plays a major role in maintaining the supply/demand equilibrium. However, regulation from the demand side becomes both undesirable and ineffective under one important set of conditions. When food price rises so high that a mere subsistence diet absorbs a large fraction of per capita income, consumers have no more freedom to reduce consumption in response to higher prices—in economic terms the elasticity of demand approaches zero. Under these conditions, supply shortages can be alleviated only by alterations on the supply side, or by malnutrition.

According to the Western Economic Model the interplay of supply and demand, if allowed to proceed without interference, will produce efficient allocation of resources to food production and efficient distribution of food to consumers. Policies based on this model tend to work toward freeing the market mechanism, both by restricting monopolization on the supply side and by opposing government interference in the market. From this point of view, interference is only permissible if it is directed toward correcting known imperfections in market operations. Buffer stocks can help smooth out weather fluctuations. Public support of agricultural research, low cost capital improvement loans, and better information systems can shorten response delays on the supply side. However, direct donation of food to poor countries would be counterproductive, because food aid would lower price, thereby destroying local incentive to invest in increased production capacity.

The Western Economic Model, focusing on the continuous and mutual adjustment of supply, demand, and price, represents the agricultural system as self-regulating and self-maintaining. According to this model, short-term adjustments keep the system at or near a desirable equilibrium at all times, so a long-term view is unnecessary. Population growth affects the agriculture system, but as long as the growth is slow enough, the system can accommodate it. More recently, however, many people who favor the Western Economic view have recognized that the system operates unsatisfactorily when supply is near subsistence and regulation from the demand side breaks down. Thus some free-market supporters advocate measures to slow population growth or to provide sufficient employment to the destitute to give them consuming roles in the market. In general, however, the Western Economic Model is associated with optimism, and not with strong or urgent recommendations to change the food-population system. The food problem, as seen through this model, is solvable. If any governmental action is called for, it should only involve protection of market mechanisms, support of basic research, administration of food buffer stocks, dissemination of new technologies, and in the poorest regions widespread employment opportunities combined with family planning [11].

The Environmental Model

> The land of every nation has a limited carrying capacity. The exact limit is a matter for argument, but the energy crunch is convincing more people every day that we have already exceeded the carrying capacity of the land. We have been living on "capital"—stored petroleum and coal—and soon we must live on income alone.
>
> The harsh characteristics of lifeboat ethics are heightened by reproduction, particularly by reproductive differences. The people inside the lifeboats of the wealthy nations are doubling in numbers every 87 years; those outside are doubling every 35 years, on the average. And the relative difference in prosperity is becoming greater [12].

Environmentalists focus their attention on real physical quantities, rather than on social artifacts such as money or prices. What matters to them is the amount of food actually available per person, which is most simply determined by the food supply and the number of people among whom the food must be shared. The world food problem can be solved either by increasing the amount of food, or by decreasing the number of people.

As does the Western Economic Model, the Environmental Model assumes that food supply will grow with increased capital, annual agricultural inputs, and land development (see Figure 1–2). However, the Environmental Model includes important limits to all these factors and therefore to the total amount of food that can be produced. Land expansion is limited by the total area of cultivable land on the earth. Capital and inputs are limited by their impact on the environment and by the ultimate resource base, the terrestrial deposits of metals, phosphate rock, fossil fuels, and other nonrenewable resources. Increasing agricultural investment as a policy may increase food supplies in the short term, but only by pushing the entire global system nearer to its limits and thereby making further increases in the long term more difficult. The economic concept of diminishing returns to investment plays a very important role in this model. Though the absolute limits may be far away, and technology may permit a closer approach to them, the cost of approaching the limits is seen to become higher and higher. In this model, technology

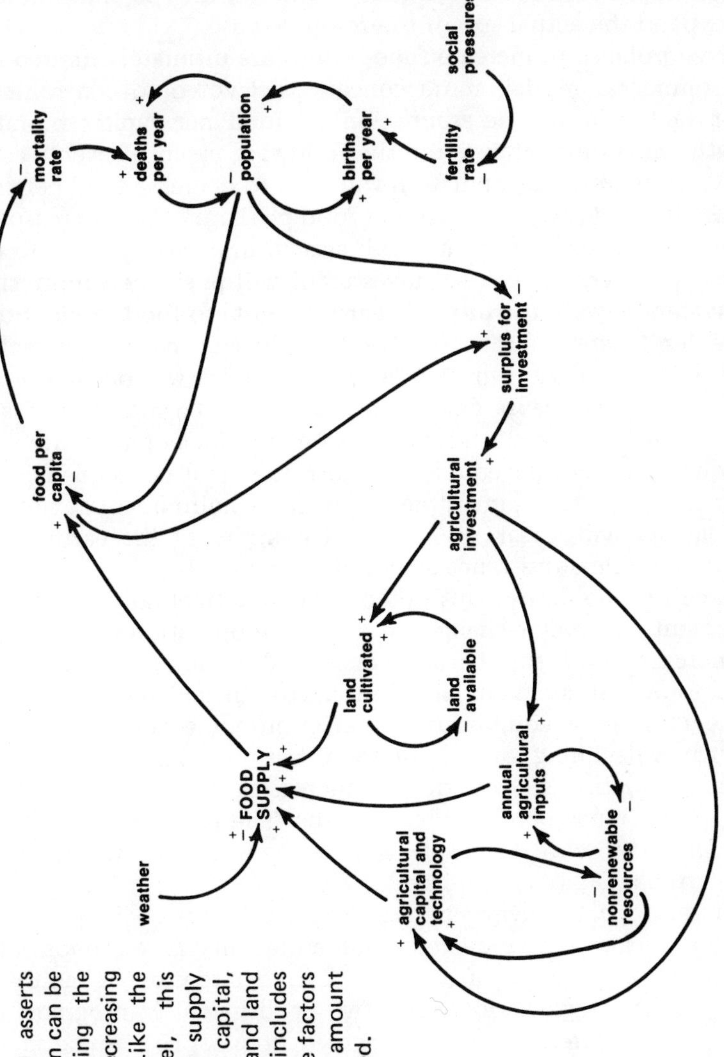

Figure 1–2. The Environmental Model

The Environmental Model asserts that the world food problem can be solved either by increasing the amount of food, or by decreasing the number of people. Like the Western Economic Model, this model assumes that food supply will grow with increased capital, annual agricultural inputs, and land development; however, it includes important limits to all these factors and therefore to the total amount of food that can be produced.

is primarily a tool for shifting from one resource to another; it does not expand the actual size of the resource base.

Since policies to increase food output are ultimately limited in the Environmental Model, more concern is devoted to controlling the other factor in the determination of food per capita: population growth. Environmentalists see the following chain of events as most likely. An increasing population will tend to decrease food per capita, all else being equal. A decrease in food per capita for any reason provides a social impetus to increase agricultural investment. However, in the long term, increased investment will push the supply side of the system toward the ultimate earthly limits to food production. As those limits are approached, food production can no longer keep pace with population growth, and food capita will decline. Finally, malnutrition will cause death rates to rise. When mortality has risen to the point where deaths balance births, the population will stop growing. The natural equilibrium and the final consequence of increasing agricultural investment, in the environmental view, is a population living near the productive limits of the earth, held in check by a near-subsistence standard of living.

Since no one desires this outcome, environmentalists see the need for urgent and major changes in the food-population system. Efforts to increase food supply are considered counterproductive, since more food just increases population growth and hastens the onset of the undesirable equilibrium. A better outcome can only be reached through a declining, or at least stabilized, population. Since no one favors population stabilization by increasing deaths, the only acceptable policy must be to decrease births. The more quickly the birth rate falls, the more favorable will be the ultimate balance between population and global resources.

Therefore, the Environmental Model calls for social pressures of one sort or another to decrease human fertility. The proposed fertility reduction policies range from further extension of family planning [13] through various incentive or disincentive programs [14], to "mutual coercion, mutually agreed upon" [15]. Sometimes the environmental argument is also accompanied by opposition to short-term measures for decreasing mortality, including food aid [16].

Environmental policies are focused on the long term and are aimed at increasing the resource/population ratio in order to improve standards of living and quality of life. Thus in addition to supporting population-control policies, environmentalists tend to favor less wasteful resource consumption habits. They promote technologies such as solar energy conversion or organic farming that rely upon renewable, rather than nonrenewable, resources. They would encourage deliberate conservation long before the market signals the need for it. They prefer living within the limits of the earth, rather than trying to push those limits outward.

This basically conservative world view leads to a radical policy position. Since the food-population system will not naturally approach a desirable state, large changes must be made. Sociocultural patterns must be altered to favor small families. Resource allocation decisions should not be made by short-term market forces alone. The world food situation is a symptom of a larger problem: the material needs of the human population are straining the sustainable physical capacity of the earth. The only solution is to stop the growth in those needs by stabilizing the human population and its material consumption.

The Socialist Model

> One of the greatest outrages of the present food situation is the excuse it has provided for muddle-headed apologists for capitalism to blame it all on the "population problem." . . . The very existence of this phenomenon described as "agricultural Malthusianism" represents the greatest *potential* leap forward in the whole of human history—it holds the promise of food productivity on a scale such that *food would become so plentiful it would not be possible even to give it all away*. But under capitalism, such a development would be intolerable. . . . The solution to the crisis of world food production can only be realized through its reorganization as social production for human needs . . . [17].

If the market system is irrelevant to the environmentalist point of view, it is anathema to the socialists. They believe the most important human goal is the provision of enough food and other goods to meet basic human needs, regardless of price or freedom of the market. The Socialist Model contains some elements in common with the two models described previously, but with some important additions and deletions (see Figure 1–3).

The central concern of the Socialist Model is distribution, primarily of the means of production (capital and land) and secondarily of the output from production (food, services, and manufactured goods). The capitalist free-market system and economic exploitation by the rich is blamed for perpetuating inequities in distribution. These inequities are assumed to be the cause of the present food problem. The millions of deaths due to hunger each year could all be prevented by a different economic world order, according to the socialist. Since the amount of food per capita available in the world today is well above subsistence, the food crisis should be solvable

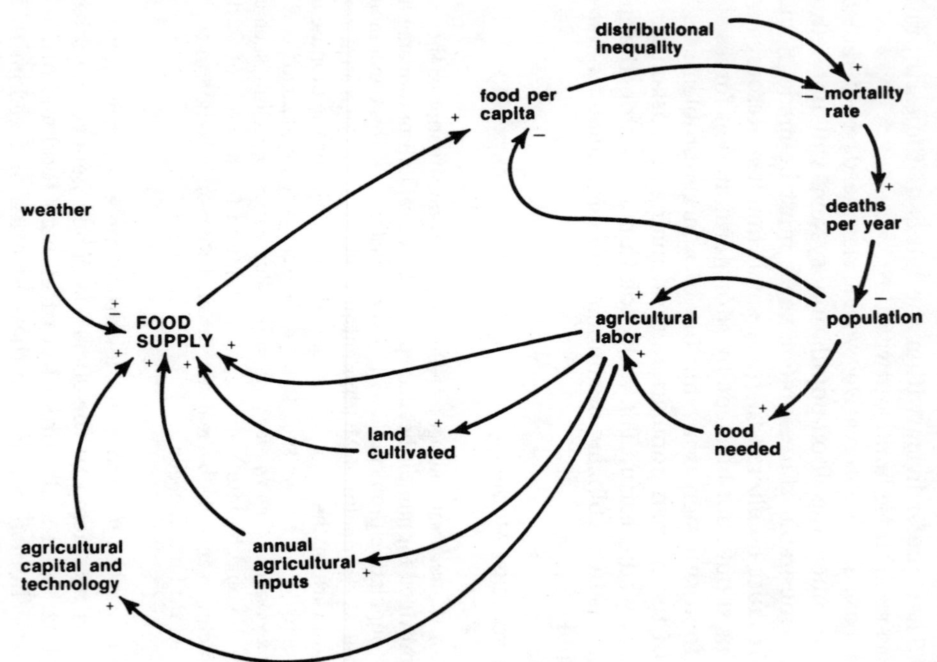

Figure 1–3. The Socialist Model

The central concern of the Socialist Model is distribution, primarily of the means of production. The capitalist free market system and economic exploitation by the rich is blamed for perpetuating the inequities in distribution which are assumed to be the cause of the present food problem.

through redistribution. The mortality rate could be reduced, not by growing more food, but by distributing it differently.

Environmentalists would answer this socialist argument by pointing out that in the long term decreasing mortality rates by redistribution would increase population, which would decrease food per capita. Socialists would agree that a capitalist regime could produce this outcome, but under a socialist system of production the additional population would provide more labor, which would be used efficiently to increase output. Food supply would grow faster than the population, and food per capita would rise. In a society truly devoted to socialist principles, population would naturally become stabilized at a point long before diminishing returns to labor would set in. In fact, many of the socialist nations of the world are now experiencing population growth rates very near zero.

No concept of global limits appears in the Socialist Model, nor does any concern for overpopulation. Of crucial importance is the addition of human labor to the factors of production. In fact, the Socialist Model elevates labor to make it the primary factor upon which all others depend. Since each new mouth comes equipped with two new hands, overpopulation is unthinkable. Recently some socialist thinkers have also embraced the idea of "intermediate" or small-scale, labor-intensive technology [18] which places even more emphasis on labor as the key to increasing agricultural output.

Policies favored by those who see the world through the Socialist Model center around economic reorganization and redistribution. Population policies are viewed with suspicion as distractions from the real issue, and perhaps as disguised genocide. Attempts to increase production under a capitalistic free market are considered exploitive. However, socialists are generally enthused about new technologies that increase output, especially technologies that are dependent on the productive factor accessible to everyone—labor—rather than on heavy concentrations of privately-owned capital. Socialists vary in the degree to which they would favor complete restructuring of the capitalist system, but most of them would agree that measures such as land reform, food aid, progressive taxation, village-level agricultural education, and alteration of international terms of trade are steps in the right direction.

The Demographic Transition Model

In order to bring the birth rate down, in order to create the conditions in which people see their own interest in having smaller families, we need a continuation of economic development, particularly in the developing

> countries. In my opinion, it is essentially impossible . . . to expect people in these countries to behave in a way that will stabilize population . . . unless they have sufficient economic development so that they see some reason for doing so [19].

The theory of the demographic transition is based upon the demographic history of nations that have undergone the industrial revolution. The historic pattern of birth and death rates for industrialized nations is taken as the pattern that all nations will follow. In the now industrialized countries, the birth and death rates were once relatively high and the population growth rate was slow. As economic development slowly permitted better living conditions, more reliable food supplies, and increased medical knowledge, death rates decreased. In the case of Sweden, the crude death rate dropped gradually from 25 deaths per 1,000 persons per year to 10 deaths per 1,000 per year over a period of 120 years.

As the death rate decreased, the birth rate followed, but even more slowly, typically with a lag of thirty to fifty years behind the death rate. The widening gap between birth and death rates during this intermediate period meant rapid population increases for many decades. Only in the twentieth century have the birth rates of the industrialized countries falled to about the same level as the death rates, so that the rate of population growth is again relatively slow.

This historic pattern of change from high birth and death rates to low birth and death rates is called the "demographic transition." The demographic transition has been observed in some form in all countries that have industrialized, although its onset, rate of development, and conclusion vary greatly [20]. The basic assumptions of the Demographic Transition Model are shown in Figure 1–4.

The Demographic Transition Model is primarily concerned with two social forces that are assumed to reduce birth rates. First, a decrease in mortality, especially infant mortality, will cause parents to perceive that they are less likely to lose a child. Since they need not have so many children to achieve their desired family size, the number of births will fall. Second, an increase in all aspects of industrialization and modernization changes the perceived costs and benefits of having children. The Demographic Transition Model assumes, and many current spokesmen for the Third World affirm [21], that large families in pre-industrial societies are needed and wanted. Children are desirable as inexpensive labor and as providers for old age, and, of course, as sources of all the noneconomic, psychic, and cultural benefits associated with children everywhere. Furthermore, in nonindustrial societies children are not regarded as a burden; they do not

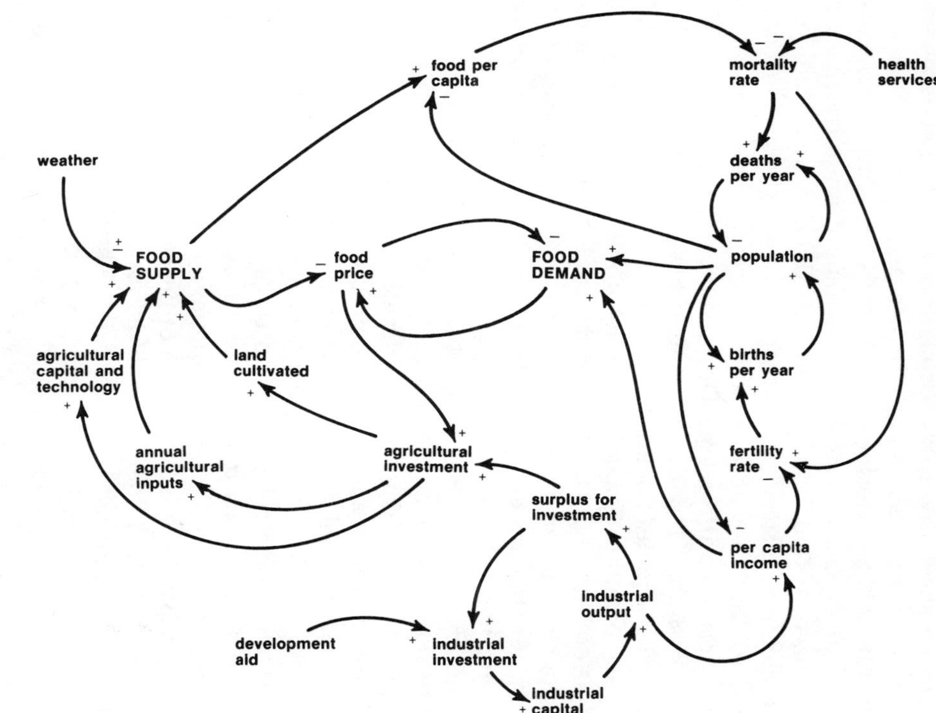

Figure 1–4. The Demographic Transition Model

The Demographic Transition Model illustrates the dynamics of a historic pattern of change in industrialized nations from high birth and death rates to low birth and death rates. Two social forces are assumed to reduce birth rates as industrialization occurs: a decrease in mortality, particularly infant mortality, and changes in the perceived costs and benefits of having children.

require much space, food, education, or other material expenditures, and their care is often shared by a large extended family or clan. As a society industrializes, however, the benefits associated with children decrease and their costs increase. The family must become mobile and urbanized to find industrial jobs, so the extended family breaks up. The children, instead of working on a family farm, must become educated so that they too can qualify for the new jobs. Alternate forms of social security emerge. On balance, children are still regarded as highly desirable, but the concept of having only as many as one can "afford" becomes dominant.

The Demographic Transition Model holds out hope for treating both the food supply and the food demand problems with the same set of policies. Increasing industrial output leads to smaller family size, and also to greater food output, through all the technologies dependent upon industrial capital.

The policies that follow from this theory are clear. First, child mortality should be decreased through public health services to start the first part of the demographic transition. Food aid will also help bring down child mortality and is therefore desirable. Second, industrial investment should be emphasized to stimulate the second part of the demographic transition, the decrease in fertility. Family planning may play a part in this second stage, but only after the desire for smaller families has been awakened by economic development. Before then, large families are desirable, and the population will not regard family planning as acceptable or necessary.

The Demographic Transition Model is usually considered more consistent with centralized, large-scale technology than with labor-intensive intermediate technology, for two reasons. First, modern capital-intensive technologies may permit more rapid increase in industrial output. And second, labor-intensive technology, with its emphasis on family-scale techniques, might maintain the desire for children as contributors to the family economic base, thereby delaying the birth rate decrease expected in the Demographic Transition theory.

A Composite Model

The four models presented here are often viewed as mutually exclusive and basically inconsistent. For example, at the World Population Conference in Bucharest no agreement was reached between Western economists and environmentalists on one side, calling for population control, and socialists and demographic transitionists on the other side, calling for redistribution and economic development. On other issues, such as resource conservation, the Western Economic and Environmental Models would lead to very different and seemingly irreconcilable conclusions. Still other issues, such as identifying the best path toward economic development, would cause those who favor the Socialist and Demographic Transition Models to part company.

When informed and reasonable people consistently maintain very different models of theories of the same underlying reality, it seems probable that no one of those models can be totally right or totally wrong. Each model is probably a correct description of part of the real system. Much can be learned by trying to combine the important insights of all the models into a composite or holistic view. I shall present such a composite model here, starting with the Western Economic Model and adding to it important concepts from the other models (see Figure 1–5).

The central structure of the Composite Model is the price mechanism of the Western Economic Model. The price mechanism can produce fine-scale adjustments of food supply and demand in the short term and eliminate the necessity for extremely detailed centralized planning. Relatively high food price is a signal that stimulates investment in agricultural factors of production and attracts labor to agricultural jobs, allowing increased food production, as long as reasonable returns to land, labor, capital, and annual inputs can be realized.

When the assumptions of the Demographic Transition Model are added to the Western Economic Model, a reassuring picture of the total food-population situation emerges. With the market to correct supply/demand imbalances in the short term and industrial growth to increase supply while stabilizing population in the long term, the food problem might be viewed as a temporary problem that is about to solve itself.

For some parts of the world, over some historical periods, the combined Western Economic–Demographic Transition Model provides a sufficient explanation of what has actually occurred. Industrialization has proceeded relatively smoothly, birth and death rates have decreased, and food scarcities have been temporary or nonexistent. The diminishing returns of the Environmental Model and the distributional problems of the Socialist Model do not seem important in representing the history of these industrialized nations. However, all nations have not followed this pattern, and future patterns need not necessarily resemble historical ones. In order to decide whether the Socialist or Environmental Models can increase the applicability of the Composite Model to the future and to the poorest areas of the world, it is necessary to examine more carefully

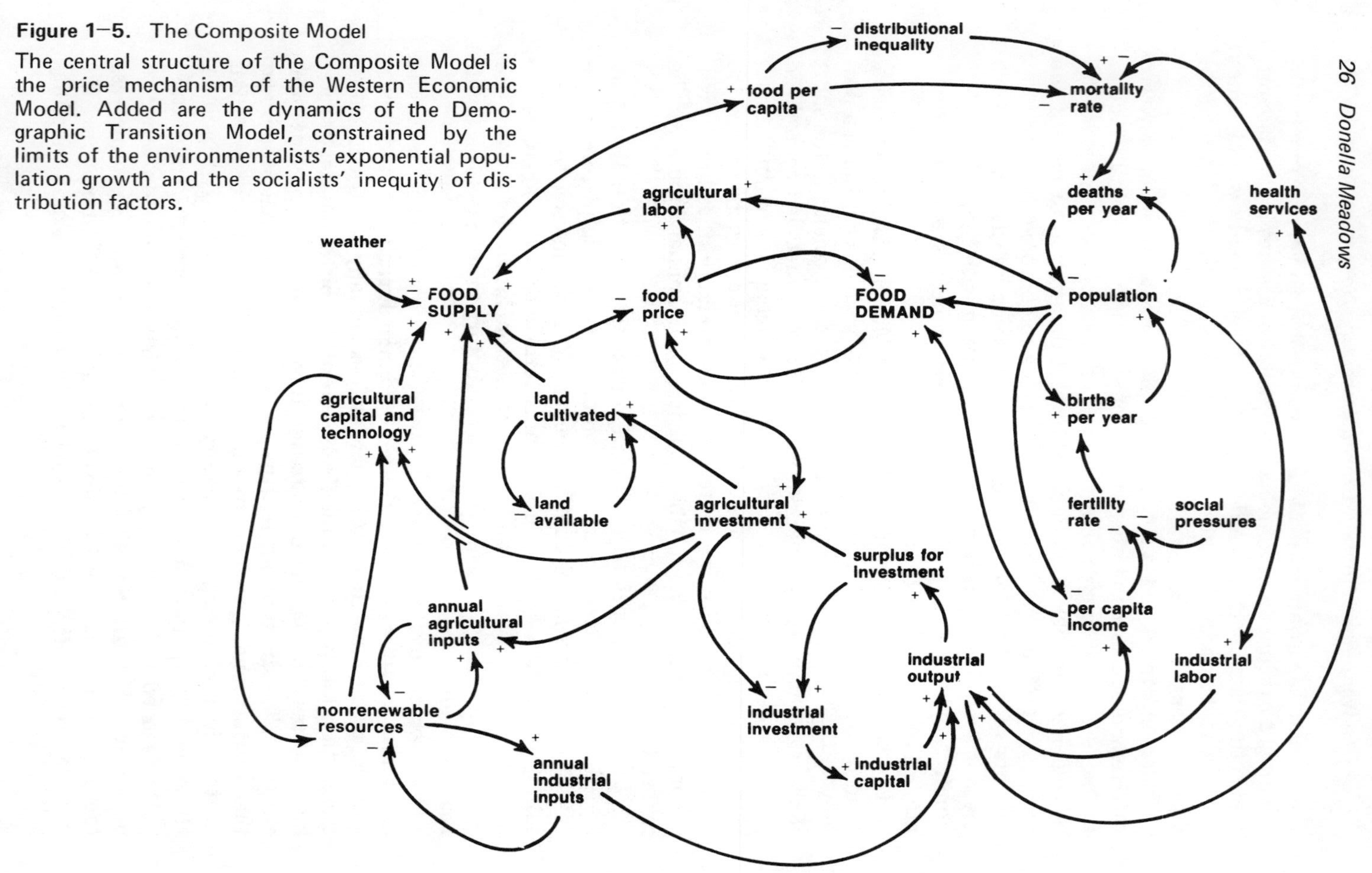

Figure 1–5. The Composite Model

The central structure of the Composite Model is the price mechanism of the Western Economic Model. Added are the dynamics of the Demographic Transition Model, constrained by the limits of the environmentalists' exponential population growth and the socialists' inequity of distribution factors.

the assumptions behind the Western Economic and Demographic Transition Models and the nature of the environmental limits and distributional inequalities that might alter those assumptions.

A point-by-point comparison (see Table 1–1) of the demographic situations in the nonindustrialized countries during their historical transitions and in the currently-industrializing countries indicates that the Demographic Transition Model may not provide a sufficient guide to future development patterns [22]. The current demographic situation in the nonindustrialized nations is not entirely analogous to that experienced by the West before and during its period of industrialization. Health services generated by industrial development in the richer countries have been transferred to the nonindustrialized countries and have altered the traditional relationship between the rate of population growth and the state of industrial development. Rapid population growth slows the rate of growth of per capita income, literacy, and industrial employment, retarding the social changes that seem to bring down birth rates. The larger population demands more food. In response to hunger and high food price, either the market mechanism or social planning diverts output from industrial investment to agricultural investment, further slowing industrial growth. The insertion of externally-generated health services in the race between growing population and growing capital has shifted the balance away from economic growth. The balance could be restored by the addition of externally-generated capital, but only if the returns to that capital are reinvested in the economy of the developing country, and if the entire population benefits from the additional output generated.

When these considerations are added to the Composite Model, the resulting theory provides both a broader description of reality and a more uncertain forecast of the future. The model now accounts for imperfections in the market mechanism and interruptions in the demographic transition. It predicts that industrial growth and demographic transition could proceed much more slowly in the future than they have in the past. This result is certainly not inevitable, but it is particularly likely if governments assume that an automatic and effortless demographic transition will solve the population-food problem, or if the capital-intensive approach to development is emphasized over the labor-intensive, or if death rates are lowered with no coordinated attempt to lower birth rates. In other words, the Demographic Transition Model, like the Western Economic Model, is valid only under special circumstances. Those circumstances include a tight linkage between industrialization and mortality, an industrial labor demand that absorbs displaced farm laborers, an internal rein-

Table 1–1. Comparison of Demographic Situations of Industrialized and Industrializing Countries

A point-by-point comparison of the demographic situations in the non-industrialized countries during their historical transitions and in the currently-industrializing countries indicates that the Demographic Transition Model may not provide a sufficient guide to future development patterns.

Industrialized Countries	*Industrializing Countries*
Decreases in death and birth rates accompanied profound social change. The process of industrialization altered nearly every aspect of the family: its organization, its economic base, its importance relative to other social institutions, and the costs and benefits of having children. All major social changes take time; this one typically extended over 100 to 200 years.	The decrease in death rate has preceded, not accompanied, the deep economic and social changes that result from industrialization. Birth rates are still high and can be expected to remain high, because the traditional family structure is still basically unchanged. The completion of the economic and social development that may bring birth rates down in these countries can be optimistically expected to require at least 50 more years.
During the transition the widened gap between birth and death rates resulted in a multiplication of the pre-industrial population by a factor of 4 to 5.	The populations of the nonindustrialized countries have already increased by factors of 4 or 5 in this century, with much of the transition still ahead of them. Assuming rapid birth rate decreases in the near future, these countries will experience a total population multiplication by at least 10 before their transition is complete.
In many European countries the population increase was counteracted by significant outmigration to the New World.	Many of the industrializing areas are already densely settled, and there are essentially no New Worlds left to absorb their population growth.
The maximum rate of population growth in the demographic transitions of the European countries was typically 1 to 1.5 percent per year. Sweden's fastest actual population doubling took 95 years; Great Britain's 70 years; Japan's 60 years.	Typical population growth rates now are 2 to 3 percent per year in the nonindustrialized countries, or about twice the rates ever experienced in Europe. Mexico's last population doubling took 20 years; Ceylon's 25 years; Taiwan's 20 years.
In most European countries the transition began from a birth rate that was already moderate—30 to 35 births per thousand persons.	The crude birth rates at the beginning of the transition are considerably higher than those that pertained in Europe—40 to 50 per thousand instead of 30 to 35 per thousand.
Because of the moderate birth rates, the fraction of the population under age 15 and economically dependent was rarely more than 35 percent at any time during the transition.	The population of dependent children in these countries is typically 45 to 50 percent of the total population.

vestment of the returns from capital, and a fairly even distribution of the increasing goods and services of the growing economy. Few of these conditions now prevail in the nonindustrialized areas of the world. Therefore distributional constraints and exponential population growth should be added to the model.

What about environmental limits? Must they also be included in policy considerations, or are they so far removed that they can be ignored? A few demographic forecasts are needed before that question can be answered. If the entire world population completes the demographic transition, so that the average global birth rate reaches replacement level by 1980 or 1985 (a development rate that most people would consider impossible), the stationary global population would total 6.4 billion. In the more likely event that the global completion of the transition takes until the year 2040, the final population will total more than fifteen billion [23]. That number has meaning only in relationship to the earth's carrying capacity, the number of people that could be sustained indefinitely by the ecosystem. If the carrying capacity is well above fifteen billion, the Environmental Model's concepts of diminishing returns and earthly limits can be left out of the Composite Model. Policies can then concentrate on establishing the proper conditions for promotion of industrialization, redistribution, and the demographic transition. If an industrialized population of fifteen billion would strain the earth's carrying capacity, however, physical limits should be included in the model and should influence policies derived from it.

Taking into account three basic resources—land, water, and solar radiation—a recent study has estimated an absolute maximum global food yield of 49,830 million metric tons per year [24]. This amount of food would support 217 billion persons at subsistence, or fifty billion at the consumption level of a typical European country today (10,000 vegetable-equivalent calories per person per day). The study assumes widespread improvements in technology, optimum weather, perfect management, perfect distribution, no damage from insects or diseases, no limit to material or energy resources, multiple cropping, no pollution problems, and no loss of cultivable land to erosion or to uses other than agriculture. The authors of this study do not themselves believe that this output is actually achievable, nor desirable from an ecological viewpoint. Let us assume for a moment that it can be achieved, and simply reduce the limit by 20 percent to allow for weather fluctuations. That gives us an estimated upper limit, on the basis of food needs alone, of forty billion persons living at industrialized standards of living.

This physical limit takes into account only land and water resources and only the food needs of the population. It assumes that energy, capital, fertilizers, and all other resources are available to the agricultural sector in whatever quantities are necessary for maximum yield, and also that arable land and fresh water are used only for food production, not for other human needs. If some other resource is more limiting than land or water, or if agricultural resources must be shared with other sectors, the real physical limit will lie below forty billion.

Whatever human economic system prevails, at some point the added cost of producing more food will be considered not worth the added gain. Resources must be used to produce other things besides food. Under any economic system and technology now conceivable, the point where the marginal cost of producing more food exceeds the marginal benefit will lie far short of the actual physical limit. Especially in an industrial society, the economic limit to food production is lower than the physical limit, simply because the list of needs of human societies contains other items than food alone. I would estimate that the economic limit might actually allow the support of about ten billion persons, a guess based on the supposition that the present global mixture of capitalist and socialist economies can support the cost of expanding cultivated land by 50 percent and global average yields by 400 percent over current values. A more careful study, based on considerations of availability of other resources, has actually set this limit at seven billion [25].

Economic decisions are seldom ideal; many human actions are based on motivations other than the desire to allocate resources rationally and equitably to recognize social goals. War, greed, corruption, economic monopoly, mismanagement, and resistance to change are inescapable social realities responsible for limiting the effective use of resources. Resources are rarely optimally distributed to production processes, nor are final products distributed so as to maximize human welfare. Furthermore, the pressures for maldistribution and the opportunities for and costs of mismanagement probably increase as physical limits are approached. Therefore, the social limit to the number of people the world food production system can support must lie somewhere below the economic limit—that is, somewhere below seven to ten billion.

The latter two limits—economic and social—could be raised by social and technological improvements; the physical limit could not, unless the human food supply is drawn from some resource base other than land, water, and sunlight. If the population actually reaches one of the lower two limits, the material standard of living would begin to fall and the resource base would erode. Eventually the aggregate death rate would rise to equal the birth rate and population growth would stop, unless social or technological innovations pushed the limit upward.

This excursion into the realm of earthly limits has been deliberately oversimplified. I have ignored the vagaries of weather, markets, and international politics that complicate the calculations by imposing short-term fluctuations. I have not distinguished the disparate subregions of the earth, some of which are much closer to their limits than others, some of which have been able to push the social and economic limits much nearer to the physical limits than others, and some of which are approaching the limits at a much faster rate than others. Since we can never know physical or social limits exactly, the only reason for considering them at all is to ask whether any limits are conceivably near enough to be included in a policy-oriented model. The estimates and arguments already presented here lead me to believe that some limits may indeed be encountered before a worldwide demographic transition can be completed. Therefore I feel that the constraints of the Environmental Model should be added to the Composite Model.

The Composite Model (see Table 1–2) leads to the following general conclusions about the future world food situation and the policies that may affect it.

Free Market Efficiency. A free market mechanism is efficient in adjusting short-term supply and demand differentials. Therefore policy should be directed to keeping the market mechanism operating and should not duplicate its role by imposing detailed, day-by-day interferences with supply, demand, or prices.

Free Market Limitations. Important long-term forces such as population growth, systematic inequities, and resource limitations tend to push the market system into regions where supply or demand is price inelastic, so that normal adjustment mechanisms are ineffective or unacceptable. Therefore, macro-level controls on distribution and total output are necessary to allow the market to work well.

Population Constraints. In all cultures children are desirable, and parents are likely to desire more than the number required to achieve zero population growth. Populations will grow until some constraint brings birth and death rates into balance. The constraint may be physical, tending to raise death rates, or social, tending to reduce birth rates. Industrialization has historically caused social and economic pressures that reduce birth rates, but not quickly, and not

Table 1–2. The Composite Model Components

When informed and reasonable people consistently maintain very different models of theories of the same underlying reality, it seems probable that no one of these models can be totally right or totally wrong. Each model is probably a correct description of part of the real system. Much can be learned by trying to combine the important insights of all the models into a composite or holistic view.

Western Economic Model

- price as a useful signal of supply/demand imbalances
- use of the market for short-term, incremental adjustments and detailed decision-making
- correction of deficiencies in free market operation

Environmental Model

- importance of diminishing returns to capital, labor, land, and other inputs
- tendency of populations to grow exponentially unless constrained by physical or social pressures

Socialist Model

- importance of labor as a factor of production
- moral and pragmatic necessity for equitable distribution
- reorganization of production through intermediate, labor-intensive, operator-owned technologies

Demographic Transition Model

- coordination of industrial and agricultural development
- role of individual motivations in determining birth rates
- association of industrial development with declining birth and death rates

necessarily to replacement levels. This demographic transition should be encouraged but may also need to be supplemented with direct population policies.

Agricultural Expansion. Considerable expansion of agricultural output is possible, but at a cost in terms of resources needed for other human desires. The marginal cost increases as the level of output increases. Technological advancements may shift the cost from more limiting factors of production (historically, labor and land) to less limiting factors (historically, capital and energy). In general, increased agricultural output should be regarded as an expensive solution to the food problem, to be replaced by other solutions whenever possible.

Distributional Equality. More people could be supported by even distribution of the earth's resources than by current patterns of uneven distribution. Distributional equality may be easier to achieve when resources are abundant than when they are scarce.

Resource Restrictions. The global resource base may not be sufficient to permit a worldwide transition to industrialization, especially given the rate at which the transition is currently proceeding, the present consumption levels in the most highly industrialized countries, and the rates of population growth in nonindustrialized countries. Therefore policies should emphasize resource conservation and efficient resource use.

International Dependence. National economies today are so tightly intercoupled that even those societies farthest from their resource limits must be concerned about societies that are close to their limits, for reasons of international stability as well as morality.

VALUES AND PRIORITIES

One of the first publications of the newly-formed United Nations was the Universal Declaration of Human Rights. This document reads, in part:

> Everyone has the right to a standard of living adequate for the health and well-being of himself and of his family, including food, clothing, housing, and medical care and necessary social services [26].

Similar statements of rights have been issued periodically by various organizations of the United Nations and by many national governments. One of the most recent was released at the United Nations World Population Conference at Bucharest, Romania, in August 1974:

> All couples and individuals have the basic right to decide freely and responsibly the number and spacing of their children and to have the information, education, and means to do so [27].

Declarations of rights are statements of fundamental policy goals, primary objectives that governmental policy should seek above all else. The right to a minimum standard of sustenance and the right to establish a family and determine its size are reiterated constantly in discussions of food and population policy. Yet the Composite Model of the food situation suggests that these two rights may come into conflict with each other, with other human goals, and with the physical laws that govern the earth. Unless by chance families choose to have on the average exactly the number of children required to balance the death rate, or fewer, the right to reproduction could lead to a population at the limits of the earth's resources, with no possibility of a right to sustenance.

If two important goals, such as freedom of reproduction and guarantee of sustenance, are in direct conflict, policies that pursue them both may waste effort at best, and fail to achieve either objective at worst. The essence of policy-making is the choice among conflicting goals. Choices cannot be made without reference to a theory that suggests what the future costs and benefits of a course of action might be, and to a set of values that indicates what is good, what is bad, and how various goods and bads should be balanced against each other. Even if the model or theory of the causes and consequences of the problem is agreed upon, different sets of values may lead to very different policies.

Models and values are certainly not independently learned or chosen. Much of the appeal of a model may stem from its congruence with a particular value set, and the model may then lead to conclusions and observations that reinforce that value set. For instance, the Western Economic Model emphasizes the values of freedom and efficiency more than equity. The Socialist Model sets equity as the highest value, while the Demographic Transition Model emphasizes material welfare and freedom. Of all the models discussed here, only the Environmental and Composite Models suggest a risk to long-term survival and weigh the value of survival against other values that a society might cherish.

I am not aware of any way of determining a single set of values and priorities that is applicable to all persons at all times. Yet each person readily forms an operational set of priorities that guides his or her choices and decisions. Discussion of policy alternatives might be enhanced if people could make their value sets explicit, not to argue their relative merits, but to increase understanding of the various viewpoints within society. To start that discussion, my own primary values, in order of priority, are:

1. survival (of the total social and ecological system);
2. material welfare (up to a level of simple sufficiency, after which this entry goes to the bottom of the list);
3. equity (equal access to other items on the list);
4. freedom (individual self-determination, diversity);
5. efficiency (maximum output per man-hour).

Of course I consider all five of these goals important and worth pursuing. However, my mental model suggests that striving for efficiency could undermine all four of the other values, a sacrifice I would not be willing to make. To me, individual freedom would be meaningless without the first three items on the list; I would give up my personal freedom, if necessary, to obtain survival, material sufficiency, and equity. Equity in poverty does not appeal to me, so I would seek basic material welfare before distributional justice. Survival is necessary before any of the other values can be enjoyed. I would not tolerate a very high risk to total social or ecological survival for any reason, even for one of the other values on the list.

My value set is included here not because it is the best or only defensible one, but because I would like to show what a value set looks like, and because my own policy recommendations depend on it. Some of the policy-relevant conclusions that seem consistent with my value priorities are:

—that the long-term survival of human society, and the stability of the natural system upon which human society depends, should be the highest goal of any policy. Therefore risks to the total system should be minimized, including implicit dependence on as-yet-unproven technologies.

—that since survival has the top priority, the costs of social change are more tolerable than the risk of physical destruction of resources or of environmental integrity. It is far better to develop new social norms and institutions consistent with zero growth than to risk the ecological damage that could result from desperate physical measures to sustain growth.

—that short-term sacrifices, especially material sacrifices, to preserve long-term stability are justified. In accordance with the goal of equity, sacrifices for the future should be borne disproportionately by the privileged of today.

—that the quality of human life is more important than the quantity; and material sufficiency is more important to quality of life than is the freedom to have more than two children. Therefore, the right to sustenance has a higher priority than the right to reproductive freedom.

—that several important aspects of quality of life cannot be measured in strictly economic terms. Therefore decisions should be made on a broader basis than simple economic cost-benefit analysis.

—that industrialization is a means to one end that can improve the quality of life, namely material welfare. It may not be the only means to that end, and it is not an end in itself.

—that in the interests of preserving individual freedom and diversity, intervention by centralized government should be minimal. Intervention is justified only to preserve the three values prior to freedom: survival, basic material welfare, and equity.

PRIMARY POLICY CONSIDERATIONS

In the remainder of this paper, I will attempt to translate these idealistic value statements into general guidelines for United States food and population policy. I shall assume throughout this discussion that the primary purpose of food-population policy is to solve the problem of world hunger, not to gain national or personal political power or to achieve any other short-term, narrowly-bounded goal.

All possible solutions to the world food problem can be grouped into three major categories:

Produce More Food. Both technological and social changes can bring more land into production and increase yields on land already cultivated. These policies aim to move the economic limit closer to the physical limit to food production. Future extensions to non-land-based food production (such as single-cell protein and hydroponics) raise the physical limit itself by substituting other resources, particularly energy, for land. Most current policy efforts fall into this category. They have the advantage of relatively short-term payoffs and of emphasizing technological sophistication, the major asset industrialized countries have to offer. The costs of these policies tend to be economic and environmental, rather than social. They require little change in the way industrial societies are used to doing things, but they demand major revisions in the life-styles of nonindustrialized populations.

Allocate Food More Equitably. In this category fall efforts to control agricultural prices and trade flows, to change nutritional habits, to establish buffer stocks, to provide famine relief, to reduce luxury consumption, and to restructure economic systems. All these policies attempt to move the social limit and, by changing priorities, the economic limit closer to the physical limit. They would allow more people to be nourished, even if food output did not increase at all. These policies could reduce hunger very rapidly, once they were actually implemented. Their costs are almost entirely social and their effect on the environment would be minimal. They require attitude changes, new institutions, and economic readjustment, but probably very little additional economic cost in terms of total investment or resources.

Slow Population Growth. Current efforts to contain population growth are dominated by family-planning programs. A few governments have experimented with rewards or punishments for large or small family sizes [28]. Population-control policies are necessarily long term, and their results may not be visible for decades. Their costs are largely social; they would probably result in new economic and environmental benefits. The aim of population stabilization is to avoid all limits to food production.

Discussions about food and population policy sometimes degenerate into arguments about which of these three options to pursue exclusively. I believe it would be more fruitful to decide which mixture of all three would be best; how much time, research, thought, and investment should be devoted to each? Current policies in most countries seem to concentrate on producing more food, with some emphasis on distributing it, rather than on controlling population. The time horizon, model, and value set I have presented here would suggest that, although all three options must be pursued vigorously, the order of priorities should be reversed. Population control is the only ultimately effective solution, and the one with lowest total costs; therefore, it should receive the most effort. Since population control measures cannot be accomplished quickly, however, redistribution and more efficient food production will be needed to minimize medium-term food shortages. Redistribution can produce almost immediate results with low ecological and economic costs, and it is also morally desirable, according to my values. Therefore, it should receive emphasis second only to population stabilization. Food production, the third priority, should be labor-intensive in order to use the major resource of the most needy countries, and should take into account conservation of energy and natural ecosystems, as well as increased output.

IMPLEMENTATION CONSIDERATIONS

One reason that current policies emphasize technological adjustments rather than socioeconomic adjustments may be that governments have already at hand the mechanisms, institutions, and personnel necessary to implement technological changes. Western governments, in particular, are accustomed to guiding technical activities. When it comes to directing a deliberate change in values, life-styles, or social arrangements, however, current governments have almost no experience and very little imagination. For example, many people can picture government involvement in population stabilization only in terms of direct dictation of individual family sizes, with punitive action for offenders who produce too many children. Visions arise of policemen in bedrooms and of forced sterilization. If Orwellian measures are the only imaginable way to implement population policy, it is not surprising that such policy is carefully avoided. Unfortunately, the very belief that no acceptable social-change policy exists cuts off all discussion of government involvement in social change, and therefore the innovative thinking that might produce acceptable policies is not encouraged.

I would like to discuss implementation considerations here in just enough detail to indicate what directions might be followed. My aim is to outline some possible programs, more to stimulate imagination and generate new ideas than to assert any completeness or uniqueness to the examples I have chosen. The programs will not be limited to foreign policy alone.

Food-population issues, perhaps above all others, are impossible to separate cleanly into foreign and domestic spheres of influence. Domestic food prices may be changed by new export arrangements or massive donations for famine relief. New agricultural technologies can alter the lives of American farmers as well as African ones. The annual increase in the United States population, because of its higher rate of per capita consumption, increases the effective demand on the world food supply by nearly as much as the much higher annual increase in the population of India. Even if the United States were primarily interested in improving the food supply-demand balance in the Third World, its influence might be greatly enhanced by consistent population and food policies at home. As George F. Kennan stated in a speech on foreign policy in 1954:

> Now this problem of the adjustment of man to his natural resources, and the problem of how such things as industrialization and urbanization can be accepted without destroying the traditional values of a civilization and corrupting the inner vitality of its life—these things are not only the problems of America; they are the problems of men everywhere. To the extent that we Americans become able to show that we are aware of these problems, and that we are approaching them with coherent and effective ideas of our own which we have the courage to put into effect in our own lives, to that extent a new dimension will come into our relations with the peoples beyond our borders [29].

Population Policy

In the spirit of the above quotation, I believe that the single most effective policy the United States could implement to promote population stabilization in the world is to announce and seek the goal of population stabilization at home. Population stabilization has already been recommended by the Commission on Population Growth and

America's Future [30], who took into consideration domestic needs alone. Stabilization of the United States population would also enhance population policy efforts abroad, by weakening suspicions of genocide and imperialism, and by providing us with practical experience in programs we are urging others to adopt. Although fertility in the United States is currently low, its population is still growing. No deliberate governmental policies have been responsible for the recent decline in the birth rate, and none have yet appeared to prevent it from rising again. What sorts of policies could possibly do that?

The birth rate is the result of millions of individual decisions made by families and affected by the complex of rewards and constraints, economic and social, perceived at the family level. Better birth control methods help families achieve the number of children they desire more efficiently and at lower cost. But birth control alone cannot stabilize population if parents desire large families.

Governments continually influence the economic and social conditions felt by families, and thus governments are already involved in determining desired family size, implicitly and almost accidentally. Such accepted governmental powers as taxation, housing policy, public health administration, highway construction, education, and monetary policy all affect family incomes, expectations, costs, and location. Any of these factors could alter childbearing decisions. For example, birth rates are known to increase in times of economic growth and to decrease in depressions [31], and apartment size may have an influence on family size in several industrialized countries [32].

Since there is no question that governmental policy will influence birth rates, we need ask only whether the influence will be accidental and unpredictable, or deliberate and consistent with other social policies. Stabilization measures in the United States could begin with reexamination of current policies that are inadvertently pronatalist, including unequal income tax rates for single persons and childless families; subsidization of middle-income housing facilities; and the remaining forms of discrimination against women. Positive steps could include demographic education both in schools and the media, and free clinics for contraception, abortion, and sterilization. Probably most effective of all would be the public acceptance of a small family norm through as many channels of public information as possible, from presidential speeches to advertising campaigns.

With respect to population growth in other countries, I feel that the United States should support all locally-originated policies to reduce birth rates. This country should not attempt to impose any particular strategies or techniques, or to oppose measures acceptable to other cultures but not to ours. An American advisory service could provide aid in family planning, demographic record-keeping, and other population-related services, but only as requested by the recipient nation.

Although I very much favor national autonomy in dealing with population questions, I believe United States policy should be insistent upon one simple condition; measures to lower death rates should be linked directly with measures to lower birth rates. All forms of death control, from public health consultations to food donations, should be available on request of any nation, but only as a package that includes serious population stabilization programs, chosen by the recipient, as well. No nation need be pressured to accept this package, but under no condition should one part of it be available without the other. The choice of high birth and death rates may be more acceptable to other cultures than it is to ours. The choice of low birth and death rates may take a long time to achieve, as it did in this country, but we should help implement it upon request. The one unacceptable choice, from a global viewpoint, is high birth rate and low death rate. No ecosystem can support that choice for long, and this country's policy should be to refuse any attempt to implement it. Clearly this policy should be followed only in combination with domestic population-stabilization efforts; the United States should not impose conditions on others that it is unwilling to impose on itself.

From a short-term viewpoint, this policy may appear coercive and anti-humanitarian. It is coercive in that it dictates one major constraint to all nations—birth rates shall not be maintained higher than death rates. That constraint is derived from the physical laws of the planet, however, not from the selfish desires of any one group of people. The conditions of population stabilization interfere with some freedoms, but it lets each nation accomplish that interference as it sees fit. At the same time, it creates other freedoms by reducing the threats to survival, welfare, and equity that overpopulation would bring. According to my value system, a nonindustrialized society might better postpone decreases in the death rate until social and economic conditions have evolved to permit concurrent decreases in the birth rate. Then both vital rates can move downward in phase, as they did in the demographic transitions of the West, and a permanent reduction in mortality and fertility can be achieved.

Distribution Policy

I believe that distribution policy, like population policy, should begin at home. The Bucharest and Rome Conferences demonstrated that a nation with 6 percent of the world's people consuming 30 to 40 percent of the world's resources can be viewed only with deep antagonism by the Third World. If the United States hopes to persuade other countries to follow long-term, globally-oriented population and food policies, it must actively try to reduce its consumption of food-related commodities, including fertilizer and energy. Measures to be considered include luxury taxes on grain-fed meat, tobacco, or highly-processed foods; limitation of fertilizer use to agricultural purposes; control of pet populations; nutrition education; and numerous energy-conservation measures, from minimum fuel-efficiency standards for automobiles to deregulation of natural gas and petroleum prices. These measures would do more than increase the international credibility of the United States. They would also improve domestic economic health by reducing dependence on imports of vital resources, and by hastening the technological transition from nonrenewable to renewable resources.

Domestic conservation policies may increase the already large amount of food the United States has available for sale on the world market. Some of this surplus should be allocated to grain buffer stocks for countering weather-induced emergencies. I believe the remainder should be sold on the international market, not given away. Donated food provides short-term aid to poor countries, but at the same time it destroys local incentives, encourages corruption, and tends to lower death rates without providing an incentive for lowering birth rates.

Reduction in food aid does not imply reduction in other kinds of aid or disinterest in the plight of the poor. Quite the contrary, if food-importing countries are to benefit from United States surplus on the international market, they must have purchasing power derived from their own economic systems. At least in the medium term, the development of those economic systems could be hastened by foreign aid, but aid of a different kind than direct transfers of Western food, capital, or technology. This paper is not meant to be a disquisition on economic development. I would simply like to mention two directions of change in aid policy that might lead to a fair and permanent global redistribution of economic power.

First, a new attitude about the ability of the United States to help other countries industrialize might be useful. Current examination of the past decades of foreign aid is producing a healthy skepticism about the general applicability of Western methods, resources, and organizational forms to non-Western societies. Out of this reassessment should come not discouragement and abandonment of effort, but a constructive humility and openness to other ways of doing things. If the United States could approach the problem of each country's development as a coexplorer with that country, willing to listen and learn as well as to teach, United States policies might be more welcome and might also make more progress. Further suggestions along this line are included in the following section on food production.

Second, a more systematic understanding of the distributional consequences of international trade is needed. The Third World countries have often complained that the international terms of trade discriminate against them. Recent studies confirm that the operations of multinational corporations [33] and of the world food market [34] both result in an effective subsidy to the rich nations from the poor. If the international economic system regularly undoes what aid programs are attempting to do, then a restructuring of trade as well as aid would certainly be in order.

Food Production Policy

Agricultural research and development is already well funded in the United States, and it has contributed greatly to increased production all over the world. I would add to the ongoing efforts only two suggestions. First, the United States needs a national policy to preserve its own agricultural land and keep it in production. Second, food production research should focus on the particular needs of nonindustrialized areas, including tropical regions, and on intermediate-scale technology. Intermediate agricultural technology emphasizes tools and inputs that are appropriate for villages and small farms and that can be manufactured and repaired locally from renewable materials. It also involves more human and less fossil fuel energy. Examples of intermediate agricultural technologies include digesters to produce methane and fertilizers from household and urban organic wastes, biological pest control, windmills for pumping water, solar grain driers, small, sturdy, hand tractors, and many sorts of handtools. Some of these suggestions may sound like a return to old-fashioned practices. But new designs, materials, and knowledge are now being combined with traditional methods in some ingenious attempts to capture the best of the new and the old [35].

Intermediate technologies are ideally suited for nonindustrialized countries with excess labor and a shortage of capital. They naturally conserve commodities whose prices are now rising, such as petroleum and natural gas. Ecologically, intermediate technologies are much more acceptable than current Western farming methods. They can combat erosion and gradually improve soil fertility, and they tend to introduce fewer foreign substances into ecosystems, since they are based on naturally-occurring renewable materials.

The intermediate scale is fully compatible with redistribution goals that call for smaller farms. Neither intermediate-technology farming nor smaller units of production are likely to reduce output. In many countries smaller farms consistently outproduce large farms on a per-acre basis, although they do produce less output per man-hour [36]. In other words, they maximize returns to an increasingly scarce factor of production, land, rather than to an increasingly abundant one, labor. These production methods are therefore capable of producing both increased total output and increased rural employment.

The most promising aspect of small-scale, intermediate-technology agriculture may be its potential for promoting self-sufficient production and maintenance on the village level. This approach may be the key to the redistribution necessary to keep poor consumers in the market. And it ultimately helps achieve the social changes that can bring about real, internally-generated development and the demographic transition. As E.F. Schumacher says:

> Give a man a fish, . . . and you are helping him a little bit for a very short while; teach him the art of fishing, and he can help himself all his life. On a higher level: supply him with fishing tackle; this will cost you a good deal of money, and the result remains doubtful; but even if fruitful the man's continuing livelihood will still be dependent upon you for replacements. But teach him to make his own fishing tackle and you have helped him to become not only self-supporting, but also self-reliant and independent [37].

CONCLUSION

There may be no more important social problem in this century than the increasing imbalance between the human population and the resource base that sustains it. This problem is creeping, diffuse, and undramatic compared with others that command attention—nuclear proliferation, international monetary disturbances, or the politics of the Middle East. Yet the food-population problem is related to all these problems, and to others now barely visible on the horizon. While solving the food-population problem is unlikely to mitigate all world problems, many problems and conflicts will certainly get worse if the food-population balance is not restored. In Schumacher's words again:

> As physical resources are everywhere limited, people satisfying their needs by means of a modest use of resources are obviously less likely to be at

> each other's throats than people depending upon a high rate of use. Equally, people who live in highly self-sufficient communities are less likely to get involved in large-scale violence than people whose existence depends on worldwide systems of trade. . . . As the world's resources of non-renewable fuels—coal, oil, and natural gas—are exceedingly unevenly distributed over the globe, and undoubtedly limited in quantity, it is clear that their exploitation at an ever-increasing rate is an act of violence against nature which must almost inevitably lead to violence between men [38].

The food-population situation will not be improved without a major global change in policies, priorities, and social institutions. No problem can be solved while preserving every aspect of the system that generated it. The system must change, but this is a statement that should be viewed not with despair but with hope. There surely can be many social systems better than one in which a large fraction of the population is poor and hungry. Some of the necessary changes, such as lower birth rates, are already happening spontaneously, but slowly, and need only be accelerated. Other changes, such as redistribution, are desirable in their own right. New technologies based on conservation of resources and preservation of small-scale control will surely be welcomed by rich and poor countries alike, as the effects of petroleum depletion and high cost resources are now widely felt.

Although many of the policies I have recommended may seem extreme from the well-fed and only slightly-worried perspective of the American middle class, all are intrinsically possible, and most are clearly beneficial to current as well as future generations. My suggestions require a shift in viewpoint, more than a sacrifice. Millions of Americans are voluntarily moving toward satisfying, productive lifestyles based on small families, less consumption, and more concern for the unfortunate of the world [39]. My own family has moved in that direction, and the result is not a loss but a clear and substantial gain in the quality of our lives.

In this paper I have followed an idealistic process and come to idealistic conclusions. I do not believe that idealism is out of order in policy discussions. Social change can occur only when there is a perceived gap between the ideal and the real. Thus any evolving and innovative society should welcome criticism of the current state of the system and descriptions of possibilities that are yet unrealized. Politics, "the art of the possible," can make no progress without occasional reminders that more is possible than is currently being done.

❋ *Chapter 2*

Technologies for a New Life-Style

John Todd

INTRODUCTION

Humanity's survival may ultimately depend upon a fundamental redesigning of the ways in which societies are sustained. A major reordering is called for—as dramatic in its own way as the societal changes brought about through industrialization and the massive use of petroleum. Beyond the need for limiting growth lies a need for a conceptual change in how planetary resources are regarded. Present day economies, including their power generation, food production, shelter, heating and/or cooling, transportation, and manufacturing depend very heavily upon finite substances, including fossil fuels and potentially dangerous nuclear materials. There is no precedent in human history for whole civilizations based upon nonrenewable fuels. Therefore, the historical past offers little guidance upon which to predict the future.

A number of years ago, a few of us, mostly scientists, began to explore tentatively the possibility of redesigning and restructuring the processes used by humans to feed themselves and fulfill their other basic physical and psychological needs. Because we respected the diversity and stability of the ecosystem, we decided to take our design strategies from a knowledge of natural systems. We set out to build communities that would function almost exclusively upon renewable energy sources, particularly the wind, the sun, and biofuels. We were seeking solutions to the problems of material poverty that would be subject to evolution over time, and that could be widely applicable throughout the world. Our thinking had to be holistic and our science and technology had to be integrative, recognizing from the outset the needs for energy, food, shelter, manufacturing, and transportation. All these needs would have to be met in a fashion that was internally consistent and reflective of institutional and personal concerns.

We sensed in biology an emerging basis for a major intellectual and social revolution capable of transforming society. We focused on discovering natural processes within ecosystems that could be combined with soft technologies to service humanity. Although these biotechnologies should ultimately have the potential to replace the energy- and resource-consuming machines presently sustaining industrial societies, they had to be designed for use initially at the periphery of industrialized societies.

We envisioned a new society, less despoiling, more conserving of the biosphere and the planet's resources: it would be one in which biological systems, driven by renewable energy sources such as the wind and the sun, would provide the food and other vital inputs for human communities. Regulation of these biotechnic support systems would be shared by living organisms, micro-computers, and people. A transformation from our current hardware-intensive and exploitative civilization to one that is informationally extensive would involve working in close partnership with nature. An intimate knowledge of organisms capable of providing energy, foods, materials, and ecological regulation and control functions would be paramount. A biologically sustained society would require a greater understanding of living systems as wholes, of their ability to function usefully for humans, and of their natural propensity for integration with appropriate technologies.

We formed the New Alchemy Institute to explore these possibilities and to pioneer for the twenty-first century; from our work at the Institute an alternative future is now emerging. The Institute was established in 1969 to explore scientifically strategies that might provide constructive alternatives for humanity in the future. This perspective was undoubtedly rather large for a tiny organization, but in an age of compounded crises and patch-it-up perspectives, some fundamental and independent scientific investigations were clearly going to be required. Moreover, we recognized that the interfaces between science, politics, and society are of legitimate concern for scientists.

At the outset our aggregate training was insufficient for designing or even comprehending the vital systems of society in their interconnectedness and entirety. We reasoned further that without some kind of holistic comprehension, no significant science for the future would be possible. For us, the key to change was linked to scale. If an adaptive future meant working with tangible wholes rather than abstractions, then the scale of our scientific inquiry would have to be much reduced; yet it should at the same time be connected to the vital systems that sustain humanity. We felt an imperative to fuse science with the practical, scholarly, and philosophic realms. There were traditions to guide us, including the Taoist in China [1] and the Hermetic in Renaissance Europe [2], that at one time embraced science. In our era, explaining the workings of natural systems through cybernetics and ecology has helped pave the way for the fusion we seek.

GUIDELINES FOR RESEARCH

Over the years we have adopted a number of scientific guidelines that incorporate political, economic, and ecological principles. We decided that our institute should begin to conduct research and design on a micro-level while maintaining a planetary perspective and a concern for linkages between levels of organization. Micro-level means the lowest functional units of society, the individual or small group, and the elements that sustain them. The assumption is that larger units of organization can be no stronger than their constituent elements, and that the microcosm can be understood in empirical terms as representing a tiny image of the larger world of which it is a part. The microcosm, if broadly conceived, can act as a model of organization. This perspective, characteristic of alchemical philosophy in several ancient cultures, inspired our name [3].

We emphasized food-producing and energy-generating systems requiring only small amounts of capital so that our findings could be widely utilized by people, institutions, or communities without substantial fiscal resources. Such a capacity would also make our work useful, although by no means exclusively so, to Third and Fourth World countries.

We seek methods for a gradual shift from a hardware-intensive to an informationally- and biologically-extensive society. The next major human advance may be the adoption of strategies deriving their primary support from natural systems instead of present day material-intensive strategies requiring high levels of energy. The design and operation of our self-contained natural systems may be assisted by micro-computers and monitors that use minute amounts of power and, like humans, act as control elements. In societies organized into micro-units, almost all the food, shelter and internal climates, power, and even transportation can be transformed to biologically- and informationally-derived support elements.

It may be more difficult to monopolize the manufacture or sale of living entities, such as contained ecosystems having a societal function as opposed to the equivalent industrial equipment or machinery that depends upon large-scale energy networks. Therefore it seems likely that a small-scale biotechnically supported society will be more egalitarian and just.

We decided to emphasize participatory solutions capable of involving large segments of society. When the petroleum era wanes, the traditional condition, in which the great majority of humanity is engaged in food raising, is likely to reassert itself. Only with the oil- and gas-based agriculture of the twentieth century has it been possible for a majority to shift to urban living. Since at some future date much of the population will probably have to return to cultivating most of their own foods, we decided to research family-level methods of food culture which would be ecologically benign and relatively inexpensive. Small-scale farming could require only part-time tending and be suitable for siting in such small spaces as suburban backyards. Further, the food-raising ecosystems would have to be designed so they could be tended by people without special training.

The Institute staff also chose to explore bioregional concepts to augment the more universal approaches outlined above. The bioregional research would determine and use indigenous environmental, climatic, and biotic elements to develop adaptive energy, food, transportation, and shelter strategies on a regional level. Toward this end the Institute has established small centers or projects in several countries and climates. In the best of all possible worlds, a balance between the regional and the global should exist. Each bioregion should be treated as physically and culturally unique, the outgrowth of an interplay among society, climate, environment, and resources. Self-reliance, pride, and independence might be restored if indigenous approaches to food production, energy, shelter, and manufacture were given serious intellectual and scientific concern. The Institute has already begun to identify and study bioregional directions in several areas as diverse as maritime Canada and the lowland tropics of Costa Rica.

Whenever possible we try to incorporate in our designs renewable energy sources and durable material, rather than finite resources and short-lived materials. Conserver societies must be founded upon such shifts in energy production and use of materials.

EARLY EXPERIMENTS

A number of key experiments that reflect the guidelines above are currently underway.

Backyard Fish Farm-Greenhouse

Several years ago we asked whether ecological principles, internal food cycles, and renewable energy sources for power could be used to meet the protein needs for a small group of people on a year-round basis in an approximately 50 × 50 foot space. Such a system might function initially as a micro-food garden or survival tool; ultimately, it could point the way to a new approach to agriculture. New Alchemy's backyard fish farm-greenhouses are an outgrowth of our attempt to answer this question.

The backyard micro-farms are semi-tropical aquatic and terrestrial environments covered by solar trapping structures that maintain and regulate year-round growing conditions for fishes, vegetables, and some fruits and grains. The aquaculture component is important for climate control. The large volume of water stores heat for cold and sunless periods. Within the ponds, dense blooms of algae are cultured, providing the feed for herbivorous fishes. Tilapia, a herbivore from Africa, has been cultured on internal food chains to an edible size in only three months. The white amur, another vegetarian fish prized in China, has grown to over a foot in length in less than a year.

Overall productivity is dependent upon internal biopurification, carried out in two small adjacent ecosystems linked to the culture pond. The first system is filled three-quarters full with mollusk shells through which the water column passes. The shells provide a substrate for aerobic bacteria. Bacterial nitrification takes place, oxidizing ammonia to nitrites and then to nitrates, forms of nitrogen less toxic to fish. High levels of carbon dioxide are a by-product. The second support ecosystem is an algae-filled pool that utilizes the high carbon dioxide levels and nitrogenous compounds from the first subelement to sustain rapidly-growing populations of algae and zooplankton. During daylight hours saturation levels of oxygen are reached. The algae, zooplankton, and oxygenated water from the second support ecosystem flows directly into the fish culture pool, providing them with feeds and purified, oxygen-filled water. The cycling is continuous.

We have not sought record levels of fish production; our emphasis to date has been on the creation of healthy aquatic ecosystems that are almost autonomous, self-regulating, and self-purifying, and that incorporate a variety of food cycles. The end points of these cycles are diverse foods suitable for human consumption, including fishes and aquatic plants such as water chestnuts. Rice has been successfully cultured in small batches using pond water. Production in shallow dome-covered ponds eighteen feet in diameter has exceeded fifty pounds per crop of tilapia. Tilapia are cultured only during the summer months. White amur and mirror carp are raised year-round in the same system, producing comparable yields.

Adjacent to and dependent upon the aquaculture are experimental terrestrial growing beds. During the summer the beds contain tropical seed-grain crops such as amaranth; vine crops such as squash, cucumbers, and tomatoes; and tropical fruits. During the winter, traditional temperate climate foods such as spinach, lettuce, onions, parsley, and chard are grown. Their overall value may exceed that of the fish. Pests upon the plants are controlled biologically; *Anolis caroliniensis*, a lizard, has proved an effective predator for most insects. Biocides cannot be used within these terrestrial capsules because they are lethal to fishes and many aquatic invertebrates.

Although our original concept has been vindicated and growing structures can now be justified at the family level, much remains to be learned. But in parts of the world where food, water, and fuels are scarce, adaptions of these micro-farms could already prove extremely valuable.

The Miniature Ark

The miniature ark—solar-heated, wind-powered, food-growing complex—was designed to study biological concepts that we hope will lead to highly productive and economically-valuable ecosystems for raising aquatic foods. The miniature ark has, in addition, a small amount of greenhouse capacity. The design was inspired by productive ecosystems in nature, in particular a river in Java, a Louisiana estuary, and a mangrove lagoon in Florida, characterized by the continuous passing of water from the ocean or upper reaches of the river. We felt an influx of water high in oxygen and free of harmful waste products was essential to sustain large animal populations. The river had high nutrient levels derived from animal and human sewage and was capable of sustaining immense populations of organisms suitable for fish feeds. The Javanese cultivate 80,000 to 90,000 pounds per acre of fish annually in floating cages along the better sections of the river [4]. Both the Louisiana estuary and the Florida mangrove lagoon were characterized not so much by high internal productivity as by accumulations of decaying detritus from surrounding terrestrial and aquatic environments [5]. Because of the influx of oxygenated water from outside, large numbers of fish and crustacea were able to thrive in these zones to feed directly on the abundant detritus and associated organisms. In the absence of flushing, decomposing organic matter lowers oxygen to levels intolerable to desirable fish and crustacea species.

The miniature ark was designed to incorporate the best bio-energetic attributes of the tropical river, estuary, and lagoon with respect to overall stability and productivity. Its aquaculture component is a circular "river" or closed loop, with solar-heated water, high nutrient levels, a rapid flow with resulting high nutrient exchange rates, detritus, organic matter, and support ecosystems for culturing additional feeds.

The flow is produced by a windmill that pumps water through the various subcomponents of the loop. Several high-capacity sailwing windmills have been developed by New Alchemy for water pumping in Third World countries and for aquaculture systems. Presently the Institute is attempting to develop water pumps to match the power and drive characteristics of the windmills. Within a year, flow rates on the miniature ark should increase fourfold with a concurrent rise in potential productivity.

Populations of Chinese white amur, Israeli mirror carp, and African tilapia are cultured together in the largest pond of the loop, which measures 15 × 15 × 5 feet. Biopurification takes place, after the water has passed through the solar heater, in five small ecosystems. These ecosystems variously house bacterial filters comprised of mollusk shells, earthen filters, open pools, and "forests" of aquatic plants arranged as alternating bacterial-carbon dioxide and plant-oxygen dominating subelements. The ability of the system to purify water laden with toxic fish wastes is exceptional. Plants from the biopurification elements are periodically fed to fishes. In this way nutrients are continuously recycled within the system.

Although small, the aquaculture component of the miniature ark has worked well as a model for larger systems. The miniature ark and the backyard fish farm-greenhouses are described in more detail in the *Journal of the New Alchemists* [6].

Solar Ponds

The recently conceived solar pond concept is an attempt to utilize living systems to serve simultaneously a number of critical functions in an integrated way. In designing the ponds, the emphasis has been on using biological entities which, in combination with an appropriate technology, can serve roles presently played by machines and fuels. The solar ponds represent an effort to create suitable climates in living and food-growing bioshelters which can at the same time perform as aquaculture ecosystems.

The solar ponds are translucent pools placed above the ground. Light can enter the ponds from the top and all sides. Their walls and tops are built from a fiberglass material which admits a high percentage of available light. Solar ponds act effectively as both solar collectors and heat storage units. The planktonic algae absorb the sun's energy in much the same way as do the black absorber surfaces of the plate collectors, a solar technology manufactured for heating houses and buildings. Within the ponds, the energy from the sun is transformed by the plants into heat and plant growth. The water medium containing the algae is an appropriate storage material; a covered solar pond 5 feet high × 5 feet in diameter heats rapidly when the sun shines brightly. During the warmer months partial shading and venting are required even when the ponds are outside.

New Alchemy's ark for Prince Edward Island—a solar-heated and wind-powered bioshelter encompassing a house, laboratory, greenhouse, and aquaculture facility—contains forty solar ponds. These ponds contribute considerably toward maintaining living and growing climates year round, and provide the backbone of the aquaculture systems.

Solar ponds represent a new approach to warm water fish culture. Because of the ponds' phenomenal light-receiving ability, algae production on a per unit volume basis is approximately ten times greater than that of our other aquaculture systems. Consequently, proportionately larger grazing populations of tilapia are being cultured within them. Within the ponds, we are also experimenting with passive versus active biopurification strategies. The "active" solar pond uses a small air pump to turn over water within bacterial filters on the bottom of the pond. This turbulence has produced extraordinarily dense algae blooms. The "passive" solar pond seems to be able to function as effectively by relying upon movements of the fishes to effect bacterial-algae nutrient recycling. Both solar ponds have an exceptional ability to take up and eliminate toxic ammonia.

We have not yet had enough experience with the solar ponds to judge their worth as solar heaters and fish culture ecosystems. However, two solar ponds with doublewall fiberglass construction and top covers, situated in an exposed outdoor location, withstood chilling winds in excess of twenty-five miles per hour when temperatures were below −10° F (−23° C). Water temperatures within the solar ponds did not fall below 40° F (+4° C); resident populations of Chinese big head and silver carp and Israeli mirror carp remained active and feeding. With more study and refinement these ponds may prove to be one of our more valuable contributions to the vexing problems of heating and food production.

The Cape Cod Ark

We intend to determine the feasibility of well-designed bioshelters that will produce foods in sufficient abundance to be economically viable, paying for themselves and providing a living income for their owners. An intensive garden/farm agriculture, based on small acreages and bioshelters containing ecologically derived food networks and powered by renewable energy sources, may be a most adaptive strategy for a future in which fossil fuels are in short supply.

The Cape Cod ark, a solar-heated, wind-powered greenhouse and aquaculture structure, was designed in collaboration with Solsearch architects to explore the micro-economic basis of the bioshelter concept. The ark has recently been completed. A small model, measuring 25 × 25 feet, was built first to test a number of concepts and materials, including the insulating and heat-trapping properties of the potentially valuable solar membrane invented by Sean Wellesley Miller and Day Chahroudi of the Solar Lab at the Massachusetts Institute of Technology. The model ark is the first test of the membrane within a growing structure. The membrane, suspended in three layers under the south-facing fiberglass wall, is an example of an effective alternative to costly, difficult-to-manage shutter systems in solar-heated growing structures.

The Cape Cod ark is a first attempt to design and build a commercial-sized growing structure incorporating the principles described earlier. Further biological and bioengineering research will ensue, including the evaluation of crops most suitable to conditions within the structure, development of biological controls for pests and disease, and internal climate regulation. Hopefully, such arks will eventually furnish an important alternative to food scarcities when cheap fuels wane, but enormous efforts will be required to realize their potential. We feel an obligation to design the arks so they will be widely useful throughout the global society.

An Ark For Prince Edward Island

The Canadian ark, a complete system for living, research, and food production, is autonomous and self-contained. It uses the sun and wind to create housing and growing climates under the rigorous climatic conditions of Prince Edward Island in the Gulf of St. Lawrence. Completed in the fall of 1976, and accepted as one of Canada's contributions to UN Settlements Year, the Canadian ark is New Alchemy's first attempt to test the feasibility of living structures which are not continuous energy drains on society. The ark will function without fossil fuels even if the sun does not shine for a month. Such hopefully long-lived structures will generate their own power, utilize their own wastes, and provide food and even commercial crops for their inhabitants. Through the ark we are trying to evolve bioshelters which are, in many respects, miniature worlds. Through tending them, their inhabitants will grow in their understanding of the larger workings of nature; out of this knowledge might arise a new-found ethic for the planet Earth.

A brief description of the ark for Prince Edward Island appears in the *Journal of the New Alchemists* [7]. A side view is shown in Figure 2–1. What makes the ark unique, apart from its self-sufficiency, is the careful integration of and the linkages between components which have not been connected traditionally. The greenhouse element, the solar ponds, and the solar collectors, for example, all trap and store the sun's heat in several subsystems which in turn will serve a diversity of vital functions. The 25-kilowatt wind-driven power plant will provide the electricity for control functions, and for air and water circulation. During critical periods in winter, the ark's electricity will be used to provide auxiliary heat to subelements that require it. The ark will be subjected to intensive testing and experimentation; various interrelationships between such external inputs as sun, wind, length of day and temperatures, and internal biochemical, biological, climatic, and storage variables will be monitored and analyzed. The emphasis will be on discovering the most appropriate ways of regulating the overall system and of optimizing food production within on a sustained basis.

During a period in history when, in temperate countries, fuel (for heating, growing food, transportation, and storage) is rapidly consuming a high percentage of the world's finite energy sources, arks may represent a major step in integrating existing knowledge with indigenous, smaller-scale approaches to the future.

Hydrowind: An Advanced Wind-Driven Power Plant

For many organizations, an occasional challenge may seem sufficiently important that a change in course may be advised to meet it. On Prince Edward Island we have been confronted with just such a challenge. The provincial government was planning to take part in a large nuclear project, but indicated to us that there was still time for other alternatives to be seriously considered. In the winter of 1975, we proposed informally to the premier and to some of his cabinet and staff that a nonnuclear future might prove the wisest course both socially and economically. The New Alchemy Institute is opposed unequivocally to nuclear-power generation. In the case of Prince Edward Island, we recommended a gradual shift to a coal-wind-solar energy future. Wind is a renewable and plentiful island resource, and coal is readily available in Nova Scotia. With about 2,000 hours of bright sun annually, the island could readily integrate

Figure 2–1. New Alchemy's Ark for Prince Edward Island

The New Alchemy's Ark for Prince Edward Island—a solar-heated and wind-powered bioshelter encompassing a house, laboratory, greenhouse, and aquaculture facility—contains forty solar ponds (center). A barn area is adjacent to the house (shown top left), above a rock-hot air storage space. The food and tree propagation area is seen on the right.

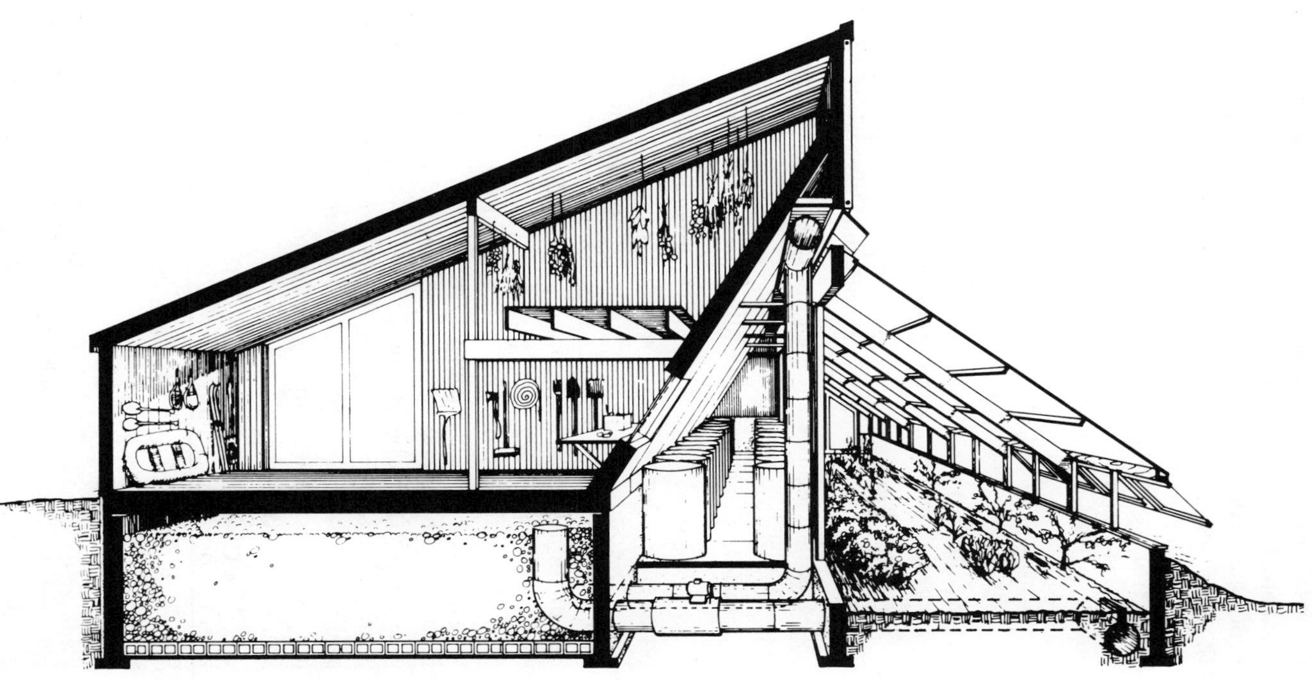

supplemental heating into its building and crop driers, thereby reducing its fuel and electricity needs. Unfortunately, our arguments were weakened by the absence of any commercially available electricity-producing windmill either large enough or suitable to demonstrate the efficacy of wind as a supplemental power source. To keep alive the ideal of a nonnuclear future, the Institute, with promised support from the Canadian government, brought together a team of engineers to develop a New Alchemy windplant. Several design criteria were drawn up for the plant. We specified:

—that it be rugged enough to withstand fierce wind and salt spray along the island's coast;

—that it have the potential without major design alterations to be scaled upwards in size to 100-kilowatt systems and larger;

—that the first plant produce enough electricity to power a sizable farm or the ark (a 25-kilowatt capacity mill was chosen);

—that the design permit the plant to be manufactured and assembled on the island; and

—that the plant's economic future look promising.

The resulting design—The Hydowind[a] electrical power system—represents a break from orthodox windmill technology. A prototype recently completed is now undergoing tests on Prince Edward Island. The Hydrowind uses hydraulics for power transfer, taking advantage of substantial improvements in hydraulics in recent years. The New Alchemy system transfers power via hydraulic pumps from the blades to a hydraulic engine on the ground, at which point the power is transformed into electricity. The system has a number of advantages, including: increased reliability and sturdiness; smaller towers and top gear; potentially better air shapes because its generators are on the ground; hydraulic tuning of the blade pitch; and opportunities for a scaling of size. Perhaps most important, inherent in the design is the ability to couple a number of windmills into the same power plant while operating a single generator.

The first power plant on Prince Edward Island will consist of four twenty-foot-blade-diameter windmills linked together. The new blade design involves an integral-core tension system and a lightweight aluminum skin.

The power plant will be connected to the ark and also to the island's power network. Testing the mill on the grid will be valuable for establishing the feasibility of windplants contributing to existing networks. We hope that an active debate will arise, on the island and

[a]A trademark of the New Alchemy Institute.

elsewhere, in response to the ark system's capacity to produce more power than it needs, leaving an option to sell the extra power to utilities.

RELATED STUDIES

The Institute is conducting a number of other studies and projects, including the culture of insect larvae as supplemental fish feeds; the study of fish diets; the evaluation of plants and animals from around the world for use in bioshelter food chains; the harvest of tree crops; and the drying and preserving of food. Efforts are underway to learn more about biological methods for increasing soil fertility and managing crops. Most of our studies are interrelated and reflect a desire on the part of the staff to find apt methods of managing living resources on a small scale. Central to our efforts is the testing of crop varieties for insect resistance and suitability to various climates.

The various systems briefly chronicled here merely represent concepts in embryo. They are not end points, but new beginnings. The various projects may seem simplistic, even quixotic upon first reading, as in some respects they are. But seeing them only in this light might be akin to judging the worth of modern physics from a painting of Newton's laboratory. Within the next few decades many of these ideas will mature, particularly if the impetus can be maintained and if others share some of the perspectives presented here.

Several years ago I should have argued that modern societies, by their nature, would be in opposition to utilizing small-scale, holistically-derived biotechnologies in designing communities of the future. At that time our research had to be justified on the grounds that a mature society should explore diverse strategies for the future simultaneously, so that when decisions are necessary a variety of options are available from which to select.

This perspective, while central to our thinking, has been transcended recently by a growing awareness that new strategies for the future are urgently required today. In part this realization arises out of a waning confidence in the ability of science and technology to salvage an industrialized growth-oriented society in an ultimately finite world. A science of steady states seems ever more needed to prepare us for the future. This new science, having been created within a framework of ethical and moral considerations, will be different from modern science. A widespread interest in building a future in which the majority of people are participants rather than spectators is emerging. If so, the work of New Alchemy and others like us may come to be considered central to the questions and problems of our time.

 *Chapter 3*

Limits to Energy Conversion: The Case for Decentralized Technologies

Amory Lovins

The recent oil embargo and the decline in United States domestic oil and gas production have led to a preoccupation with the physical limits to energy use inherent in finite fuel resources. But there would be many limits to energy use even if fuel resources were essentially infinite. In this discussion I survey some of the more critical constraints on mankind's conversion of energy (assumed in this context to exclude food, water, and materials). Some of these limits are general, some are specific to centralized and electrified high technologies, and some are even more specific to nuclear fission technology. In other works, I discuss in more detail various strategies for energy use and development [1, 2, 3, 4, 5].

GENERAL ENERGY LIMITS

Despite local shortages—becoming global over the next few decades—of oil and gas, physical stocks of fuels are not a fundamental limit to energy growth over the next few centuries, since substitution of more abundant fuels and fluxes is possible in theory. The limits to substitution, and hence to maintaining or increasing present levels of energy conversion, are biophysical, social, ethical, economic, technical, and political. Particular patterns of fossil-fuel scarcity make particular constraints more important, and these constraints, not aggregate fossil-fuel abundance, should be the focus of policy interest.

Biophysical Limits

The most fundamental biophysical limit to energy conversion arises from the inevitable degradation of all energy to low-temperature heat, regardless of the energy conversion technology used. All energy converted from chemical or nuclear fuels, or obtained from geothermal heat or from solar collectors in outer space, must end up as low-temperature heat added at the surface of the earth, in most cases immediately upon use. This extra heat causes complex and poorly understood climatic events, and, despite increased infrared radiation away from the earth, probably tends to increase the earth's surface temperature, particularly at high latitudes. Intricate feedback effects may enhance such an increase.

At levels of energy conversion between perhaps ten and one hundred times those of today, the warming would certainly suffice to affect some leverage points of global climate—for example, by melting the sensitive Arctic pack ice, thereby profoundly altering climate over at least the Northern Hemisphere and perhaps triggering longer-term effects. Many climatologists now agree that, at historical growth rates, major global effects may occur some time during the next century. These effects may be even more imminent than now thought if other deleterious influences (such as increased levels of CO_2, particulate emissions, and diversion of Arctic rivers) continue to destabilize the Arctic pack ice. Unfortunately, such influences tend to be concentrated at high northern latitudes where they are more damaging. Such heat limits can be avoided only by using natural energy flows that are already present at the surface of the earth, via direct and indirect solar collection, with due care to disturb the natural geographic distribution of that energy as little as possible.

Burning any carbon-based fuel (thus excluding hydrogen) produces carbon dioxide, as well as small particles that make the air more turbid and change its optical properties in very complex ways. Control of these emissions is impracticable for a number of reasons, one being that the control process would require more energy than the fuel yielded. (Burning fuels derived from biomass does not give rise to the CO_2 problems of burning fossil fuels, since biomass contains only photosynthetically fixed carbon that is "on current account" and would have been oxidized soon even if it were not burned.) Both kinds of emissions have intricate climatic effects, sometimes competitive and sometimes reinforcing. Whatever these effects might be, they are bound to include changes in the geographic patterns of temperature, rainfall, and storms—changes to which agriculture could not readily adapt.

Such climatic changes, like those caused by man-made heat, are already observable locally and regionally. Some respected climatologists think that large-scale effects, for example on monsoon rainfall, are already occurring. By wide agreement, in any case, global climatic problems could be expected fairly early in the next century if energy use were to continue growing at historical rates. The climatic effects of CO_2 emissions alone ensure that only a rather small fraction of the coal in the ground can be safely burned. Accordingly, it would be exceedingly imprudent to assume that the comparative ignorance of climatic constraints—which are extremely hard to compute—constitutes a license to commit society to a large-scale, long-term coal economy. So far, the knowledge gained through further research has only made climatic problems seem worse.

Some possible climatic limits to energy conversion are very specific. For example, it appears that the delicate Arctic pack ice can be directly endangered by spilling oil in the Beaufort Sea. Oil emulsions can probably work their way to the surface of the ice, darkening it so that it irreversibly melts in the intense spring sunshine.

More proximate than most climatic limits are the biophysical public health limits to the use of traditional energy technologies. The ill effects of oxides of sulfur and nitrogen are well known and rapidly becoming more obtrusive, owing in part to the tardiness of most utilities in using available combustion and cleanup technologies. Some of the more subtle and disquieting health effects of submicron particulates (which are very hard to control), of sulfate aerosols, and of the many heavy metals present in fossil fuels are just being realized. For example, the heavy metals, or even more toxic radioactive substances, can absorb on the surface of submicron particles and consequently be carried to the bronchi or deep into the lungs. Likewise, though the occupational hazards of coal mining are well known, those arising from carcinogenic chemicals produced in coal-conversion plants are still speculative. For most health effects, whether occupational or public, further research has again tended to make the technical and political limits on energy expansion seem closer than expected.

Social and Ethical Limits

The effects of traditional energy technologies on land, water, ecosystems, and wilderness are perhaps the best known and historically the most important source of social limits. Problems arise at each step along the long continuous chain of energy conversions stretching from fuel in the ground via "sources" to "uses" to low-temperature heat. Whether the harm is obvious—as in oil spills, coal stripping, water pollution, Arctic abuse, deforestation of fragile uplands, hydroelectric flooding by large dams—or more subtle—as in acid rainfall, or the settlement patterns made possible by the existence of cars—the damage has produced, and will continue to produce, major social limits to energy growth.

Less readily perceived than chronic effects, but ethically at least as important are the acute effects of singular events to which many large-scale and sophisticated energy systems are particularly prone. For example, people living a few miles downwind of a harbor where modern cryogenic tankers deliver liquefied natural gas (LNG) might eventually discover, empirically or otherwise, that a ground-level plume of cold methane gas boiling off from a spill after a collision, hard grounding, or sabotage of one such tanker could reach them in ten or twenty minutes and, in burning, could release as much energy as about fifty-five Hiroshima bombs, causing an unprecedented firestorm. The prospect is not conducive to easy urban siting of LNG terminals; nor should it be.

Economic and Technological Limits

Many modern energy technologies superimpose high economic and technical risks on a substratum of high cost, technical difficulty, and complexity. The result is a tangle of economic, logistical, and net-energy constraints that severely limit the ability of large-scale, high-technology energy systems to sustain rapid growth for long enough to attain nationally significant size.

The capital intensity of energy technologies was not a major policy issue until perhaps a decade ago. Capital was plentiful and major energy-supply transitions were smooth, owing largely to the subsidy provided by fossil fuels costing at most a few dollars per barrel equivalent. According to present plans, however, the capital of the 1980s and beyond will instead be created increasingly from economic activity fueled by, say, synthetic high-BTU gas at perhaps \$20–\$25 per barrel equivalent and nuclear electricity at perhaps \$65–\$120 per barrel equivalent. Because of the rapid increase in the cost of high-technology fuels, coupled with an order-of-magnitude increase in the capital intensity of new energy supplies and drastic increases in the capital intensity in other major sectors, capital will no longer be plentiful. To illustrate, the 1976–1985 phase of Project Independence (as proposed by former President Ford) would cost nearly one year's GNP at current level, or roughly two-thirds to three-fourths of cumulative net private domestic investment over that decade. This contrasts sharply with the energy sector's historical requirement for one-fourth of that investment. Diverting so much capital from competing sectors, particularly for enterprises that could not pass the test of the marketplace, clearly requires centralized control of national capital allocation and therefore raises deserved political difficulties. Proposals to set up a \$100 billion slush fund to make huge blocks of capital available to places where, for excellent reasons, they would not otherwise go—for instance, economically and technically risky nuclear, oil-shale, or coal-conversion investments—will be wholly inadequate to the task. The proposals are, however, a sign that the capacity of fiscal institutions is being exceeded.

Along with prohibitive capital intensity (and with a correspondingly formidable intensity of requirements for scarce materials and skills) comes a general level of technical complexity that increases the likelihood and effect of mistakes and that constrains practical rates of large-scale deployment. The comparative simplicity that has allowed natural gas to sustain a seven-year doubling time, so long as reserves were abundant—long enough to account for two-thirds of United States energy growth in the past few decades—is not an attribute shared by synthetic fuel, oil shale, or nuclear technologies. And even if an unprecedented mobilization of resources permitted rapid, sustained growth in these more complex technologies, the quantities of resources required would be so prodigious that it would be physically impossible to shift major blocks of supply before fluid-fuel depletion became severe.

On a world scale, for example, a simple rate-and-magnitude calculation shows that if world energy conversion increased by the annual 5 percent that many governments still desire, and if 1,000 megawatts of new capacity to supply useful energy—for example, a large reactor—were commissioned each day, starting now, then in the year 2000 primary energy would still come mainly from fossil fuel, which would be consumed more than twice as fast as now. Likewise on a national scale, if energy and electricity demand in Denmark (the Japan of the West) were to grow at 3 percent per year and 4 percent per year, respectively, both far slower than historical rates, and if a maximum credible nuclear program of 1,000 megawatts every other year were to start being built now, then in the year 2000, Danish power stations would burn nearly as much fossil fuel as they do now. Indeed, Denmark would still be more than 90 percent dependent on imported fossil fuels for her national energy supplies. (The remaining 10 percent would come from imported fuel-cycle services, reactor technology, and perhaps uranium.)

The complexity and capital intensity of modern energy systems give rise to a further property that is the physical analogue of a problem with a profit-and-loss or a cash-flow account: namely, net-energy problems, either in the "static" case of one energy facility in isolation, or in the "dynamic" case of an expanding program of facilities. In the static case, the fiscal unattractiveness of some marginal fossil-fuel technologies, as with the deeper or poor oil shales and tar sands, reflects a small or perhaps negative yield of net energy from a large gross resource. Not only is a great deal of shale or sand consumed to produce a barrel of oil, but indirect energy inputs can also be large. To oversimplify a bit, one reason that the cost of producing a barrel of shale oil rises when the price of the Organization of Petroleum-Exporting Countries (OPEC) oil rises is that there is a substantial fraction of a barrel of OPEC oil in each barrel of shale oil, embodied in the machinery and fuels required to produce the shale oil. Owing to market imperfections, it is quite possible to make money on a technology that loses energy. Energy analysis is a tool for identifying such market imperfections.

Even in the case of energy facilities (such as nuclear power stations fueled from high-grade uranium ore) which may be substantial net producers of energy, "dynamic" net energy problems can still arise. Just as a profitable but rapidly-expanding business can have cash-flow problems, so a rapidly-expanding energy sector can produce national energy shortages lasting for decades. For example, Project Independence entailed an energy investment, just to build and commission the facilities, on the order of 10 billion (i.e., 10^{10}) barrels equivalent, or the best part of a year's oil consumption in the United States. If the United States Energy Research and Development Administration (ERDA) or Électricité de France calculations of nuclear net energy are correct, then ERDA's nuclear program may require about two-thirds of its own output just to maintain its own growth, and probably cannot clear its cumulative energy deficit in this century. In fact, no large-scale, high-technology energy system seems capable of providing timely and significant substitution for oil and gas while simultaneously producing substantial amounts of net energy—unless energy demand is meanwhile stabilized, or preferably reduced. People who rely on nuclear or other energy-intensive energy technologies as a prompt, independent, and abundant substitute for scarce fluid fuels have forgotten some basic facts about the timing of fossil-fuel inputs to and outputs from the industrial economy.

Political Considerations

Most modern energy technologies pose difficult policy problems of public acceptance. Local or regional resistence on social, environmental, and economic grounds is more frequent and seems increasingly justified, particularly in such fragile areas as the western United States coal fields and the Scottish coast. Inevitably, many countries will have energy-exporting and energy-importing regions. Central governments will try to impose energy facilities on recalcitrant people. Within many industrial countries today, the resulting centrifugal force of federal, local, and interregional confrontation coincides with grassroots distaste for big government, for concentrations of economic or political power, and for remote administrative interference with individual or local self-reliance. In my opinion, these potent political forces will prove one of the most effective energy constraints, and, where suppressed or ignored, will tend to cause major political upheavals.

Somewhat related political forces have already shown their power on a world scale. Oil is an uniquely useful and valuable resource; its sources are geographically concentrated, and it can be replaced only by investing enormous amounts of money, skills, and time. Thus, its owners, with a certain Sophoclean inevitability, have sought to extend their resource's lifetime and to avoid selling it at a price that is clearly detrimental to some of their own economies. At the same time, the principal buyers of OPEC oil are finding it harder to obtain money to buy oil from the countries that increasingly have most of the global stocks of both money and oil. Now there are few assets, and ultimately there will be none, that oil producers consider attractive and that oil consumers can continue to pay. The OPEC nations' well-founded fear of expropriation precludes their acceptance of many kinds of assets in exchange for oil. The West's dependence on OPEC oil will be lasting and costly, so generating a substantial risk of further and extremely hazardous Middle Eastern military adventures—not necessarily by the traditional parties only.

More generally, concentrations not only of fuels but of technologies, skills, and capital, and the susceptibility of most modern energy technologies to commercial monopoly or technical dependence, all produce inequity that is bound to be a basis for conflict. In a world where inequity both between and within countries is already rampant and worsening, and where those who control strategic commodities (whether Persian Gulf oil, Siberian gas, Chilean copper, or American wheat) are increasingly willing to make them an instrument of political policy, the fragility of peace and tolerance may be the most stringent limit to the further growth of the gluttonous and the starving alike.

LIMITS TO CENTRALIZED ELECTRICITY

Virtually all industrial countries, and many others aspiring to imitate their mistakes, are seeking to electrify as much of their economies as possible. Some, such as the United States, have even defined their energy policy goals so that any energy technology that is not electrified (and preferably large scale) is considered incapable of having a major long-term impact. That is, ability to provide large blocks of electricity, rather than sufficient amounts of energy, is the first criterion. The rationale for pervasive electrification appears to be that electricity is convenient to use and control, can be generated in several ways, and can be generated remotely from its use. It is thus easier to inflict the side effects of generation on a politically weak minority of rural dwellers rather than on the politically strong mass of dwellers in suburbia. Yet other features of centralized electric grids that may be equally important for policy have so far received scant attention.

Scale

With isolated exceptions, all governments have assumed that energy systems must be large scale, with capacity in blocks of hundreds or thousands of megawatts. Accordingly, the waste heat into which two-thirds of the fuel consumed is transformed comes in such large blocks that it is very hard to use even though it can be economically transported for many tens of kilometers. Most or all of the waste heat must therefore be dissipated somehow. The latest official proposals for energy supply in the year 2000 envisage dissipating enough waste heat to raise the temperature of the entire freshwater runoff of the forty-eight coterminous states by an average of about 34°–49°F. Such an electrical system would also occupy a land area roughly equivalent to southern New England, and would partition the country with linear barriers such as megavolt transmission lines, whose electrical fields are so strong that roads, footpaths, and the like reportedly cannot go underneath them. Since power-station boilers generally require considerably more fuel than does direct combustion by the end user, the land destroyed by unreclaimed coal stripping or by subsidence over underground mines would be enormous. Already in the United States alone an area about the size of Massachusetts has been thus despoiled. Indeed, sustained coal-stripping or uranium mining for making electricity would need about as much land as—and perhaps more than—equivalent centralized solar-thermal-electrical capacity. Likewise, more energy falls as sunlight on the exclusion area of a typical temperate-latitude nuclear power station in a year than that station sends out in a year.

Requirements of Capital, Skills, and Materials

The capital intensity of electrical systems is qualitatively different from that of direct-combustion systems. For example, building a complete energy system to deliver to a consumer an extra barrel of refined oil or its heat equivalent per day used to cost several thousand 1976 dollars with the traditional direct-fuel systems on which industrial countries have long relied. But it costs perhaps about $10,000 for the more profitable of the North Sea oil fields, about $20,000 to $70,000 for synthetic fuels, and about $200,000 or more for a typical nuclear electrical system, with coal electrical systems not so very far behind at $150,000. Such enormous capital intensity led the strategic planners of the Shell Group, among others, to conclude several years ago that no major country outside the Persian Gulf could afford to electrify most of its economy—a conclusion consistent with the observed inability of utilities, even those backed by national treasuries, to afford even the early stages of the process. Yet some still try: of the $1 trillion-odd total capital cost (in 1976 dollars) of Project Independence during 1976 to 1985, three-fourths lay in the electrical sector. From that sum, over $140 billion could be saved at the margin by reducing the ten-year average electrical growth rate from an absurd 6.5 percent per year to a merely ridiculous 5.5 percent per year.

Accompanying this capital intensity, too, are formidable requirements for skills and materials. Electrical technologies tend to be more demanding of both, particularly at large scale, than classical direct-fuel technologies; they are slower to build and repair owing to their greater complexity and more stringent technical requirements; and they are more prone to unforeseen large-scale failures. Unfortunately, institutional failures are also common in this sector. Many of the electrical utilities that governments rely upon to implement simultaneously a dizzying array of novel, unforgiving, and very costly new technologies and practices currently lack the money and ability to operate their way out of a paper bag.

Political Considerations

Perhaps most disquieting, however, are the sociopolitical implications of centralized electrification. Electrification encourages or demands extensive changes in the nature and patterns of end-users—including settlement patterns—in order to make them conform to the requirements of the source of supply, the extreme capital intensity of which necessitates near optimization of use. Centralized electrification is not a local and understandable technology, but one administered from afar by an elite (and, in times of stress, perhaps paramilitary) technological priesthood likely to be socially remote from much of its clientele. Such energy systems greatly concentrate administrative and economic power at a time when many people want it diffused. Even now, some policymakers in Washington are thinking, albeit vaguely, about central regulation of domestic-scale solar technology, lest mass defections from the utility grid deprive utilities of revenues essential to many state and municipal cash flows and, presumably, of power to regulate who will get how much energy at what price.

Moreover, centralized electrical grids are vulnerable to mistake or disruption—a handful of people can turn off a country, and a single rifleman can black out most cities. Stringent social controls akin to a garrison state therefore become necessary to prevent the disruption. Centralized electrical systems are also perhaps the most prone of any to technical dependence and commercial monopoly and tend to be used to maintain or promote social inequities. Today's appeals for more electricity to help the poor are touching to hear—from utilities that have consistently charged the poor several times more than large industrial users for the same unit of electricity. Electrical grids are unlikely to be run by the poor. Quite the contrary, the politically weak and poor often suffer most of the unpleasant side effects and the rigors of roughshod siting of centralized facilities.

Limits to Adaptive Change

Those who pin their hopes for sustaining growth on the adaptive potential of new technologies overlook the fact that institutional and political forces inherent in the development of one energy source may preclude the development of other necessary techniques. These forces thus become effective limits to growth. Because centralized and electrified high technologies demand so much money, skill, and time to develop and implement (especially if they are nuclear technologies, and above all if they are the exceptionally difficult breeder technologies), any commitment to them—even if precommercial and represented as mere development of an option—tends effectively to foreclose other options. Such commitments also rapidly develop large and powerful constituencies of those who link the commercial success of the project both with the public welfare and with their own livelihoods. These beliefs, often sincerely held, and the harsh demands that development itself places on time and energy tend to discourage such persons from acquiring a thorough knowledge of alternative technologies or policies or of perceiving the need to explore or even discuss them.

Furthermore, the intense social pressures within committed institutions managing large cash flows tend to discourage deviance from official promotional policies, reinforcing them with apparent consensus whether deserved or not and perhaps seriously compromising individual professional ethics. Such effects, common today in nuclear safety programs, occur throughout large industries, especially those feeling the energy sector's sense of mission. The resulting institutional and political conflicts have a major bearing on society's ability to manage the development of large energy systems and to cope with their structural and political consequences.

The money and talent invested in an electrical program tend to convey a disproportionate influence in the counsels of government, often directly through the incestuous relationship of policy-making bodies with mission-oriented agencies and through their tendency to swap staff. This position, now well developed in most industrial countries, further distorts both social and energy priorities and excludes nonconformist opinions in a way that has proved peculiarly intractable to the usual political remedies. For example, changing the legislatively mandated function and name of the United States Atomic Energy Commission does not seem to have helped much, largely because no administrator can change the perspectives inherent in an agency that has retained more than 90 percent of its staff from the old AEC. The indirect effects of such political and policy commitments are pervasive and lasting. So long as federal research and development interest seems to be directed mainly toward fission technologies, for example, it will be hard to persuade first-rate technologists to devote their careers to small-scale solar technologies, thereby limiting the long-term ability of that sector to absorb research and development funding effectively.

The foreclosure of options by commitments of resources and time is a crucial point with enormous social implications. Further pursuit of the centralized/electrified/nuclear approach, of which the liquid-metal fast breeder reactor (LMFBR) is the keystone, will in practice make it impossible to return later to a different policy path [6, 7] relying on conservation, rapidly deployed "soft" energy-income technologies that are relatively decentralized and nonelectrical, and efficient transitional fossil-fuel technologies of modest scale. Resource and political investments in the LMFBR program alone would suffice, if redirected, to make this "soft" path a prompt reality—or, if retained, to make it forever unattainable. Such investments tend in international history to follow the manner of sheep, with each government pointing to similar commitments elsewhere, either as examples of wisdom or as threats of competition. Wiser decisions by even small countries can thus catch disproportionately the attention of the flock. Some countries are already realizing that competitive folly is beyond their means.

LIMITS TO NUCLEAR FISSION TECHNOLOGY

It is impossible to discuss the biophysical, social, and ethical implications of and limits to nuclear fission without intermingling some technical facts and opinions, particularly since my assessments differ from those of some other analysts, and we cannot all be right. I suggest that much of the disagreement in policy interpretations of agreed-upon physical facts arises from a difference described by Harold Green: "To some, the absence of evidence that there will be injury connotes the belief that injury will not in fact result; to others, the absence of proof that injury will not result connotes the belief that injury may result" [8]. This difference in treating scientific uncertainty is especially important in nuclear matters, where many fundamental data are not only unknown but also likely to remain so for a long time, and where some are probably unknowable in principle. In the low-level radiation controversy, for example, some people say that safety has not been proved while others say that harm has not been proved. Both are correct; and one must decide for oneself which position is ethically preferable.

The biophysical hazards peculiar to nuclear fission grow out of a unique combination of range in space, range in time, and moral significance (for example, genetic transmissibility) in the potential effects of accident or malice involving toxic or explosive materials unavoidably present in the nuclear fuel cycle. Unique sociopolitical hazards in turn arise from the measures likely to be taken to reduce perceived biophysical risks. Before discussing these broad issues, I should mention a few more specialized, less philosophical problems.

Biophysical Constraints

Potential biophysical constraints on the practical use of nuclear power include the transitional issues mentioned earlier for larger power stations in general (some, such as local heat dissipation, being somewhat exacerbated) plus several that have been realized only recently. For example, emissions of 10.8–year krypton–85 from nuclear facilities over the next fifty years, according to classical projections, should increase the electrical conductivity of the entire atmosphere below the tropopause by about 15 percent, with unknown but possibly substantial effects on nimbus rainfall or on other events that depend on nucleation and charge-separation phenomena. This risk is not easily avoided, since control technologies for krypton–85 would be expensive. Likewise, when uranium is mined its chemically different decay product, thorium–230, remains behind in the tailings, generating (with a 78,000-year half-life) radium–226, which (with a 1,620-year half-life) generates radon–222 gas. Some of this gas (with a 3.8-day half-life) escapes from the tailings piles into the air. The radon from western tailings is typically passing over the eastern seaboard while decaying into extremely radioactive products, such as polonium–218, which tend to absorb onto submicron particles and to irradiate sensitive tissue such as the bronchial epithelium, thereby causing cancers. Data on the escape and effects of radon gas are very uncertain, but the total deaths caused might be more than those caused by uncontrolled emissions from an equivalent coal-fired power station.

The amounts of materials involved in the nuclear fuel cycle are substantial. Mining enough uranium to operate 1,000 megawatts of electric capacity continuously for a year typically requires 85,700 metric tons of ore to be crushed and treated after it has been removed from under about 2.5 million metric tons of overburden. For comparison, an equivalent coal-fired station burns about 4.7 million metric tons of coal per year. Chattanooga Shale, which some enthusiasts of fast breeder reactors foresee as their eventual source of uranium, would have to be mined in approximately the same quantities as coal for equivalent coal-fired stations.

The more familiar radiological hazards of the nuclear fuel cycle arise from its extremely large inventories of radioactive materials that must be isolated from the biosphere for periods ranging from seconds or less to around a hundred million years. Contrary to some facile opinions, it is not technically practicable to reduce significantly the hazard of the very long-lived transuranic isotopes by separating them and fissioning them in a reactor, as this process would create roughly comparable amounts of transuranic-contaminated low-level wastes.

By way of illustrating the magnitude of hazard involved, a 1,000 megawatt light-water reactor at equilibrium contains enough iodine–131 (to mention just one isotope) to contaminate the air over the forty-eight coterminous U.S. states to a height of 10 km to eight times the maximum permissible concentration for that isotope. The same reactor contains enough strontium–90 to contaminate the annual fresh-water runoff of the same area to 12 times the maximum permissible concentration for that isotope. A large reprocessing plant contains about 150 times more strontium than the reactor. Of course, dispersion could never actually be so thorough, widespread, and uniform, but the size of the numbers suggests a need for the most diligent containment.

Plutonium–239, a 24,400-year hard alpha emitter that is the most plentiful of the transuranic isotopes in the nuclear fuel cycle, further illustrates the exquisite care demanded in preventing the escape of nuclear materials. Pu-239 is chemically reactive and can, in various ways, form respirable aerosols. Its chemistry is extremely complex, and knowledge of its environmental pathways and medical effects is sketchy. Corresponding knowledge for the many less common transuranic isotopes, many of which are more hazardous, is almost nil. It is known that a few ten-millionths of an ounce of plutonium-239, if inhaled, can cause lung cancer, but nobody knows whether a quantity hundreds or thousands of times smaller would also do so under certain circumstances. Several independent hypotheses to this effect have not so far been proved or disproved by any direct experiment, but if any were correct, then inhalation doses of plutonium-239 capable of inducing lung cancer in 3.9 billion people could be contained in a piece about the size of a marble or a cherry. If the hypotheses were completely wrong and the present standards, recently attacked on several independent grounds, were completely right, then the piece involved would be more the size of a beachball. This is still not very reassuring, since a typical modern power reactor contains about half a ton, and an equivalent fast breeder reactor would contain several tons of the material. To make matters worse, the scientific uncertainty over plutonium toxicity is likely to persist for many years, or more likely decades. Nuclear decisions must be made meanwhile; and, since the levels of plutonium presently allowed in air or lung are barely detectable, even slightly more stringent standards would lack operational meaning because the amounts involved would be undetectable in principle.

The large inventories of persistently radioactive, and often biochemically active, materials in the nuclear fuel cycle, and the presence also of internal energy (chemical, mechanical, thermal) which could aid release of such materials from their containing structures, give rise to unique sociotechnical issues of transcendent importance. The central issue, one not faced with any previous technology, is whether fission technology is too demanding for society's management skills. Are its safety problems too difficult to solve? If so, then as Hannes Alfvén points out, it is futile to claim that they are solved by pointing to all the efforts made to solve them [9]. Both the literature of nuclear experience and analogies with other engineering experience suggest that nuclear safety is not a mere engineering problem that can be solved by sufficient care (though it certainly has unresolved engineering problems in profusion) but rather a new type of problem that could be solved only by infallible people, none of whom currently exist. This constraint appears to be a new and awkward type of limit to a technology.

Sociopolitical Constraints

Nuclear systems must be protected not only against malfunctioning machines but also against malfunctioning people. Toxic and explosive materials in the nuclear fuel cycle offer new and unprecedented opportunities for high technology violence and coercion, as well as for international proliferation and blackmail of the type cogently described by Robert Heilbroner [10]. For example, a few kilograms of reactor-grade plutonium in any chemical form can be made into a crude but convincing atomic bomb by a talented amateur, or into a rather predictable and efficient bomb by a government. On present plans, twenty years from now, some 20,000 bombs' worth of strategic material will be in transit annually within the same international community that has consistently failed to halt bank robberies, aircraft hijackings, and the heroin traffic. Once generated, this material will remain explosive not just for the short lifetime of political arrangements, but for the foreseeable lifetime of our species.

Careful analysis of present or proposed safeguards against theft of strategic materials suggests that, especially if viewed internationally and in the long term, the problem is insoluble in principle. The safeguards are bound to be ineffective, repressive, or most likely both. Nuclear technology places some absolute constraints on society by making technically possible some events that absolutely must not happen. The natural response of threatened societies, and a response that is already under way, will be to sacrifice traditional values and institutions—ranging from civil liberties to the competitive market system—in order to make diverse, disinclined, or disgruntled people safe for the technology. The civil liberties implications of nuclear deployment are so disturbing that it is hardly an overstatement to suggest that a large civilian nuclear sector could bring about precisely those political changes that our costly military nuclear deterrent was intended to prevent [11]. As Alfvén remarks, it is necessary to envisage "very strict police control of the entire world. . . . This will be difficult to achieve and does not lead us to a very attractive future society" [12].

Anyone who feels that references to a potential police state are exaggerations need only ponder the changes introduced by federal governments and the airlines in response to a few hijackings. In every airport armed guards are instructed to shoot to kill under certain circumstances, all luggage and passengers are subjected to search through either physical body inspection or electromagnetic sensors. Even joking about a bomb or gun is an offense punishable by immediate arrest. And hijackings have not one ten-thousandth the potential of nuclear sabotage to damage property or to kill.

Moreover, for society (in Kneese's words) to "exercise great vigilance and the highest levels of quality control, continuously and *indefinitely*" requires specific mechanisms for perpetuating personal dedication and skill by "creating a continuing tradition of meticulous attention to detail" [13]. But technologies are run by people, not by whole societies, and the burden falls on both. People in the nuclear enterprise must not make serious mistakes, become inattentive or corrupt, disobey instructions, or the like. Their standard of personal conduct must differ greatly from historical norms for the general population. The society that provides context and incentives for such personal conduct and that insulates nuclear workers from political or commercial pressures must also provide the tranquility to avoid wars, guerrilla movements, specialized strikes, terrorist attacks, and other threats to the persistently vulnerable nuclear inventories. It is hard to envisage a credible set of policies for achieving these management goals—particularly without degrading pluralism, social diversity, and freedom of personal choice. It is also apparent that in the absence of strong compensatory mechanisms not yet identified, both the impact of human fallibility or malice and the social difficulties of reducing that impact are bound to increase as reactors proliferate, nuclear salespeople outrun engineers, investment conquers caution, routine dulls commitment, boredom replaces novelty, and less skilled and motivated technicians take over, especially in countries with little technical infrastructure or tradition.

Even the way in which many governments now try to make nuclear decisions can erode democratic principles. Since nuclear technology poses compulsory insensible, exotic, long-term hazards that depart from social experience and are difficult to subject to political judgment, and since the size and nature of these hazards are disputed or unknown or unknowable, there is a temptation, to which many governments have succumbed, to leave the decisions effectively to self-appointed experts rather than to the public political process. The powerful constituencies engaged in the nuclear debate, the misguided urgency of many autarchic governments in allaying public apprehension, and the superficially technical and esoteric nature of the issues together create a danger to democracy by limiting the effectiveness of political discourse.

Unfortunately, although most proponents of nuclear power are honest and competent, few appreciate that others with similar qualities have very different, perhaps broader, views that merit detailed exploration. The difficulty of shifting one's paradigms (a point of which I am particularly mindful as one who used to welcome nuclear power) is impeding good-faith discussion of alternative policies even within the technical community, and thereby contributing to many politicians' impression that soundly based alternatives are not available. In reality, sensible alternative energy policies can be devised, not by a continuation of incremental ad-hocracy, but only by working backwards from a long-term goal to what must be done, or omitted, in order to retain necessary options. This argument should receive particular consideration in the nuclear debate because fission technology requires so many scarce resources that a substantial commitment to it can effectively foreclose all other options.

Ethical Constraints

Many policymakers today consider the most important and difficult questions of energy strategy to be technical and economic. I believe, on the contrary, that they are mainly social and ethical, and cannot be framed by people whose vision is purely technical. The basic questions are in the sphere not of reactor engineering but of human capability and behavior: of history, psychology, law, common sense, even poetry—in short, in the realm of the ordinary political thought and speech of generalist citizens. To move from the democratic principle that the essence of public policy determination is the optimal public resolution of conflict toward the scientific principle that the technical truth (as perceived by that scientific group currently enjoying political credence) is the ultimate desideratum for policy is to remove public accountability and judicial review in favor of government by elite, an approach incompatible with democratic principles [14].

Leaving our descendents irreversible nuclear commitments that society does not know how to handle seems to me to be ethically unacceptable. So does squandering fossil fuels. Moreover, there is an important link between the two issues. Fossil fuels could be used not to build a highway off the edge of a cliff, but rather to build a bridge to a worthy goal. That is, they could be used as briefly and sparingly as possible to buy the few decades needed to deploy fully the relatively decentralized technologies based on renewable energy sources. But this is a real option only if resources and time have not earlier been preempted by nuclear power. Only then can good use be made of the last opportunity for an energy transition subsidized by cheap fossil fuels—by going as directly as possible to ultimate sources, meanwhile using transitional technologies adaptable to these sources.

Most governments publicly regret, but officially accept,the inevitability of a world where all governments desiring nuclear weapons can obtain them and, presumably, can sooner or later use them. Many nations are making such a world inevitable. Each claims that if it does not proliferate nuclear technology, the others will do so anyhow. The conventional wisdom is that the multiplicity of nuclear exporters and their independence of United States policy makes this country unable to demand a particular moral tone of the rest of the world in these matters—that is, to demand that proliferation stop. But I believe that this view is, and must be exposed as, a disingenuous fiction. For the next few years at least, the dependence of all nations' nuclear programs on the United States for materials, for technical services and support, and above all for political support is so great, and true metastasis of the technology and of its essential political base has been so small, that a principled decision by the United States alone to discourage fission everywhere could virtually solve the nuclear proliferation problem.

SOME PREVENTIVE MEASURES

A unilateral effort in the United States to turn off nuclear power all over the world should be part of two packages of policies, of which the first could undoubtedly succeed and the second might. First, both by its own strong example and by direct help, the United States should make available to all countries technical, political, and perhaps fiscal support for wide-ranging energy conservation, indeed frugality, and for deploying technologies based on renewable sources, particularly the kinds that most people throughout the world need to meet their everyday requirements for heating, lighting, cooking, and pumping. Such an approach seems sounder for all countries, even Japan or India, than the nuclear approach. The traffic of help would, of course, be two-way. The United States and other technically endowed countries are skilled at technical innovation, but most of the social innovations everyone needs will probably continue to come from the smaller countries.

The United States, as the country with most fat in its energy budget, should commit itself to energy stability by about the mid-1980s and to substantial energy shrinkage thereafter. With what is now known about energy efficiency, Americans could without doubt be at least as well-employed and as uncomfortably comfortable as now with only about half as much primary energy. The United States in the early 1960s used only about half as much energy per person as now—inefficiently, too—and that was not a period of massive unemployment or physical hardship. The time is here, indeed long past, to devote resources and ingenuity to this most cost-effective path. The attendant social problems would be substantial, but they seem more tractable than those of a vulnerable and probably coercive high-energy path. A lower-energy path offers opportunities for greater pluralism, for more meaningful social roles, and for reversing the degradation of the social milieu that acute energitis has produced by mechanizing and fragmenting work. This change of direction would be profound, but I think a concerted effort at both political leadership and grassroots lobbying could accomplish it. To a surprising extent, the needed values and perceptions are already appearing through society, and will accelerate as more energy strategists develop and provide the catalyst of explicit alternative models.

The second policy initiative that should accompany the termination of the fission experiment is to begin at last to discuss strategic arms reduction, nonproliferation, and control of civilian nuclear technology all together as inseparable parts of the same problem. A clear commitment to solving this problem, by the country that has the most commercial profit to lose by solving it, could meet with a more constructive reception from all countries than the piecemeal and hypocritical approaches tried so far. Moreover, the energy conservation and supply policies mentioned above should go far to reduce the international tensions that now make nuclear proliferation attractive to many countries.

There are deep differences between advocates of high- and low-energy futures, of high and intermediate technologies, of large and small scale, of centralized and local decision, of political reflex and social inquiry. The differences impede the adoption, even the serious discussion, of such United States policies. The vigorous and informed use of the democratic political process could go very far to resolve such differences: whether this will happen soon enough, and whether the conclusions will be determined by events meanwhile, I cannot say. But as I suggest in my introduction to *Non-Nuclear Futures*, the differences really boil down to a more fundamental limit of human perception.

> At the root of the issues we discuss here is a difference in perspective about man and his works. Some people, impressed and fascinated by the glittering achievements of technology, say that if we will only have faith in human ingenuity (theirs) we shall see the Second Coming of Prometheus, bringing us undreamed-of freedom and plenty. Other people think we should plan on something more modest, lest we find instead undreamed-of tyrannies and perils, and that even if we had an unlimited energy source, we would lack the discipline to use it wisely. Such people are really saying, firstly, that energy is not enough to solve the ancient problems of the

human spirit, and secondly, that the technologists who claim they can satisfy Alfvén's condition that "no acts of God can be permitted" are guilty of hubris, the human sin of divine arrogance. We have today an opportunity—perhaps our last—to exercise our responsibility to foster in our society a greater humility, one that springs from an appreciation of the essential frailty of the human design [15].

 *Chapter 4*

Economic Growth, Energy Use, and Altruism

Bruce Hannon

This paper explores the idea of substituting energy content for price as the basis for consumer choices among alternative goods and services. The objective is to coax into being a form of altruism leading to effective energy conservation programs in this country. Thrift rather than consumption is suggested as the behavior more deserving of social status, but this change in goals would necessitate a thorough understanding by the three major classes of consumers—individuals, industries, and government—of the stock of available energy, the rate of use of that stock, and the stability of that rate of use. My own work, and that of the Energy Research Group, is dedicated to these ends.

ENERGY CONSERVATION

The limits to United States energy resources are becoming clear. To cite only three of the many indications of this trend: first, most energy-independence scenarios depend heavily on nuclear energy as the energy form of the future for the United States; however, Michael Rieber and Ronald Halcrow have shown that the energy spent launching the nuclear plan will be greater than the energy produced, at least until the late 1980s [1]. Second, Rieber has also shown that the available quantity of low-sulfur coal in the United States is considerably less than formerly expected [2]. Third, the U.S. Geological Survey recently announced a drastic reduction in its estimates of the total recoverable United States oil and gas reserves [3].

Given these known limits and the uncertainty of available quantities from these sources, plus the projected limits to the flow of solar energy [4], a strong energy conservation policy should be adopted in order to ease the trauma of transition to life on a constrained energy budget. The United States should assess the stored energy resources clearly available to it today, set aside a quantity sufficient to meet national security needs, and decide on a maximum rate of consumption annually that will guarantee a sustainable state for present and future populations.

The political uncertainty about foreign sources of energy, as well as our own dependence on these sources, increases the necessity for a domestic energy conservation policy. In 1973 the energy used to make exported goods (about 7 percent of total United States domestic energy production) approximately equaled the energy used to make imported goods. But direct imports of energy into the United States exceeded exports by about 25 percent of all United States domestic energy production in 1973 [5]. Since then the dependence on imported sources has grown rapidly.

This proposed conservation policy heading towards equilibrium should become a generalized national aim rather than a goal, in the same sense that material economic growth is now a national aim. The policy could not help but have a direct impact on economic affairs; energy has now taken on such importance that material economic activity for the nation is the basic correlate of the rate of energy consumption. The interrelationship between energy growth and economic growth is explored in a 1975 paper showing that, for the period from 1963 to 1967, the rise in per capita consumption—rather than technological change, shifts in the composition of consumption, or population growth—accounted for almost all of the 24 percent increase in energy use [6].

Three basic levels of voluntary energy conservation activities are possible. First, technological innovations can improve the efficiency of energy use. These might include more efficient airconditioners, better insulation for houses, smaller autos, and demechanized production activities. These changes would not have a radical effect on the pattern of living in the United States. Even so, they would reduce energy demand and produce dollar savings for consumers—the latter being a mixed blessing, as I will show later in this paper.

At the second level of energy conservation, consumers would improve the efficiency of product use—for example, by using an urban bus instead of a car and by choosing refillable instead of throwaway containers. These choices represent ways of substituting one entity for another in order to reduce the energy consumed per unit of the product or service delivered. Changes in product use require greater personal life style changes than do changes in technology.

Third, it is possible to save energy by persuading people, industries, and governments to substitute different consumption objectives for those often pursued now—for example, to vacation at home instead of in the Bahamas, to read a book instead of drive in the country, to invest in a solar-energy company instead of an auto company, or to spend the federal budget on national health insurance instead of the Highway Trust Fund. All of these decisions represent alternate uses of income that would consume less energy than the choices usually made today. Changes in consumption objectives would have a greater impact on the nation's life-style than the other two levels of energy conservation activities.

Conservation offers certain and immediate relief from the energy crisis, rather than the uncertain and long-delayed respite that could be produced by opting to increase energy supplies. However, adopting conservation on any piecemeal basis is fraught with difficulties. These problems are explained by examining three potential obstacles to voluntary energy conservation, all of which will require the development of an altruistic consumer consciousness if they are to be overcome. The obstacles are:

1. the tendency of consumers to spend more energy as their incomes increase;
2. the long-established industrial practice of using cheap energy rather than more expensive capital or labor;
3. the wasteful respending of money (energy) saved through conservation measures.

While these three obstacles complicate the design and implementation of new policies to achieve energy savings, several viable program options still exist, although these require federal intervention to reduce demand. In concluding this analysis I will examine two non-voluntary energy conservation measures. The first is an energy tax, geared to wage levels. The second is a rationing or quota system using energy coupons.

To explore the nature of these three obstacles and to provide a means for calculating the effects of energy-conservation schemes on employment and income, the Energy Research Group has devised large and effective models to quantify the concept of "energy cost," an idea I have been developing since 1969. Each good and service, including energy itself, contains embodied energy, in the same sense that a product, service, or energy unit possesses a dollar cost.

MODELING ENERGY CONSUMPTION AND EMPLOYMENT

The production process is made up of all the industrial and commercial establishments and public enterprises, government and nonprofit, that carry on the highly complex exchange of raw and intermediate products and services. Its primary goal is to supply the demand for the array of consumption activities in which society engages.

All domestic and imported energy is processed and distributed either to various industrial, commercial, and government establishments or directly to individual consumers to provide energy for home heating, cooling, lighting, cooking, and transportation. In the production process, energy is consumed and is thus embodied in the manufactured product or the service. Therefore, as resources are transformed into useful products and services, their embodied energy and dollar value increase. Imported products are considered to have been made by production processes similar to those used in the United States; therefore, we assign to these products an embodied energy value similar to that of their United States counterparts. Embodied energy, plus directly imported energy, plus energy mined from the earth in the United States, constitute the total flow in the American economy of non-solar energy, which, like dollar income, can be accurately assigned to the various items of final consumption.

These energies can be quantified by the technique of input-output modeling. Immense amounts of dollar data about the detailed demand and output of the United States industrial-commercial activity are gathered routinely. The dollar data are organized by the government into a matrix of transactions within the various sectors for a given year. By using computers for specialized data collection and matrix manipulation, the Energy Research Group transforms the dollar flows into energy flows, using units of energy (Btu's) to measure the input and output of the energy sectors—such as coal, crude oil, refined petroleum, natural gas, and electricity—and dollar values to represent the quantities of all the other inputs and outputs. This set of activities is then transformed into a matrix representing the total energy requirements for the various activities of final consumption. In this manner each activity of final consumption in the United States is assigned an appropriate level of energy, direct or embodied. In a somewhat similar manner, embodied employment—total or by occupation—can be determined for the activities of final consumption. We have described this process in detail elsewhere [7].

Using the energy model, we allocated energy and employment over the various activities of final consumption for 1963 and 1967.

Because of the complex and expensive process of gathering data, no more recent data are available from the federal government. Sensitivity, error-analysis, and projecting techniques have been developed to help overcome older and potentially inaccurate data; linear modeling of this kind is not done without difficulty. But in spite of these modeling problems, there is no other practical method of calculating the direct and indirect energy and employment demands.

To summarize the energy and employment modeling: for both 1963 and 1967, nearly two-thirds of all energy and employment was used directly and in embodied form for personal consumption [8]. (Data for 1967 are shown in Table 4–1.) Capital-formation and net-inventory changes required about 13 percent of all energy and employment. Government activities—federal, state, and local—consumed about 16 percent of all energy and about 21 percent of all nonmilitary employment.

Personal consumption is clearly the dominant form of energy use, consuming 63 percent of all United States energy in 1967. In our energy model, the personal consumption activity can be broken down into eighty-three separate parts, with total energy and employment demand calculated for each. For our purposes, the most effec-

Table 4–1. Percentages of Total[a] Energy and Employment (Direct and Embodied) for Final Consumption Activities, 1967

Personal consumption is clearly the dominant form of energy use, consuming 63 percent of all United States energy in 1967.

Activity	*Total[b] Primary Energy*	*Total Employment[c]*
Personal consumption	63.0	59.5
Capital formation	10.1	12.3
Inventory change	3.1	1.4
Exports	8.3	4.1
Federal, defense	6.6	8.6
Federal, other	1.6	2.5
State and local governments	7.5	11.6
Total Final Demand	100.2	100.0

Source: Robert Herendeen, "Energy Impact of Final Demand Expenditures, 1963 and 1967," Technical Memo 62, Center for Advanced Computation, University of Illinois (1975).

[a]Domestic base: All figures contain estimates of energy and labor embodied in imports.

[b]Coal plus crude petroleum plus natural gas plus the hydro power of electricity converted at the fossil conversion rate.

[c]Jobs basis: All figures contain estimates of energy and labor embodied in imports.

tive form of comparison is on the basis of energy intensity, measured in Btu's per dollar.

The energy and labor requirements of the twenty most significant activities of personal consumption, in terms of dollars, were ranked according to decreasing energy intensity, as shown in Table 4–2, by dividing the Btu's and jobs by the dollars spent on each activity. Interspersed for comparison are aggregated activities of personal consumption, auto and home ownership, average investment, and federal spending. Total employment intensities are also shown.

The conservation-minded consumer with extra income could use the data in Table 4–2 to control his impact on energy use and employment. When the total energy and employment intensities of the eighty-three activities of personal consumption are plotted against each other (see Figure 4–1), the data seem to fall along two basic lines [9]. One is roughly horizontal, representing the low-energy-intensive services. The other is nearly vertical, representing the low-labor-intensive products. The services range from low-labor-intensity, high-wage activities such as physicians' care to high-labor-intensity, low-wage activities such as hospital services. Similarly, the products vary from those with high energy intensity and low energy cost per unit such as energy directly supplied (for example, home heating oil), to those with low energy intensity and high energy cost per unit such as furniture [10]. A similar pattern emerges when industrial consumption data are plotted along the same axes. This pattern is a key finding in our research: goods or services may be energy-intensive while not labor-intensive, or the reverse, but not both.

Figure 4–1 does not show all the effects of a shift in consumption patterns. Suppose, for example, that an individual purchases a new car. The energy and employment effects reflected in Figure 4–1 are only those produced in the web of industries that supply the auto industry—including fabricating, transporting, and retailing. These effects do not include the energy and employment created by the demand for goods by the workers who receive the money from the new car purchase, or the energy and labor demanded by the workers employed by the producers of these goods as they, too, spend their wages. This process is analogous to the multiplier effect, which refers to the amplification of dollar expenditures in the economy. Energy, like money, passes through many sets of hands; some is saved, some is spent, and some is taxed, until eventually the effect of the original purchase dies out.

If one assumes that for every dollar spent on a new car, two more are spent via the multiplier effect on average personal consumption,

Table 4–2. Total Energy and Labor Intensity of the Activities of Personal Consumption, 1971

The energy and labor requirements of the twenty most significant activities of personal consumption, in terms of dollars, are ranked according to energy intensity. The conservation-minded consumer with extra income could use this data to control his impact on energy use and employment.

Activity	*Energy Intensity* *Btu/$*	*Labor Intensity* *Jobs/Hundred Thousand $*
Electricity	502,500	4.4
Gasoline and Oil	480,700	7.3
(Housing)	(144,000)*	(N/A)
(Auto Ownership)	(111,500)	(8.1)
Cleaning Preparations	78,100	7.3
(Average for all Personal Consumption)	(70,000)	(8.0)
Kitchen and Household Appliances	58,700	5.5
New and Used Cars	55,600	7.8
Durable House Furniture	54,600	8.9
(Private Investment)	(45,600)	(6.6)
Food Purchases	41,100	8.5
Furniture	36,700	9.2
(Federal Spending)	(36,300)	(8.2)
Women and Children's Clothing	33,100	10.0
Restaurants	32,400	8.8
Men and Boys Clothing	31,400	9.8
Religious and Welfare Activity	27,800	8.6
Private Hospitals	26,100	17.2
Automobile Repair and Maintenance	23,500	4.8
Financial Interests Except Insurance	21,500	7.8
Tobacco Products	19,800	5.8
Telephone and Telegraph	19,000	5.9
Rented Home (Interest Plus Some Utilities)	18,300	3.5
Physicians	10,700	3.3
Own Home (Interest Charges Only)	8,300	1.7

Source: Bruce Hannon, "Energy Conservation and the Consumer," *Science* 189 (July 11, 1975): 95–102.
*Numbers in parentheses are for aggregated activities.

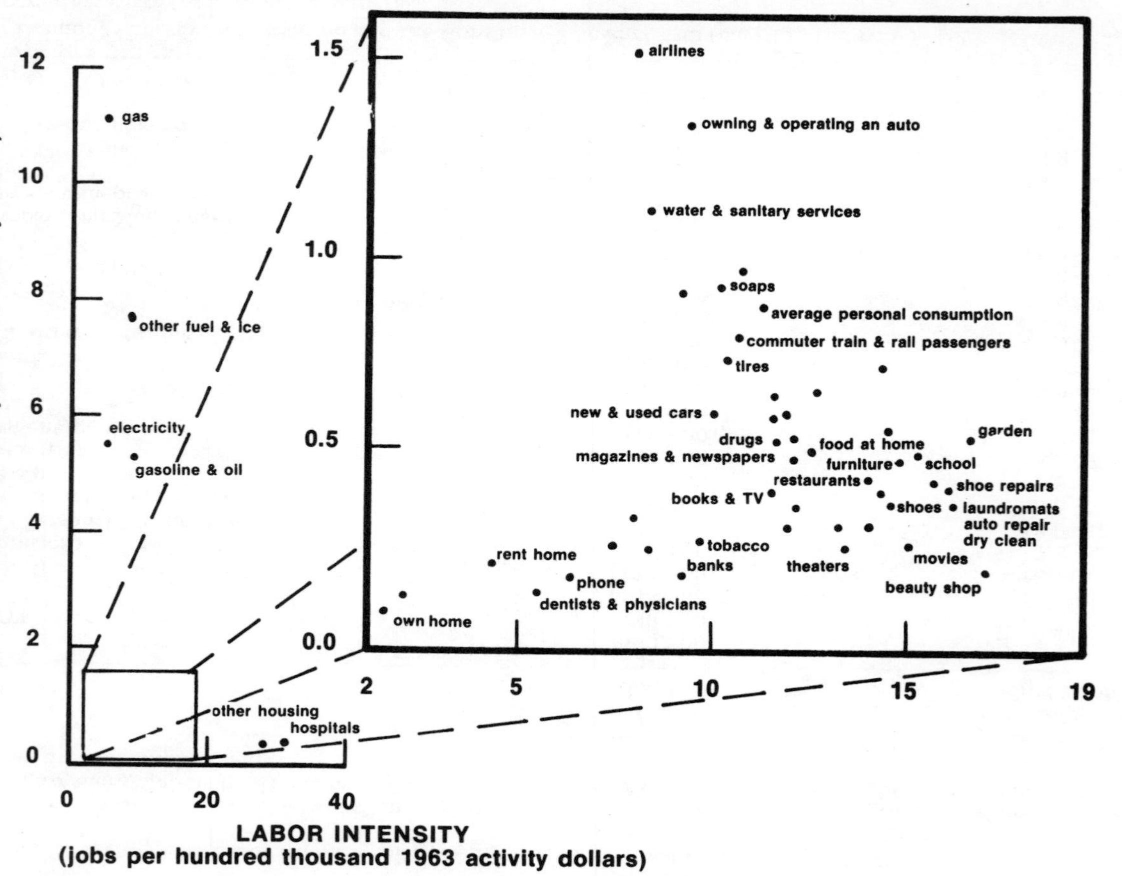
TOTAL ENERGY INTENSITY
(hundred thousand BTU per 1963 activity dollar)
LABOR INTENSITY
(jobs per hundred thousand 1963 activity dollars)
0
2
4
6
8
10
12
0
20
40
0.0
0.5
1.0
1.5
2
5
10
15
19
gas
other fuel & ice
electricity
gasoline & oil
other housing
hospitals
airlines
owning & operating an auto
water & sanitary services
soaps
average personal consumption
commuter train & rail passengers
tires
new & used cars
drugs
magazines & newspapers
food at home
furniture
garden
school
restaurants
books & TV
shoe repairs
shoes
laundromats
auto repair
dry clean
movies
beauty shop
tobacco
banks
theaters
rent home
phone
dentists & physicians
own home

Figure 4–1. Total Energy and Labor Intensity of Various Personal Consumption Activities, 1963 (The inset is an enlargement of the central portion of the data.).

When the total energy and employment intensities of various activities of personal consumption are plotted against each other, the data seem to fall along two basic lines. One is roughly horizontal, representing the low-energy-intensive services. The other is nearly vertical, representing the low-labor-intensive products. This pattern is a key finding; goods or services may be energy-intensive while not labor-intensive, or the reverse, but not both.

Source: Bruce Hannon, "Energy Conservation and the Consumer," *Science* 189 (July 11, 1975): 95–102.

then each new car dollar spent demands 60,000 Btu's for the new car (see Figure 4–1) and 172,000 Btu's (or two average 1963 personal-consumption expenditure dollars) for a total of 232,000 Btu's. The expansion from 60,000 to 232,000 Btu's demonstrates the effects of increased money flow on energy demand. The effects are similar on employment demand. The multiplier effect also works in reverse; as a dollar is removed from the economy, it reduces energy consumption both directly and indirectly.

THE FIRST OBSTACLE: INCOME AND ENERGY

The first obstacle appears immediately in the initiation of the energy conservation process—reducing energy consumption requires changing spending patterns in this society, and this is not likely to be a process popular with individuals, industrial decision makers, or government policymakers. People will resist radical changes in their lives, changes that might mean more work, less convenience, and greater variability in their day-to-day routines. However, the direct correlation between income and energy consumption dictates that people must consume a different set of goods and services if energy is to be conserved.

Consumer Spending

Most people do not associate income spending and energy demand. Income is easily measured, whether in the form of a paycheck, revenue from taxes, or money from stocks and bonds. Spending is more difficult to trace, especially spending for personal consumption, and most difficult is making obvious the energy which individuals, as well as industries and governments, expend as they spend their money.

One way to analyze energy consumption is to examine spending patterns, the best-known measure of which was a detailed survey of expenditures by income class made in the early 1960s [11]. We calculated the direct and embodied energy connected with income after taxes to discover that direct energy use—home heating, cooling, lighting, appliances, and auto fuel—leveled off with rising income [12]. Embodied energy consumption—such as the energy in foods, cars, furniture, and the tickets for buses, trains, and planes—tended to rise with rising income, leaving a nearly linear connection between total energy demand and income. When income doubled, energy demand nearly doubled. Clearly, current consumer preferences dictate a high level of energy consumption.

The data also indicated that direct energy taxes would be very unfair to the poor, who consume two-thirds of their energy directly in the form of oil, gas, gasoline, or electricity used in their home furnaces, appliances, or automobiles. Those of average income consume about 55 percent of their energy directly, while those in the wealthiest class use only about one-third directly.

These data should force a closer look at other calculations of income and energy consumption. For instance, Resources for the Future reported that the average New Yorker exceeds the national average in per capita income by some 25 percent, but uses considerably less energy than the average person [13]. This energy calculation was made by dividing all direct energy used in New York by the number of residents. By this method, those who live near the high-energy consumptive steel mills in Gary, Indiana, have the country's most energy-intensive life-style. Obviously the dynamics of embodied energy consumption were ignored in the RFF calculations. If the consumption of the average New Yorker could be studied in terms of embodied energy, it would actually be nearly 25 percent above average in total energy demand, simply because his income was that high.

Governmental spending styles would also have to change under a successful energy conservation program. Thus those who will be setting United States energy policy may consequently be opposed from within the government itself.

Table 4–3 shows estimates of the total energy and labor requirements demanded directly and indirectly by the spending of five billion 1975 dollars on seven different federal programs, including tax relief [14]. In normal economic times, the Highway Trust Fund clearly creates less employment demand and more energy demand than such projects as building educational facilities or sewage-treatment plants. Also, railroad building provides more jobs and uses less energy than highway construction. When the total system of rail passenger and freight is compared with that of cars and trucks, the railroads use less energy per unit of service. However, changing the spending priorities of the government to less energy-consumptive activities and policies has been and will continue to be a formidable task.

A Starting Point

Our data indicate that the upper-middle income class is the most fertile area for energy conservation. This class demands the most total energy due to the combination of a large number of consumers with relatively high energy-intensive consumption patterns. Psychologists intent on studying class behavior for the purpose of enhanc-

Table 4–3. The Impact on Energy Consumption and Employment of a Five Billion Dollar[a] Investment (1975 dollars) in Seven Federal Programs

In normal economic times, the Highway Trust Fund clearly creates less employment demand and more energy demand than such projects as building educational facilities or sewage treatment plants. Also, railroad building provides more jobs and uses less energy than highway construction.

	Energy Consumption		*Employment Demand*	
Federal Program	*Requirement (Btu per 1963 dollar of program)*	*Total requirement (trillion Btu)*	*Jobs per $100,000 of program (1975)*	*Total number of jobs*
Highway construction	112,200[b]	409.53	8.1	256,180
Railroad and mass transit construction	43,100	157.32	8.4	264,430
Water and waste treatment facilities construction	65,400	238.71	8.2	259,490
Educational facilities construction	70,600	257.69	8.5	268,980
National health insurance	40,400	147.46	13.4	423,220
Criminal justice and civilian safety	118,500	432.53	12.4	393,520
Personal consumption expenditures (tax relief)	86,000[c]	313.90	8.7	275,120

Source: Bruce Hannon, "Bottles, Cans, Energy," *Environment* 14 (March 1972): 14–19.

[a] Five billion 1975 dollars are equal to $3.65 billion in 1963 and $3.165 billion in 1958. No attempt was made to correct for the technological impact on energy use efficiency between 1963 and 1975. It is generally expected that 1975 technology will be more energy intensive.

[b] As in all programs this number is for a technology of estimated efficiency. The actual energy intensity of all highway construction in 1963 was 98,000 Btu per dollar. Similar construction (Army Corps of Engineers) caried from 92,000 to 146,000 Btu per dollar, the highest of all government programs.

[c] Includes direct energy purchases and the energy and labor required for trade and transportation margins.

ing energy conservation should focus here rather than on the very rich, the very poor, or even on the average consumer. This class is also the likely reference group that directs the goals inherent in the rising expectations of the average income group. Reducing the energy consumption patterns of the upper-middle income group therefore could have significant secondary effects. Such a reduction, however, would involve developing an altruistic consciousness in these people such that they voluntarily reduce their spending and/or their incomes.

If this first, and significant, obstacle were overcome, and energy conservation policies were accepted at the consumer level, pressure would still have to be applied to industry to abandon certain energy-expensive practices. One of these practices—the substitution of energy for labor—is the source of the second impediment.

THE SECOND OBSTACLE: TRADING ENERGY FOR LABOR

Economic forces have made the substitution of low-cost energy for labor a pervasive pattern throughout industry, agriculture, and commerce. As steps are taken to reverse this pattern, significant opposition is likely to develop, creating another major obstacle.

Measuring Output in Terms of Energy

The standard economic production equations relate output to various expressions involving the input of labor and capital, the factors of production. Great attention is paid to their productivity—that is, how much of each factor is required to produce a unit of output—and to marginal productivity, the change in output with respect to the change in the use of each factor. In theory producers will use increasing amounts of an input, until its marginal productivity falls to the same level as its marginal price.

In our calculations we have introduced energy as a primary factor of production because of its obvious physical importance in production processes [15, 16], and have developed a time series of the ratio of the cost of capital to the cost of a kilowatt hour of electricity. Electricity was chosen for comparison because it is almost totally available for mechanical work, and represents the most logical substitute for labor. The data suggest that the optimal capital/electricity ratio did not change very much until about 1955. Since then the cost of capital has risen much faster than that of electricity, encouraging the substitution of electricity for capital. This trend aids in explaining such phenomena as the general tendency in the United

States to pay for heat loss rather than install adequate building insulation [17], and to centralize industries, allowing full-time use of capital equipment that is capital-efficient but requiring large transportation networks that are energy-inefficient.

The most consistent pattern in the capital-labor-energy comparison is the ratio of hourly wages to the cost of electricity, which has grown by a factor of 12 since 1935, indicating a continuous pressure to substitute electricity for labor. The capital/electricity ratio indicates that the rising relative value of capital could be a deterrent to the substitution of machines and electricity for labor. However, the share of the average production dollar allocated to capital, electricity, and all other forms of energy for that matter, is a small fraction of that going to labor [18]. The overall effects of economic growth on energy and labor demand were suggested by the results of an earlier paper which stated that, if each economic sector were allowed in turn to grow and increase its proportionate share of GNP, most industries would be led by short-term economic incentives to become more energy-demanding and less labor-intensive, the opposite directions from those required by the economy's long-term needs [19].

Conserving Energy

In order to conserve energy, it should be accorded a high value relative to labor and capital. However, two important events would take place as real energy shortages pushed the economy toward being more labor- and capital-intensive and less energy-intensive.

First, since labor and capital productivity would be decreasing in relation to energy productivity, real wages and real proprietor income would decrease in the long run. To maintain a constant output if energy use were reduced, more workers would be required at a lower average wage. This long-term decline in income would not imply a reduction in total national production and consumption until the supply of either labor or capital were fully utilized, but there would be downward pressure on the incomes of those currently employed. While the shift toward labor-intensive production does effect a more equitable compromise between current and future energy needs, it is a shift that would be resisted by many today.

Second, there would be an occupational shift from the highly mechanized industries to more decentralized, labor-intensive enterprises. A particular case study showed that the system producing beverages would be less energy-demanding and more labor-demanding if the beverages were delivered in refillable containers, rather than in throwaways [20, 21]. In fact, the substitution of throwaways for refillable containers some years ago disemployed thousands of relatively unskilled workers. If the change back to refillables were made, jobs would be lost again, but this time in the highly-organized, high-wage plants of the can makers. Jobs would be gained in the relatively nonorganized, low-wage retail sector. It is not surprising then that legislation to restrict the use of throwaways has been directly opposed by organized labor.

The Obstacle

The second obstacle to energy conservation becomes clear at this point. Labor and capital owners will naturally tend to resist a relative increase in the economic value of energy. As production processes become more highly mechanized, a decreasing number of highly paid workers is required. Consequently, these workers develop powerful unions that bargain well for high pay in return for a thinning of their ranks. Effective bargaining for high wages simply insures a continuation of the substitution process. Likewise, low-cost energy is substituted for high-cost capital wherever possible.

It is also generally true that capital- and, therefore, energy-intensive processes are large and highly centralized in order to obtain economies of scale—that is, to increase capital productivity. Such industries have relatively large work forces and are therefore easiest to organize. The bulk of the service industries are highly diffuse and their wage level is generally low relative to wages in manufacturing. The low wage obtains because of the general skill level required and the widely separated work areas.

The unions of service industries also have difficulty organizing because of a high turnover rate and because the low wage does not allow substantial union financial support. Yet service industries are low in energy intensity and are typical of the decentralized, labor-intensive production that would be increased by an effective energy conservation program. Consequently, reducing energy use is likely to be opposed by the most powerful unions, which are understandably unwilling to give up high paying jobs so that more people might work. This phenomenon represents an almost total concern with present union membership and a nearly complete discounting of potential members, behavior that is strongly reminiscent of the way in which the present generation discounts future generations. The solution to this second problem again calls for an altruistic attitude, this time on the part of the unionized workers and capital holders, both of whom would have to accept a drop in income.

Even if this obstacle were overcome—and it is dubious whether it can be overcome through solely voluntary measures—the third obstacle provides a frustrating stumbling block in the efficiency of any energy conservation policy, whether it is oriented toward consumers, industry, or government.

THE THIRD OBSTACLE: RESPENDING DOLLARS SAVED

Imagine the United States as an altruistic society. The President makes an impassioned plea for all consumers to reduce energy consumption by 10 percent, and each person does so immediately. Each citizen would soon find he had saved money and he would spend it, but not on gasoline, electricity, or any direct form of energy consumption. Perhaps he would dine out more or buy new furniture, a new car, or a color television set. However, these products contain embodied energy, and their purchase would reduce and perhaps nullify the voluntary energy savings of 10 percent.

This situation exemplifies the obstacle to conservation inherent within any conservation program: any generation of additional income saved by conservation will provoke additional spending, which in turn will result in energy expenditure. How can the consumer be armed with the information he needs to become aware of embodied, as well as direct, energy consumption and to change his behavior to realize net energy savings? Ultimately he must realize that he will never be able to save as much energy by redirecting certain portions of his income as by choosing to live on a lower economic standard.

Energy and Dollars

Using the energy model, we have calculated the energy cost of various consumer options, as shown in Table 4–2. All transportation activities in 1963 required about 42 percent of United States energy used, directly or indirectly [22]. Table 4–4 shows the dollar, energy, and employment costs of ten alternate passenger modes. The intercity modes were investigated for an approximately 300-mile intercity distance in order to allow the five modes to be considered competitive. All costs are very sensitive to load factors. In terms of dollars and energy, the airplane is easily the most expensive and the train the most employment-intensive. As one moves down the list, the modes are increasingly unpopular but decreasingly energy-intensive. The intercity bus costs the least in dollars and in energy per passenger mile.

The important factor in energy conservation is the ratio of energy saved to money saved in the transfer from one activity to another. Using the data from Table 4–4, calculations show that except for the urban transportation shifts from car to bus, dollars are saved

Table 4–4. Total Dollar, Energy, and Labor Impacts of Consumer Options in Transportation, 1971. *(Data are expressed in terms of the requirements to move one million people one mile.)*

In terms of dollars and energy, the airplane is easily the most expensive mode of transportation and the train is the most employment-intensive. The intercity bus costs the least in dollars and in energy.

Transportation Mode	*Load Factor*	*Thousands of Dollars (1971)*	*Energy** *Million Btu*	*Energy** *Direct* (%)*	*Jobs*
		Intercity Transportation			
Car	2.9 people	55	5900	51	3.7
Plane	53% full	58	9800	73	3.8
Bus	47% full	39	2700	51	3.1
Train	37% full	44	4000	58	7.2
Electric Commuter†	31% full	128	9900	11	8.5
		Urban Transportation			
Car	1.9 people	69	8900	58	4.2
Bus	12.0 people	105	5300	57	8.3
Motorcycle	1.1 people	57	4200	49	1.6
Bicycle	1.0 people	26	1300	59	1.7
Walking	1.0 people	NA	710	51	0.7

Source: Bruce Hannon, "Energy Conservation and the Consumer," *Science* 189 (July 11, 1975): 95–102.

*Vehicle transportation fuel only.

†The "PATH" commuter system, New York–New Jersey, 1971.

if energy is saved, and vice versa. For example, the traveler who switched from urban bus to bicycle would save energy and dollars at the rate of 51,000 Btu's per dollar. In an energy-conservation sense, if he carelessly spent the dollars he saved on an item of personal consumption with an energy intensity of over 51,000 Btu's per dollar, then his shift to the bicycle would have been in vain. In terms of Table 4–2, his dollar savings could be spent on anything below and including "private investment" and still some energy would be saved. If, for example, he spent his savings on "restaurants," the net energy savings in Btu's would be 51,000 minus 32,400 or 18,600 Btu's per dollar saved. However, this reduction in energy use is still far below the original 51,000 Btu's.

From Table 4–2 it is obvious that the worst choice he could make would be to spend the money he saved directly on electricity or on gasoline and oil. However, if he purchased an extra car, for example, indirectly he would be purchasing gasoline and oil. It is necessary to remember that the items listed in Table 4–2 have a varying degree of interdependence.

In general, this applies to energy conservation policies in industry and government too. Changes in purchasing habits made to conserve energy, whether direct energy or energy embodied in material and service purchases, might also save money. The allocation of that money would consume more energy. Note in particular from Table 4–3 that, if the government had not collected revenue for the Highway Trust Fund, the consumer would have spent or saved the money. If this spending diversion happened, total energy use would have decreased and total employment would have increased. There are, however, governmental programs—for example, national health insurance—that per dollar would require more employment and use less energy than personal consumption.

The previous examples have presumed that the consumer can be educated to make voluntary choices for the purpose of energy conservation. Now let us assume that the consumer reduces his use of energy by 10 percent, but still pays the same dollar amount for it. The energy companies would have increased their profits, which they could invest or could return to their stockholders and employees. Either choice will cause energy to be used, and will reduce the effectiveness of the 10 percent energy reduction. If the money is spent abroad, its absence from the United States economy will cause a decline in employment and a further energy reduction through the multiplier effect mentioned earlier. Globally, this effect would be canceled by a roughly opposite impact in the foreign economy. In other words, it does not matter if savings accrue to individuals, industries, or governments: the money is likely to be spent in ways that offset potential energy gains.

CONCLUSIONS

The obstacles outlined here are not presented to create discouragement, but rather to identify clearly the problems of implementing energy conservation programs. In the decade ahead the United States will have to determine whether its democracy can function with scarce energy resources. If the individuals who make up the society cannot be convinced by argument that the use of energy must be steadily reduced to meet specified conservation goals, and if they cannot overcome the three obstacles by demonstrating the necessary altruism required to spread the effects of a reduction in material growth equitably, then some form of government intervention will become necessary. In lieu of any better alternatives, such intervention then becomes the price of living in a highly complex, resource-constrained society [23]. The government's highest purpose now should be to reach prescribed energy-conservation goals—one being an energy steady state for the future—and to increase total employment in an equitable manner. This may well be the government's most important and difficult function. The real meaning of permanent energy scarcity is that everyone will have to work longer and probably harder to use less energy while also preserving real income. This is the absolute dimension of the situation, and is implicit in all three obstacles. Equitable distribution represents the relative dimension. If all else fails, some form of taxing or rationing of energy, or both, may become necessary. Even these measures will require altruism, however, if they are to be widely accepted by society.

The Energy Tax

As I pointed out earlier, to reverse the trend of substituting energy for labor and capital, the cost of energy must increase in relation to labor and capital. Energy cost could be increased by employing an energy tax, based on the energy content of fuel in its primary form, and geared to rise continually with the cost of labor and capital. The cost of energy need rise no farther than the cost of the most appropriate renewable energy replacement. As the cost of energy-intensive products and services increases, a bias would be produced toward their low-energy-intensive substitutes, which are also generally high in labor intensity, and toward renewable energy sources. Labor would have no reason to ask for a subsequent cost-of-living increase if the energy tax were redistributed as a reduction in corporate and personal income tax, especially if the tax and the reduction were designed to offset each other exactly.

The tax concept is based on the assumption that:

—the energy decisionmaker is more price-conscious than income-conscious;

—the prices of non-energy-intensive goods will not rise because of increased demand;

—any regressive return of the tax, in which the poor would receive less than a proportional share (based on income) of the returned taxes, would be intolerable for reasons of social equity;

—any progressive return of the tax, in which the poor would receive more than a proportional share, would increase overall energy consumption slightly;

—the individual can be more efficient than the government in reducing the cost of living.

The tax level should be regularly adjusted to reflect the degree of conservation achieved. However, during the recent oil price rise other primary energy forms, principally coal, rose in price to a level that would not quite discourage the substitution of coal for oil. This price equalization process should set the principle for governing the relative tax levels on different energy sources in order to prevent both the creation of excessive profits for energy resource owners and also undesired fuel substitutions [24].

Historically, the government has acted directly to insure that the technology of substituting energy for labor would continue by allowing tax deductions for artificially high depreciation rates, by permitting investment tax credits, by maintaining high payroll taxes, and by regulating the cost of important energy forms. However, in a time of energy shortages, careful adjustment of these allowances could be used to ease the change to a technology that is less energy-intensive and more labor-intensive.

An advantage of the tax is that it can be raised or lowered, theoretically with great ease, and depending on the progress made in achieving the established conservation goal and the desired level of equity. When applied to energy imports, the tax also provides an important buffer against the shock of a sudden externally-caused price increase. The principal disadvantage of the tax is that it translates the energy problem into dollars. Energy users would likely have difficulty understanding the connection between the tax and the pervasiveness of the energy crisis. Also, since the tax is likely to make energy and energy-intensive goods significantly more expensive, these goods would attain much more status in the eyes of those with average and lower incomes. Thus, the tax could maintain and perhaps even widen the gap between reality and expectation for some individuals and groups. Under the taxing plan it would seem appropriate, therefore, to control commercial advertising about energy-intensive products and services, with the intent of holding the forces of stimulation in check.

The effect of the tax would be diminished as the income it generates is spent by the government. Also, because the tax is returned to the economy, it does not solve the third problem—the need to control total spending.

The Energy-Rationing Scheme

To use energy wisely, consumers must be aware of the storage, flow, and flow stability of energy in the economy. Only one of these elements has been brought forceably to their attention—the stability of energy flow—and that by foreign governments. Much of the discussion here has concerned methods of advancing consumer awareness of energy flow. An awareness of the stock of available energy resources, analogous to the perception of a savings account or a woodpile stacked by the fireplace, is also needed. The absence of this awareness is the root of the problem.

The size of the energy-resource base, even without the complex connection between total remaining energy and the cost of the next energy unit consumed, is difficult to grasp. Energy is the only truly nonrecyclable resource. The ignorance of the fact that there is a finite quantity of energy available is perhaps the greatest tragedy of this age.

The taxing scheme mentioned above would control the consumption of energy by controlling its price. At the other end of the spectrum of conservation possibilities is a personal energy rationing coupon system providing direct consumer control of the quantity of energy used. Under this scheme, people would work for energy coupons, each representing a specified number of energy units. These coupons would be traded for the direct and indirect energy embodied in the goods and services we purchased. The national government would own the energy sources and issue new coupons to meet targeted energy use rates.

Note that this rationing proposal assumes a theory of energy currency, not of energy value. The latter theory assumes all human needs can be stated in terms of energy, while the former holds that the true finite resource—energy—should be the basis for exchange. As such, energy should be the true control variable in the economy, and people should have an explicit control over its flow. Voluntary energy conservation will come about only when the consumer is convinced that he owns, until consumed, a certain quantity of energy. Rationing promotes the consumer's awareness of the availability and flow of energy resources, allowing him to make a personal contribution toward revoking the Tragedy of the Commons [25].

The administrative history of rationing, however, is bleak. The distribution system has been imperfect, and nongovernmental blackmarkets always develop. However, instituting a coupon system in a time of relative plenty paves the way for more equitable distribution in periods of severe shortage. The scheme, if properly implemented, would avoid all three obstacles. Rationing energy implies an increase in its value relative to labor and capital. Rationing also skirts the need to control directly the total spending and the energy consumption of dollars freed by changes in the pattern of consumption.

Herman Daly has suggested an intermediate rationing approach [26]. He suggests the annual federal purchase and auction of a controlled amount of energy. The buyers at auction would be the present energy companies, who would then proceed to sell the energy to consumers. This system would control the quantity of energy flowing into the economy and the price at which it was sold. Because the government would be in effect skimming off part of the energy owners' profits, it should then redistribute these monies equitably, subject to the respending obstacle.

In the long run, people must become materially poorer to avoid the trauma of a complete and sudden collapse of the stored energy resource base. The United States must, in the long run, shift completely to renewable resource bases; however, in the meantime, energy, the surrogate in the production of goods and services, must be accorded the real value it deserves as a scarce resource. Even though every conscious and inadvertent reaction would seem to resist reduction in energy use—hence the three obstacles—the reduction must be made. Energy rationing is a complete solution in theory, but there is no assurance that people can muster sufficient will to self-impose so pervasive a restriction equitably in practice. They have not in the past. This may have been from a lack of altruism; it may also, hopefully, have resulted from the absence of compelling data on which to base decisions and of sensible alternatives from which to choose. If the latter is the case, there is hope that the continued work of the Energy Research Group and other conservation-oriented organizations will build a case strong enough to spark the consumer altruism necessary to make energy conservation policies work.

 *Part II*

Economic Alternatives in an Age of Limits

Introduction to Part II

Dennis L. Meadows

> Given new conditions, desirable economic concepts will have to be expanded to embrace more external variables. Since this probably cannot be achieved without sacrificing some of the pretensions to rigor that have seemingly separated economics from its humbler sister disciplines in the social sciences, economists will have to moderate their claims to value-free scientific method if they are not to further confuse government policymakers and themselves.
>
> *Hazel Henderson*—Chapter 6

Economics is the study of criteria and procedures for allocating scarce resources among competing needs; that is, how to decide the type and quantity of goods and services to be produced, the inputs to be employed in their manufacture, and the distribution of products across the members of the population. This abstract definition of the field would seem to leave little outside its purview. But in practice, contemporary economists have chosen to focus on a very narrow set of goods—those that are easily measurable in financial units and contained within the system of national statistical accounts—and to deemphasize an important set of inputs—those derived from the natural world. Moreover, they have been preoccupied with only two inputs, capital and labor, and have placed only secondary emphasis on the equitable distribution of final output. For these and other reasons, contemporary Western economics has come to focus on the short-term, material consequences of economic activity and to stress the importance of continued growth.

The classical roots of modern economics extend back to John Stuart Mill, David Ricardo, and Adam Smith, who were not reluctant to base their analyses on concepts difficult to express mathematically and in monetary units, concepts such as scarcity, equity, quality, and sustainability. And a few contemporary economists—Georgescu-Roegen, Schumacher, Daly, Boulding, and Galbraith—have once again begun to search for principles of the steady-state economy. There is certainly no reason to believe that current economies cannot be modified to function effectively with zero growth in capital, labor, and energy. The social unrest, inefficiency, and unemployment that accompanied the recessionary part of recent business cycles are not necessary attributes of zero economic growth, any more than the damage sustained in an automobile collision is characteristic of a controlled stop. The trick lies in understanding the economy's control system well enough that the brake can be substituted for the brick wall.

So long as the myth of a "guiding hand" coordinating the myriad, personal, short-term economic decisions still prevailed, there seemed to be no need for any sort of long-term social image, goal, or plan. But whatever their benefits over the short term, it is now clear that market-price-oriented decisions do not necessarily produce a long-term social evolution beneficial to anyone. A sequence of short-term, individual optimizations can easily lead to long-term, collective disaster. It is necessary to learn much more than economists know now about the real, physical consequences of current economic decisions. It will be necessary to revise current economic theory and institutions and to augment them with deliberate, long-term planning. The former task is addressed in the following four papers, the latter is the focus of Part III.

Jay Forrester's paper summarizes several insights gained from his computer models of growth and decline in social systems. His chapter draws most directly from a model of global population growth completed for The Club of Rome several years ago and from a model of national economic life cycles currently under development within his group. From the perspectives afforded by this work, Professor Forrester concludes that the limits-to-growth debate has focused too exclusively on purely physical limits. More attention should be placed on important social limits and on their interaction with physical constraints. He suggests that national leaders should be much more cautious in assuming that domestic limits can be ameliorated by drawing on international resources and markets.

Forrester stresses that current economic trends must be viewed with at least a fifty-year perspective if their true significance is to be understood. He describes some preliminary conclusions from his study of socioeconomic interactions that occur over the 200-year cycle of economic development. Business cycles, Forrester suggests, combined with a longer-term periodicity, the Kondratieff wave, may have confused both proponents and opponents of the limits-to-growth thesis in their thinking about the significance of recent growth trends. He believes that the industrialized world may be entering several decades of low growth, which will provide time for the formulation of more sustainable steady-state options.

Elaborating on Forrester's criticisms of Keynesian economics, Hazel Henderson suggests that more research should be undertaken to clarify understanding of declining capital productivity, rising social costs of production and consumption, and the structural tendency to overinvest in capital. She indicates several symptoms of failure in modern macro-economic management: stagflation, inequality, spiraling government costs, and periodic business cycles. She identifies three areas for renewed economic research and puts forward a concerted program she believes would tide the country over the short term, while the process of more fundamental structural reform required to achieve a sustainable economy over the long term was initiated. Henderson advocates programs to maintain consumer purchasing power, to achieve significant conservation of oil, to increase the labor-intensity of production, and to educate the electorate about the forces that mandate more substantial structural reform.

It is useful to compare her paper with that of Davis and Mauch in Part III. Though they summarize two efforts conducted in different countries and in complete isolation from each other, both reports present several similar ideas. They both suggest the economic system has become insulated from real human needs and now acts to sustain its own growth in directions quite unrelated to basic social and political goals; industrialized societies have become so complex that the costs of controlling them may soon rise above the productive capacity of their economies; and it is necessary to adopt a set of short-term measures to sustain the society while beginning more fundamental and long-term structural reforms.

Should the economic decline described by Forrester or the deceleration policies discussed by Henderson begin to take effect, much more concern will be evidenced for the distribution of economic output. Donella Meadow's paper examines the relation of economic growth and free-market mechanisms to equity. Drawing on theory and empirical data, she concludes that free markets tend to widen the gap between the rich and the poor, especially when important inputs to the productive process become limited. She identifies four attributes of the market system—delays, unequal access to resources, externalities, and a preoccupation with capital efficiency—that all make equality more difficult to attain. Her conclusion is supported by reference to two case studies of agricultural production, one in Vermont and the other in the Punjab of India. Agricultural production is typically used by economists to exemplify the free market; thus the fact of growing inequality of wealth and income among both Punjab and Vermont farmers does warrant some doubts about the ability of the pure free market to bring about equity.

Professor Meadows describes the efficiency and flexibility inherent in a market-price system. She proposes several policies that would retain the advantages of the market economy while improving its equity, including limitations on the size of productive units and establishment of minimum and maximum boundaries for individual wealth.

To introduce his analysis Professor Daly evokes the parables of the monkey trap and the sorcerer's apprentice, analogies that appear in other chapters as well. The central point of each anecdote is the need to have a longer-term image of the purpose behind a current activity, and to make certain that short-term tactics do not defeat more fundamental objectives. The purpose of economic activities is not to produce more output, but to satisfy basic human needs. Daly suggests that some changes in current tactics might help to attain that goal.

He echoes Jay Forrester's call for less emphasis on solving a country's problems by drawing on resources from outside its own borders, and then describes three institutions that could help satisfy more social needs with a given stock of resources. The first institution would enforce maxima and minima on personal wealth and income. The second involves depletion quotas to govern the amount of nonrenewable resources available to the economy as inputs each year. The third proposal would bring market forces directly to bear on the goal of stabilizing population. As the first and third have been discussed by Daly elsewhere, he uses this essay to elaborate on the second. He describes the effects of depletion quotas on equity and efficiency and closes his discussion with an exploration of the factors that would govern the implementation of the three proposals. His recommendations could be implemented without fundamental changes in the current United States economy. They should not require large bureaucracies, and they would provide the macro-level controls necessary for any sustainable state, while preserving micro-level freedom for producers and consumers.

 *Chapter 5*

New Perspectives on Economic Growth

Jay Forrester

The debate on limits to growth needs a sharpened focus. Much past discussion, because it has been so general, has failed to couple with practical issues. A more effective resolution of growth questions might follow from changes in perspective that include:

—more emphasis on social limits and on the tradeoff between physical limits and social limits;

—more attention to solutions at the national level where effective institutions exist rather than at the world or regional levels where institutions are weak compared to the forces created by growth and by limits;

—more awareness of intermediate modes of dynamic behavior that may lie between the short-term business cycle and the long-term life cycle of growth.

SOCIAL LIMITS

The first change should shift attention from physical to social limits. Much debate on limits-to-growth issues has focused too narrowly on physical constraints. Restricting debate to physical limits invites hope that technology can circumvent such limits. Indeed, technology might do so for quite some time. But any expectation that shortages of energy and food can be overcome will be used by people and governments as an excuse to avoid facing the issues posed by growth of population and social stress.

Through growth in population, a reduction of physical pressures can be transformed into an increase in social pressures. If physical limits seem less threatening, then concern about population growth will be temporarily relaxed. If physical support appears possible, the easy course is to ignore population growth. But rising population density is surely at the root of many social stresses. Crowding, psychological pressures, and lack of individual purpose, arising from increased population and a more complex technological society, accentuate frustration and antisocial behavior.

Social limits already exert growing pressure in the form of drug addiction, kidnappings, aircraft hijackings, sabotage, revolution, and a growing threat of atomic war. Technological complexity also brings forth more subtle pressures in the form of questions that challenge the legitimacy of institutions. Social limits are not relieved by more emphasis on technology. Quite the contrary, increased technology has increased per capita income while creating a more complex and vulnerable society. A complex technological society is at the same time harder to understand, more difficult to accept, and easier to disrupt. Complexity increases frustration and disenchantment, while also increasing vulnerability to either individual or organized interference.

In public debate over physical limits, desirability of technological success is seldom questioned. For example, in the present energy shortage, the first question should not be, "Can technology provide unlimited energy?" Instead, we should ask, "If unlimited energy were available, should we want it?" To ask for unlimited energy is to favor shifting the restraint on growth from physical limits to social limits. Energy can be converted to food for support of a population that will then be more apt to grow until social breakdown occurs. Society should want to choose the least traumatic mix of growth-limiting pressures. A smooth path of nonsustainable growth is more likely with distributed than with concentrated pressures. Technological policies for removing physical barriers implicitly will limit growth by radically increasing social stresses, but a combination of social and physical pressures probably will generate a smoother transition from growth to equilibrium. Some social threats, some energy and materials shortages, some inadequacy of food, and some pollution would exert a balanced set of restraints until people begin to accept the inherent tradeoff between rising population and falling quality of life.

So, the debate over physical limits seems unbalanced. It can divert governments and the public from the ultimate necessity of striking a compromise between population, standard of living, and quality of the natural environment. The preoccupation with physical limits obscures a rising threat from social limits. As population growth continues, aided and abetted by intensifying technology, complexity increases. With greater complexity come stronger tendencies for social breakdown and at the same time more vulnerability to disruption. The debate on growth has so far been largely between environmentalists on one side and economists and technologists on the other. But the issues should be broadened to include more input from sociologists, political scientists, and theologians. The nonphysical side of man needs stronger representation.

NATIONAL FOCUS FOR ACTION

The second change in attention should be from world limits to national limits. Although the problem of growth in a finite world can be stated on a one-world basis, solutions seem likely to come only on the national level, because only national institutions possess the power to act.

The limits-to-growth debate has concentrated on the entire world or on major regions. *The Limits to Growth* focuses on the world as one system [1]. Such a single aggregate view is useful for stating the problem. The United Nations debates food shortage and economic development as world problems. Such broad and general treatment is useful for alerting member nations to the issues. The book *Mankind at the Turning Point* divided the world into several regions [2]. Subdivision into major areas is useful for looking at differences between dissimilar regions. But implementation of effective policies for restraining growth and achieving a desirable equilibrium cannot be expected on either a uniform world or a regional scale. For areas larger than countries, there is no authority with the capability to deal with growth. Neither the United Nations nor any of the regional confederations have the charter to determine and enforce a balance in the tradeoff between population and standard of living. A wide range of compromise is possible between size of population and conditions for living. Different cultures would choose different compromises. Some countries would allow a higher population and accept a lower standard of living. Others would take steps to stabilize population before the capacity of their geography had become so fully committed.

If countries retain freedom to choose the tradeoff between population and standard of living, then physical equality between countries is not possible. Different countries will arrive at different balances. Freedom of choice and worldwide equality are incompatible. If there were to be physical equality on a global scale, some authority would be required to impose uniform standards for the balance between population density and geographical capacity. But such external imposition of population standards is most unlikely to be accepted. However, without such standards, material equality will be impossible.

Most countries are now acting as if their shortages could forever be met from the outside. But, as worldwide limits to growth are ever more closely approached, there is less slack in the world system. International trade has depended on such slack. Many countries have supported their population growth with imports. However, as every region becomes more densely populated, food and material surpluses decline and less is available to export to others. The time is approaching when each country must more and more meet its growth-induced needs from within its own borders.

If a country believes that solutions for its stresses can be found outside, then failure to achieve solutions will naturally be attributed to others. When both the source of the problem and the potential solution are believed to lie across the border, war appears to be the only answer. Unless population is to be restrained by war and genocide, nations must look inward. Only if each nation accommodates its needs to its own geographical capacity, can international tension be reduced.

Suggesting that nations think in terms of self-sufficiency is a proposal unpalatable to the developed countries. Most industrial countries have been living beyond their geographical means. They have imported energy and resources at low prices, depressed by excess world supply. They have exported manufactured goods at high prices, sustained by a world shortage of industrial capacity. But the imbalance is reversing. Energy and resources are becoming scarce, and in the long run their prices will continue to rise. Manufacturing capacity and technical skills are becoming widespread, and their relative prices will fall. To live within their own capabilities, most industrial countries face a more traumatic transition than many developing countries. Of all countries, Japan is probably most vulnerable. Without foreign energy, foreign resources, and foreign markets—and that time is approaching—life in Japan will be far different. Close behind Japan in vulnerability comes Western Europe, and then the United States. Countries with sufficient energy and resources are fast acquiring industrial knowledge and plant capacity to manufacture basic goods with their own labor for their own markets.

If industrial countries see their plight as having been caused by countries that withdraw supplies and markets, then war is apt to be chosen as the obvious solution. But if industrial countries recognize their own growth as having been the cause of social and economic pressure, then internal adaptation, with any necessary reduction in quality of life, becomes an appropriate solution. Through a general recognition that pressures come from national growth, not international actions, atomic war may be avoided as the ultimate limit to growth.

This proposal to put limits to growth in the national context is quite the reverse of most present discussions for sharing and for human equality. It rejects the common implication that others have created the problems and must be responsible for solutions. Such is the basis for distrust and conflict.

Any course of action has weaknesses and disadvantages. Three would be of particular concern in choosing the national route for dealing with growth. First, countries that limit population and thereby sustain attractive living conditions must be able to police their borders and prevent inundation by people from countries where population has grown beyond the national capacity. Some countries may be so small, or may have such unfavorable border conditions, that they cannot adopt policies of self-sufficiency. Such countries will probably be absorbed into larger political units. Second, individual freedom to migrate across national borders will be severely restricted when overpopulation is recognized as the critical limit in every country. Third, some international discipline will still be needed to prevent any one country from serving itself at the expense of other countries. For example, a country must not be allowed to discharge pollutants that threaten foreign populations or interfere with the rights of equal access to the oceans and atmosphere. But these issues are more limited and manageable than trying to cope on a uniform worldwide basis with population control, equality, common standards for quality of life, and yielding of national sovereignty to a powerful central authority.

This second change, reduced emphasis on limits to growth as a single world issue, would lead to decentralization and diversification of limits for separate handling by individual nations. Each nation could then address the questions of how much population it could support at a desired standard of living; how to develop its future without taking environmental capacity from others; and how to discourage population from rising above the target level. No country, rich or poor, seems to have accepted such internal questions as top priorities. Instead, most countries are using external issues of world energy, distribution of food, and international investment as ways to divert their citizens from the difficult task of shaping their own future. I see no promising avenue but to reverse foreign adventurism, turn inward, establish national self-sufficiency in each country, and solve global problems by taking appropriate action separately in each part of the world. This position should enhance national and global stability in a world of geographic and cultural diversity.

INTERMEDIATE-TERM DYNAMICS

The third change in perspective should be from exclusive concern with the life cycle of growth to the multiplicity of dynamic modes inherent in a national economy. Different groups tend to be concerned with different time behaviors in the social system. A growing minority is presently concerned with the very long run, while most people in commerce and government do not look beyond the short-term business cycle. For those reacting to stresses arising from growth and seeking a viable long-run equilibrium, the relevant time horizon is the "two hundred-year present" mentioned by Elise Boulding in Chapter 15. It extends one hundred years into the past and at least one hundred years into the future. Their perspectives encompass the period of exponential growth, the transition period during which growth is suppressed by environmental forces, and a future equilibrium. In contrast, the business-cycle perspective encompasses periods only five to ten years in duration. With such different time horizons, lack of serious communication between the two groups is almost inevitable; they fail to view the world in the same way, and they have few concerns in common. Much of the debate on limits to growth results not from disagreement over facts, but from the disjointed time horizons of the debate participants.

The economic system does contain intermediate modes of behavior that may serve to bridge the gap in viewpoints. The literature of politics, public attitudes, and economics is rich in discussion of important changes occurring over several decades. Social systems contain the diversity of cause and effect relationships necessary to create many simultaneous modes of behavior—exhibiting patterns from a few months to a few centuries in duration.

However, the intermediate modes have been relatively neglected. Historians treat the rise and fall of civilizations—the time span of growth, equilibrium, and collapse. The business press, economics books, and political debate all emphasize the three- to seven-year business cycle. But dynamic modes of behavior lying between the short-term business cycle and the long-term life cycle receive less than their due attention.

The intermediate dynamic modes in society are important. Not only do they fill the behavior spectrum between the extremes, but, more importantly, they generate symptoms that confuse and mislead those who focus on either extreme. Changes with characteristic time intervals in the fifteen- to sixty-year range can easily be misinterpreted as belonging to either the business cycle or to the life cycle of growth. When intermediate modes are attributed to one extreme or the other, the extremes are incorrectly perceived and the middle ground of dynamic behavior is lost as a common basis for communication.

After the work on *World Dynamics*, the M.I.T. System Dynamics Group has been looking at the full range of time spans of behavior in social and economic change at the national level [3]. We believe that social and economic change must be studied together and that design of improved national policies will be of the greatest practical effectiveness in ameliorating problems related to growth. System dynamics models have been used in the past as effective tools to study a number of variables simultaneously [4, 5, 6, 7, 8, 9, 10, 11]. At M.I.T. we have been developing a system dynamics model of the national economy. The model contains some fifteen industrial sectors, worker mobility networks between sectors for both labor and professionals, and household, demographic, financial, and government sectors. When fully assembled, the model will have nearly a hundred times as much detail as the Limits to Growth model.

Simulation studies have so far been conducted with one and two of the fifteen industrial sectors of the National Model. Even this limited part of the whole economy generates simultaneously a wide range of periodic fluctuations. Several different modes of cyclic behavior originate from the interactions of inventories, production rate, acquisition of labor and capital, and supply interconnections between different sectors. In a complex economic structure, many different dynamic modes of fluctuating activity can exist simultaneously. Much puzzling economic behavior probably arises from multiple modes superimposing their patterns of interaction. If identities of the separate modes are not recognized, symptoms arising from one part of the system may be misinterpreted and applied to policy control points in some entirely different part of the system. Policy is then ineffective because it only remotely relates to the symptoms that inspired the policy.

An extensive literature deals with each of three different modes of periodic fluctuation in the economy—the business cycle, the Kuznets cycle, and the Kondratieff cycle [12].

The business cycle, the well-known short-term fluctuation of business activity, appears as varying production rates and employment, with peaks of activity separated by some three to seven years. Business cycles lie within the experience of most persons and are the focus of attention in the press and in governmental policy debates.

Support for the existence of the much less generally recognized Kuznets cycle [13, 14] exists as an observation that many time series in the economy seem to exhibit a periodicity of fifteen to twenty-five years. The source of the Kuznets cycle has been a subject of debate. It has received little public attention because other cyclic modes in the economy are of sufficient magnitude to mask the Kuznets cycle from popular awareness.

The Kondratieff cycle [15, 16], to be discussed in the next section, is a fluctuation in the economy characterized by intervals of about fifty years between peaks, which are separated by long valleys of economic stagnation.

Simulation studies with the new M.I.T. system dynamics National Model of the economy have shown that physical relationships and decision-making policies in the production of consumer durables and capital equipment can generate simultaneously all three major periodicities—business cycle, Kuznets cycle, and Kondratieff cycle [17]. The short-term business cycle can be generated by interactions among backlogs, inventories, production, and employment without requiring involvement of capital investment or changes in consumer income. The Kuznets cycle is consistent with policies governing production and the acquisition of capital equipment. The fifty-year Kondratieff cycle can arise from economic and physical relationships between the capital-equipment sector and the sectors procuring capital equipment from it. Those relationships influence the competition for the output of the capital-equipment sector between the customer goods sectors and the capital-equipment sector itself.

The well-known business cycle need not be elaborated here. The Kuznets cycle seems less important to questions of growth and can therefore be omitted from this discussion. But the Kondratieff cycle may be of major significance in coupling short-term national decisions to long-term growth policy.

The Kondratieff Cycle

The Kondratieff cycle, also known as the "long wave," was forcefully presented in the literature by Nikolai Kondratieff in the 1920s. Kondratieff, a Russian economist, made extensive studies of long-term behavior in the Western capitalist economies. His statistical analyses of economic activity showed that many variables in the Western economies had fluctuated with peaks about forty-five to sixty years apart. Such peaks of economic activity occurred around 1810, 1860, and 1920. Kondratieff believed that the fifty-year cycle was caused by internal structural dynamics of the economic system, but he did not propose a sharply-defined set of causal mechanisms. Some other economists agreed that the long-term fluctuation had occurred but believed that it was caused by events external to the economy, such as gold discoveries, wars, major technical innovations, changes in financial institutions, and fluctuations in population growth.

The Kondratieff wave has not been taken very seriously because no one has presented a persuasive theory of its causes. Nevertheless, events since Kondratieff first discussed long waves are bringing the subject back into the public press. After the peak in economic activity around 1920, the Great Depression of the 1930s represented a typical low point in such a cycle. Now, some fifty years after the preceding peak, economic activity has again risen to a high level, but exhibits many signs of faltering. It is appropriate to ask whether the Kondratieff wave has underlying structural origin, and if it has significance for current national policy.

The Kondratieff cycle is of special interest in the discussion of limits to growth. Much apparent industrial growth of the last several decades may merely reflect the rising phase of the fifty-year cycle emerging from the depression of the 1930s. If so, recent growth trends will not be sustainable into the future regardless of long-term limits. A downward phase in the Kondratieff wave, if such lies in the near future, could produce a few decades of industrial equilibrium during which a sustainable future could be charted.

Recent computer simulations with the National Model suggest that long-period cyclic behavior can arise from the causal structure connecting consumer-goods sectors and capital sectors. A sufficient cause for a fifty-year fluctuation appears to lie in movement of people between sectors, the long time required to change production capacity in capital sectors, the way capital sectors provide their own input capital as a factor of production, the need to develop excess capacity to catch up on deferred demand, and the psychological and speculative force of expectations that may induce overexpansion in central sectors.

Figure 5–1 shows behavior in one model configuration of a consumer-goods sector connected to a capital-equipment sector. A fifty-year periodicity appears in the capital sector. Although the behavior in Figure 5–1 is not yet well understood and does not occur in all simple two-sector configurations, it seems reasonably certain that the processes of production and capital equipment procurement, and the relationship between consumer and capital sectors, have the potential for producing a Kondratieff-like cycle.

Figure 5–1. Kondratieff Cycle Appearing in the Capital Sector

Recent computer simulations with the National Model suggest that long-period cyclic behavior can arise from the causal structure connecting consumer-goods sectors and capital sectors. Sufficient cause appears to lie in the long time required to change production capacity in capital sectors and the way capital sectors provide their own input capital as a factor of production, as well as in other dynamics of demand and speculation.

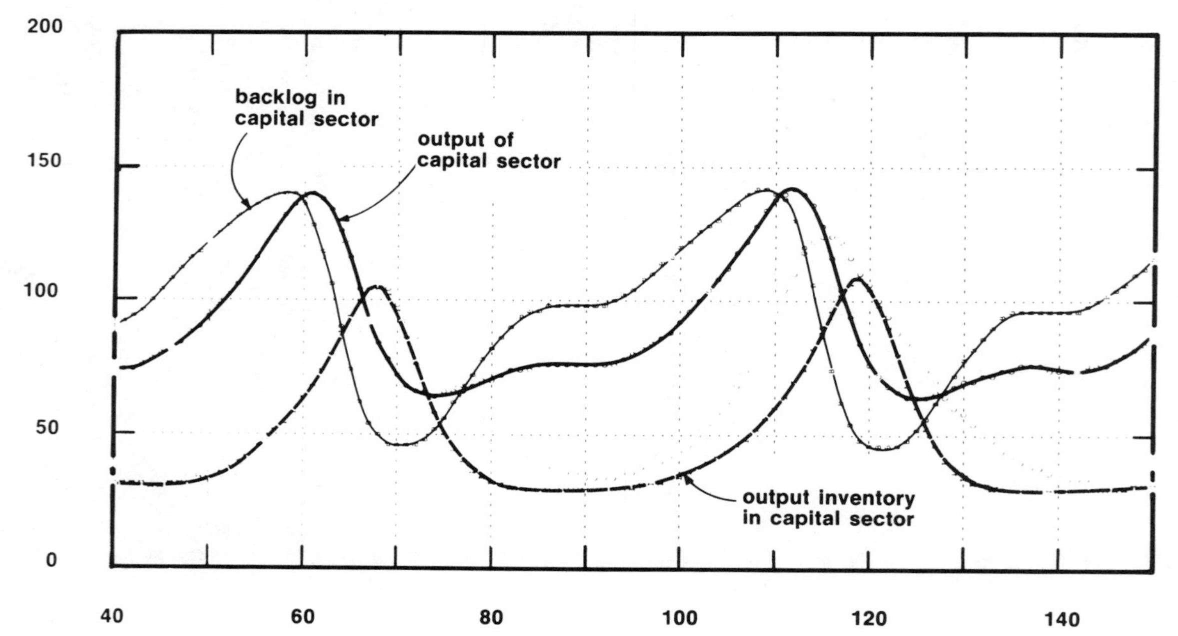

The cyclic mode in Figure 5–1 is unstable for small amplitudes. Any small disturbance can initiate the fluctuation, which then grows in amplitude until bounded by nonlinear restraints. Such a mode is especially persistent and not easy to influence. If such a mode exists in real life, it is probable that changes over the fifty-year interval in psychological attitudes, propensity to take risks, and efforts to sustain the economy's upward growth phase by monetary expansion all tend to accentuate the fluctuation.

Investigation of this long-wave mode is at present incomplete. Yet a substantial fifty-year fluctuation is of sufficient potential importance that even preliminary hypotheses are worth presenting for discussion. The most fundamental sequences in the long-wave mode, starting from the depression years at the bottom of the cycle, seem to be:

—the slow growth of the capital sector of the economy;

—gradual decay of the entire capital plant of the economy below the amount required, while the capital sector remains unable to supply even replacement needs;

—initial recirculation of output of the capital sector to its own input whereby the capital sector at first competes with its own customers for capital equipment;

—progressive increase in wages and development of labor shortage in consumer sectors, both of which encourage capital-intensive production and still higher demand for capital equipment;

—overexpansion of the capital sector to a capacity greater than required for replacement as a consequence of effort to catch up on deferred needs;

—excess accumulation of housing and capital investment by consumers and of plant and equipment by manufacturers;

—eventual failure of capital-equipment users to absorb output of the overexpanded capital sectors;

—sudden appearance of unemployment in the capital sectors;

—reversed change in relative costs to favor more labor-intensive consumer production that further diminishes need for new plant;

—rapid collapse of the capital sector when demand falls below even the long-term average needed by the economy;

—spreading discouragement and slow decline of excess capital stock through physical depreciation.

Present symptoms in the economy seem consistent with the top of a Kondratieff wave if the top is a period of excess capital expansion. New tankers are leaving the shipyards and going directly to anchorage. Aircraft are going into storage. For the first time since the late 1920s, many cities have an excess of office space. The interstate highway system has been built and another will not be needed soon. The condition of the auto industry is partly due to the consumer stock of automobiles having been adequately filled. The financial plight of real-estate investment trusts and the decline in home construction suggest that we already have more housing than the economy can support.

The presence of a long-wave fluctuation involving a rise and decline in the capital sectors would significantly affect thinking about both business cycles and the life cycle of growth. Business cycles have usually been interpreted without regard to the possibility of their being superimposed on a long wave. On the other hand, part of recent apparent growth may have come from the fluctuating long wave rather than from the life cycle of growth.

Business-cycle Stabilization Versus the Kondratieff Cycle. Interaction between the Kondratieff cycle and business cycles may have produced confusing symptoms that have been interpreted as erroneous explanations of recessions and depressions, leading to inappropriate policies for economic stabilization. Recessions since World War II have been less severe than those in immediately preceding decades. Anticyclic monetary policy and fine tuning of the economy have often received credit for reducing business downturns between 1945 and 1970. But another explanation would be justified if we consider how different kinds of economic fluctuations can combine.

Figure 5–2 shows three simple curves as stylized representations of the business cycle, Kuznets cycle, and Kondratieff cycle. Figures 5–3a and b show the three curves added together on an expanded time scale. The numbers in heavy print along the curves give the time in years for economic expansions and contractions. Figure 5–3a covers the rising segment of the long wave and Figure 5–3b the falling segment. The upward thrust of the long wave before the peak in Figure 5–3a causes business cycles to seem to have strong and long expansions with weak and short recessions. On the other hand, after the peak in Figure 5–3b the long-term decline weakens and shortens expansion phases of business cycles and deepens and lengthens recession phases.

By itself, superposition of business cycles on a long-term fluctuation can explain milder recessions since World War II, and also the

Figure 5–2. Three Curves Representing Business, Kuznets, and Kondratieff Cycles

Simulation studies have shown that physical relationships and decision-making policies in the production of consumer durables and capital equipment can generate simultaneously all three major periodicities—business cycle, Kuznets cycle, and Kondratieff cycle.

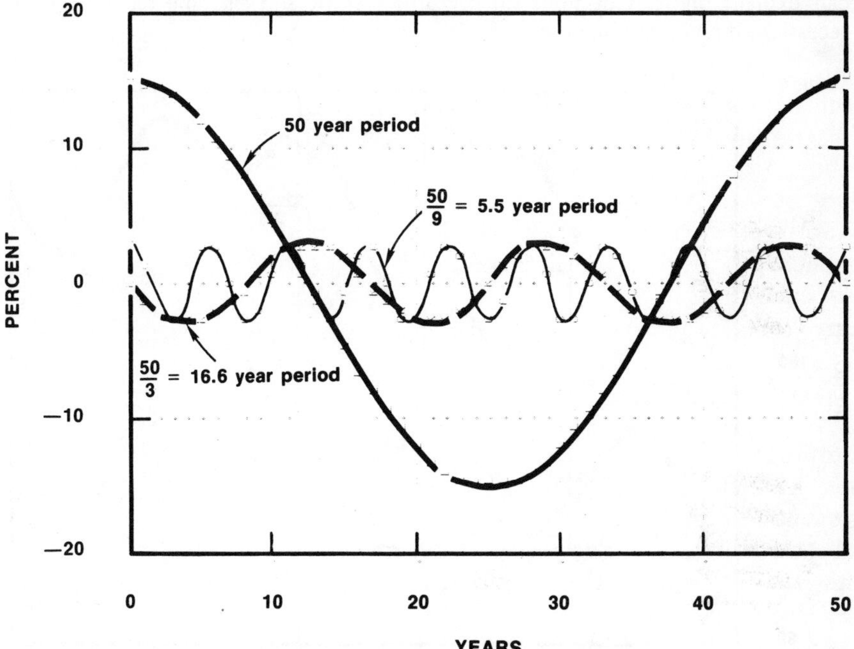

recent deeper recession, if an underlying long wave is now topping out. On the basis of simultaneous fluctuating behaviors having different time durations and coming from different parts of the economic system, monetary policy need not be invoked to explain either milder recessions in the 1950s and 1960s nor the worsening recession now.

Growth Versus the Kondratieff Cycle. Those concerned about the hazards of growth may also be misled by the Kondratieff cycle. Much of the upward thrust of economic activity in the last three decades may be a consequence of expansion in the capital sectors that seems to go with the rising phase of the long wave. If so, the economic processes will not sustain themselves forever. When capital expansion has run its course, accompanied by heavy debts and non-

Figure 5–3. Combination of Three Curves During Rising and Falling Part of Long Wave

The upward thrust of the long wave in Figure 5–3a causes business cycles to seem to have strong and long expansions with weak and short recessions. On the other hand, after the peak in Figure 5–3b, the long-term decline weakens and shortens expansion phases of business cycles and deepens and lengthens recession phases. By itself, superposition of business cycles on a long-term fluctuation can explain milder recessions since World War II, and also the recent deeper recession, if an underlying long wave is now topping out.

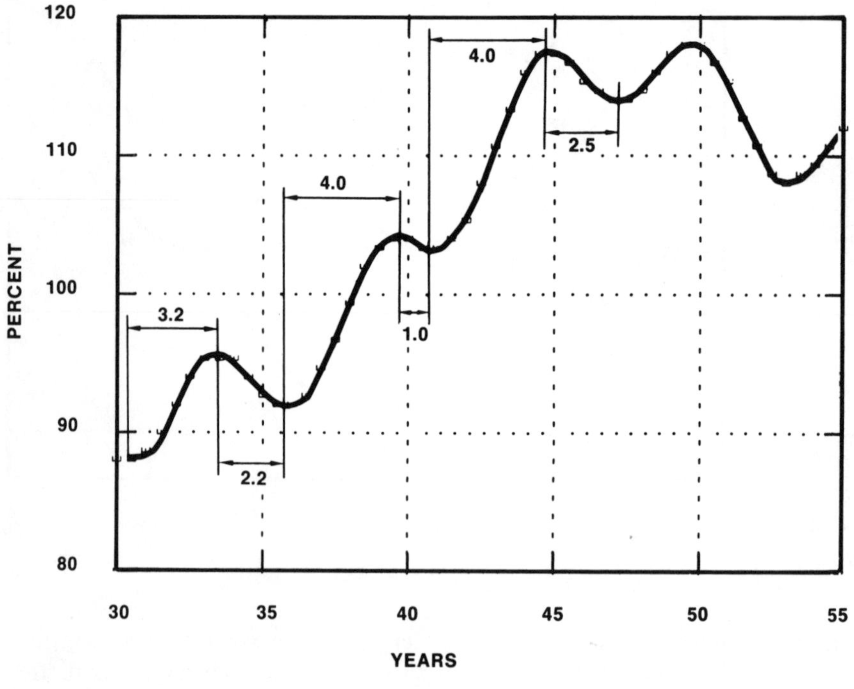

Figure 5–3a

sustainable rates of public and private borrowing, an internal readjustment must begin. In such a readjustment capital sectors decline, unemployment increases, people move back toward food and consumer-products sectors, and growth is suspended or reversed. But such conditions may confuse the debate on limits to growth. Those attempting to reduce unemployment and increase short-term economic growth may blame the downturn on environmentalists and adherents of an equilibrium society. On the other hand, proponents of equilibrium may misinterpret a downturn in the long wave as arrival of a nongrowth future. Instead, the downturn, like the upward

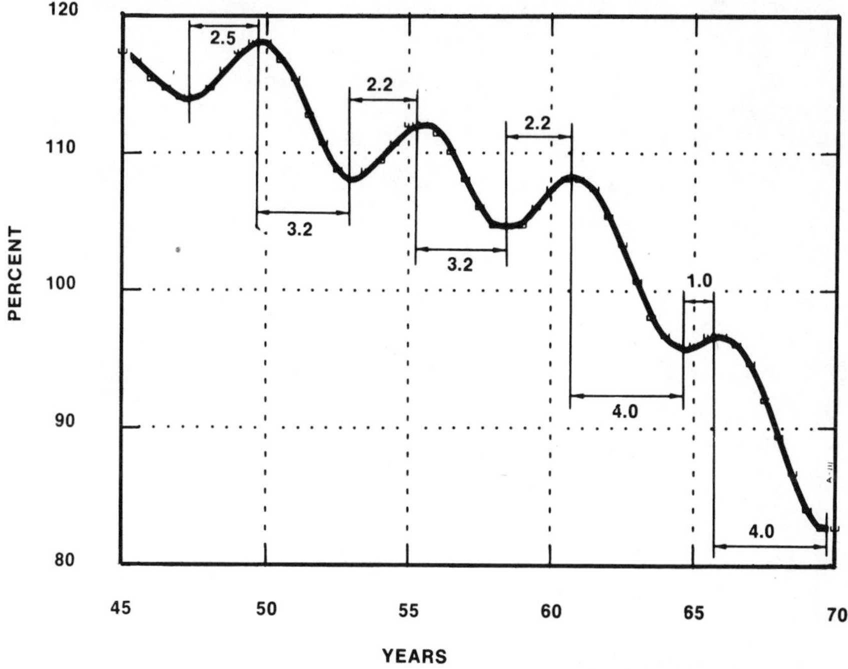

Figure 5–3b

phase, may be only a consequence of imbalance. If so, the end of growth would not represent a sustainable equilibrium. A period of slackening growth, arising as a consequence of internal dynamics of the Western economies, should be taken instead as an interlude in which to accelerate discussion of future alternatives.

SUMMARY

The limits-to-growth debate deals with the most important issue of our times. But the particular form of the debate often fails to bring forth effective action. Discussion could be led into more practical channels by three changes in perspective—less emphasis on physical limits and more on social limits, less concentration on world limits and more on national limits, and less attention to a single dynamic mode and more to the interaction of short-term and long-term forces in the economy. Those who would be leaders toward a sustainable future must thread their way through the multiple cross-currents in social and economic change. Effective leadership must be built on sensitivity to important tradeoffs, awareness of institutional influence, and knowledge of the social and economic processes shaping the future.

SUMMARY

Chapter 6

The Coming Economic Transition

Hazel Henderson

If the present "slumpflation" is over, can the next one be far behind? Or will our latest turn of the Keynesian crank lead us back to the good times? I believe that it will not. I think that instead it will clearly reveal the inadequacy of traditional Keynesian policies, and, indeed, the bankruptcy of macro-economic management itself. In spite of an unemployment rate hovering around 9 percent and a federal budget deficit on the order of $60 billion, officials pronounce that the light is now visible at the end of the tunnel. Meanwhile, traditional economic advice is rigidifying the responses of both Congress and the administration, continuing to generate policies that are counterproductive and that often lead to exacerbation of the problems.

The new malaise of "stagflation" or even "slumpflation" is inexplicable by traditional economic theory [1], but it has now been experienced by virtually every Western economy, as well as Japan. Inflation, no longer understandable as the tradeoff for unemployment, has now become a structural feature of many industrial economies, and recession hits all industries dependent on heavy use of increasingly scarce and expensive energy and resources. Although resource prices have fallen of late due to worldwide recession, as soon as the latest shot of Keynesian adrenalin takes hold, resource prices are likely to surge again and the now familiar shortages to reappear.

It is no longer unthinkable to speculate whether industrial societies are approaching some sort of evolutionary cul-de-sac. Instead of moving onward to Daniel Bell's salubrious vision of the post-industrial state, the end-game of industrialism might well be that of the "entropy state" [2]. Simply put, the entropy state is the stage at which society's complexity and interdependence have reached such unmodelable, unmanageable proportions that the transaction costs generated are equal to or exceed its productive capabilities. In a manner analogous to physical systems, the society winds down of its own weight and the proportion of its gross national product that must be spent in mediating conflicts, controlling crime, footing the bill for all the social costs generated by the "externalities" of production and consumption, providing ever more comprehensive bureaucratic coordination, and generally trying to maintain "social homeostasis" begins to grow exponentially [3]. Such societies may have already drifted to a soft landing in a steady state, with inflation masking their declining condition.

GOVERNMENT-POLICY ECONOMICS

Business cycles in these mature industrial economies are now created by economists and governments rather than by market forces, and therefore market forces can no longer be relied on to right things. In their frantic efforts to deal with what they perceive as the three-headed monster of inflation, recession, and energy supply problems, government policymakers, caught in a conflicting chorus of advice from economists, heroically man the money pumps and fiscal machinery and alternately inflate and deflate their respective economies. Sadly, after each one of these artificially-created business cycles, the economy undergoing such treatment is left in a more feverish, flabbier condition than before, with residually higher levels of both unemployment and inflation. Obviously the problems are structural; the aggregate policies which pump up the whole system to ameliorate structural pockets of unemployment and distributional inequities are now too costly. The accompanying increased rates of inflation and resource consumption cannot be maintained. Conversely, trying to deflate the whole economy will not touch structural causes of inflation—such as monopolistic pricing, government protectionism, and other excesses in the wielding of institutional power—nor will it deal with rising global competition for scarce resources or the newly-perceived social costs involved in expanding world trade: the phenomenon of excessive interdependence and synchronously oscillating economies.

The short-term, artificial oscillations brought on by applications of conventional economic wisdom obscure longer-term cycles and inexorable realities, such as the declining global resource base, a climatic cooling trend, and unabated population growth. The real prospect of a massive world food shortage and widespread famine suggest that Malthusian predictions cannot yet be wished away by the technological optimists. Reality is what people attend to, and not only economists, but most other people, attend too much to short-term oscillations. In Chapter 5, Forrester points out how important the longer-term cycles may be.

Oscar Morgenstern recently underlined the absurdity of fixations on the short-term by pointing out that even data on these oscillations which most frequently occupy economists are often little better than statistical illusions, replete with leads, lags, and perceptual errors [4]. It is now self-evident that there will be no solution to current economic discontents unless some cherished assumptions are jettisoned. One of these must be the elegant, free market equilibrium model of supply and demand, which has permitted economists to discount possibilities of absolute scarcity of both resources and capital on the supply side. Such unrealistic models of how the economy works are now short-circuiting new formulations of the dilemma.

Fortunately, the current policy confusion and official resignation to dangerously high unemployment levels is at last opening up the debate to expression of new economic thoughts, formerly considered heretical and often suppressed. Those jumping into the vacuum range from well-known advocates of national planning, including Wassily Leontieff and Senator Jacob Javits (Chapter 10); to Keynesian purists, including Paul Davidson of Rutgers, Kenneth Boulding, and E.F. Schumacher; and finally to the almost underground views of the young radicals of the Union for Radical Political Economics and Paul Sweezy, the Marxist editor of the *Monthly Review.*

Unfortunately the prescriptions of these heretics are inadequate because they still lie within the confines of the discipline of economics, and incorporate historical lags that do not capture the changes in context that have occurred since Keynes wrote his *General Theory of Employment, Interest and Money* in 1936. This radically-changed context includes the worsening global population/resource ratio, the limits of human adaptation to rationalistic, massively-scaled organization and production systems, the mounting environmental disruption, and the new global interdependence and rising militancy of the less-industrialized world. Thus today the policies that are hailed as good economics—such as placing reliance on the free market or vetoing legislation for public service employment—are becoming more obviously nonviable politics, poor sociology, inadequate systems theory, and almost incompetent science—psychologically, ecologically, and even simply physically.

Given new conditions, desirable economic concepts will have to be expanded to embrace more external variables. Since this probably cannot be achieved without sacrificing some of the pretensions to rigor that have seemingly separated economics from its humbler sister disciplines in the social sciences, economists will have to moderate their claims to value-free scientific method if they are not to further confuse government policymakers and themselves. More uncertainties will have to be acknowledged, and the paradoxical fact will have to be faced that much of today's research into policy-related questions, using environmental impact and technology assessment methods, actually increases uncertainty, only revealing more of what is not known. For example, the cluster of related problems economists define as inflation, recession, and a shortage of capital require explanations from beyond traditional economics. While many economists have recognized the role of the Vietnam War, global interdependence and rising expectations, and, of course, the oil producers cartel in increasing rates of inflation, few have explored the following underlying problems:

Declining Productivity of Capital Investments

This phenomenon is rooted in the declining resource/energy base, which necessitates using more capital to extract resources that are more inaccessible, diffuse, and degraded. This decline in the productivity of capital investment is visible in the food system. For example, yields for many crops can no longer be increased by massive increases in fertilizer inputs, and destructively overmechanized fishing boats destroy fingerlings and diminish the available catch. Ecologists Howard and Eugene Odum drew attention to the same problem in the energy extraction process, where increasing quantities of capital investment yield less and less net energy [5]. These new conditions, this "gnawing on the bone" in many energy and resource extraction processes, mean that more of society's activities, wealth, and income must be diverted into getting the energy to get the energy. The GNP continues to climb and people work harder, but their money simply becomes worth less in real terms.

Social Costs of Production and Consumption

Economists dismiss the mounting social and environmental costs in an almost Freudian slip as "externalities." Economic activities, especially when defined in free market terms, treat not only air, water, and the absorptive capacities of the environment as free goods, but also the delicate web of the social system—the human relationships of the family, community cohesiveness, and the network of social sanctions that enables societies to maintain order without constant recourse to police and courts. The maximizing of profits stresses the social fabric in many costly ways; for example, excessive mobility demanded of corporate employees can result in less stable communities, less committed voters and citizens, alcoholic wives, and disturbed children and schools. Technical and managerial scale and complexity exacts its toll in dropouts, drug addicts, and criminal behavior and alienation. In addition, such diseconomies of scale, complexity, and interdependence mandate the soaring transaction costs I spoke of previously.

Capital Investment and Employment

There has been little examination of the structural tendencies of the United States economy to overinvest capital: for example, the favored tax treatment of capital investment and income; the ability of large corporations to retain earnings and thus generate their own internal capital; and definitions of productivity and efficiency skewed toward the substitution of capital for labor. This trend is exemplified in the normative assumptions equating technological innovation with "progress," as illuminated by Francois Iletman in *Society and the Assessment of Technology*. It becomes clear that both market-oriented and Marxist economists share this latter confusion. Marxists still believe in the labor theory of value, even though in the intervening period since Marx's analysis, the population/resource ratio has shifted drastically. People are now plentiful and resources are scarce, and as a consequence the capital/labor ratio has now shifted back toward increased labor in varying degrees all over the planet.

On the other hand, the confusion of market-oriented economists is based on their belief in the equilibrium model of supply and demand, which leads them to view capital and resource inputs as expendable. Thus, all that appears to be needed to call forth more supplies of raw materials is to hurl more capital into the extraction process, even when it becomes little more than a sink. This accounts for the conventional expressions of optimism rather than the more realistic worries when aggregate capital expenditures rise, no matter how frivolously or wastefully allocated. Similarly, the constant demand of business and economists for increased tax favoritism to capital investments is based on a Keynesian, trickle-down theory of job creation; in lending, capital is made available to affluent, large savers and owners of existing capital rather than to alternative ventures via credit allocation and social investments.

Concomitant confusion exists over the correlation between capital investment and employment. In fact, capital is often invested to reduce employment, as in the case of oil-refining processes, automation of supermarket check-out lines, and banking institutions' drive to install electronic funds transfer systems. The Report of the National Commission on Technology, Automation, and Economic Progress tried to lay this issue to rest in 1966, but it will not go away in an economy with 9 percent of its labor force unemployed. Even a cursory critique of this report reveals its conceptual flaws: for example, accepting free market assumptions in viewing the labor market, rather than the more persuasive case that labor markets are highly imperfect and much unemployment in technologically-advanced countries is structural.

All of these confusions rest on a more profound misunderstanding of "efficiency." Rarely do economists ask, "Efficient for whom and for what system or subsystem?" Corporate efficiency often results in less social efficiency if costs are externalized to taxpayers, as they frequently are. Such fuzzy definitions of efficiency in an interdependent economy lead to chronic suboptimization, since it is axiomatic in many other disciplines such as general systems theory, biology, and ecology that optimizing subsystem goals is always done at the expense of the larger system. The word "efficiency" is quite meaningless until related to time and space coordinates.

Similarly, other value-laden words, "productivity" and "profit-maximizing," are indefinable unless a system boundary and a time horizon are specified. In an even wider, longer-term context, the question arises of whether what capitalist countries call "profits" and centrally-planned societies call "economic growth" do not always incur matching, but unrecorded debit entries in some social or environmental ledger. It seems more likely that as socioeconomic systems approach boundary conditions—such as those imposed by the laws of physics and cited by Dr. Alfred Eggers, director of the National Science Foundation's RANN Program, in his warning to economists at the Senate Conference on Economic Planning [6]—the concepts of "profits" and "economic growth" become little more than anthropocentric figments of human imagination. In the relatively brief decades of maneuvering time available, I hope that the technologists can repeal these basic laws of physics, but prudent economic planning suggests that society had better not count on it. Furthermore, options for technological substitution are fast eroding since it is now clear that a wide range of potentially substitutable resources are becoming scarce simultaneously.

POLICY DIRECTIONS FOR THE COMING ECONOMIC TRANSITION

An economy that has been riding on a cornucopia of resources and that has enjoyed a long historical period of growth cannot be shifted drastically to a new course without dislocation and hardship, at best. At worst, there will occur widespread social unrest, depression, and economic gyrations, and, paradoxically for economists, continued inflation. Therefore a series of stop-gap policies is called for to ease passage and enable a rolling readjustment, while attention is turned to needed long-term structural changes in consumption patterns, life-styles, and values. At the same time a mandatory shift to sustainable forms of production and energy based on renewable resources is vital, along with a corresponding reduction of rates of materials throughput and maximum conservation of all nonrenewable resources. Such interim policies during the vital readjustment decade ahead should be geared toward the following:

Maintaining Consumer Purchasing Power

Consumer purchasing power must be maintained even at minimal levels, by extending unemployment benefits to those in dislocated, resource-intensive industries, and by providing a comprehensive system of negative income taxes for those for whom jobs cannot be found. Such uncomfortably austere but basic economic security for all citizens would act as a stabilizer, permitting phasing out of old production processes and allowing orderly transition without unacceptable individual hardship and the danger of widespread social unrest.

Conservation of Oil

Vigorous conservation measures geared toward the concept of reducing throughput should be taken to preserve maximum options in dealing with oil producers (and other likely cartels) and this country's declining resource base. As Amory Lovins points out in Chapter 3, a Btu of energy saved is always cheaper than a Btu generated. Specific policies might include:

1. Bringing domestic natural resources such as public lands, publicly-owned oil, and gas and coal reserves under greater democratic control; tightening up on leasing practices geared to rapid exploitation or speculation—for instance, separating exploration from leasing and retaining exploration in the hands of government to determine exactly what is being leased and assure the public a fairer return; and bringing all major components of the energy industry under much

tighter government surveillance and control, not excluding nationalization.

2. Initiating mandatory fuel allocation programs less penalizing to colder climatic regions than higher import tariffs.

3. Rationing gasoline and taxing horsepower and fuel inefficiency. Rationing is in effect more of a "market" solution to gasoline conservation than raising prices and attempting to offset social inequities by setting up complex systems of transfer payments to the poor. Not only would raising prices set off another inflationary surge, but the need for compensatory transfers to the poor would endanger higher transaction costs than a system of rationing; moreover, the taxes to be collected and transferred would probably prove an irresistible pork-barrel and their transferral to the poor would be unlikely. A rationing system, based on the issuance of a prescribed number of ration coupons covering the total consumption rate targeted, would be made available to all citizens over the age of eighteen, rather than merely drivers. This removes a major inequity, since some 20 percent of United States families do not own a car, and at the same time assures enough ration coupons in circulation to make counterfeiting and black-marketeering marginally unprofitable. Such a scheme has the additional advantage of providing not only a "stick" for reducing consumption, but also a "carrot" rewarding nonconsumption, by permitting those who do not own vehicles to sell their coupons to those who do at free market prices. This would also do away with rationing boards and costly administration because there would be plenty of extra coupons available to those willing to pay for them. Coupons could be issued each month at post offices or through other means, and any citizen who wished to turn them back at an established price could immediately do so, or otherwise sell them to friends, neighbors, or employers. Thus a socially equitable solution to gasoline conservation might be possible without adding to inflationary pressures.

4. Introducing tax and credit allocation programs to reduce energy consumption and materials throughput—for instance, repealing depletion allowances and tax credits for capital investments which may be wasteful or unproductive in net energy terms; directing and encouraging investments in the needed new industries geared to recycling and based on renewable resources, such as solar, wind, and geothermal energy and methane conversion, with selected tax credits for such investments and government research and development funds targeted to meet similar criteria; repealing taxes favoring use of virgin materials and exploring amortization taxes to increase product

durability; requiring full disclosure of corporate research and development investments and using technology assessments to determine likely social and environmental impacts, which would shift the burden of proof, in recognition of capital shortages, to the instigator of technical change.

Shift to Low-Investment, Labor-Intensive Production

Policies recognizing the need for replacing capital with labor might include:

1. Retraining programs for all workers dislocated from resource-intensive production, including the reorientation of highly-skilled engineers trained in esoteric, high-technology fields where job opportunities will temporarily shrink. This will occur as emphasis in investment is placed on achieving economies of scale in manufacturing cheaper and less complex solar, thermal, and wind energy components and recycling systems.
2. A federally-funded program of public service employment, similar to that vetoed by President Ford or modeled after the Humphrey-Hawkins Bill, to finance productive human service jobs—particularly to fill pressing needs in cities for restoring services cut by layoffs in police, fire, sanitation, hospital, and education services, and to restore confidence of urban populations that cities will not be abandoned by federal and state governments, as they pursue economic policies based on free market assumptions. Human service jobs must be recognized for their advantages in the economic transition, as well as for their social and humanitarian benefits.
3. Funding and initiation of federal programs now authorized, which create needed public facilities in labor-intensive, capital-conserving, energy-conserving, and environmentally-benign ways—for instance, the $6 billion authorized water-treatment facilities; funds provided in the Railroad Reorganization Act for repair of roadbeds; and Highway Trust Funds for repair, maintenance and setting up of express bus lanes on all arterial roads. The Council on Environmental Quality has prepared a summary review of all such mandated programs that can be initiated without further legislation, finally laying to rest the artificial conflict often fomented by special interests between labor and environmentalists [7]. Conversely, all resource- and capital-intensive projects, such as new highways, space, and other high-technology programs should be reassessed in light of capital shortages and competing needs. Mass transit expenditures represent

a gray area, since many projects are overly capital-intensive boondoggles geared to Buck Rogers schemes more suited to the capabilities of high-technology vendors than the needs of riders.

4. Tax policies and expenditures to restore neutrality in the treatment of capital income and wage income, treating dividends at the same rate as wages [8]; repeal of across-the-board tax credits for capital investments, however wasteful or socially marginal, and replacement by credit allocation to essential industries and tax incentives to needed new industries geared to a declining resource base; repeal of favored tax treatment permitting wasteful real estate speculation, ruining of agricultural land, and all accelerated amortization which encourages unnecessary write-offs and capital replacement. Tax credits should instead be enacted to give incentives to hire labor and replace capital—for example, credits to those who are self-employed and employ others, with a cutoff aimed at encouraging small business and preventing the program from subsidizing large companies' payrolls unduly. Such a program would help reduce the disastrously high unemployment rates among minorities, teenagers, women, and other special and unskilled categories, by making it more feasible for people to hire each other in child care, yard care, home repairs, and small proprietary retail businesses. If capital is scarce, such a package of policies will raise capital's marginal cost relative to labor inputs, thus conserving it for more optimal productive uses.

5. Reform of banking institutions to limit bank holding companies and excessive speculation; repeal of regulations limiting interest payments to small savers, in order to encourage more decentralized capital formation. Rather than thus forcing small savers to underwrite cheap mortgage funds, specific subsidy of mortgages for home construction may be needed.

6. Anticipatory studies on the employment ramifications of all public and private investment over a certain size, such as the Employment Impact Statements, as proposed by Environmentalists for Full Employment, in testimony before the United States Congress [9].

7. More vigorous antitrust enforcement to prevent corporations with undue market power from exercising it for internal capital investment, and to restore market competition under the new tax constraints to prevent development of socially costly and wasteful goods and services.

8. Studies on controlling the volume of product advertising on radio and television through the Federal Communications Commission and the Federal Reserve Board, to develop this as a new means of aggregate demand management. No First Amendment principles

would be violated, since total advertising time available is already limited by regulations and the limits of the electromagnetic spectrum. Space and time would still be available to all commercials on a competitive basis, as today, but limiting the total time and ceilings for advertisers as a means of reducing inflationary demand would tend to prevent saturation advertising by powerful corporations to achieve rapid penetration and domination of market share, which in turn, would favor small businesses which cannot compete with such massive advertising budgets. Accompanying this, corporate advertising expenditures would be disallowed as tax write-offs.

9. Policies designed to encouraging the wider diffusion of capital ownership, such as the Employee Stock Ownership Trusts recently enacted, based on the ideas of Louis O. Kelso in *Two Factor Theory: The Economics of Reality* [10]. Diffusing capital ownership and encouraging small savers with the same rates as large savers would tend to restore the vitality of capital markets and reduce the concentration of wealth and maldistribution of incomes.

LONG-TERM GOALS

The *sine qua non* for the successful transition to a sustained yield economy based on renewable resources will be leadership and programs of public education to explain the basis for such apparently drastic policy shifts. The current vacillation in economic policies is heightening the atmosphere of fear and the loss of consumer confidence. An all-out program is needed to illuminate the new contexts and the need for change, and to reassure people that a gentle, managed economic transition can sustain full employment, if the tough choices are now made and if current wastes of energy and materials are foregone in order to allow investment in the new productive base. It should even be possible to portray the advantages gained in less pollution and environmental disruption, not to mention the psychic relief in store for those who relinquish the destructive, exhausting game of keeping up with the Joneses [11].

Longer-term structural readjustment to a sustained yield economy, restoring lost flexibility, will require decentralization of population and industrial activities. Such moves are now under discussion in Congress, where the House Committee on Public Works last year appointed a scientific advisory panel to explore how public works investments could direct and distribute growth more rationally to uncrowded, less developed areas of the United States. Chairman John Blatnik voiced concern over increasing urbanization, and the panel's report reviewed the trend to centralization [12], citing the potential of performing "carrying capacity" assessments of the environments of many overcrowded regions, so as to set limits on their growth and redirect it to sparsely-developed areas. Many other lawmakers, including Vice President Mondale, Senators Humphrey, Hartke, Jackson, and Bensen, as well as Congressmen John Dingell and Morris Udall, have focused on more rational growth policies. The political viability of such policies is argued by the victory of Governor Richard Lamm in Colorado, who campaigned on a platform of reduced, balanced growth that has also proved popular in Oregon and California.

Lastly, it is vital that the long-accepted notion that economics is a science be contradicted; this idea is now proving destructive in that it is preventing Americans from talking to each other and debating the important subject of what is valuable. Economists must be called to account for their field's unnecessary mystification, so that there will be no more concealment of value conflicts under the guise of technical or economic efficiency. Two policy suggestions for making the normative nature of economics explicit are:

—To amend the Employment Act of 1946 so as to expand the Council of Economic Advisors from three to seven persons, and include economists from labor, consumer, minority, and environmental constituencies [13]; and

—To assure that the Federal Reserve Board members are selected from major constituency groups, instead of from banking, financial, and business-oriented organizations exclusively, as they tend to be at present.

The aforementioned proposals by no means exhaust the possibilities of steering the economy through the dangerous shoals ahead. All of them need to be explored for unanticipated impacts in other areas and for second order consequences that require careful further research. Recognizing the inherent difficulties of implementation, there is no choice but to accept the challenge.

Chapter 7

Equity, the Free Market, and the Sustainable State

Donella Meadows

Neither the book *The Limits to Growth* nor the computer model underlying it contains much information about, or insight into, the global problem of distributional inequity [1]. In one sense this omission is understandable; the *Limits* project was intended to be a study of growth, not of distribution. Yet in a larger sense, growth of population and capital are closely related to distribution of scarce resources. Any plan to deal with the problems engendered by material growth on a finite planet must take into account the interconnections between growth and economic distribution. In particular, any design for a sustainable, steady-state society must be based on some understanding of the sources of inequity in the current society and on some plan to keep these sources under control.

This paper explores the relationships interlinking growth, equity, and various economic systems—in particular, the free market economy. I am interested here in three questions:

1. Is a nongrowing economy likely to be an equitable one?
2. Is nongrowth consistent with a market economy?
3. Is a market economy consistent with equity?

Before pursuing the answers to these questions, I should begin by defining the slippery concept of inequity.

WHAT IS INEQUITY AND WHY SHOULD WE CARE ABOUT IT?

Inequity is a subjective concept, related to ethics and values and undefinable in any exact terms. For the purposes of this paper, inequity shall mean the distribution of anything people value in a way sufficiently unequal to disturb a significant number of people. Note that by this definition, inequality can exist without inequity. Inequity is inequality that is strongly resented.

I have two reasons for caring about inequity, one individual and one social. The first arises from the simple moral outrage I feel about some forms of inequity. I am not comfortable living in an inequitable society, even when I do not suffer personally from the inequities. Everyone has a different moral threshhold, however, and the source of my discomfort may not particularly bother others or vice versa. My second concern may be more widely shared because it is not moral but practical. Inequity may be a cause of destructive social instability, for it is self-reinforcing and self-magnifying, as Kenneth Boulding has pointed out: "Unfortunately, the principle: 'To him that hath shall be given', has a good many examples; it is one of the systems increasing inequality. It is easier for the rich to save than it is for the poor; it is easier for the powerful to conserve and expand their power than it is for the powerless to increase what little power they have" [2].

Boulding describes a positive feedback loop that can feed upon itself and turn a small inequality into a great inequity. Unequal distribution of any resource that increases relative power (education, money, influence, credit) permits the successful competitor to gain ever-increasing power to win further competitions.[a]

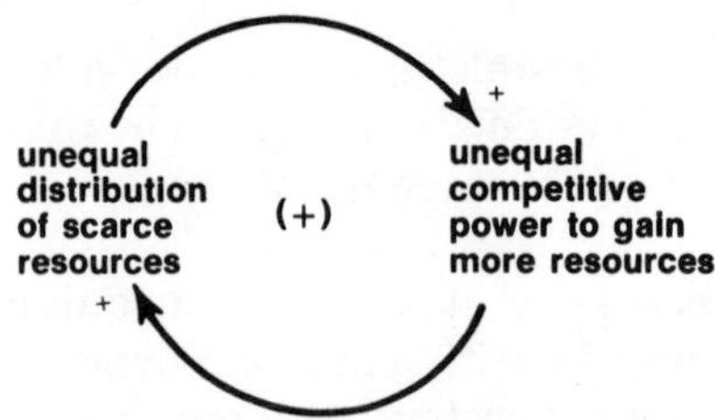

[a]In all diagrams in this paper, an *arrow* indicates that a change in one element causes a change in the other. If the arrow bears a + sign, the two elements change in the *same* direction; if a – sign, they change in *opposite* directions. The (+) or (–) sign in the middle of a closed loop indicates whether the entire loop is positive or negative. Positive loops are self-reinforcing viscious circles that tend to grow or decline exponentially (explosively). Negative loops are self-balancing circles that tend to seek a level and maintain it.

Aside from escalating a tolerable inequality into an intolerable inequity, this positive feedback loop of power could eventually create enough dissatisfaction to produce social conflict. Boulding even claims that conflict can create still further inequality: "A simple, but very depressing, model would be one in which conflict creates inequality, especially if one side wins and the other side loses. The resulting inequality would lead to further conflict, and so on. We have here an unfortunate example of destabilizing feedback, which can increase both inequality and conflict until some limit is reached" [3].

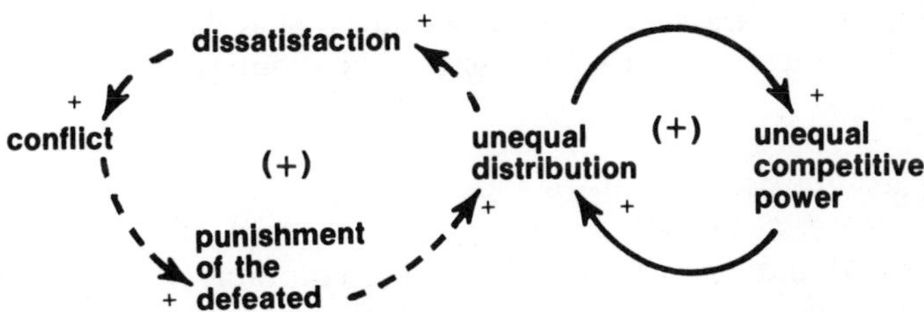

These positive loops need not escalate until they destroy society; their effect can be neutralized in several ways. Underprivileged people could be convinced not to be dissatisfied, dissatisfaction could be resolved by responses other than conflict, conflict could result in something other than a clear set of winners and losers. Or inequality could be reduced in the first place by any number of redistributive mechanisms that allow the less privileged to compete more effectively for scarce resources. However, these positive loops are germane to the discussion that follows. The message of *The Limits to Growth* was that the present social system is unstable, in part because of the positive feedback loops that cause population and capital to grow exponentially. In a stable, steady-state society where those material growth loops are restrained, the positive feedback loops of power and of conflict must not be left free. Therefore, it is important to know more about how they are related to material growth.

One Theory that Does Not Work: Growth Leads to Equity

For some time now I have been searching for a theory that explains the dynamics of the distribution of social goods and bads. I have found few explicit theories but many conclusions drawn from unexpressed assumptions. The most-often-voiced conclusion is that an end to material growth will worsen distributional inequities. Here are two expressions of this point of view:

> If we were to accept . . . the thesis that the world cannot be saved except through zero growth rates, we must also demonstrate that world income redistribution on a massive scale is possible. Otherwise, freezing the present world income distribution would not save the world; it would only bring about a confrontation between the haves and the have-nots. . . . While income redistribution is a desirable objective and must be pursued with full vigor, we must recognize that it is going to be even more difficult to achieve . . . if there is no prospect of future growth [4].

> It is most doubtful that the elimination of economic growth could create equality between the advanced and less advanced countries. In fact, the ability of the advanced countries to help the less advanced countries would significantly decrease. Moreover, international redistribution of wealth is unlikely to occur on a significant scale without further economic growth [5].

The assumption behind this argument seems both reasonable and simple: material growth leads to an abundance of things to be distributed. Abundance of anything makes equitable distribution more likely, because it is a natural human trait to be generous with something in surplus and stingy with something scarce. The causal links of this theory would look like this:

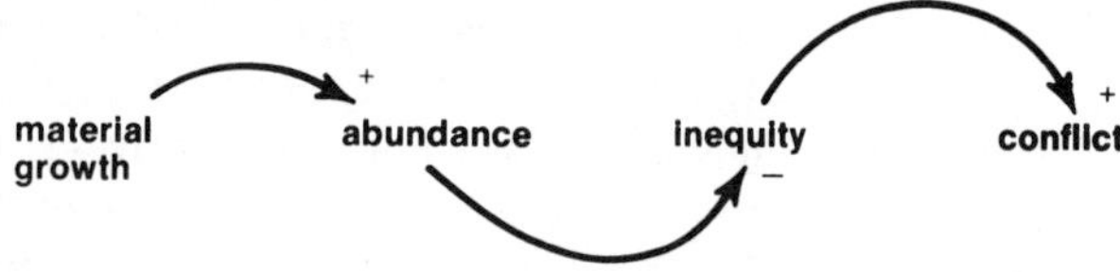

The second link in the chain makes perfect sense; abundance decreases inequity because the necessity for competition is decreased. Land in America was probably distributed much more equally two hundred years ago, when it was in greater abundance relative to the population than it is now. Studies conducted by the UN Food and Agriculture Organization show that food distribution is more unequal in famine areas than in areas where food is sufficient [6].

These examples raise a puzzling contradiction, however. Land and food are not becoming more abundant or more equally distributed in the world, in spite of a hundred or so years of significant material growth. The problem comes from the assumption represented by the first arrow in the causal chain; material growth does not necessarily lead to abundance. The two exponentially-growing physical quantities discussed in *Limits to Growth* are population and capital growth. Putting these explicitly into the causal diagram gives a more complete picture:

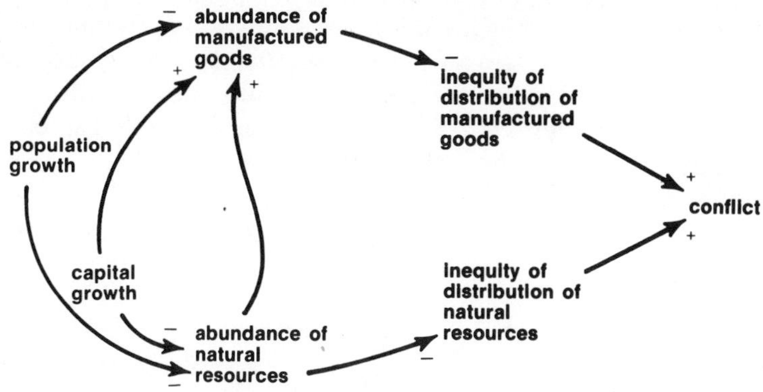

If the index of "abundance" is taken as *per capita* availability, then population growth automatically decreases the abundance of finite natural resources such as land, fresh water, clean air, petroleum, and ore deposits. Population growth may add to the abundance of manufactured goods by adding to the labor force, but since labor is rarely the limiting factor in production these days, the net effect of population growth on per capita abundance of manufactured goods is also negative. Thus, according to this theory, population growth—by creating two kinds of scarcity—is doubly a cause of inequity.

Capital growth increases the abundance of manufactured goods; if capital grew faster than population, everyone could become richer in manufactured goods, and inequity in distribution of those goods could decrease. This set of causal links must have been the dominant influence in the historic experience of our culture, since it is the one so often seized upon as an argument to promote growth. Nevertheless, it is the only one of the four effects of material growth in the diagram that is favorable to equity. The other result of capital growth is a diminishing abundance of natural resources. Factories and machines use land, air, water, energy, and ores just as the population does, and the richness in manufactured wealth produced by capital is inevitably accompanied by an impoverishment in natural wealth. Furthermore, since the manufactured wealth is ultimately derived from natural resources, capital growth that depletes those resources will decrease even manufactured wealth in the future.

This analysis leads us to a conclusion opposite from the argument that growth is needed to attain equity. Continued material growth may create a temporary illusion of abundance and equity, but in the long run it will worsen distributional equality by increasing scarcity, first of natural, then of manufactured resources. Increased scarcity forces greater competitiveness, activating the positive feedback loops of power and conflict that further increase inequity. Technology can prolong the process by allowing more abundant lower grade natural resources to be substituted for depleted prime ones, but not indefinitely. And technology can in itself be an instrument for creating inequity, as it increases the competitive power of those who possess and understand it over those who do not.

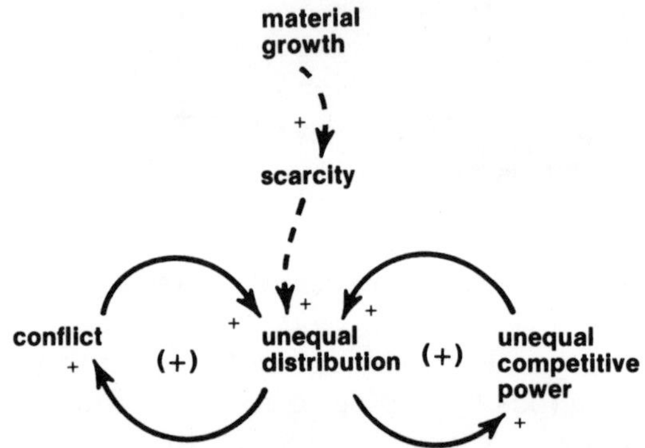

According to this theory of distributional dynamics, a non-growing economy may not improve distributional equity, but it will at least keep inequalities from getting worse quite so fast. That may be comforting news, but it is hardly the basis for the design of a sustainable state. That requires further examination of the basic distribution mechanism of the capitalist world, the market system.

Another Problematic Theory: The Free Market

The ideal distribution of society's scarce resources, according to Western economic theory, is attained automatically through the mechanism of the decentralized market system. To understand how the free market fits into the design of a sustainable state, it is useful to begin with a brief description of how it works in theory:

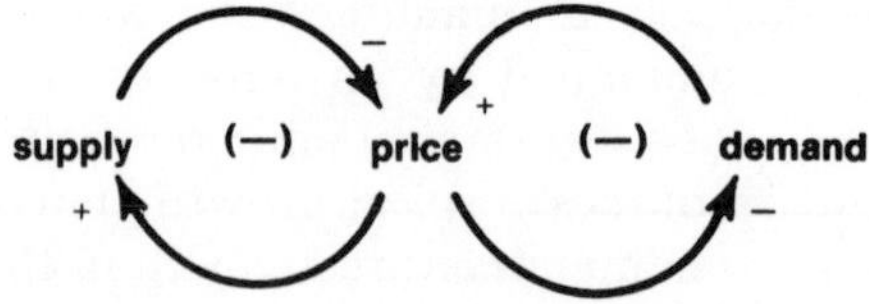

If at any time the demand for any item on the market is higher than the supply of that item, its price will rise. The higher price stimulates more profit and thus more production of the scarce item. On the demand side, higher price causes some prospective purchasers to buy something else instead, or to do without. Thus supply rises and demand falls until the initial imbalance is corrected. At that point supply equals demand, the price is stable, and the system is in equilibrium. The market adjustment mechanisms also work in the opposite direction; when supply is higher than demand, prices fall—causing, on the supply side, a cutback in production, and on the demand side, more customers, attracted by the bargain price.

The supply and demand sides of the market system form two stabilizing negative feedback loops, acting in concert to pull the price of every economic good and service to the exact point where supply equals demand. This point will also represent the most efficient, but not equal, distribution of resources, producing maximum possible income to the suppliers, maximum possible utility to the consumers, and greatest possible total output. The beauty of the idealized system is that it is self-regulating. No one needs to plan or control anything. Price acts as a signal of relative scarcity or oversupply, and then consumers and producers, acting in their own best interests, correct the imbalance by producing or consuming more or less, whichever is required.

That is the theory, and it is a very appealing one. If one attempts to imagine a centralized planning bureaucracy trying to control prices, production, and consumption of many million different goods and services without the market system, one can understand why there are often long queues and barren store counters in the Soviet Union and other nonmarket economies. It would seem that decentralized allocation decisions based on these two stabilizing negative feedback loops are ideally suited for a society that emphasizes long-term stability. After all, their very function is to maintain a stable and optimal equilibrium.

However, if one looks not at the theory but at the way real markets work, four important problems are obvious. These problems are well known and often discussed. In fact, they are so pervasive that one must believe they are intrinsic to the market system, not accidental flaws that can be easily repaired.

Delay in Response. Response on the supply side to a changing price, especially a higher one, rarely can be instantaneous. Producers may have to perceive the higher price long enough to believe it, decide to expand capacity, obtain financing, build new machines or factories, and hire new workers before a larger supply actually appears on the market. This response delay may easily be several years, especially in complex, high-technology productive processes. Delays in a feedback response may actually destabilize a system by causing overadjustments and oscillations [7]. Similar oscillations can be experienced by anyone who tries to adjust the temperature of a shower with a very long pipe between the faucets and the showerhead. This basic instability can be countered somewhat by the addition of a planning or forecasting ability that supplements the backward-looking price signal with additional information gained from looking ahead. If this projective mechanism is perfect and if everyone trusts it, the system will be stabilized. If, however, forecasts take the form of blind extrapolations or rumor-prone futures markets, small signals may be amplified into large ones, and the system may be further destabilized.

Cost and Income Bounds. A more complete representation of the market system would include the constraints of cost and income:

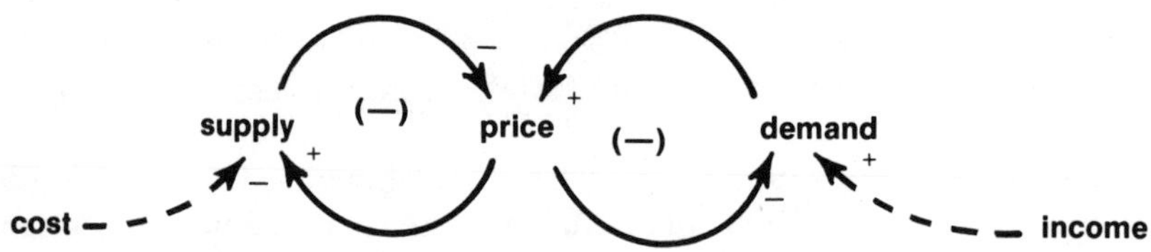

If the price of an item ever falls below the marginal cost to the producer of making it, he will shut down. If the price of a product ever equals, or even approaches, the total income of a consumer, he will stop buying it. Under either of these conditions, one of the regulatory loops becomes inoperative; no one can produce or consume less than zero. Thus cost and income act as two bounds or walls limiting the regulatory capability of the system. At low prices the cost barrier deactivates the supply loop. At high prices the income constraint nullifies the demand loop, as price rises to the point where consumers are priced out of the market. The grain market in India is near the income wall because demand chronically exceeds supply. The cost and income constraints are normally no problem as long as there is a substantial middle region, far away from the walls and as long as the system operates in that region. As we shall see in the discussion on equity to follow, the system may not naturally stay away from the walls; under some conditions it drives itself toward them.

False Costs. The "cost" that influences profits and the expansion decision of suppliers is only the perceived immediate cost to the supplier. Since the system is competitive, each supplier is effectively rewarded for cutting costs and thus continuing to realize a profit at price levels that shut down his competitors. A very effective way to cut costs is to transfer them to other parts of the system. The market gives producers strong incentives to do this: to release pollution that must be cleaned up by public agencies, to convince the government to subsidize exploration for new oil wells, to avoid installation of capital that would increase worker safety, to create toxic waste products that must be safeguarded by future generations. These "externalities," as they are called, are widely recognized as basic faults of the market system. They result in prices that are lower than true total costs. This false price information induces consumers to buy products the full price of which they actually cannot afford. There are many ways to correct externalities, most of which require government-established standards and constant inspection and enforcement. The effort must be vigorous and continuous, because a competitive system *rewards* externalities; they are an intrinsic and logical result of the free market.

Efficiency Versus Equity. A fourth complaint about the market system is that it is blind to considerations of equity. The elegant market allocation mechanisms may result in maximum overall "efficiency," but nothing in the workings of the market guarantees that the efficient allocation is "fair," that it results in maximum satisfaction of real human needs, that it properly rewards real productive contributions to society, or that it does not lead to the positive feedback loops of power and conflict. Critics have observed the real market allocating grain to some people for the production of beef to feed their pets, while it denies other people the grain required to feed their children. They see the market rewarding with a pittance the man who works all day in the field to produce that grain, while greatly enriching the man who does nothing more than buy it and hold it off the market until the price rises. Two questions are raised by these observations. First, is the market system really rewarding productive efficiency, as it must to function well? Second, even if it is, would a society that allocates its output efficiently in the market sense be stable, equitable, or desirable to live in?

HOW DOES THE MARKET DISTRIBUTE THE MEANS OF PRODUCTION?

Two nearly-perfect market systems provide answers to that question. I have studied dairy farms in Vermont and wheat farms in the Punjab of Northern India, in order to analyze two problems raised by government officials in the two widely-distant areas. Why is the number of dairy farmers in Vermont decreasing so precipitously? Why is the rural-urban migration rate in the Punjab so high? To my surprise, the answers to both those questions turned out to be quite similar, and both of them could be traced back to the operation of the market.

The Vermont and Punjab agricultural economies both consist of many small-scale producers, and their product is undifferentiable; one farm's milk or wheat is essentially indistinguishable from that of another. There has been some governmental interference in each system, but in each case the effect seems to have been to enhance, not impede, market function. The price of New England milk is governmentally fixed, but primarily to smooth out fluctuations due to weather variation; the fixed prive has tracked the equilibrium market price [8]. In the Punjab, a massive land reallocation at the time of India's partition resulted in more equal land holdings. Since then the government has intervened primarily through educational efforts and in promoting credit systems.

In Vermont the number of dairy farms has decreased from 22,000 in 1950 to 6,000 in 1975. The average number of cows per farm has tripled over the same period. Farmers can handle much larger numbers of cows either by hiring labor or by mechanizing many farm operations from milking to manure handling. Most Vermont farmers have followed the second option; the average value of farm machinery has increased, in real dollars, from $20,000 in 1962 to $37,000 in 1973, and the average indebtedness per farm has increased since 1950 by a factor of six.

Vermont farmers are not at all happy with these changes, and neither are their nonfarming neighbors. The farmers complain of the debt loads, of the increasingly tight management needed to make ends meet, of the high risk of bankruptcy, and of the impossibility for a young new farmer to raise the funds, an estimated $250,000, required to start in business. With few exceptions, the only young farmers in Vermont are sons of old farmers who have inherited their farms or received low-interest, start-up financing from their fathers. Nonfarmers in Vermont are unhappy with the trend away from dairy farming for both economic and esthetic reasons. Economically, although the total dairy income to the state in real dollars is about the same as it ever was, it now supports far fewer people. Much of the money flows out again, to bankers, feed distributors, and tractor factories in other states. Esthetically, Vermonters like the look of dairy farms. Over the last twenty-five years, two million acres of dairy farm, amounting to 30 percent of the state's area, have been converted to other uses—typically scrub forest, recreation developments, or shopping centers, none of which, according to opinion polls, especially appeals to Vermonters [9].

Many factors are blamed for the decline of the dairy industry in Vermont. Some say the trouble is the burdensome property tax that hits farmers especially hard. Others blame rising land prices, or avaricious developers, or higher prices of midwestern grain, which is fed to Vermont cows. In our study of Vermont farm economics we found that all of these factors were indeed involved, but none was very important. The real problem was the functioning of the market mechanism.

Vermont milk goes to a market called the "Boston milkshed," where the total demand for milk, the average real price, and the total supply have not varied significantly in twenty years. The real cost of producing one gallon of milk has risen steadily over this period. Since the price (in constant dollars) has been constant, the profit per gallon must be falling. To maintain a constant income, every farmer must then produce more gallons of milk. But demand is constant; no more gallons will be bought. So for every farmer who successfully expands his production, another must decrease his. For every farmer who successfully maintains or expands his income, another finds his income decreasing. Almost without exception, it is the larger farmer who expands and the small farmer who is squeezed out.

One might think that the main problem in the Vermont dairy system is the constant demand for milk. If the market could expand in some way, then all the farmers could get rich together instead of some forcing others out. However, in my second example, wheat in the Punjab, the market is by no means saturated, yet the same process is occurring.

The Punjab is one of the great success stories of the Green Revolution. From 1960 to 1968 wheat production in one district there increased by 300 percent [10]. At the same time, the price of wheat doubled, indicating a strongly rising demand. In such booming circumstances everyone in the district benefited, but some more than others. Wages for landless laborers doubled, but the price of farm land quadrupled, as did the income of landholders. The distribution of land followed a pattern similar to the one I have already described in Vermont. Farms of twenty acres or more expanded in area by an average of 9 percent in twelve years by buying out smaller farms. The proportion of landless laborers in the male work force increased from 9.2 to 19.8 percent (in a period of net outmigration) [11]. In the Punjab wheat market, demand is not fixed—all of India's burgeoning population must be fed. But there is one fixed factor at the center of competition, and that is land. Arable land in the Punjab is fully occupied. If any farmer expands his land holdings, he must do so by buying acreage from another farmer. And, as in Vermont, it is the large farmers who are expanding and the small farmers who are selling out and leaving for the city.

If we look again at the diagram of the market system, we may be able to summarize more clearly what is happening in Vermont and the Punjab. Previously I drew the system with only two loops:

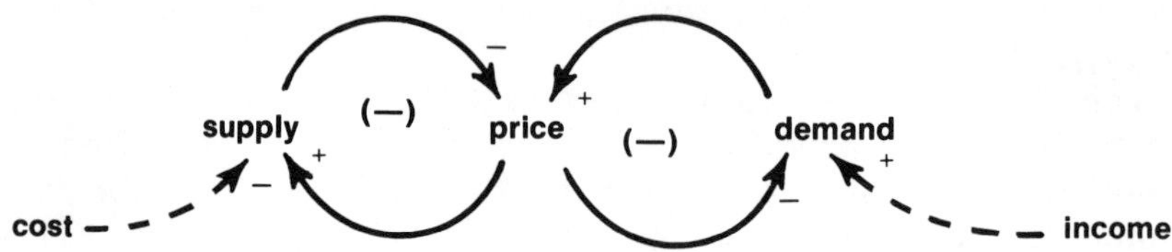

Looking more closely into what is really happening within that lower arrow on the supply side, we can expand the diagram:

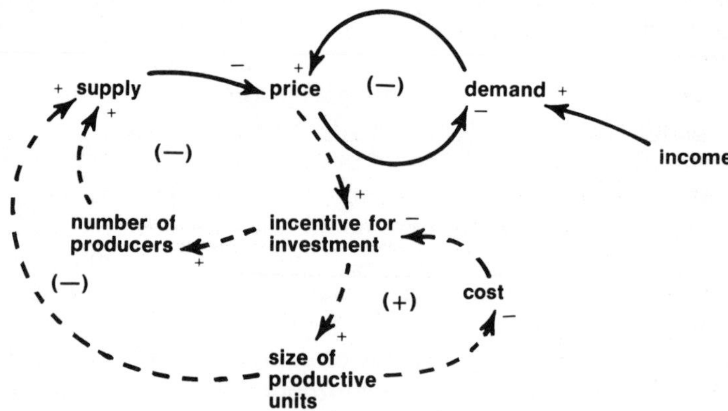

If the price is high enough to trigger an incentive for investment, the supply side can respond in two ways. Either the number of producers can increase, or the present producers can expand their output. In terms of market performance, it does not matter much which happens, except that there may be economies of scale that allow larger suppliers to produce wheat or milk at lower cost. If so, the supply system will expand almost entirely by the outer path, and the size of productive units will increase.

Notice that a small positive feedback loop has appeared at the bottom center of the diagram. If larger farms can indeed lower costs, they reap higher profits, which gives them both the incentive and the means to expand still more. This positive feedback loop will operate, even if there is no change in price, shifting the supply side from inefficient small producers to more efficient larger ones, until productive units are so big that further expansion will not lower costs. If the figure above included all important influences in the system, there would be no problem; the number and size of suppliers would settle into a low-cost, high-efficiency optimal equilibrium. But other factors must be at work because in both Vermont and the Punjab the average size of productive units already far exceeds the lowest-cost size and is still increasing.

Checking the Vermont statistics in detail, one finds that the average herd size per farm increased from thirty-two to fifty-three cows between 1960 and 1973, and it is still rising rapidly. The number of twenty-cow-or-less herds dropped from over 3,000 to about 200 during the same period. Yet there is no indication that small herds are less efficient than larger ones. In fact, in 1973 the total cost of producing one hundred pounds of milk was less for small (thirty-two-cow average) farms than for medium-size (fifty-seven-cow average) farms, and still less than for large (115-cow average) farms. Small farms spent less per pound of milk on labor, fertilizer, trucking, and interest, and slightly more on utilities, gas, and oil. The two major costs of running a dairy farm—feed and capital purchases—were almost exactly equal (per pound of dairy product) across all farm sizes [12].

The same conclusion can be gleaned from the less detailed Punjab statistics. The small farms selling out to large neighbors are not less efficient in terms of total cost per unit of product. They do tend to be less efficient in output per man-hour, but far more efficient in output per acre or per dollar of capital investment [13]. Since the scarcest resources in India are land and capital, not man-hours, small farms should be competitive in the market.

Why are these two market systems moving toward larger productive units when there is no economic reason for doing so? I can only guess that the actual market system, as opposed to the ideal one we have been discussing so far, must be influenced by more relationships than were shown above:

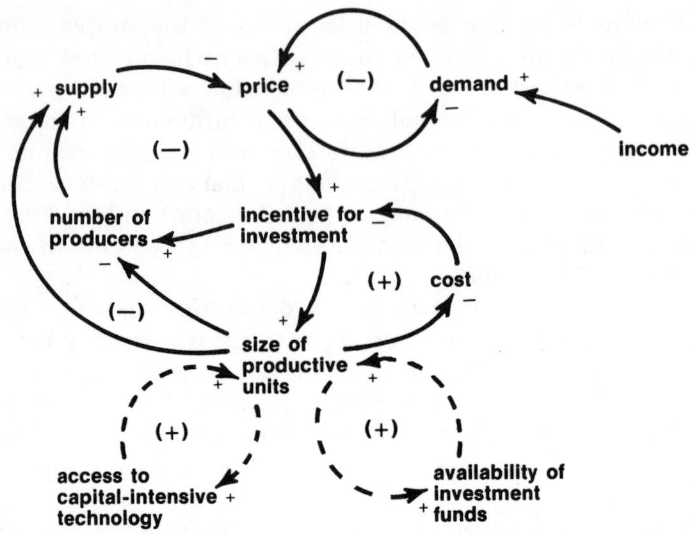

Added here are two positive feedback loops. The first positive feedback loop at the bottom right simply indicates that big farms, or factories, are more likely to get loans for expansion than small ones. That fact may stem initially from the supposition within lending organizations that economies of scale make bigger units better investments. Vermont farm loan agencies have been known to declare publicly that farms with less than fifty cows are, in their views, simply not viable. It is also true that bigger units generally possess more social power, contacts, collateral, information, and political strength. That is certainly the case in both the Punjab and Vermont. This positive feedback allows large farms to grow preferentially, primarily because they are large, not because they are more efficient.

A single arrow has been added to the diagram—a negative one leading from size of productive units to number of producers. It indicates that as some producers expand, they decrease the number of their competitors. This need not always happen, but it must happen in any market where the productive sector has run into any kind of limit. In Vermont the limit is total demand and in India the limit is land; in both cases the limit means that an increase in one farm's size must be bought by decreasing another farm's size (or eliminating it entirely).

The second new positive loop, in the lower left-hand corner, indicates why farm expansion in Vermont and the Punjab are both relatively recent phenomena. For at least a century, both of these systems possessed all the characteristics that I have said might cause farm size to expand: a competitive market system, an intrinsic limit to the market, and a credit advantage to larger farms. But another limit prevented farms from expanding; no farmer, even with a big family, could handle very many cows or harvest very much wheat. Labor could be hired, but there is also a limit to how much labor can be managed effectively. Only recently have new capital-intensive technologies permitted farmers to expand their operation without hiring many more laborers. Of course, those technologies are always more accessible to farms that can take risks. Furthermore, the new machinery adds to the capital value of the farm, and it thus increases the resources required to purchase an average productive unit. As a consequence, it is quite effective in prohibiting any new small competitor from entering the market. Note that the capital-intensive technology need not lower production costs to have this effect. It need only prevent newcomers from entering the market or permit a farmer to expand faster than his neighbor.

The diagram shown above now contains three positive feedback loops. One of them, involving cost, is a beneficial mechanism, selecting higher efficiency techniques through the price system. The other two are positive feedback loops of power. One expresses the ability of large producers to dominate financing resources and thus to become larger. The other represents the ability of large producers to gain preferential access to new capital-intensive technology. The diagram does not include other positive feedback loops respresenting the less legitimate modes by which large producers may use power to displace small ones from the market. To the extent that any of these loops exist, and they do exist demonstrably in Vermont and the Punjab, they push the size of productive units even further above the optimal size that would reduce cost and price. Allowed to operate indefinitely, they can create oligopoly and monopoly, which destroy the perfect market system entirely.

At least in the two systems I have studied, the market system has a flaw that not only balloons productive units far beyond their most efficient size, but that also could lead to the destruction of the competitive market system. There is still competition in the Vermont dairy industry and the Punjabi wheat markets, although both supply sectors seem to be moving rapidly toward oligopoly. It has been estimated that 14 percent of United States crop production and 36 percent of livestock production now take place under formal contracts and vertical arrangements that can no longer be called market operations. About 95 percent of vegetables for processing and 50 percent of citrus cruits are controlled by vertically-integrated firms and never see a market until they are differentiated by brand [14]. I would hesitate to generalize from these to other markets, but the evidence is suggestive. The competitive market system has already essentially vanished in the markets for automobiles, beverages, petroleum, and aluminum. John Kenneth Galbraith claims that 50 percent of the American economy has already entered the oligopolistic category [15]. One wonders why more notice has not been taken of this potentially self-destructive characteristic of the competitive market system [16]. But my theme here is equity, and although monopolies have highly inequitable consequences, I believe that the competitive market may produce inequity long before it evolves into a monopoly. To demonstrate, I need one more expansion of the diagram:

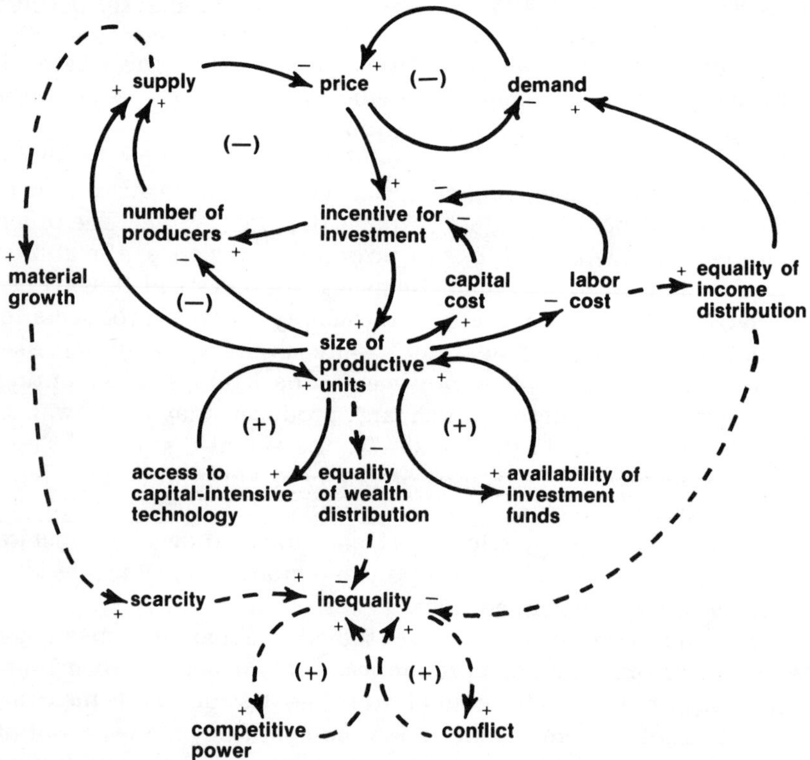

The additional links make apparent more of the connections between supply and demand, production and equality, equality and stability. As I have indicated, in the Punjab, Vermont, and probably most other regions, farmers expand not by hiring more laborers, but by replacing laborers with machines. This choice is sometimes justified by economic calculation, but often the economic gain is not apparent. I suspect that farmers are attracted to machines for two nonquantifiable but very real reasons; machines reduce hassles and increase status. It is easier to be master of a machine than boss of a man, and the neighbors admire you more for it.

So as productive units expand, unit labor costs decrease while capital costs increase. But these costs are no longer paid to thousands of farmers or farm laborers in Vermont. Instead, they go to tractor producers, oil companies, chemical plants, and especially bankers. The distribution of the *means of production*—wealth, farms, or factories—necessarily becomes more unequal as the size of productive units increases. And the distribution of income also becomes more uneven. In effect, the increasing size of productive units is producing reallocation of both wealth and income from the relatively poor to the relatively rich, another very subtle, nearly-invisible positive feedback loop of power. Of course, some of the reallocation does go to laborers in tractor factories, oil refineries, and banks, but these units are also increasing in size, replacing labor with capital, and returning more of their income to the owners of capital.

IS THE FREE MARKET CONSISTENT WITH THE SUSTAINABLE STATE?

The market system, as I have described it, is inherently inequitable and unstable. It is certainly not consistent with a social system dedicated to sustainability. That does not mean, however, that the idea of decentralized economic allocation should be discarded entirely. What is needed is a better understanding of the strengths and weaknesses of the market system and ways to emphasize the strengths while eliminating the weaknesses. As Joan Robinson has said, "a pricing system based on supply and demand, though a bad master, may be a useful servant" [17].

The market's tendency to generate inefficiency and inequity, the weakness I have explored in this paper, results directly from the character of competitive market interactions. The market provides successful competitors with the means to become even more effective competitors in the future. The competition need not be ethical or even efficient; it need only permit one producer to expand faster than another.

Two possible adjustments might correct this deficiency. One would be to design a system that rewards cooperation instead of competition. That is what various socialist and communist movements have tried to do, with varying degrees of success. Cooperation seems to work better on a small scale than a large one. But I prefer decentralized solutions, so I find a new sort of small-scale socialism to be an attractive design for a sustainable state. Such a plan would have to be seen as a long-term solution, however, because it would require deep changes in values, education, and nearly every institution in Western society; such changes would take a generation to implement.

The second approach is to accept competition, but to interrupt or continually counteract the undesirable positive feedback loops it involves. Several methods for doing this have already been instituted, weakly, in our society. Some examples are the progressive income tax, antitrust legislation, and various legal or social sanctions against overly aggressive ways of doing business. We could use more of these constraints, more vigorously enforced.

A more direct correction, applied to a central and easily measurable part of the system, would be a limit on the size of productive units. I have rigorously studied the detailed effects of such a limit in only one case, dairy farming in Vermont. The limit there could be applied in many ways—on acreage, on number of cows, or on total milk production per farm. The latter seems most desirable because it allows each farmer to adjust his factors of production as he sees fit [18]. When a production limit is combined with protective zoning for agricultural land and financial aid for young farmers, both measures that deactivate two other power-based positive feedback loops, the number of farmers in Vermont stabilizes, and milk price is essentially unchanged.

In addition to, or in place of, limits on size of productive units, the sustainable state could impose upper as well as lower limits upon both income and wealth. Herman Daly has suggested this policy as one of the three controlling principles of the steady-state economy:

> The basic institution for controlling distribution is very simple: set maximum and minimum limits on wealth and income, the maximum limit on wealth being the most important. Such a proposal is in no way an attack on private property. . . . According to [John Stuart] Mill, private property is legitimated as a bastion against exploitation. But this is true only if everyone owns some minimum amount. Otherwise, when some own a great deal of it and others have very little, private property becomes an *instrument* of exploitation rather than a guarantee against it [19].

A steady-state society would automatically make the attainment of equity easier by limiting the population and capital growth that creates physical scarcity. These limits would also tend to decrease the inequitable effect of capital-intensive technologies. But fixed population and stabilized material standards of living would automatically limit markets, intensifying the competition that thrives on the positive feedback loops of power. Therefore, if a steady-state economy is to utilize a decentralized market system, it must incorporate an effective redistribution mechanism. This mechanism could be an upper limit on the size of productive units, or upper and lower limits on personal wealth and income, or some combination of these.

There is no question that the thoughts and policies posed here conflict with some freedoms that many have come to believe are important: freedom to make a profit, freedom to manage individual businesses for maximum profit, freedom to gain and wield power, freedom to expand. At the same time, a sustainable state that deliberately interferes with these freedoms would release others that we have forgotten about: freedom to define and create meaningful, dignified employment; freedom from want; freedom from the gainers and wielders of power; freedom from the pressures and long-term threats of growth.

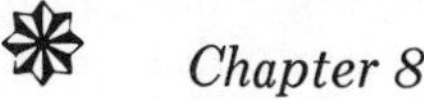

Chapter 8

On Limiting Economic Growth

Herman Daly

In 1936 John Maynard Keynes remarked that "the part played by orthodox economists, whose common sense has been insufficient to check their faulty logic, has been disastrous to the latest act." The same words ring true today. Economists have become trapped by the excessive rigidity of their own paradigms, values, and goals. The South Indian Monkey Trap is a good example of the danger inherent in this inflexible orientation. A hollowed-out coconut is filled with rice and fastened by a chain to a stake in the ground. There is a hole in the coconut just large enough to allow the monkey to insert his extended hand, but not large enough to permit withdrawal of his clinched fist full of rice. The monkey is trapped by nothing more than his refusal to reorder his goals and to realize that in the given circumstances freedom is more important than the fistful of rice. The industrialized nations are trapped in a similarly greedy growth-dominated economic system that is causing ever more depletion, pollution, and disamenity, as well as increasing the probability of ecological catastrophe. Society must open its collective fist and let go of the doctrine of perpetual growth, or else be trapped by the consequences.

CURRENT EMPHASIS ON ECONOMIC GROWTH

Economists have produced a large literature on how to increase growth, but, like the sorcerer's apprentice, have not considered the need to stop the process at some point. Yet, by a short chain of reasoning from the laws of diminishing returns and diminishing marginal utility, it is clear that growth in physical commodities and in population will eventually begin to cost more than either is worth. But the ideology of growth as a substitute for sharing, coupled with the cardinal idolatry of the present age that science and technology are omnipotent, has distracted or intimidated economists from considering the problems of transition to a mature, steady-state economy.

In view of the popular belief in the omnipotence of science and technology, it is ironic to recall that the most basic laws of science are statements of impossibility: it is impossible to create or destroy matter-energy; it is impossible to travel faster than the speed of light; it is impossible for an organism to live in a medium consisting of its own waste products; and it is impossible to measure anything without in some way altering the thing being measured.

The relevant challenge is not to torture the economy by attempting the impossible task of perpetual growth, but rather to learn how to maintain the highest level of living that can be universally shared and ecologically sustained over the long run. Economics, like other sciences, should identify some impossibility theorems. A good one to begin with would be: a United States-style, high-level, mass-consumption economy is impossible to achieve for a world of four billion people; and even if by some miracle such a state were achieved, it would be impossible to sustain.

The establishment worldwide of the Western material life-style is the explicit goal of most of our aid and development programs. As a means to that end, as well as an end it itself, rich countries are urged to continue growing. According to the former chairman of the Council of Economic Advisers, Dr. Paul McCracken, "The action most urgently needed in the world economy is for the strong economies to be willing to accept higher levels of living. Their reluctance to do so seems to be of Calvinistic proportions" [1]. Evidently it does not matter that the 6 percent of the world's population residing in the United States already requires over 30 percent of the world's annual production of nonrenewable resources to sustain its current level of living. The duty of the rich is to consume more, not less!

How could a respected economic adviser make such an apparently absurd statement? Or, more instructively, what premises must be accepted for McCracken's statement to be reasonable? If resources were unlimited in supply and the only limiting factor in economic growth were aggregate demand, and if the distribution of income were unimportant or did not matter as long as the absolute incomes of all were increasing, and if only the short run were of concern, then the McCracken statement would make sense. But these assumptions are grossly unrealistic.

Resource supplies are in fact increasingly limited, distribution is at least as important as absolute level, the long run cannot be ignored, and enough should be permitted to suffice for the rich. The wealthy should not be urged to sacrifice their leisure to meaningless consumption. Better that they should consume less, freeing resources for the poor who can create their own markets by selling necessities to each other, rather than by selling more extravagant luxuries to the rich.

The Level of Control

The first order of business for any community is to free itself from the knee-jerk reactions and self-serving compulsions of growthmania, to help its economic advisers get their hands out of the monkey trap, and to realize that in the long sweep of history stability and small scale are the norm; the large-scale growing industrial economy is a temporary aberration.

Assuming that a community has taken these first emancipatory steps, the difficult next question is what specific policies should be taken to achieve stability. The answer depends critically on the scale of the community: is it municipal, state, national, or global? At the global level all growth in resource use comes from natural population increase and new production. There is no problem of interplanetary migration of people or transfer of products. At the local level, however, growth is often mainly the result of migration and transfer, rather than natural increase or new production. Consequently, what is seen locally as a growth problem may appear from a global perspective as a distribution problem, and corrective policies will differ accordingly. National laws already govern migration and international trade. In Chapter 13 Tanton has suggested even more stringent restrictions on population flows. But at no level of government are there currently any effective limits on natural population increase, or on growth in commodity production. Only the nation-state seems to have the authority to impose these necessary constraints; no world authority with sufficient power exists.

Aside from these pragmatic reasons for emphasizing national over state or local policies, two general principles also point to the same conclusion. First, local policies could have self-canceling effects, since the solution to one community's growth problem may be to shift the problem to another community (for example, zoning out the poor or excluding a new power plant while having it close enough to supply electricity). Second, it is a general principle of system design that personal freedom and system viability are enhanced by providing the maximum freedom and variability at the micro-or individual level that is consistent with the general stability of the system at the macro-or aggregate level. If aggregate growth is controlled at the national level, then the growth problems of local communities will be rooted entirely in distribution issues and will be less severe. If one community still grows too much, unhappy residents will always be able to move to a declining community, and vice versa. Microfreedom makes macro-control less onerous, while macro-control makes micro-restrictions less necessary.

National control, however, would not preclude such tried and true local mechanisms as zoning ordinances, sales and severance taxes to limit energy use, pollution-emission standards, as well as citizen opposition to nuclear-power plants and to other salient manifestations of particularly irresponsible growth. Cognizance of the local costs of growth often has a greater pedagogical value in liberating the public from growthmania than awareness of abstract global phenomena, such as the greenhouse effect or ozone depletion. Arguments for "not doing it here" often lead to recognition of sound reasons for "not doing it at all." Municipalities seeking to limit growth have been criticized by developers for their unwillingness "to bear their fair share of the burden" of development. Once development is conceived as a burden to the community, it is but a short step to ask how that total burden can be minimized, in addition to how it can be fairly allocated. In Chapter 9, Finkler explores this issue in depth.

MODEL FOR A STEADY-STATE ECONOMY

To control growth at the national level there is required an institutional model for achieving a steady-state economy: that is, an economy characterized by a constant population and a constant stock of physical artifacts, each maintained at some desired level by low rates of throughput. Low throughput for the population means low birth rates that are equal to low death rates so that average life expectancy can be high. For the constant stock of artifacts, low throughput means low production rates that are equal to low physical depreciation rates so that artifacts are on the average long-lived or durable. The throughput is of the cost of maintaining the stock in the face of wear and tear, rust, depreciation, decay, accident, and all the other ravages of time and entropy. The throughput flow begins with depletion of low-entropy (concentrated, structured) resources, and ends with pollution from high-entropy (dispersed, unstructured) wastes. Throughput is the physical entropic flow of matter-energy by which all structure, order, and life is maintained.

Since both the sources and the sinks of throughput are limited, it must be treated as a cost, and should be minimized for any chosen level of stocks. Since throughput makes up a large part of GNP and since modern societies usually strive to maximize GNP, present behavior is much closer to maximizing, rather than minimizing, throughput. For example, if cars could be made to last twenty years rather than ten, it would be possible to maintain a stock of one hundred cars by producing five new cars per year rather than ten. Production would fall by one-half, yet car owners would be better off, not worse off, since they would still have the services of one hundred cars, yet would be maintaining those cars with a lower throughput cost. Employment would not necessarily decrease; it could even increase if it took more labor to maintain a car for ten more years than to produce a new one.

Three Institutions for Zero Growth

Three new institutions seem necessary to provide adequate social control of growth with a minimum sacrifice of individual freedom [2]. I shall explore only the second in depth in this paper.

Distributist Institution. A distributist institution to limit the range of inequality to some functionally justifiable degree is the first innovation required. This end might be accomplished by setting a minimum income floor and maximum income and wealth limits for individuals and families, and imposing a maximum size limit on corporations. I pursue this point further in my chapter "The Steady-State Economy" in *Towards a Steady-State Economy* [3].

Depletion Quotas. Second, it is necessary to limit aggregate depletion of each of the basic minerals by setting depletion quotas to be auctioned in conveniently divisible units by the government. The resource market would become two-tiered. To begin with, the government as a monopolist would auction the limited quota rights to many buyers. Resource buyers, having purchased their quota rights, would then have to confront many resource sellers in a competitive resource market. The competitive price in the resource market would tend to equal the average cost of the marginal producer. More efficient producers would earn differential rents, but the pure scarcity rent resulting from the quotas would have been captured in the depletion-quota auction market by the government monopoly. The total price of the resource—quota price plus price to owner—would be raised as a result of the quotas.

All products using these resources would become more expensive. Higher resource prices would compel more efficient and frugal use of resources by both producers and consumers. But the windfall rent from higher resource prices would be captured by the government and become public income, a partial realization of Henry George's ideal of a single tax on rent [4]. The major advantage is that higher resource prices would bring increased efficiency, while the quotas would directly limit depletion, thereby increasing conservation and indirectly limiting pollution.

Pollution would be limited in two ways. First, since pollution is simply the other end of the throughput from depletion, limiting the input to the pipeline would naturally limit the output. Second, higher prices would induce more recycling, thereby further limiting pollution and depletion, though at the cost of increased energy throughput. The revenue from the depletion quota auction could help finance the minimum income component of the distributist institution, offsetting the negative effect of the higher resource prices on income distribution.

Higher prices on basic resources are absolutely necessary. Any plan that refuses to face up to this necessity is worthless. Back in 1925, economist John Ise made the point in these words:

> Preposterous as it may seem at first blush, it is probably true that, even if all the timber in the United States, or all the oil or gas or anthracite, were owned by an absolute monopoly, entirely free of public control, prices to consumers would be fixed lower than the long-run interests of the public would justify. Pragmatically this means that all efforts on the part of the government to keep down the prices of lumber, oil, gas, or anthracite are contrary to the public interest; that the government should be trying to keep prices up rather than down [5].

Ise also went on to suggest a general principle of resource pricing: that nonrenewable resources be priced at the cost of the nearest renewable substitute. Amuzegar, Iranian delegate to OPEC, has emphasized this principle more recently [6]. Therefore, virgin timber should cost at least as much per board foot as replanted timber; petroleum should be priced at its equivalent of sugar or wood alcohol, assuming they are the closest renewable alternatives. Renewable resources should be exploited on a sustained yield basis.

The Ise principles could be used in setting the aggregate quota amounts to auction. For renewables, the quota should be set at an amount equivalent to some reasonable calculation of maximum sustainable yield. For nonrenewables with renewable substitutes, the quota should be set so that the resulting price of the nonrenewable resource is at least as high as the price of its renewable substitute. For nonrenewables with no close renewable substitute, the quota would reflect a purely ethical judgment concerning the relative importance of present versus future wants. Should these resources be used up by this or by future generations? The price system cannot decide this because future generations cannot bid in present resource markets. The decision is ethical. It has been too easy to assume that future generations will be better off due to "progress," so that there need be no worry about the unrepresented claims of the future on exhaustable resources.

In addition to the Ise principles, which deal only with depletion costs that fall on the future, the quotas must be low enough to prevent excessive pollution and ecological costs that fall also on the present. Pragmatically, quotas would probably at first be set near existing extraction levels. The first task would be to stabilize, to get off the growth path. Later quotas could be reduced to a more sustainable level, if present flows proved too high. Abundant resources causing little environmental disruption would be governed by generous quotas and therefore relatively low prices. Depletion quotas would capture the increasing scarcity rents, but would not require expropriation from resource owners. Quotas are, however, clearly against the short-run interests of resource owners, but not unjustly so, since rent is by definition unearned income from a price in excess of the minimum supply price.

Transferrable Birth License Scheme. The third and final institution required to attain the steady state must provide for population control. A stationary population can be achieved by various means consistent with the first two institutions. My own favorite is the transferrable birth license scheme first proposed by Kenneth Boulding. But important as the subject is, population control lies outside the scope of this paper. In any event, I need not argue for a specific population-control plan, since the distributist institution and depletion-quota system could function under a wide range of population-control programs in no way requiring the transferrable-license scheme [7, 8, 9].

Efficiency and Equity

The depletion-quota scheme allows a reconciliation between the two conflicting goals of efficiency and equity. Efficiency requires high resource prices. But equity is not served by high prices because they affect income distribution in the same way that a sales tax does—namely, to the disadvantage of the poor—and also because the windfall rents arising from the higher prices accrue to resource owners, not to the poor. The latter effect can be reversed by capturing the scarcity rent through the depletion quota auction and using it to finance a minimum income, and/or to eliminate the most regressive taxes.

In addition to raising the efficiency of material use, the quota scheme should lead to two further efficiency increases. First, taxing rent causes no allocative distortions and is the most efficient way to raise government revenue. To the extent that a rent tax, or its equivalent in this case, replaces other taxes then allocative efficiency should be improved. Second, as conservatives and radicals alike have noted, the minimum income could substitute for a considerable number of bureaucratic welfare programs. Of course, the major increase in efficiency would still result directly from higher resource prices which would give incentives to develop resource-saving techniques of production and patterns of consumption. Equity is not served by low prices which in effect give a larger subsidy to the rich than to the poor, since the rich consume more resources. Equity is served by higher incomes to the poor, and by a maximum limit on the incomes of the rich.

The allocation among firms of the limited aggregate of resources extracted during the time period would be accomplished entirely by the market. The distribution of income within the maximum and minimum boundaries imposed would also be left to the market. The initial distribution of reproductive licenses is done outside the market on the basis of strict equity—one person, one license—but reallocation via market exchange is permitted in the interest of efficiency. The combination of the three institutions presents a nice reconciliation of efficiency and equity, and provides the ecologically necessary macro-control of growth with the least sacrifice in terms of micro-level freedom and variability. The market is relied upon to allocate resources and distribute incomes within imposed ecological and ethical boundaries. The market is not allowed to set its own boundaries, but it is free within those boundaries.

No one has ever claimed that market equilibria would automatically coincide with ecological equilibria, or with a reasonably just distribution of wealth and income. Nor has anyone ever claimed that market equilibria would attain demographic balance. The very notions of "equilibrium" in economics and ecology are antithetical. In economics "equilibrium" refers not to physical magnitudes at all but to a balance of desires between savers and investors. To maintain investment equal to some positive level of saving requires growth in productive capacity. This implies, under current institutions, a growing flow of physical inputs from and outputs to nature—that is, economic equilibrium is biophysical *dis*equilibrium.

Physical conditions of environmental equilibrium must be imposed on the market in quantitative physical terms. Subject to these quantitative constraints the market and price system can, with the institutional changes just discussed, achieve an optimal allocation of resources and an optimal adjustment to its imposed physical system boundaries. The point is important because the belief is widespread among economists that "internalization of externalities" or the incorporation of all environmental costs into market prices is a sufficient environmental policy, and that once this is accomplished the market will be able to set its own proper boundaries automatically. This is not so, nor, in any case, is it possible to incorporate all ecological costs in rigged money prices.

Applying the Steady-State Economy Model

Two distinct questions must be asked about these proposed institutions for achieving a steady state. First, would they work if people accepted the goal of a steady state and perhaps voted the institutions into effect? Second, would people ever accept either the steady-state idea or these particular institutions? I have tried to show that the answer to the first question is probably "yes." Let the critic find any remaining flaws, or, better yet, let him suggest improvements. The answer to the second question is clearly "no" in the short run. But several considerations make acceptance more plausible in the not-too-long run.

The minimum-income side of the distributist institution already has some political support in the United States, but the maximum limits will at first be thought un-American. Yet, surely, beyond some figure any additions to personal income would represent greed rather than need, or even merit. Most people would be willing to believe that in most cases an income in excess of, let us say $100,000 per year has no real functional justification, especially when the high-paid jobs are usually already the most interesting and pleasant. Maximum limits on personal and corporate wealth would also tend to reduce the inflationary pressures exerted by large accumulations of surplus funds seeking ever new ways to grow exponentially, and would help to rescue the economic and political system from the excessive power of oligopolistic corporations. The exact limits should be subject to debate and compromise, as well as arithmetical consistency, but probably a minimum income of $7,000 and a maximum of $70,000 would be reasonable. It is even possible to be pragmatic and begin with much wider limits, gradually narrowing the range. Moreover, it would be possible to put responsible social limits on the exercise of monopoly power by labor unions since the countervailing monopoly power of corporations will have been limited, and since all workers are protected by a minimum income floor.

The depletion-quota auction is more radical, in the literal sense of going to the root of the problem, than the economists' favorite recommendation of pollution taxes. Depletion quotas place quantitative limits on the input end of the depletion-pollution pipeline, while pollution taxes place price limits on the output end. The input or depletion end offers greater leverage for the simple reason that there are fewer mines, wells, and ports of entry than smokestacks, drainpipes, and garbage cans, not to mention such diverse sources of pollution as auto exhausts and fertilizer runoff into rivers and lakes. The input end is clearly the best point at which to control the throughput flow. But why quotas? Why not severance taxes? Many of the benefits of quotas could in fact also be attained by means of severance taxes. But taxes limit quantities in only an elastic, indefinite manner. Would-be buyers can always arrange financing to purchase just as much as before, even at the higher price. According to Say's Law, in the aggregate, the economy always has sufficient income to purchase whatever it produces, regardless of price. For example, the government could tax resource extraction and then spend the tax receipts to buy, either directly or indirectly, the same resources being taxed. Taxes can reduce the throughput per dollar's worth of GNP to some minimum feasible amount, but cannot limit the GNP, and thus cannot limit aggregate total throughput, nor, of course, aggregate depletion and pollution. Furthermore, quantity, not price, impinges on the ecosystem. Therefore, it is ecologically safer to control quantity directly and let errors and shifts in demand work themselves out through unanticipated price fluctuations rather than unanticipated quantity fluctuations. Also, Hannon's discussion in Chapter 4 lends strong support to quotas in preference to taxes.

Technological optimists suggest that resource scarcity will be offset by resource-saving technical progress induced by rising resource prices. My proposal simply asks the optimists to live up to their faith. If resources really are so unimportant or easily substituted for, then why object to quotas that would stabilize resource usage? Technology would still be free to perform its miracles, and the price incentives for doing so would be strengthened. At the same time, society would be hedging its bet on technology by slowing down the rates of depletion and pollution.

In spite of their somewhat radical implications, the proposals presented in this paper are based on impeccably respectable conservative institutions: private property and the free market. If private property is good, then everyone should share in it. Moreover, making allowances for a range of legitimate inequality, no one should be allowed to hog too much private property, lest it become an instrument of exploitation rather than the barrier to exploitation that was its classical justification. Even orthodox economic theory has long recognized that the free market fails to deal adequately with depletion, pollution, and distribution. These proposals would supplement the market at its weak point, yet would allow the market to allocate resources freely within the imposed ecological and ethical boundaries.

To show how a proposal could work if accepted is to take at least a small step toward making it acceptable. The remaining steps may well be hurried along by the soaring ecological and moral costs of economic growth. Also, when and if economists begin to discuss these issues seriously, better suggestions might be forthcoming.

The model outlined here requires sharing, population control, and stabilization of average per capita resource consumption. It is impossible to escape these basically moral demands, no matter how much money government and the foundations pour into the quest for clever technical fixes. The past practice of substituting physical growth for moral restraint cannot be continued forever. Moral problems have only moral solutions, not technical solutions. The major problem and the first priority should be to reform values and end the idolatrous national worship of economic growth.

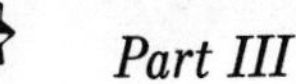

Part III

The Politics of Equity and Social Progress in a Finite World

Introduction to Part III

Dennis L. Meadows

> What are ultimately necessary are strategies that eliminate the roots of coercion to material growth in the social, political, and economic systems, such that goal-seeking mechanisms compatible with long-term stability evolve from within. Thus, society faces the problem of reforming from the inside a closed system of which mankind itself is a part.
>
> *Joan Davis* and
> *Samuel Mauch*—Chapter 12

A growing recognition of the problems engendered by the short-term perspectives of the electoral and free-market systems has produced increasing pressure for longer-term, comprehensive social plans. All planning processes have in common the identification of goals and the design of policies for attaining them. But actual planning efforts can differ very widely in form. Current planning programs encompass the rigidly centralized, comprehensive, nationwide, five-year plan of the Soviet Union as well as the indicative plans of several United States communities that merely state the preferred form of growth within a specific locality.

Opponents of national planning proposals have grounds for their fears that a new bureaucracy, instituted to provide longer-term guidance, might instead merely hamper market mechanisms without correcting any of their fundamental flaws. But it is increasingly hard to deny the necessity for some sort of supplemental process that will, for example, provide investors with greater confidence about the future course of government policy, reduce the inconsistencies among the goals of the private and public sectors, and facilitate the structural changes inevitably required within any dynamic economy. Because the pursuit of growth is usually the path of least political resistance in the short run, any long-term effort to attain a steady state will require enhanced planning capacities.

In this section are five papers that describe the rationales, the mechanisms, and the implications of various planning proposals. Earl Finkler has studied a number of United States communities that have already instituted local planning programs to achieve control of their own demographic and economic growth. His interest is in identifying the motivations behind local planning, characterizing local nongrowth activities, and resolving the potential conflicts between nongrowth and social equity movements.

Finkler concludes that the poor may be better served in localities where there is no longer any pretense that continued growth will itself reduce social or economic inequalities. When growth controls are sought, a community must deal directly with the demands of its less advantaged residents. The result in many cases has been greater provision of low income housing and services than is found in comparable cities without growth restrictions. Finkler thus suggests that those lobbying on behalf of the poor and those arguing for controlled growth might be natural partners for political coalition.

United States Senator Jacob Javits is coauthor of a recent congressional bill that would create a national institution to facilitate balanced growth and economic planning. His paper is a defense of the principle of long-term planning by the federal government. Citing inflation, housing shortages, economic cycles, and the energy crisis among other chronic problems, he contends that the economic system by itself is incapable of attaining social justice and bringing long-term consistency to economic policies. He responds to five criticisms often leveled at planning proposals:

1. Planning implies government dictatorship over the economy.
2. The free market is already an effective system.
3. Planning implies loss of personal freedom.
4. Effective planning programs cannot be implemented by government.
5. Government forecasts are not accurate enough to permit planning.

Javits' paper is brief and thus unable to provide the details of his planning proposal. But his defense of planning does include an extensive explanation of the advantages he seeks from his planning initiative, and the contents of his list illustrate a crucial problem. The goals of increased capital formation and industrial decentralization, improved public services and lower rates of inflation, greater economic growth and improved environmental quality, reduced resource depletion and lower structural dislocation are inconsistent with one another. Determining where goals conflict and how compromise is to be attained will be one of the most important phases in the design of viable planning systems.

Success in developing alternatives to growth will certainly require the ability to look back over past initiatives and learn from their successes and failures. In his paper, Canadian Senator Maurice LaMontagne presents a retrospective analysis of a major experiment in national planning instigated by Canada in 1963, similar in form and function to the institution proposed by Javits. Senator LaMontagne describes the reasons for rising acceptance of planning in the market economies, and describes the goals of the Canadian Economic Council: to produce more broadly-based public and private decisions, to extend the time perspectives of federal policies, and to help attain better economic performance. The Council has facilitated dialogue among diverse sectors of the Canadian economy, it has produced in-depth analyses of specific economic sectors, and it has put forward numerous significant policy recommendations. However, it has failed in its basic goals—Canada still has no comprehensive plan, and governmental decisions are based on rather narrow and short-term considerations. The country's economic performance, as a consequence, has not improved.

Several problems are identified by LaMontagne to explain this outcome. International factors have introduced uncertainty into domestic plans, the goals of the Council were too narrowly expressed in economic indices, its forecasts spanned too short a period to permit early warnings about fundamental problems, forecasting procedures were inadequate even for short-term predictions, and there was no attempt to develop a comprehensive plan. Most fundamental of all, however, has been the growing factionalism of the Canadian society. With the growth of numerous, distinct interest groups, there have come diverging goals, and increasing conflict. Without the will and the mechanisms to attain social consensus on fundamental goals, no society can pursue an internally consistent, long-term policy. Senator LaMontagne concludes his paper with a brief discussion of a proposed new organization which would help structure debate and facilitate the attainment of agreement among diverging interest groups.

The fourth paper in this section draws from a study of Switzerland several conclusions about the nature and implications of the centrifugal forces that are producing factionalism and growing alienation among the different sectors of society. Joan Davis and Samuel Mauch summarize the results of their government-sponsored project to design sustainable futures for the Swiss society.

They began their research with two questions: can technology extend the limits of growth, and will the economic system automatically reduce its growth rate as it reaches important limits? They concluded that new technologies probably could be developed to postpone the physical necessity of halting growth until long after irreversible social and psychological damage had been done. They also concluded that the long delays and narrow goals of the economic system will lead it to pursue further material growth long after the point of increasing diseconomies to society has been passed.

To understand the incentives for growth, they analyzed interactions among the three aspects of human society—economic, sociocultural, and political-administrative. They discovered that the economic system, originally developed to provide an efficient means for attaining social and political goals, has increasingly dominated the determination of goals, substituting its own internal needs for more humane demands. This has been caused by (and has reinforced) the disintegration of society into mutually distinct and inconsistent goal sets. The result is concentration of centralized power, specialization of function, and growing use of policies that stifle symptoms rather than eliminate problems. Meanwhile, the population has lost its sense of control, responsibility, and involvement. The result is a vicious cycle in which citizens increasingly relinquish to organizations control over more and more important parts of their lives, producing a culture that fails to meet basic human needs and that is thus unsustainable, even if it can avoid encountering physical limits.

The authors believe the consequences they describe are inherent in any program of sustained industrialization and economic growth. Thus they suggest three policy programs that could ameliorate short-term difficulties and redirect society along a more viable path: controls that reduce the environmental damage caused by physical growth, barriers that hold economic growth within limits, and structural reforms that eliminate the coercions to growth while initiating the reintegration of the technical, administrative, and psychological spheres of life. The resulting paper was awarded a Mitchell Prize.

The fifth paper, by John Tanton, illustrates the need for long-term planning through reference to a specific problem. Because they have not been developed within the context of a long-term plan, current policies guiding international migration have led to a "no-win" situation for both sending and receiving nations. Tanton argues that new United States' policies ought to seek the end of significant immigration. He defends this proposition through a discussion of the original purpose of migration, the effects of migration on both sending and receiving countries, and the consequences of large-scale population movements for world stability.

Much migration today is composed of highly talented people leaving the Third World and moving to more advanced nations. This movement robs capital from the poorer countries and reduces the pressure for social change and population stabilization in the countries of origin. It also removes personnel who could be most helpful in developing family planning programs. Because young adults are most free to leave their home countries, migration serves to increase the dependency ratios of the poorer areas and to stimulate growth in the receiving nations. Immigration exacerbates unemployment and thus inequality in the richer nations and worsens already serious urban problems. The addition of new cultures to established nations also makes it more difficult to form social consensus about significant problems.

Tanton asserts that the receiving nations must be the ones to exert control, and that they can do this without violating the legitimate rights of refugees or losing any real benefits commonly attributed to cultural diversity. Once a global system of sustainable societies has been attained, Tanton suggests that no restrictions on migration would be necessary. But the transition to a steady state will require very different perspectives on migration from those that have characterized past policies. Tanton's paper was awarded a Mitchell Prize.

One fact is made clear by the contributors to this section: adding a new bureaucracy to the current political system will have little effect on the implicit time horizon of current political and economic decisions. Reorganization and a thoughtful redesigning of society is called for. Some new institutions may be required, but many old ones will also have to be eliminated. And, most importantly, political and administrative change will have to proceed in concert with new social perspectives and personal values. The nature of these social and personal values and the paths toward realizing them are elaborated in Part IV.

Chapter 9

Lessons in Equity from Local Communities

Earl Finkler

AN INTRODUCTION TO LOCAL NONGROWTH INITIATIVES

Nowhere is the limits to growth debate more alive than in local communities in the United States and other countries such as Canada. Their interest in "nongrowth" should not imply that communities want to stop any and all future growth. Rather, it means that the rate, amount, location, and type of future population and economic growth have become items of open and legitimate public concern. A number of managed or controlled growth options are being considered, including the stopping of growth in some cases [1]. Heedless population growth, economic development, and local government expenditures are viewed more as problems than panaceas by an increasing number of citizens.

The nongrowth movement has developed rather spontaneously in a variety of communities, mostly within the past five years. I suggest these local areas could serve as laboratories, or test cases, whose results can provide guidance for other communities and for higher levels of government facing larger, broader problems such as the need for material equilibrium. Local experiments with reduced growth may provide particularly useful information on policies to ensure equity in the absence of continued economic expansion. The nongrowth movement has spawned concern and criticism on the matter of gaps between the rich and the poor. The overt symptoms of inequity are in relative deficiencies of goods and services available to those with low incomes. The proposed remedy has always been to distribute more of the fruits of growth to the poor. Though it has not been especially effective, even during periods of rapid growth, this strategy becomes obviously invalid when there are fewer prospects for growth. Thus, the charge has been made that local nongrowth works to restrict opportunities for those who have less income, or who live in poorer environments [2].

Nongrowth advocates such as Herman Daly, Carl Pope, and William Toner have responded to such charges by noting that rapid growth will not by itself guarantee improved social equity in the future any more than it has in the past [3]. Some economists point to the fact that income distribution in the United States has remained virtually static since World War II. According to one analysis, "The poorest and wealthiest fifths of American families had roughly the same proportion of national income in 1972 (5.4 percent and 41.4 percent, respectively) as in 1947 (5.1 percent and 43.3 percent)" [4]. At the community level, moreover, some of the most rapidly growing areas in the country, such as Orange County, California, and the newer Chicago suburbs, remain almost exclusively white. A recent Rand Corporation study of San Jose, California, concluded that rapid growth there had actually increased inequality between Anglos and Chicanos [5]. The Rand report found that Chicano incomes declined relative to Anglos, and ethnic segregation increased during a period of rapid local population and economic growth between 1960 and 1970.

But to criticize the past track record of unchecked growth is not enough. The local nongrowth movement will have to demonstrate clearly its commitment to some real redistribution of resources. I contend that the local nongrowth movement provides more of an opportunity than a problem for those striving to increase social equity. The key to the opportunity lies in some of the attitudes underlying the movement and some of the policy and regulatory innovations in nongrowth communities. The same spirit of community identity and innovation that has challenged the growth ethic could stimulate a better distribution of resources in and around those communities.

Local communities do not have all the answers. But, as real-world groups of people, institutions, and interests, they are exploring various new strategies to control their population and economic growth. These strategies usually involve increased, direct control over land use and public services. The pursuit of nongrowth can put more policies, including those affecting social equity, under improved local control. Widespread monitoring, analysis, and discussion of local efforts to stabilize communities can stimulate the design and diffusion of new solutions for the twin problems of wasteful growth and social equity.

The argument that local community experiments and innovations can enrich each other and influence larger units of government is supported in a recent book titled *From Know-How to Nowhere* [6] by Professor Elting E. Morison of M.I.T. Professor Morison's work is rather theoretical, but he contends that such problems as runaway technology and the energy crisis are too vast, complex, and varied for the federal government to prescribe a cure. Rather, he would have cities, towns, and states develop their own solutions. His advice is first to think small, not to attack the entire global problem head on.

The existence of concrete, nongrowth programs in a number of communities provides the opportunity for a real test of Morison's proposal. This paper reviews a variety of current local nongrowth activities and concludes with recommendations for immediate action by those eager to build on what has already been learned.

THE NEW MOOD

Randall Scott has written:

> In more and more communities across the country, the costs and benefits of continued growth are emerging as major public issues. There is hesitation over accommodating further development with its attendant consequences of greater numbers of residents and higher densities, economic expansion, rapid consumption of land, and alteration of the environment. Time and time again—in public hearings, in elections, and bond referenda, and in the professional literature as well as the press—there is manifested strong resistance to unbridled growth and inadequate land use management [7].

Local communities are becoming more receptive to nongrowth initiatives for a variety of very positive reasons. People want:

—more control over their neighborhoods, their communities, and their lives;

—adequate open space, nature preserves, and recreation facilities;

—good access to their jobs, commercial areas, schools, and the great outdoors;

—safety and some feeling that they can control or influence their immediate environment;

—low taxes;

—decently-priced housing;

—good schools and public services, such as police and fire;

—clear, accurate information on where their community is heading, and the chance to participate in future plans and decisions.

A growing number of people believe nongrowth will help to bring forth or maintain these kinds of amenities. While there is a negative strain to nongrowth—"stop that freeway," "delay that shopping center," "tie it up in court"—the movement also has strong positive aspects. If goals of nongrowth such as those just listed are realized, the benefits can be shared by all local residents, regardless of income or race. This is something that is often ignored in the heated pro-growth-nongrowth debates. Concern for the poor also tends to get lost in rapidly-growing communities. Such places tend to be preoccupied with overloaded sewers, overcrowded schools, congested streets, and a host of daily crises. Nongrowth can keep the general community living conditions and the rate of change and development under control. A community in control of such factors can deal more openly and directly with local equity.

While the precise number of growth-challenging communities is difficult to assess, the movement seems to be growing. For example, in 1973, the Urban Land Institute assembled a list of thirty-nine cities, counties, and townships that had enacted some kind of growth constraints. Another seven were listed as possibilities [8]. A survey by the International City Management Association indicated in early 1974 that 258 cities—23 percent of the 1,115 cities surveyed—had enacted some form of growth control. Of the 258 growth-limited cities, 170 were suburbs, 51 were independent cities, and 37 were central cities [9].

In 1975, another list was compiled as part of a research project funded by the National Science Foundation. This list contained 138 cities, counties, and towns described as "Growth Control Localities" [10]. The list included large communities such as Los Angeles, Denver, Miami, Honolulu, and Minneapolis, as well as smaller communities such as Belle Terre, New York; Eugene, Oregon; Gillette, Wyoming; and St. George, Vermont. It included communities in twenty-nine of the fifty states. Only a few of the communities listed had any kind of explicit or proposed population quotas or limits such as those of Boca Raton, Florida; Petaluma and Santa Barbara, California; and Carson City, Nevada. Almost all were either implementing or considering much stiffer controls on land use and development, including urban limit lines,[a] phased development, downzoning to lower densities, and interim moratoriums against all or some new development. An interview with one of the NSF researchers indicated that 300 to 400 communities were also being analyzed at the time for possible addition to the list [11].

Innovative land use controls and other public antigrowth actions have gained limited publicity, but they have also taken a long time to implement and have sometimes gotten bogged down or obscured in local politics or bureaucracies. However, national and local citizen-attitude surveys have shown that the foundations of the nongrowth movement are broad, and that people are eager to explore the new directions and potentials it offers.

The 1973 Rockefeller Brothers Task Force report entitled *The Use of Land: A Citizen's Policy Guide to Urban Growth*, based in part on field interviews in a number of nongrowth communities, verified the presence of a new mood against community growth. The report described some of the deeper attitudes behind this new mood, including aspirations for a more humane environment:

> This mood [against growth] defies easy generalization because it springs from a mélange of concerns—many that are unselfish and legitimate, some that are selfish and not so legitimate. The mood is both optimistic and expansive in its expectations of the future, and pessimistic and untrusting about inevitable change. . . . The new mood reflects a burgeoning sophistication on the part of citizens about the overall, long-term economic impact of development. . . . But the new attitude toward growth is not exclusively motivated by economics. It appears to be part of a rising emphasis on humanism, on the preservation of natural and cultural characteristics that make for a humanly satisfying living environment [12].

Perhaps people do not want to see their communities grow larger because they fear a lower quality of life. In 1973, pollster George Gallup, Jr., gave some support to this view, finding that over one-third of the residents of cities of one million or more were dissatisfied with the quality of life in their community. This percentage

[a] An urban limit line is an actual line which is drawn around an urban area to contain higher density urbanization (inside) and protect agricultural land or open space and lower density development (outside). It can be a general line or it can be precisely applied to actual property lines, streets, and natural features such as rivers. The line can be implemented by zoning regulations which strictly restrict development beyond the boundary. Annexation policies can also be used. A very important implementation tool is a policy which refuses services such as water and sewer beyond the line. Urban limit lines have been approved for Salem and Eugene, Oregon; San Jose, California; Boulder, Colorado; and Manatee County, Florida.

generally fell with city size, down to a figure of only 13 percent dissatisfied in communities under 2,500. Nationally, the percentage of dissatisfied was 21 percent, but for non-whites the percentage rose again to 44 percent [13].

Gallup also reported that another one of his national surveys showed that "fully half of all persons interviewed believed that it will be necessary at some time to limit human population if present living standards are to be maintained." In addition, three out of four persons favored setting aside more public land for conservation purposes [14].

A more recent Gallup survey, commissioned by Potomac Associates in April 1974, asked the following question of a nationwide sample:

> Speaking now of the general area where you live, some people say population and industrial growth in this area should be regulated in order to prevent more pollution and improve the quality of life. Others say this would mean fewer job opportunities and slower economic progress. Do you yourself feel that population and industrial growth in this area where you live should be or should not be regulated? [15].

A majority of respondents, 54 percent, favored regulating population and economic growth in their home communities. Nine percent had no opinion and the remainder, 34 percent, were against regulation [16].

The Potomac Associates–Gallup survey found considerable antipathy toward direct federal government involvement in the regulation of growth, through actions such as national land-use legislation. This reluctance correlates with the same Potomac survey findings that people were more inclined to trust local and state governments than the federal government. Over 60 percent expressed trust and confidence in state and local governments, compared with 52 percent for the federal government in the area of domestic problems [17].

Pollster Louis Harris told the U.S. Conference of Mayors meeting in Boston in 1975 that "confidence in government at all levels in this country has hit rock bottom," but he added that there was still hope for the local community. Harris noted that 69 percent of the respondents to his survey would opt for strengthening local government, if the right leadership asked for it, and, most important, by a 90 to 5 percent margin, an overwhelming majority still have the faith that local government can be made to work well [18].

Public attitudes on social equity were unfortunately not directly related back to attitudes toward local population and industrial growth in the Potomac Associates–Gallup survey. Respondents indicated general support for the continued spending of more tax money to alleviate many of our domestic problems. According to William Watts and Lloyd A. Free, who interpreted the Potomac Associates survey, people do not want to end many of the New Deal social programs, but generally take them for granted [19]. One of the least favorable scores on spending to alleviate domestic problems came on "welfare programs to help low-income families." The predominant opinion expressed was that the present level of such expenditures should be maintained. However, Watts and Free emphasized that "prevailing views do not favor reducing, let alone terminating, our society's obligation to help the poor in some way or other" [20]. What the public may really be looking for is a new and more effective attack on the problem—for example, the use of a guaranteed minimum family income. This strategy outpolled retention of the current welfare system by a margin of 47 percent to 39 percent [21].

Finally, the Potomac Associates–Gallup survey showed that sentiment for control of community growth apparently springs from roots other than racial prejudice. When people were asked whether they would be happy or unhappy to see black families of lower income and educational levels move into the neighborhood, only 4 percent said they would be happy, but 48 percent said it would not make much difference. Forty-one percent said they would be unhappy. When blacks themselves were asked the same question about lower-class neighbors moving in, 70 percent said it would not make much difference. Less than 20 percent said they would be unhappy [22].

A related question showed that whites would be less opposed to sharing their neighborhood with equal-status blacks than with lower-status whites [23]. Consequently, the controlling influence seems to be more socioeconomic than racial. A near majority, in fact, seems to feel that neither factor would make a difference in its happiness with the neighborhood.

A number of more localized polls, some random samples and some not, have shown that a majority of the population wants to slow or stop community population growth. For example, a 1974 random sample of the Tucson area population showed that almost 70 percent of the respondents wanted policies established to slow down the population growth rate. The same respondents, however, backed several programs to increase social equity. "More public housing for low income people" was ranked sixth from the top on a list of forty-five programs and services needing public support. Job-training programs for local residents was ranked seventeenth, but promotion of tourism ranked forty-fifth. Almost 94 percent of the respondents wanted improved bus service, while less than 40 percent favored more freeways [24].

In Orange County, California, one of the more rapidly growing areas of the country, a 1974 questionnaire returned by nearly 1,600 respondents indicated that over 65 percent of the respondents thought continued population growth would worsen the current lack of low- and moderate-income housing. Only 8 percent thought that continued population growth would result in improvement of this housing problem. The percentages were roughly the same for the problem of unemployment [25].

NONGROWTH AND CITIZEN PARTICIPATION

A strong, revitalized spirit of innovation and citizen participation characterizes most nongrowth communities. Growth-associated projects such as freeways, high-rise buildings, and even entire new towns, bring out unprecedented numbers of citizens to public meetings. Citizens up and down Long Island, New York, for example, have appeared in great numbers at public hearings to protest rezonings for higher-density residential units, shopping centers, and even new industries.

Citizen Initiatives

But public meetings represent only the tip of the iceberg as far as increased citizen participation in nongrowth goes. Citizens do not always wait for planners or politicians to move into action, but rather take the initiative themselves. In 1972, voters in the San Francisco Bay Area communities of Livermore and Pleasanton approved initiative measures that prohibited the issuance of residential building permits until double sessions in the schools were ended, sewerage facilities met the standards of the Regional Water Control Board, and adequate reserves of water existed for fire protection, as well as irrigation and human consumption, without rationing.

Citizens have also demanded funds from their local governments to further their own nongrowth activities. For example, in Orange County, California, in the early 1970s, planners worked with a special nineteen-member Citizen's Direction Finding Commission that included one black, one university student, and several Chicanos. Using some county funds and some federal funds, the Commission developed a public dialogue program on future growth alternatives for the county.

In Boulder, Colorado, citizens have spoken at the polls on growth issues a number of times. In 1967, they approved a referendum to use a portion of city sales-tax funds to purchase greenbelt lands. Low-income people receive a rebate on this portion of the sales tax to keep it from being regressive. In addition, in 1971 the citizens of Boulder (a community of some 70,000) placed a designated optimum population size of 100,000 on the ballot as a charter amendment. While the proposition lost in the election by a 6 to 4 ratio, nongrowth citizens were still able to obtain $100,000 from the city and a federal planning grant to continue their own study of growth-slowing alternatives.

Citizens also elected nongrowth or managed growth representatives in a variety of local, county, and state elections in the 1970s. These included Governor Richard Lamm of Colorado, Governor Jay Hammond of Alaska, and a good number of county and city officials, including Mayor Pete Wilson of San Diego, Mayor Jeffrey Friedman of Austin, Texas, and Councilperson Margot Garcia of Tucson.

Florida, the fastest growing major state, saw some strong new citizen efforts emerge to combat destructive growth in the early 1970s. In Dade County, Florida, one of the most densely populated areas of the state, growth caused severe environmental damage—beaches were lost, major waterways polluted, and drinking water contaminated [26]. In early 1972, citizens initiated and overwhelmingly passed a referendum that legally allows the county manager to impose a moratorium on building permits in certain unincorporated areas to prevent irreversible environmental damage. The moratorium ordinance had previously been voted down by the County Board.

Pressure from Dade County and other rapidly growing areas prompted much more sophisticated regulation at the state level. In 1972, the Florida legislature passed one of the strongest set of land and water management laws in the nation; unfortunately the legislation came only after numerous local areas had already been disgracefully ravaged by growth and development. According to one report:

> The new mood in Florida means a kind of "guerrilla warfare" against countless rezoning attempts. . . . It means a shift for old-line conservationists from polite living-room meetings to aggressive political action. It means increasing numbers of people taking up the arguments of the conservationists. . . . What is most distinctive about Florida today is the re-

sponse of government to citizen pressures. All over, in cities and towns, in counties, at budding regional agencies, there are new regulations and new procedures; *people who have in the past stayed out of local government are now attracted to elected and appointed posts, and the old-liners are being challenged.* (emphasis added) [27].

Much that is positive in the experiences of Florida and other rapidly growing areas seems to have escaped outside commentators. Citizens often appear to support nongrowth in response to problems from past growth and in the context of rather traumatic new development proposals. They respond to such problems and threats with direct negative action such as an injunction, a moratorium, or a packed public protest meeting. But the same citizens also often advocate improved and innovative planning for the future.

The positive citizen support for nongrowth may also have potential for powerful new coalitions. The Florida experience shows the broadened wave of citizen support for nongrowth, in contrast to the narrower base of the older environmentalist movement:

In Florida, the 1972 vote on the bond issue for purchasing endangered areas was overwhelmingly favorable. Virtually every precinct in Dade County backed the bond issue, including those made up primarily of blacks (although the margin of victory was narrower in Cuban and Spanish neighborhoods) [28].

The experience of Florida was also reflected in California, where a successful 1972 initiative to regulate growth and development along the coast received substantial support from a variety of political and social groups, including blacks and Chicanos [29]. Blacks and other minority groups have allied with environmentalists at public meetings to oppose certain types of development. In Tucson in 1975, one young radical Chicano leader appeared at a packed public hearing, at the request of a liberal political-action group, Volunteers in Direct Action, to protest a rezoning for a far-flung new town proposed by the Dow Chemical Company. Construction of the new town would draw away more services and resources from the inner city barrios, he contended. He acknowledged that some construction jobs would be gained by the development, but added that they would not emerge for several years, would be of relatively short duration, and would probably go to local Chicanos on a last-hired, first-fired basis [30].

The Rockefeller Brothers report noted that although the nongrowth movement "has broadened considerably, in many areas it still has not shed its white middle-class image." But the report also recognized the appearance of several types of new coalitions:

> A few issues have transcended economic and social barriers. The use of pesticides is one. Transportation is another. New roads have often been cut through poor neighborhoods, destroying decent housing and communities without any plans for relocation or rejuvenation. Now, civil rights groups and environmental organizations are pushing the alternative of mass transportation in a combined effort to cut down pollution and to preserve neighborhoods [31].

Power Struggles and Obstacles

Local nongrowth has stimulated innovations in planning and in social equity, including the inclusion of quotas for low- and moderate-income housing in new development. Quotas are explicit tools used to provide some housing within specified price ranges. When used by nongrowth communities, quotas make it possible to slow the rate of new housing construction, but in a more socially responsible manner.

But nongrowth innovations threaten many established interests. Nongrowth activists are really telling both private developers and public planners either to improve the results of development and growth or to stop expansion. Entrenched interests are offended by citizens throwing past failures in their face, and fearful that the new mood could lead to a virtual veto over economic expansion. Therefore, the rhetoric and legal battles are heating up.

For example, Petaluma, California, a rapidly growing community of some 30,000 people in the San Francisco Bay area, enacted an Environmental Design Plan in 1972, in response to overcrowded schools, overloaded sewer and water facilities, disappearing agricultural land on the urban fringe, and a declining downtown. The plan, which was much more comprehensive and sophisticated than plans for most cities of Petaluma's size or larger, set an annual limit of 500 new dwelling units to be constructed by developers over the following five years. The city established a process for potential residential developers to compete for annual allocations, based on the best project designs, environmental considerations, contributions to citywide services, and provision of low-income housing units. Developers who gained the most points awarded on the basis of such criteria were allocated a certain fraction of the yearly quota. This new regulatory system was approved by 82 percent of the voters in an advisory ballot item in 1973.

Rather than working within the new system, builders took the community to court and assisted in a national publicity campaign characterizing the community as elitist. In 1974, a federal trial court judge ruled for the developers. According to the judge, a community must grow at the rate dictated by prevailing market demand or else the Constitutional "right to travel" will be infringed. However, in 1975, a federal appeals court reversed the earlier decision after finding that a community does have some rights to preserve its small-town character and open spaces and to grow at a more orderly pace. The builders appealed to the U.S. Supreme Court, but in early 1976, the Court decided not to take the case, thus upholding the appeals court decision. One of the developers predicted that unless the Petaluma ordinance were overturned, many other communities throughout the country would be encouraged to enact similar ordinances [32].

The real significance of the Petaluma system has generally been obscured by builders, planners, and lawyers who criticized the community for being parochial and exclusionary. The competition process for prospective residential development appears to be a fair and innovative way to improve the quality of new development and minimize negative environmental impacts. The Petaluma system accounts for social equity by specifying that 8 to 12 percent of each year's new housing quota be allocated to low- and moderate-income housing. Perhaps the percentage should be more, and perhaps the city should have supplemented this with more public housing of its own. But Petaluma is more progressive socially than its neighboring communities in the San Francisco Bay area. Most of them have neither voluntary low- and moderate-income housing goals nor local mechanisms to achieve them.

Ramapo, New York, also responded to rapid growth with an innovative growth-management system for its unincorporated areas. This town of 75,000 includes about 4,500 black residents and is located some thirty-five miles from New York City. Starting in 1965, Ramapo spent several years developing a comprehensive plan and phased development regulations that included a pioneering concept which coordinates capital improvements planning with the phasing of new construction. But Ramapo was still taken to court by landowners. The highest court in the state of New York upheld the Ramapo system in 1972, giving rise to a flurry of criticism of this "elitist" community by builders and some of the more conservative national planning and zoning professionals [33].

Under the Ramapo system, the city will not grant a residential development permit for any project failing to score at least fifteen points on a scale awarding points for availability of sewer and drainage facilities, schools, adequate roads, and other public services. If services are not available for a proposed development, the town will agree to provide them over an eighteen-year period, according to a local capital improvement program. A developer who does not want to wait must put in the services personally.

Ramapo was one of the first communities to implement a policy of actually phasing population growth according to the community's ability to service it. Ramapo officials also took favorable positions on construction of public housing, in stark contrast to many neighboring jurisdictions in the suburban New York City area. The town has a low-rent public housing authority and 198 units of such housing. One commentator on Ramapo acknowledged the social-equity potential of the Ramapo system, although he was quick to dismiss it as tokenism:

> Proponents of development timing believe that this limited amount of public housing was more acceptable politically in the town because of the controlled growth ordinance. In other words, some opponents of lower income housing were mollified by the prospect that the controlled growth policy would contribute to preventing the influx of additional lower income people after a token number were included [34].

Another innovation developed in a growth-conscious region is the areawide tax-base sharing plan adopted by the Minnesota legislature for the Minneapolis–St. Paul area in 1971. The same metropolitan area is also presently developing a variation of the Ramapo timed-development approach. According to the tax-sharing law, which was also legally challenged but upheld in court in 1974, all communities in the Twin Cities area pool 40 percent of their net commercial-industrial property-tax valuation. Each community then receives a share of that pool, based on its population. An adjustment factor weighs the allocation so that a community receives a larger share if its per capita property valuation is below the metropolitan average and a smaller portion if the valuation is above the metropolitan average.

The anecdotal evidence cited above suggests that communities exploring nongrowth options are among the more innovative in the country and that nongrowth programs can provide new and effective means to improve social equity. But the picture is still fragmented, and it may be that communities successful in their efforts to manage a deliberate end to growth and a reduction in inequality may remain the exception rather than the rule. To obtain a more systematic set of data regarding the current importance and future prospects for nongrowth-social equity conditions, I surveyed fourteen cities, counties, and regions known to have had experience with some form of nongrowth initiative, at least in the discussion stage. Responses came from decisionmakers in political jurisdictions ranging from small cities of 30,000 up to large cities and counties with populations as great as 2.5 million. The details of the survey are reported elsewhere [35], but the results may be briefly summarized. Nongrowth sentiment is not restricted to elitist or exclusionary communities. Many of the most successful nongrowth movements have occurred in localities of increasing racial and economic diversity. Many respondents even stressed the difficulties rapid growth had visited on the poor during earlier phases of this community's development. The respondents expressed varying degrees of enthusiasm for the idea of nongrowth-social equity coalitions. However, not one of the jurisdictions reported formal private or institutional coalitions between groups seeking those two ends. While a number of planners seemed to feel that the idea of a coalition had considerable merit, they believed real progress in cooperation will be possible only after the poor and the minorities have become convinced that nongrowth advocates are sincerely concerned about their welfare. I believe the genuine concern that does exist, plus the political advantages inherent in a coalition of the two groups, should increase the importance of their formal collaboration in the future.

TRANSITION—THOUGHTS ON THE NONGROWTH-SOCIAL EQUITY FRONTIER

Cooperative, local nongrowth-social equity efforts could mean a better life for both rich and poor. A strong, positive social equity effort may keep nongrowth communities out of lengthy and costly court battles, and help environmentalists and other nongrowth advocates gain political strength. Moreover, to the extent that redistribution takes place locally in a nongrowth community, the donors can be more certain of its limits, effects, and efficiency. Alliance with nongrowth advocates would give the poor some powerful and knowledgeable new allies. Nongrowth policies could also generate more local housing and job opportunities than the trickle-down process associated with random, uncontrolled community growth.

But if such open cooperation is a good idea, why has so little been done about it? Why have not more of the hundreds of nongrowth communities developed explicit redistribution concepts and goals in their plans? Why have social equity advocates forged more coalitions with builders than with environmentalists?

The answer seems to lie in ignorance, misunderstanding, and fear. Until recently, local communities have been ignorant of their full prerogatives. Without power, there cannot be much sense of responsibility. As long as local communities feel powerless to influence their growth and social equity, they can easily shrug off such responsibilities and defer them to a higher level of government. But nongrowth pioneers have shown that community action has much more clout than federal policies, even if only in employing primitive land-use regulations to shut off or delay development. Such powers probably will not remain primitive or misunderstood for long. As local power increases, so will local responsibility.

The disadvantaged have also failed to realize the full extent of the power inherent in local institutions. Much of the information about nongrowth initiatives has come from proponents of growth and development who use social equity as a rationalization for their desire for profits. Thus the poor and their advocates are often suspicious of the local nongrowth movement. Few attempts have been made to show how zero population growth locally might benefit them, and only a limited number of local experiments are available to serve as models. Consequently, the poor often see their only salvation in the expansion of their region's population and economy.

Fear is also a major obstacle to nongrowth-social equity coalitions. Some nongrowth proponents may acknowledge the need for redistribution, but they still fear that it may be ineffective or uncontrolled. Social equity advocates, on the other hand, may have suspicions about new paths of development. They generally prefer the familiar, uncontrolled pattern of growth which its proponents claim will cause benefits to trickle down to the poor. Overcoming these conceptual obstacles will require action at the personal, local, and national levels on several fronts all designed to facilitate understanding of nongrowth options and to educate those with a stake in their community's development. Programs in each of these areas can be usefully initiated now.

Since the nongrowth movement is newer and less well established than the social equity movement, nongrowth proponents should take the initiative on social equity issues. I have described a number of local initiatives on social equity; analysis of these efforts could be implemented in most communities. One additional way for local nongrowth advocates to show initiative and sincerity would be personally to reduce their consumption of energy and materials. Proposals for programs that support high and wasteful consumption rightfully attract suspicion and mistrust.

Economic Measures: Land Use Control and Other Local Powers

To control growth in a socially responsible manner, community members will have to become much better informed about their local economy. Land-use controls, the principle tool of the nongrowth movement to date, will continue to be important. But if land-use controls are not reinforced by other measures, they will ultimately be eroded under the pressures of rapid economic growth, major new industries, and accelerated inmigration. Land-use controls need not discriminate against the poor as much as their critics claim, but they are by themselves a rather weak and cumbersome means of dealing with a maldistribution of resources.

It is frequently claimed that restrictions on local land use drive up the price of housing beyond the means of the poor [36]. In fact the relation between land-use controls and housing costs has not been studied sufficiently to permit any firm conclusions. But the effect of controls is likely to be small. Land acquisition and site improvement costs generally account for less than 30 percent of the total cost of a single-family house [37]. Many other factors such as interest rates, rising material costs, and taxes are more important in raising new housing costs well beyond the reach of the poor.

Those really interested in equity must consider an individual's total economic well-being. That is much more influenced by total income than by the amount that has to be spent on housing. The movement of hard dollars from one set of hands to another is a much more effective redistribution strategy than the lowering of land-use standards to provide slightly cheaper housing. Thus the local economy is a critical concern.

Precise economic strategies will vary according to the nature and location of the nongrowth community. If a community faces a substantial amount of private employment growth or turnover, it could emphasize a policy of continued economic growth and slower population growth, especially from inmigrants. A key to this strategy would be to hire and train the resident unemployed, rather than inmigrants.

This strategy, which resembles that advocated in Jay Forrester's book *Urban Dynamics* [38], has already become a goal in the future planning efforts of the city of Boston. Boston now has planning policies and financial tools to encourage work centers that will offer jobs to neighborhood unemployed. The city chose this strategy over one favoring large industrial parks or more high-rise office buildings, both of which provide jobs primarily for suburbanites [39]. One meeting in 1974 between M.I.T. academicians and Boston planners and leaders found the former mayor John F. Collins questioning one of the housing renewal concepts carried out during his tenure. If he were to do it over again, Collins noted, he would use the cleared land for creation of industries for job growth and would have lived with a temporary housing shortage [40].

Each city has land-use and fiscal tools that can help implement its economic and equity goals. Land-use controls can be used to deny a rezoning for a new industry unless certain local manpower training goals are accepted. Fiscal powers can relate to the substantial amounts that each city spends on contracts. Local leaders can follow the example of Atlanta Mayor Maynard Jackson who required that any firm winning a city contract share 15 to 25 percent of the jobs with the city's blacks. Cities can use such fiscal and legal powers to allow and encourage growth that directly benefits the poor or minorities, rather than giving all growth a blank check in hope of some trickle-down benefits.

Local communities can gain more control over their local economies and remain socially responsible in the process by:

—gauging economic development according to what it does for residents at the low end of the economic spectrum, rather than what it will do in gross numbers;

—requiring large new employers to prepare an economic impact statement outlining the likely population, as well as economic, social, and ecological effects of the project;

—encouraging the development and expansion of small resident industries, such as solar energy operations, rather than attempting to attract large outside manufacturing firms;

—providing more and better public services for the local poor and disadvantaged, including services which previously were available only in the private market. Local capital improvement programs should emphasize poorer neighborhoods.

The private economy is the place to start in real nongrowth-social equity efforts, but the public economy can interact with the private sector. It is possible to make approval of new developments contingent on the projects' compatibility with the community's long-term growth and equity objectives. To do this efficiently, each community will have to distinguish between large and small employers. A guideline might be to classify any firm with more than twenty-five employees as large. Smaller employers should be exempt from the regulation process, both to avoid overloading the system and to recognize that small firms tend to hire locally and be more responsive to local goals than larger employers. Improved or new services might include day care centers and special services for the local elderly and handicapped. Residential bedroom communities could also agree to supply land or other free services to developers willing to build lower-income housing.

Local Community Focus

Implicit in my analysis is the assumption that the federal government will not assume leadership in developing new programs to control growth and maldistribution of resources. The failure of past federal social equity programs almost parallels the complete failure of the federal government to take action on growth issues. The federal government and a majority of the states have not passed even elementary land-use legislation. Both these levels of government will probably remain fairly conservative and isolated from local experience. Their greatest contribution can lie in actions that facilitate local initiative.

Some local communities may be able to take primarily symbolic actions on nongrowth and social equity at present because they lack dollars or have highly restricted or antiquated legal powers. But the future seems to look the brightest for local action. City and even neighborhood powers seem likely to increase during the coming years as information moves faster and people are less docile and more identity-conscious.

The federal government and state governments can assist local efforts by:

—collecting and disseminating information on nongrowth activities and their results. The dissemination should be widespread and rapid. Innovations that cover both nongrowth and social equity should be stressed.

—requiring social equity-nongrowth assessments for all relevant local grant and loan programs. The Housing and Community Development Act—which offers, in theory at least, grants through which a community could manage growth and increase social equity—would be a good place to locate such a mandate.

—adopting the new Model Land Development Code prepared by the American Law Institute as state-enabling legislation for zoning, subdivision, and other land-use powers. The ALI Code encourages the transfer of greater powers to communities that have more sophisticated land-use and development plans.

—avoiding interference with local growth controls unless the community in question has clearly rejected efforts to attain better equity for its own residents. Even then, states should consider overriding local opposition to major developments only when the states have developed clear policies and priorities of their own in close coordination with the local communities involved.

The emphasis on the local focus raises the question of relative inequities among communities. Many central cities, for example, have a higher percentage of poor people and fewer per capital fiscal resources. Many suburbs, on the other hand, have a lower percentage of poor people and more per capital fiscal resources. Obviously, social equity goals would not be met by an enhancement or continuation of such patterns, although complete interjurisdictional equity is not likely ever to be achieved, either naturally or through federal action. To deal with relative inequities a local community should assess specific negative impacts on the social equity of the surrounding region that result from local nongrowth policies and take some concrete remedial actions.

No one local community should be expected to solve all the problems of its region. Nongrowth calls for limits and controls. But positive initiatives should also be undertaken. Quotas for low- and moderate-income housing in all new residential developments are one approach. If a formal redistribution structure such as the Minnesota tax sharing technique is not available, concerned communities could band together and contribute to a fund for a park, a housing project, or improved transit in a neighboring older central city.

A more rural community could develop a nature preserve and an environmental education program designed especially for inner city children and their parents. Outlying communities could seek out minority entrepreneurs for new shopping areas. They could also develop express bus service or some kind of transit to enable the poor or minority central city residents to obtain jobs in suburban industrial parks. More exclusive resort areas such as Aspen, Colorado, and Martha's Vineyard, Massachusetts, could acquire and rent out a certain number of homes and cabins at reduced rates for the poor, perhaps under a reservation or lottery system. Obviously, if a community does absolutely nothing in terms of social equity, it cannot hide behind a facade of nongrowth, and its efforts will deservedly be subject to legal and political checks. But communities have wide latitude and room for innovation in both nongrowth and social equity.

CHALLENGE TO ACT

This paper sketches out some ideas that can lead to constructive community responses to problems associated with growing populations and resource shortages. Unfortunately, there are no quick and easy answers, even in the smallest community on the most remote island. Growth will in any event come to an end. I believe it can be halted through means more acceptable than throw-away cities, urban bankruptcy, and environmental deterioration, if vigorous alternatives are pursued. As Albert Camus put it, action and courage are everything. It is urgent to start trying out new ideas in actual communities, not just in textbook models. People should start where they live, and they should start now.

Chapter 10

In Defense of Long-Range Federal Planning

Jacob Javits

On May 21, 1975, Senator Hubert Humphrey and I introduced the Balanced Growth and Economic Planning Act [1]. At the time we introduced this legislation I felt that it was one of the most important bills I had ever introduced. The reduced prospects for future growth of the United States' economy, the lack of a coherent national energy policy, and the severity of this country's structural problems in employment, capital formation, inflation, industrial concentration, international trade, and municipal financing all pointed to the need for this measure. In this paper I will demonstrate the very real need for such long-range economic planning measures in the United States and will attempt to answer some of the recurrent arguments of the critics of federally-initiated planning programs.

THE NEED FOR LONG-RANGE PLANNING

The planning concept envisages a process for taking a longer-term view of our economic problems. Most economic policy-making for the United States is short term and conducted primarily through the annual preparation of the President's Economic Report, which is designed to deal with only the most immediate problems. Longer-term analyses normally are narrowly focused on only one area, such as energy. Both approaches are required, but something more is also needed—a mechanism that provides a longer- and a broader-term view of the economy.

The United States economy is increasingly afflicted with great swings between rapid expansion, which leads to inflation, and excessive restriction, which brings widespread unemployment and severe recession. The country cannot continue to ride this roller coaster indefinitely. What it needs is a national policy on growth and a mechanism to implement it. Such a balanced growth policy would strive to meet Americans' basic needs for decent housing, quality education, meaningful jobs, effective public services, and a clean environment; would set out priorities in these areas and develop proposals for achieving selected goals; and would illustrate the tradeoffs and the costs of such proposals.

The policy must take into account the rapid exhaustion of this country's nonrenewable resources as well as its increasing reliance on imported materials (some of which are under monopoly control), and must develop measures that will conserve these resources and use them wisely. Some means must be found of reconciling a lower growth rate with greater, not less, equality of opportunity and a decent standard of living. This must be done without sapping the individual initiative, creativity, and pluralism which have been the mainsprings of this society.

Many Americans believe that the best way to deal with this complex issue is to free the business community from the "shackles" of government regulation. There is a certain truth in their arguments, especially given the blizzard of paperwork created for business by the federal government in recent years. There is little information to suggest, however, that the unseen hand of market forces will solve many of this nation's most serious problems in a manner consistent with social justice.

Government must provide direction and impetus for the market. In the last few years the country seems to have moved away from some of its most important goals, such as the employment promise contained in the Employment Act of 1946 or the housing goals of the Housing Act of 1968. The financial crisis facing New York and a number of other large cities will make still more difficult the provision of a decent living standard for many of our citizens. A satisfactory balance must be found between the beneficial aspects of private enterprise, upon which 90 percent of the American people depend for a livelihood, and the essential guidance that a balanced economic growth plan would contribute to the treatment of this country's most serious, complex, and long-term problems.

THE CRITICISMS OF LONG-RANGE PLANNING

The debate over the need for a balanced economic growth plan has raised a number of interesting arguments against planning, the most representative and compelling of which will be discussed here.

The Police State

Critics argue that national economic planning will lead to a governmental dictatorship over the economy. Opponents do not seem to believe that planning can be a force for improving competition and abolishing outdated or counterproductive government regulation.

There is good evidence, however, that planners do not necessarily have a proclivity toward total government control or "police state" behavior. For example, the Council on Wage and Price Stability has been successful in forcing other government agencies to examine the economic impact of their rules and regulations on business and consumers. Recalling the hue and cry raised in Congress by conservative forces and the business community when the Council was established, there is some irony in its actions having more recently drawn praise from the business community. Just as business has discovered that the Council on Wage and Price Stability can be a flexible tool to make the operation of government more efficient, the business community might discover the same capabilities in an economic planning board.

In an analogous vein, business representatives expressed alarmist fears about the Employment Act of 1946. For example, James Donnelly, executive vice president of Illinois Manufacturers Association, testified that: "The result would be a system of so-called planned economy with lower standards of living, more government spending, an avalanche of legislative panaceas and bureaucratic mandates, impairment of confidence, and eventually, the destruction of economic and political freedom" [2]. Likewise, according to Nathan S. Sachs, a corporate leader: "This bill, if enacted, would ultimately lead to such planned economy and regimentation which is dramatically opposed to the free enterprise that has made this country so great. Under such a planned economy and regimentation, our very democratic way of life might ultimately be in the balance and lost to us forever" [3].

Senator Robert Wagner, my predecessor from New York, knew how to reply to such arguments:

> In earlier years, it was customary on the part of those who yearned for the past and feared the future to brand every proposal as being a step toward regimentation and the destruction of the American system. More than a century ago this argument was used against those who proposed free public schools. Later, it was used against Abraham Lincoln when he campaigned for internal improvements for the country. The same argument was made against the creation of the Federal Reserve System, the enactment of the income tax law, the regulation of the stock exchanges, and the establishment of the right to collective bargaining [4].

This exchange sounds as if the needle had been struck in the same record groove for thirty years. Just as the Employment Act of 1946 did not bring about the disastrous "destruction of freedom" Donnelly feared, a balanced economic growth plan would not mandate government's totalitarian manipulation of the economy.

Interference With the Free Market

Other critics assert that the free market, while not perfect, is the best system available and should not be disturbed by attempts at planning. The real fear behind this complaint is that if the government does not dictate economic policy by planning, at least it will intervene more frequently and systematically in the economy, upsetting an otherwise smoothly-functioning system. But without planning, the government will follow its consistently inconsistent course of limited intervention in certain areas and times, especially hard times, without, however, an orderly approach.

In some major sectors, such as oil and transportation, the free market already fails to operate. It may be possible to secure greater competition through more careful planning, but merely getting the government out of certain aspects of the economy will not restore competition; in fact it may reduce competition.

Nor does more reliance on the creative characteristics of small business provide the answer. Although small businesses numerically constitute an overwhelming proportion of private enterprises in the United States and even employ somewhat more than one-half of the work force, small business by itself is not primarily responsible for and cannot solve the nation's economic problems. Indeed, small business is a concern precisely because big business has acquired such a predominant role in determining markets and the direction of the economy. Individual initiative and hard work are certainly admirable, but the importance of these individual attributes in the economy is consistent with the theory of a stable economy made up of multitudinous private transactions, an essentially pre-World War I idea that is far from an accurate model of the economy today.

Economic decision-making today is heavily concentrated in large corporations, many with an economic output greater than most nations. In many cases, big businesses are impervious to the normal market pressures of a free-enterprise economy. For example, they are often able to increase prices while demand declines, as recent experience in the automobile and energy industries demonstrates, and they can frequently create artificial demand for their products. Their size and wealth enables corporations to manipulate public opinion and public officials to ward off efforts at ending abuses and righting the economic balance on behalf of workers and consumers.

If all government regulations were removed to allow big business perfect freedom, the results might include: unchecked competition to develop energy resources without regard for the social and environmental costs; continued production of pollution-generating automobiles and other consumer products with unexpected and unsafe side effects, such as aerosol sprays with ozone-destroying capabilities; production of outrageously priced or downright dangerous drugs; sale of nutritionally inadequate, but heavily energy-intensive, packaged foods; more consumer fraud; and the starvation of already inadequate public services. This society has determined not to accept privation for the many in order to permit the perfect operation of a free enterprise economy, with its great swings from prosperity to recession and major benefits for the few. Government is presently more involved in the economy because the dynamics of the economy have become so complex, because environmental and resource limitations have been recognized for the first time, and because social objectives are being pursued more vigorously.

Freedom of Choice

A third school of critics says that planning would substitute government choice for individual decision-making. The implicit assumption in this argument is that people are now truly free to make a vast variety of meaningful choices. I wish first to challenge this assumption. A television advertisement proclaims that a leading fast-food chain gives Americans "freedom of choice." It is a bit pathetic that "freedom of choice" extends only to such items as deodorants, hair sprays, frozen foods, tires, oven cleaners, and hamburgers. The right to these kinds of choices should not be regarded as the ultimate justification for an economic system. Americans should have more fundamental options, rather than trivial choices, among consumer products. They should have better options in employment, housing, education, and use of leisure time. Americans are fortunate to have great scope of freedom in these significant areas, but such freedom is closely related to one's economic prosperity. At the most important level most lives may actually offer very narrow options, or perhaps no choice at all.

The current economic system is not adequately equipped to deal with tradeoffs between public and private services. There is a vast market for canned dog food, but why should the elderly have to subsist on inadequate diets? The dogs have owners who care for them; has society less concern for the elderly? Vast sums are expended on violent television programs, but the educational system produces virtual illiterates in far too many cases. Does society have any choice in striking some better balance? Americans cannot even choose between less polluted air and big, gas-eating cars because someone else's choice forecloses the option of clean air.

While offering rhetorical praise to "free choice," the critics of planning should take a closer look at the choices that corporations offer the consumer. Planning might be a better mechanism than the not-so-free market for letting people register their feelings and express their choices through means other than their pocketbooks.

Inefficiency of Government

Yet another group of critics argues that while planning is perfectly acceptable for corporations, it is quite unworkable for government. As stated by a *Wall Street Journal* editorial, "Unlike corporate planning, which generally leads to decisions with an eye to maximizing efficiency and profits, government economic planning is dictated by political goals that are often inimical to efficiency" [5].

True, political goals sometimes may be inimical to efficiency, but efficiency is neither the exclusive property of private enterprise nor necessarily the highest virtue in our society. America is not yet a corporate state. In fact, one source of its current economic problems may be too great a concern with "efficiency" in government. In the name of efficiency, millions of Americans have been consigned to the scrap heap of endemic unemployment. But even if the tradeoff worked, this society should have more humane goals than efficiency alone. Economic policies must serve social ends, not vice versa.

The government already makes hosts of legitimate and necessary economic decisions: the rate of growth in the money supply, tariff levels, income-tax regulations and collections, international monetary matters, bank credits, investment insurance, and so on. Plainly, the government will make thousands of economic decisions in the future. The question is whether these decisions will be informed or haphazard, coordinated with other economic decisions or unrelated, based on adequate data or unsubstantiated, future-oriented or shortsighted.

If corporations can take a look at where their companies and the economy are heading, then the government should do the same. In fact, corporate planning might be more successful if corporations knew what the government intended. For example, both corporate planners and an economic planning board ought to consider the implications of slower economic growth on employment opportunities and the educational system. The manipulation of aggregate demand alone is inadequate to deal with a lower growth trend. The planning process can help both Congress and the public to choose more wisely among alternative growth courses. No planning mechanism can prevent Congress from acting in willful ignorance, but at least with formalized planning the public will be able to see the relative benefits and shortcomings more clearly. Both Congress and the private sector, including labor, would be able to reach a consensus on the available options.

Quality of Government Planning

The final group of opponents to planning points out that recent government economic policy does not inspire great confidence in the ability of government to be either accurate or farsighted in its predictions. The corollary is that if the plan and the economy began to diverge, the government would be tempted to enforce rather than change the plan. In many ways, this argument is the most compelling because America's economic policy has been rather erratic in the past. Economic planning would introduce no rigidity into the decision-making arena, but it would offer a new mechanism for stability coupled with well-thought-out change.

Past events suggest that planning might have helped the country avoid some poor decisions. For example, the devaluation of the dollar and the imposition of wage and price controls on domestic sales in 1971 caused an unexpected and very substantial outflow of basic materials and food from the United States, contributing to shortages at home and ultimately to higher prices. An economic planning board might have anticipated and pointed out the likely consequences in advance. Agricultural policies have also been extremely shortsighted and ill-planned. The Russian grain deals provide an obvious example; another is the freeze of meat prices, which led to meat shortages in 1974. Acreage restrictions were maintained long after the grain shortage was well known. Finally, despite a plethora of reports on the shortage of natural resources and especially on the possibility of energy-supply disruptions, no coherent national energy and resource policy has been enacted. This government failure is perhaps the most discouraging of all. Planning is no panacea, but it might force federal decisionmakers to deal with issues like shortages much earlier, with more attention to the totality of the problem and with a more realistic perception of our options.

PLANNING IN THE TWENTIETH CENTURY

Planning should not be an ideological issue. Since it must be in keeping with the character of the society, planning will not alter the nation's fundamental values. No one wishes to see the balance between government control and private decision making destroyed by bloated government slowly squeezing out the private sector. But the current balance cannot be maintained through ignorance. Nor will critical problems vanish in the absence of planning. It is impossible to turn the clock back to the often romanticized agrarian society of open spaces and clean air and water at the time of independence.

The greatness of the United States has rested on an ability to interpret continually its constitution and revise its institutions to meet changing political circumstances. No one can pretend that eighteenth century economic solutions are adequate to today's world. To follow such an antiquated path would cause ever-increasing numbers of Americans to become misfits in the economic system, with the end result that their economic powerlessness could very likely vent its frustration in political nihilism. A balanced growth and economic planning policy could help provide the public with information, analysis, and alternatives so that this society can continue to nourish its traditional dedication to human freedom in the midst of technological change in this frighteningly complex world.

 *Chapter 11*

The Pitfalls of National Planning

Maurice LaMontagne

The recent rapid economic growth experienced by the industrialized nations has created the vital necessity for these nations to face the future. Like past civilizations, the present one is limited by its physical, institutional, and human constraints. If it is to avoid the chaotic decline of its predecessors, it must be able to predict the future outcome of its economic policies. This paper focuses on the newly-emerging acceptance of national planning to describe a Canadian planning experiment which failed, to discuss the reasons for its failure, and to examine the crucial obstacle to planning in a horizontal society—lack of consensus.

PLANNING IN A NEW PERSPECTIVE

Before World War II planning was seen by business, the public, and government in many Western countries as a system of coercion incompatible with private initiative and democracy and, as a substitute for the market mechanism, closely associated with socialism. Soon after the war, however, France developed the concept of indicative planning as a tool to complement and improve the market mechanism [1]. As implemented in France, the planning process indicates the goals of development and the steps to be taken in achieving them. However, the government cannot force the private sector to adhere to the plan, though it can exert an indirect influence on business decisions through monetary and fiscal policies.

In many Western European countries planning ceased to be identified with socialism and coercion and gained approval as a means of reconstructing a war-destroyed economy and of maximizing quantitative growth. In this perspective, however, planning still appeared unduly complicated, unnecessary in countries that were already growing rapidly, and ineffective in countries highly dependent on world markets.

More recently, the awareness of rapid and pervasive material growth and its negative side effects has been expanding. Planning is gaining acceptance as being indispensable for reducing uncertainty, organizing change, and providing for more sustainable and harmonious growth. This new justification will undoubtedly contribute to a greater interest in national planning as a basis for concerted and future-oriented action.

For instance, the advocacy of effective planning could become a practical rallying point for most of the participants in the growth debate, except for those who argue that the global society is irremediably doomed and those who contend all current problems can be solved eventually by the present political and economic system. Proponents of less, quantitative growth or more, organic growth should become strong advocates of planning [2]; nations that begin to plan systematically will become in the process more conscious of the limits to growth and will learn how to adjust to these constraints. Adherents of the "technological fix," including supporters of Seaborg's "recycle society" [3], should also be ardent supporters of planning—even technology requires successful planning to accomplish its wonders.

Therefore, planning can become a crucial step in the implementation of any action-oriented program, even if divergent views persist regarding treatment of the world *problématique*. Moreover, planning should become not only a problem-solving technique, but also a learning process. Planning provides a deeper understanding of current problems and opportunities and a better chance to reach an informed consensus on diagnoses and prescriptions.

Wider acceptance of planning is already noticeable even in political circles in the United States. For example, in 1975 Senators Hubert H. Humphrey and Jacob K. Javits introduced a bill to create an economic planning board in the President's office [4]. This board would develop a procedure to produce a six-year national plan to be reviewed biennially by Congress. Although the proposal of such a bill bodes well for national planning, the enactment of such legislation will not automatically solve the nation's problems. Many pitfalls await such a complex undertaking, especially in a democracy facing for the first time the challenges of the post-industrial revolution. A superficial analysis of the Humphrey–Javits bill suggests that its provisions are quite similar to those of the Canadian model developed in 1963, which failed. In this paper I will describe several lessons taught by the Canadian experiment, in order to illuminate the planning problems that most industrialized Western countries, and particularly the United States, will have to face.

THE CANADIAN PLANNING MODEL

In 1963, as a minister in the Lester Pearson government, I introduced a bill, unanimously approved by Parliament, establishing the Economic Council of Canada. Having previously indicated some of the difficulties faced by the Canadian economy, I remarked at the time, "To overcome our present difficulties, we need new policies applied in a new spirit and within new administrative structures. In other words, we need a plan so that the various aspects of economic policy may be well coordinated and so that the private sector can work in the same direction as the government towards the common objective of harmonious growth . . ." [5].

Prime Minister Pearson also expressed the hope that the Council would become an effective instrument for creating an economic consensus: "Planning, as we mean it, means consultation in order to replace haphazard influence by conscious guidance. It means both government and private policies will be more broad-based and long-sighted than at present" [6].

To meet these objectives, the Council was required "regularly to assess, on a systematic and comprehensive basis, the medium-term and long-term prospects of the economy, and to compare such prospects with the potentialities of growth of the economy," "to recommend what government policies . . . will best help to realize the potentialities of growth of the economy," and "to study and discuss with representatives of the industries concerned and with representatives of labor, farmers, and other primary producers, and other occupational groups and organizations, what specific plans for production and investment in major industries in Canada will best contribute to a high and consistent rate of economic growth" [7].

Although the Council is a government agency and has been reporting directly to the prime minister since 1966, it has operated with a large degree of independence. The chairman and two directors are appointed on a full-time basis for renewable terms of seven years. The twenty-five other part-time members are selected after formal consultation with appropriate organizations to assure representation of the various segments of the private sector. For all practical purposes, the Council is free to hire its own staff, to publish its studies, and to select its program of activities, including the launching of research projects and the holding of conferences and seminars.

Over the years, the Council has substantially ignored the long term, while concentrating its attention on the medium term. In this context, the Council has made valuable contributions. In the area of statistical information and analysis, it has promoted the collection of new and better data and the development of techniques for the convenient storage, retrieval, and manipulation of economic time series. This effort led to the development of a new and greatly enlarged computer-based information system. The Council also developed CANDIDE (Canadian Disaggregated Interdepartmental Econometric Model), a medium-term model designed to portray actual and possible changes in the structure of the Canadian economy and to assist in the preparation of detailed assessments of economic potentials, including the depiction of possible future patterns of employment, investment, and productivity growth in groups of industries [8]. More recently, the Council designed a set of fifteen interrelated economic indicators to serve as performance objectives for a period of three years into the future. The Council has also begun to identify and measure selected social indicators.

At the outset, the Council defined five major economic goals: full employment, a high rate of growth, reasonable price stability, viability in the balance of payments, and an equitable distribution of rising incomes. Several years later, it sought to extend its conceptual framework by identifying well-being and equity as the two basic goals of society, and by designating nine major areas of concern—including individual and social rights, health, access to knowledge, and preservation of the natural and human environment—in an effort to build a social accounting system. The Council has published a series of assessments of the performance of the Canadian economy in light of the economy's potential, the Council's designated goals, and annual reviews of medium-term problems and prospects.

In its advisory role, the Council has insisted on a new policy-formulation framework: a shift from concentrating exclusively on poor performance in relation to one goal, such as full employment or price stability, to focusing simultaneously, consistently, and continuously on several major objectives. The Council has proposed that policy formulation become more future-oriented rather than reactive, so that the economy can be steered in desirable directions into the future. It has stressed the need for potential-oriented policy formulation in order to reach what is possible and desirable. It has underlined the necessity of coordination in policy formulation within particular governments, among governments, and between government and private decisionmakers.

In the hope of enhancing its policy-advisory role, the Council recently proposed the establishment of "an appropriate parliamentary setting" for improved policy evaluation. In such a setting, medium-term economic priorities and prospects would annually be discussed so that Parliament could improve its evaluation of government policies and acquire broad guidelines for the preparation of the budget. With a similar purpose in mind, the Council recommended that ministers of finance establish indicators of future government expenditure in the light of medium-term economic priorities and prospects, and as a means of seeking better coordination of federal and provincial financial policies.

The Council has also maintained contacts with the academic world, industry, labor, and other private groups. This dialogue culminated in the calling of the first National Economic Conference sponsored by the Economic Council of Canada in December 1973. During the Conference, according to the Council's *Eleventh Annual Review*,

> A number of delegates expressed the view that the individual industries and interest groups would benefit from a continuing organization that would consider, in a systematic way, the industry's perspective in the light of the developing economic situation and government policies. The continuing industry organization could be made more effective, in the view of some delegates, if its deliberations were set within the comprehensive analytical framework of the Economic Council of Canada. In that setting, an objective evaluation could be made of each industry's perception and of its relationship with plans and activities in other industries and sectors [9].

Such a "continuing industry organization" having close association with the Economic Council could have provided the essential basis for concerted planning in the private sector. Unfortunately, after a second conference held in December 1974, the Council decided not to continue to sponsor such meetings.

On the whole, the Council has accomplished an impressive amount of work and has taken substantive initiatives. It has produced a series of studies on the Canadian economy which have given careful readers a much better understanding of the economy's problems and prospects. It has made significant policy recommendations and has provided a new and broader framework for policy formulation. On several occasions, it has brought together decisionmakers of the private sector, mainly labor and management, to discuss their respective goals and problems.

In retrospect, however, the Canadian experience in planning has failed to meet its major objectives as set out in 1963. Canada still lacks an integrated plan. The economic consensus initially sought has not been created. Government and private policies have not become more broad-based, more long-sighted, or better coordinated. The performance of the Canadian economy has not improved and, in this respect at least, the impact of the Economic Council has been marginal. The Council itself acknowledged failure in its *Eleventh Annual Review* published in 1974. The *Review* noted "the absence, within the consultative and decision-making process, of any clear perspective of longer-term, comprehensive objectives for individual industries, of government policies, or of economic and social goals and targets more generally" [10].

THE FAILURE OF THE CANADIAN MODEL

The factors accounting for the failure of the Canadian planning effort reveal the pitfalls that successful indicative planning has to overcome. I will examine five such pitfalls one at a time.

Uncertain International Factors

International factors produce uncertainty. The Economic Council underlined this first pitfall in its very first Annual Review:

> A set of policies, programmes, and plans can be directed to the attainment of certain objectives, but they cannot guarantee success. The actual outcome will depend in considerable measure upon the unfolding events, many of which are beyond Canada's control. . . . For the purpose of our analysis we have assumed the maintenance of peace and of favorable conditions in world trade and in our principal markets, especially the United States. If these assumptions prove to be wrong, the task of achieving our goals becomes vastly more difficult and more complicated. Also an analysis can help to identify problems, but it cannot contribute much to their solution if political and social tensions make it impossible [11].

One must recognize that the expectation of the maintenance of a favorable international environment was unrealistic, even in 1964. The population explosion, the oil and food crises, chronic inflation, the growing dependence of most industrialized countries on imports of raw materials and mounting dissatisfaction in the underdeveloped world were already prevalent or germinating. Many people argued then and still argue that, without a favorable international environment, planning for a country like Canada is bound to be rather ineffective. This defeatist view engenders an attitude of helplessness and passive fatalism.

Successful national planning cannot be based on the assumption of a favorable world environment. It must be conceived within a realistic international perspective, and rest on the best possible anticipation of medium-term and long-term prospects and problems. Nations having a significant external economic sector have an additional need for planning. When the international environment is unfavorable, they must be prepared to minimize the internal impact of that environment. Moreover, national planning by a growing number of countries is probably the most practical way to build a stable world order. A favorable international environment cannot be established on national disorders. Finally, learning to organize a national economy in the perspective of the medium term and the long term will almost inevitably foster a national conviction that interdependence in the absence of close international cooperation means eventual ruin for all.

Narrow Targets

The Canadian planning strategy does not have a sufficiently broad perspective in the formation of "targets." The medium-term targets have consistently been identified as "potential" growth rates at full employment levels and expressed in terms of the major components of the GNP. The failure of the Canadian economy to attain these targets has been measured in terms of GNP "gaps."

But this overly narrow approach does not take into account physical and social limitations which also determine "potential" economic growth. For instance, it neglects the resource sector, implicitly assuming (in line with conventional Canadian wisdom) that Canada is endowed with "boundless resources." The analytical framework must be broadened in the general direction indicated by Wassily Leontief a few years ago:

> To deepen the foundation of our analytical system it will be necessary to reach unhesitatingly beyond the limits of the domain of economic phenomena as it has been staked out up to now. The pursuit of a more fundamental understanding of the process of production inevitably leads into the area of engineering sciences. To penetrate below the skin-thin surface of conventional consumption functions, it will be necessary to develop a systematic study of the structural characteristics and of the functioning of households, an area in which description and analysis of social, anthropological and demographic factors must obviously occupy the center of the stage [12].

The Canadian planning model is also too narrow in that its targets are not expressed in terms of specific industrial components. The GNP framework may be useful for the formulation of government policy, but it cannot easily be used to derive targets for specific industries. Therefore, it has only a very limited value for private decisionmakers. The main participants in the enactment of a plan must be able to perceive clearly the role they are supposed to play and the targets they are expected to achieve.

Neglect of the Long Term

The Canadian experience has not sufficiently emphasized the long-term perspective. In practice, planning must be conceived within a medium-term framework; however, a serious effort must be made to identify as precisely as possible the long-term prospects and objectives that should serve as a broad context. Although directed by the act which created it to look into the long term, the Economic Council has done very little in this area.

A short-term view can be very deceptive, especially in times of deep and rapid change such as the present, when industrialized countries are beginning to feel the full impact of a third major technological revolution, of scarcity, and of the post-industrial era. A long-term perspective could have warned us of the exponential era more quickly; then, much earlier, we should have realized that exponential quantitative growth cannot last forever. Canada would have been in a better position to anticipate logistic trends or slower growth in areas such as population, thus avoiding some costly mistakes in certain sectors of social-capital investment, such as education.

Inadequate Short-term Control

The Canadian planning effort has also neglected the short-term situation. The Economic Council was not directed to look into short-term problems and prospects, but it did recommend the establishment of an independent research institute to analyze and report regularly on short-term economic trends and problems. Several such institutes now exist, but they have not yet created a better basis for understanding and forecasting the business cycle.

Since World War II, the forecasting record of government and private institutions has been very poor. The techniques used have systematically failed to anticipate the amplitudes and the turning points of cyclical fluctuations. For example, although a recession clearly began in the United States in late 1973, almost one year later Milton Friedman is reported by the press to have said: "We are not, and I emphasize *not*, in danger of a major depression or even of a severe recession."

In the immediate postwar period most governments in the West proclaimed their intention to use fiscal and monetary policies to minimize cyclical unemployment and inflation. This they have done. But their forecasting techniques have always recognized turning points too late, and the Western governments have thus tended to fight recessions and booms when these movements were practically over. Countercyclical policies applied at the wrong time have achieved the exact opposite of what was expected, and have helped to accentuate recessions and booms, cyclical unemployment, and inflation.

In Canada, as a result of such untimely interventions, the Economic Council and the government have seldom been on the same wavelength. For instance, the Council was urging the government to abandon its role as a "balance wheel" in the economy and to direct its efforts more to "steering the economy along a smoother underlying growth path in final demand, in line with the economy's continually expanding potential" [13]. Meanwhile, however, the government was engaged in an almost day-to-day fight to reduce the inflation and unemployment that its policies had helped to intensify.

The lesson to be learned from this experience is that attempts at medium-term planning will fail in the absence of a greater measure of short-term economic stability. Consequently, governments should not abandon their balance-wheel role, but instead should be prepared to fulfill the role more effectively by improving their short-term forecasting systems and learning how to intervene more quickly. Thus, a serious obstacle to medium-term planning would be overcome.

Lack of a Comprehensive Plan

A more basic and paradoxical reason for the failure of the Canadian effort is that it has never really produced a comprehensive and widely-accepted plan. At best, the Economic Council has developed an analytical framework for planning which was, as mentioned before, better suited for government policy than for the guidance of the private sector. But even the government has not used the planning framework for the formulation of its goals and policies.

PLANNING VERSUS FACTIONALISM

In retrospect, it is doubtful whether the Council would have been more successful even if it had produced a better analytical framework or a more comprehensive and detailed plan. Planning in a democracy cannot be purely technocratic and elitist. It must be participatory and must rest on the active cooperation of public and private decisionmakers, not only in its conception, but also in its implementation. In this context, an agency such as the Economic Council can never be much more than a springboard, catalyst, and clearinghouse closely linked with an effective network of decisionmakers.

Unfortunately, the Council has operated most often in a vacuum. Especially in the beginning, the Council wanted to keep government at arm's length, feeling that it could not act simultaneously as a private government adviser and a public government critic, without destroying its credibility. But then it had to face the resistance, or what Donald Schon has described as the "dynamic conservatism," of bureaucratic baronies [14]. Nor has reporting to the prime minister, as the Council does, helped to improve communication channels with the government, because he is too busy, especially when Parliament is sitting. Annual assessment of the medium term by members of Parliament has not succeeded either.

The Economic Council of Canada may be reduced to little more than a research academy or a permanent Royal Commission on economic problems and prospects unless it succeeds in establishing continuing links with a national network of public and private decisionmakers. Indeed, the basic condition for success of indicative planning is broadly-based participation in its inception and concerted action in its implementation. But can a horizontal society characterized by widely diverging interests, and based on an adversary system of checks rather than a cooperative system of balances, meet that basic condition?

With the benefit of hindsight, most of the pitfalls of indicative planning outlined above might seem relatively easy to overcome. However, the innate planning capacity of horizontal societies becomes a crucial question. It can be argued that effective long-term planning cannot be achieved in Western democracies because the systematic pursuit of distant goals is incompatible with frequent elections. This conflict can be all too real, especially in the United States: elections bring frequent turnovers in personnel; politicians have to run continuing electoral campaigns; and legislative and executive powers frequently override each others' decisions in a struggle for control. The veto, if applied too often to important issues, produces negative government which is certainly incompatible with planning. The American system does not seem much more ineffective than other political regimes, however, so frequent elections probably do not really lie at the root of the problem. Modern democracies are based to an increasing extent on a continuing referendum symbolized by public opinion polls. Politicians must remain close to prevailing public opinion in order to survive. Insofar as they do, people get the governments they create, and elections do not unduly influence this process.

The heart of the planning problem, then, lies closer to the inherent structure of the society than to its election mechanisms. The historical transition from vertical to horizontal societies brought about a democracy characterized by the participation of an increasing number of people in collective decision-making. However, the ballot box has proven a poor mechanism of effective and continuing participation.

The successful fight for the right of association brought the equal-participation-by-voting dream to an end. An increasing number of individuals discovered that association meant power, and that in order to achieve effective membership in participatory democracy they had to belong to a group. A multitude of special groups gradually developed to meet the new need in various ways, according to the specific preferences and requirements of individuals. Horizontal societies changed radically into fragmented societies.

Today, the list of special groups defies enumeration. Most share common features; they have short-term goals and sponsor special interests or causes, and in their zeal they tend to be intolerant, dogmatic, and uncompromising. When their leadership becomes too soft, more activist elements come to the fore. Evidence of this dynamic is the view of a Canadian labor leader, who termed his organization a mob rather than a union. Significantly, he had already decided to retire when he made that observation.

With the rise of facionalism, horizontal societies have become more unstable. Cyberneticist W. Ross Ashby claims that "when a whole system is composed of a number of sub-systems the one that tends to dominate is the one that is least stable" [15]. The tendency has been reinforced by the acquisition of a powerful platform for factionalism in the media. Television puts the emphasis on conflict: beneficial events are not news; conflicts and disasters make the "best" news.

As human conflict widens, various segments or factions of society can always find another group to blame for failure to achieve their objectives. Frustration impels factions to appeal to the state to resolve private conflicts, although they are quick to resent government interference if the decisions are not in their favor. The state cannot solve all conflicts nor satisfy everybody and ultimately the state becomes a scapegoat. Moreover, the state itself becomes the victim of factionalism. Growing bureaucracies fight each other to preserve or extend their respective territories. Time-consuming legislative processes are too often dominated by the negative forces of the adversary system.

Most Western nations, then, have become fragmented and subject to "the tyranny of the majority." Unable to keep all factions equally satisfied, governments try at best to keep them equally dissatisfied; like fire brigades, governments solve crises as they arise without the benefit of planning. At worst, since getting a majority consensus is becoming increasingly more difficult while lining up opposition to a position is getting easier, governments tend to provide negative leadership.

My picture of the situation may seem unduly bleak and pessimistic. Nevertheless, I believe that it is realistic. The conflict between distant goals and frequent elections is largely a symptom. The real and more fundamental incompatibility is between planning and horizontal societies as they have developed, with ever more factionalism and increasing pains caused by uncontrolled growth and emerging scarcities. Such societies are bound to experience even more chaos if much slower growth replaces exponential expansion. Those already conscious of this serious danger and not prepared to abandon their social membership realize that planning has become an urgent necessity. As George Meany has observed: "We need long-range economic planning and priorities to minimize unforeseen major developments and reduce the degree to which American society has stumbled and fumbled along in the past few years" [16].

However, does Mr. Meany really want the consequences of what he suggests? Obviously, private leaders will not accept compulsory planning by the state, not only because such a turn of events would make their own role obsolete, but more importantly because it would be incompatible with basic freedoms and democracy. The only alternative is indicative planning based on a broad consensus and compromise. To fill the vacuum of leadership and to satisfy the basic prerequisite for successful planning, it is essential to break through the barrier of factionalism to achieve mutual persuasion and to produce the shared perceptions crucial to concerted action.

THE NEED FOR CONSENSUS

A growing number of observers recognize the urgent need for consensus. Alvin Toffler calls for "a continuing plebiscite on the future" [17]. Sir Geoffrey Vickers contends that the containment and resolution of conflict depend more and more on persuasion through dialogue:

> Mutual persuasion depends on a shared universe of discourse, whereby it is possible for the parties to enlarge their shared view of their situation, their shared repertory of acceptable responses, even their shared valuation of the always-conflicting results to be expected from any course of action or inaction [18].

Claude Gruson, an influential French former public servant, attaches great importance to the setting of the continuing plebiscite:

> The organization of the debate holds a crucial place. It is this debate which must identify conflicts, prepare the bases of agreements or delimit disagreements, and which must in any case allow each interested party to understand the nature of the problems raised, to design the solutions which appear the best to him, to measure his agreement and disagreement with the solution being implemented, and to evaluate the political importance of this agreement or disagreement [19].

The continuing debate, dialogue, or plebiscite will not come to life spontaneously. For reasons mentioned previously, it should be organized on neutral grounds rather than under government auspices. Governments must, of course, be active participants, but as partners not leaders. Required, therefore at least to start with, is a new type of private nonprofit anticipatory institution operating at the national level with a representative membership of public and private decisionmakers. The institution should not be a research organization. It should function both as a relay station, using the best techniques of information technology to develop among its membership a common awareness of prospects and problems, and as a rallying station, organizing periodic meetings to maintain Gruson's continuing debate in the hope of achieving mutual persuasion and a broader consensus.

Such an organization should not be expected to accomplish miracles. But, at least as a seed operation, it could start an amplification process and what John Platt calls "a social chain-reaction with positive feedback" [20]. Several countries, including Canada and the United States, have reached the stage where such an operation could have a large multiplier effect.

Like all past civilizations, this one is on the road to chaos. Today's horizontal societies desperately need planning. But they have not yet developed the necessary basis for success in this difficult task. The Canadian planning model, while making a constructive attempt, failed to establish the crucial broad consensus on future-oriented action. Societies must develop and promote this consensus. If they can replace collective irresponsibility with collective leadership, they can develop alternatives to unexpected and uncontrolled growth.

 *Chapter 12*

Strategies for Societal Development

Joan Davis and Samuel Mauch

While we have lips and voices
Which are to kiss and sing with
Who cares if some oneeyed son of a bitch
Invents an instrument to measure Spring with.
e. e. cummings

INTRODUCTION

Contributing toward global stability has become the goal of countless scientists, politicians, and concerned individuals. The strategies range from global approaches, often criticized as unrealistic, to local activities, criticized as insignificant. It must be taken as a valid point that solutions which extend beyond national boundaries raise the problem of enforcement, since there is no "multinational" government that can enforce such policies. The first concrete steps that can be taken are thus restricted to those which can be taken within national borders. For this reason, concrete strategies must be compatible with national and local needs, resources, and institutions, if they are to be amenable to implementation. Analyses based on highly aggregated models may predict with some accuracy future developments, since they tend to reflect the increasing influence of a few industrialized countries upon all other countries. For specific policy development at the national and local level they are, however, at best indirectly useful. Perhaps global stability becomes possible only as a product of stable local and national situations, rather than as a goal to be approached monolithically.

In order to design solutions for the current situations in industrialized countries, it is necessary to understand the bases of their problems of economic growth, political, social, and human development, and environmental quality. Much information can be gained by considering the mechanisms creating such problems in industrialized countries. However, some of the more significant problems are derived from conditions that are specific to each particular country. We took Switzerland as an example for our study and looked at the characteristics she shares with other countries as well as at her special problems. This paper focuses on local problems, but attempts to propose solutions applicable to industrialized countries in general.

Industrial and Post-Industrial Switzerland

Switzerland is a typical Western European industrialized country in many aspects of its socioeconomic development. It manifests the fundamental socioeconomic dynamics of modern post-industrialization: education serves essentially scientific, technological, and economic objectives related to material demands; productivity of labor has increased, and, at the same time, labor is increasingly replaced by capital and energy. Trends run toward automation, extreme specialization of labor, assembly-line-type jobs for more and more workers, and increasing "distance" between jobs and their socioeconomic goals. Production, capitalization, and most socioeconomic functions are concentrated in ever-larger corporations and government institutions. The need for superimposing more, larger, and more complicated technocratic control structures onto the changing economic and sociocultural system is perpetuated.

In certain aspects, however, the Swiss situation is unique. Switzerland has 6.3 million people, of which about 1 million are foreign. The 6.3 million live on 41,000 square kilometers, corresponding to a density of 150 people per square kilometer. The settlement area comprises about 3 percent of total land area. One-quarter of the land is unproductive. Virtually the only domestic natural resource is hydroelectric power, accounting for 80 percent of electric and 14 percent of total energy demands. Only 50 percent of the consumed food and 10 percent of the consumed energy are domestically produced; the rest is imported. The direct energy use is three kilowatts per capita—three times less than in the United States at essentially the same annual GNP per capita of $9,000. However, an additional 1.5 kilowatts per capital of energy is imported indirectly in the form of products: steel, autos, fertilizer, meat, grain, and other goods.

Switzerland's economic structure is unlike that of most highly industrialized countries. The country has virtually no heavy (i.e., heavily polluting) industry such as mining or steel fabrication. The emphasis is on industries which process imported raw materials into tool-making machines, watches, instruments, turbines and generators, chemicals, and pharmaceuticals. Other major export sectors are tourism and banking. As a result, Switzerland has a significant net resource and energy import and a net pollution export. While the value of Switzerland's imported goods exceeds that of exported goods by some six billion Swiss francs, or 15 to 20 percent of import-export values, the country has nonetheless traditionally shown a positive balance of payments. This favorable balance is due to the positive balance of the capital-transfer sector and the service sector, especially banking. The Swiss working force, 3 million strong, includes 700,000 foreign workers, who are employed in low-skilled jobs in the construction industry, tourism, hotels and restaurants, and agriculture.

During the boom period of the 1960s and early 1970s, the government stood by and watched industry expand its labor force and production at fantastic rates. During this time, the construction industry expanded at a world record of 20 percent of GNP. This rate is now painfully shrinking to more normal proportions. Imports and exports are about 35 percent of GNP, as compared to 2 percent for the United States. The concentration and the monoculture characteristics of Switzerland's technological and economic systems are in marked contrast to the characteristics of her geographical, ethnic, and political structures, which show high degrees of diversity and decentralization. The country has four different ethnic groups, each with its own language; yet there are few incidents of unhealthy competition or tension.

Politically, the federal unit is divided into twenty-five states and three thousand communities, with very high degrees of self-determination and sovereignty. These structures have shown a remarkably high degree of resistance to the technological, economic, and sociocultural system of bigness, concentration, central control, and monocultures. Admittedly, the very incompatibility between the traditional sovereignty at the local level and the current trend toward gigantism is often a source of difficulty. Economic growth and technological advances produce environmental effects which evoke increased control, power, and legislation at the federal level. Increased socioeconomic and geographic mobility call for federal "coordination" of, and/or federal intervention into, the twenty-five state school systems. As in other industrialized countries, Swiss universities mainly serve economic, not sociocultural needs. They produce scientific and technical specialists who know more and more about less and less. University attendance is made attractive and trade schools are neglected. Technology promises to replace handwork and arts by industrial production, machines, and energy. Too little reflection is given to the long-term implications of these policies. All in all, development goals for education, research, health, and other domains of human activity are set by the economic, rather than by the sociocultural system.

National priorities in research and development, foreign policies, economic policy, social goals, environmental standards, and energy policy tend to be set de facto more and more by experts in the federal administration and by powerful lobbies. This happens in spite of the fact that Switzerland formally still practices one of the world's most direct democracies. Popular referenda and initiatives are used at all three political levels. At the federal level, 50,000 signatures suffice to bring almost any major issue to a popular vote. In addition, many issues, such as international treaties and legal acts in all fields, can, by means of a referendum, be brought to public vote. Each year, the Swiss vote on ten to twenty such issues.

The rate of change and the complexity of technological, economic, social and political systems have outrun the comprehension of man. He is simply no longer able to understand the mechanisms of the world around him. Science and technology seem slowly to be undermining the fundamentals of democracy. This alienation, we believe, is the major reason for decreasing participation in Swiss votes and elections, especially among people between twenty and thirty. The overall percentage of participation is down to 30 or 40 percent. Most of the pending initiatives deal with the broad issue of environment, growth, and quality of life. The marked increase in initiatives is an indication of the restlessness of many elite peer groups who perceive the general course of economic development as a malaise.

Opinions regarding the implications of these current trends vary according to the thesis upon which they are based. Our analysis must begin with an explanation of the thesis of the limits to material growth, as growth itself may be seen as one of the bases for the increasing disintegration of the industrialized world.

The Thesis of Limits to Material Growth

The general thesis of limits to growth states that material growth is not forever possible in a finite world. It must lead to ecological collapse at some point in time. This thesis is uncontested, but it has no practical value for decision-making without substantial elaboration. In this paper, we present a study which does offer some positive basis for decision-making. Starting with an examination of the Malthusian thesis in relation to the growth of modern industrialized societies, we recommend several concrete strategies that can be adopted to help mitigate the crises being fostered by unlimited growth.

In order to judge whether or not the continuation of present trends in industrialized countries will necessarily lead to ecological and/or socioeconomic crises or collapses, initially we must determine:

—to what extent technology is capable of extending the various ecological limits to growth;

—to what extent the total economic demand for material goods and services will saturate the economic system automatically at a level consistent with the capacity of the environment, technological progress, and social values.

We approach these questions as theses often expressed by those who believe that no fundamentally new strategies are needed to avoid a crisis. The technological optimists believe that growth in the production of goods and services can be continued indefinitely because technological progress will always be capable of limiting the potential negative side effects of larger material flows. They believe the environmental reproductive capacities will not be destroyed by material growth because it is possible to allocate sufficient financial and energy resources to environmental protection and resource conservation without significantly slowing the growth of individual wealth. Many traditional economists also believe that the demand for all goods and services will automatically show self-saturation without economic or social crises. The economy will logistically approach some finite level compatible with technological capabilities, environmental capacities, and social values.

From the standpoint of the long-term biophysical stability of environmental systems, the refutation of both theses is necessary and sufficient to prove the necessity of fundamentally new strategies, if environmental damages leading to ecological catastrophes are to be prevented. However, for those interested in enhancing the comprehensive quality of life for the human population, this refutation is sufficient but not necessary. The proof or disproof of these theses becomes irrelevant if it can be shown that the continuation of current growth trends leads to an inhuman society, even with clean air and water. Under such conditions, the quality of life deteriorates whether or not acceptable biophysical environment quality can be achieved. Therefore, investigations of limits to growth must consider not only the quality of the biophysical environment, but the comprehensive quality of human life for all members of society [1].

For example, even if nuclear technology could provide all the energy society ever demands, it would not be attractive if the safety and safeguard mechanisms for the technology would necessitate a police state. Weinberg's Faustian bargain is not worth it [2]! It is essential to consider the economic and sociocultural crises that could be induced by continued growth as well as those which could arise from an all-too-abrupt transition from growth to equilibrium.

Objectives of the Study

In the light of these thoughts, the objective of our study has been developed in the following iterative steps.

1. Assume that a desirable course of development leads toward a sustained equilibrium between man and his natural environment, where all members of society can achieve a high quality of human life.
2. Analyze the intrinsic dynamic mechanisms of the ecological, economic, sociocultural, and political system of a Western industrialized country in order to judge the validity of the theses of "unlimited technological progress" and "self-saturation."
3. Investigate other conditions which might be necessary to justify or impel the development of new societal strategies.
4. Develop societal, i.e., technological, economic, sociocultural, and political, strategies which optimally lead towards the desirable course of development in the examined country.

The analyses and the strategies we have developed are applicable in general to most Western industrialized countries. They have been applied here to the situation in Switzerland. With respect to these specific strategies for Switzerland, it must be emphasized that their implementation often depends on the state of development of those countries with which the Swiss development is economically, technologically, socially, and culturally interdependent. Furthermore, the present must be accepted as the initial condition of an inertial dynamic system when strategies for change are developed and assessed. History cannot be undone. The fundamentals of the strategies developed here are similar for all industrialized countries, East and West, because the dynamics of the development have become more and more the same in these countries.

The study group whose work provided the background for this paper encountered, in the course of its work, problem situations which in many ways resemble those facing our societal system. First, for the type of problem approached here, neither the right questions nor the appropriate methods were known at the beginning. As a result, the process had to be iterative between asking questions and giving answers to them. We believe that major progress in our study took place through asking new and better questions, rather than through developing even more exact answers to the same wrong questions. As a result of this process, our focus shifted significantly from the natural to the social and human sciences.

Second, this iterative process compelled the various specialists to accept new ideas from other disciplines, leading to drastic revisions in their views of the problem. This often required individuals to be tolerant and to reevaluate their own contributions. Our small group became a mirror reflecting the necessary and desirable changes in societal problem-solving methods; we gave up some *efficiency* in busily solving problems preformulated by leaders, in favor of *effectiveness* in developing better questions during open and democratic discussions. As a result, the artificial divisions of the total societal system shown in Figure 12–1 (and reflected in the divisions in our study group) were gradually connected by a strong network of small interdisciplinary subgroups, overlapping in topics and in members. Thus the initial multidisciplinary team had evolved into an interdisciplinary team.

There seems to be an important analogy between the methodological problems that confronted our research team and the problems facing society. Our conclusions were that methods of problem-solving characterized by hierarchical division of labor and decoupling of information and responsibility cannot generate effective solutions: the methodology itself is part of, if not responsible for, the problems.

SOCIETAL STRUCTURE

Ecological Constraints and Technological Limits

The main issue underlying the ecological dynamics outlined above in Figure 12–1 is the validity of the first thesis: is technological progress unlimited, and can it solve social problems? For the sake of analysis, it is assumed that society currently opts for a strategy of continued material growth, with technological progress and technological fixes as tools for maintaining environmental quality. We even assume that technology is capable, under this strategy, of providing virtually unlimited energy to control technically the various problems of food supply, of air, water, and soil pollution, of solid waste

Figure 12–1. Societal Subsystems

The fundamental dynamics of the societal system in industrialized countries is the result of an historical process. Originally the three subsystems—economic, sociocultural, and political-administrative—formed one integrated whole, whereby the sociocultural domain clearly could perform its function of specifying and developing societal objectives. At present, the three subsystems are far along their development into separate systems.

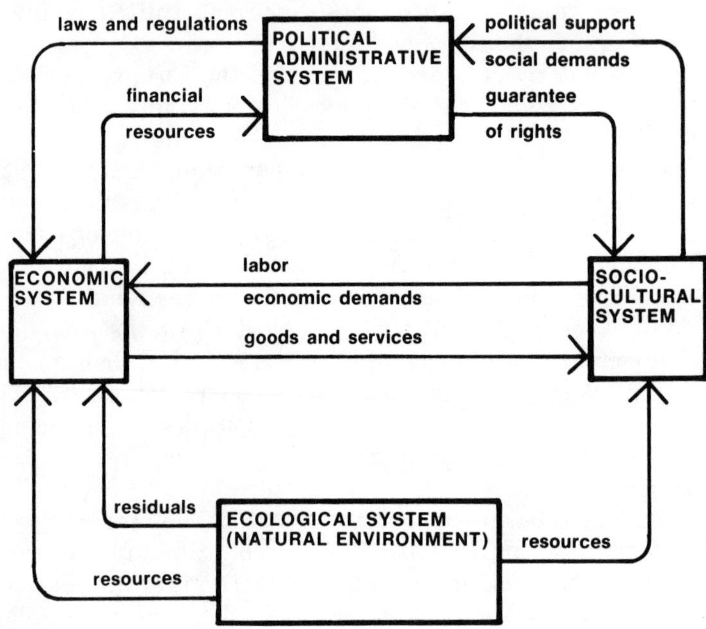

management, and of recycling and natural resource depletion. Under these assumptions, only a few quasi-absolute material limits to growth would remain for discussion, such as thermal limits, finite land area, and the economic cost of this "limitless" strategy. With constantly increasing energy and financial costs, the possibility must be considered that a point of energetic or economic "idling" would result. This would occur when any additional energy or economic input into the system had to be totally directed toward environmental control, in order not to violate the requirement of constant environmental quality. Henderson also points to this possibility of an "entropy state" in Chapter 6.

Our analysis shows that new devices and problems could conceivably be capable of allowing further material growth for at least the next generation or so in Switzerland, without further deterioration of the natural environment. The economic price of this could, however, be up to 10 percent of the GNP. Assuming society were willing to pay the price, the critical issue is whether the economic, sociocultural, and political system is capable of or willing to develop, apply, and pay for the necessary investments in pollution control in time. The character of the present crisis reflects the psychological reason behind society's unwillingness to attack the problem objectively. In contrast to other crises in history, which have been caused by visibly negative factors—such as plague and drought—the "cause" of the current crisis—material growth—is generally considered "good." It is obviously difficult to obtain the same cooperation and commitment in fighting something "good."

Apart from the question of willingness, the ability to deal with the problem must also be strongly questioned. For one reason, there is a time lag between initiating a harmful process—for example, releasing toxic chemicals into the environment—and recognizing the danger, and then further, identifying the causal factors. After identification, an additional lag exists in achieving the legal-political changes required to eliminate the harmful factor. For the case of DDT, the delays totaled more than thirty years. A second reason is the time required by nature to dissipate the toxin. The chemicals, all too readily applied, become locked in the trophic cycles, exerting their effects over generations. Thus, even if it were possible to apply the pollution controls in what seemed like adequate time, the momentum of the affected system might well prevent the measures from having the needed results in time. Previously, man's capacity to impact his environment was not comparable in magnitude to the assimilative capacities of the environment. Now, the magnitude of forces available to man are comparable to the forces of nature. Not only is his impact on the environment beyond his comprehension, but also the effects extend beyond the horizon of his active concern. He cannot really imagine the problems involved in the 24,000-year half-life of radioactive material. Also, because of the alienation created by the complexity of technological and bureaucratic structures and centralization of decision-making, he no longer feels actively responsible for his interference in the ecological system.

As the time horizon is extended to more than one generation, no one living now can prove whether or not the technological breakthrough strategy will be successful. A finite risk of not meeting the requirements remains, and this risk increases with the extension of the time horizon. In the long run, a finite probability, however small, of environmental catastrophe remains. *The decision whether to accept such a risk can no longer be based on a scientific basis alone.*

The decision involves unknown risks with extremely high values at stake. The decision is whether present generations would forego further material growth and thereby reduce risks for future generations. This is a moral and ethical question, not a scientific one.

Dynamics of the Economic System

Analysis of the dynamics of the economic system can help determine whether the thesis of self-saturation can be proved or refuted. Such an analysis is possible at the macro-level of a nation's economy and at the micro-level of the individual firm and employee. Basically the question is whether or not those forces which now coerce the socioeconomic system to material growth will automatically develop in such a way that a state of quantitative equilibrium, compatible with ecological constraints and social values, is approached.

Macro-level. At the macro-level, the historical analysis of the long-term evolution of all three subsystems shown in Figure 12–1 brings out their key determinants and major evolutionary steps. In simplified form, the overall conclusion of the analysis is that the mechanisms in the evolved economic macro-system do not stabilize the growth of its material throughput. Two factors imbue the system with an intrinsic tendency to overshoot its limits.

First, the continued process of concentration of production into ever larger, centrally-controlled units completely separates the producer from the consumer. Thus, the producer produces a good or a service not for a consumer, but for an anonymous market. He produces not because he recognizes a social need or value, but because he must produce in order to cover his financial outlays, capital costs, and wages. He will work to create the demand for his products, and he will demand more labor when he can make an economic profit from its use, even if society is impoverished in the process.

Planned technological obsolescence accelerates this process. Recently a computer firm in Zurich disposed of most of its office equipment related to punch cards because new data storage technologies had made it all obsolete. The most economical way for the company to get rid of each 200-kilogram, 1,000-franc steel file cabinet was to sell it for ten francs. Although only six or eight years old and in perfect condition, the equipment had become useless scrap to the economy. This waste is an outgrowth of technological "progress," increased productivity of labor, and decreased productivity of raw materials and energy. What does it concern the worker in the file cabinet industry that he produced for obsolescence? He will never know.

Because growth has led to the concentration of economic power, many economic entities are now large enough to exert substantial political power. This power can be used to nullify or circumvent the economic forces that economists expect will lead to orderly saturation of growth processes.

As an example, in the present phase of recession, perhaps some 30 percent of the capital equipment of the Swiss construction industry is idle. This causes capital losses to the enterprises. But rather than accepting a reduction in growth, the industry coerces the government to increase investment limits, which means new capital to revive this infinite process of: capital investment, production, technological progress and increased productivity, new capital investments, and thus new coercion for higher production. It is ironic, but under this coercion the Swiss government in early 1975 passed a bill which would free several hundred million francs to increase the production of housing units, at a time when Switzerland had a record high of unoccupied apartments. Could one find a better example to illustrate the systemic coercion to material growth in the economic system?

Switzerland's problems with foreign workers show how the pursuit of economic profits typically pushes growth beyond the point where governments can deal with the social side-effects. Yet, the government does not interfere to prevent these problems before they begin. During the boom period of the last decade, the limiting factor for the expansion of the Swiss economy was labor. Energy and capital were abundant. The rational decision of individual firms was to import labor in order to achieve higher growth rates and higher profits. The extent of the social problems and individual hardships provoked by this rapid expansion is becoming visible only now, some ten years later. Swiss industries wanted to import labor; they did not take into consideration that those who came were human beings. These people were put in lower standard housing and used for lower quality jobs than the Swiss. They were also restricted in changing jobs. Their children are disadvantaged at school because of language problems. They are not socially integrated and thus tend to form ghettos. In many cases they are separated from their families. All in all, this economic "progress" has led to one of the country's most severe social problems, and the burden has fallen on the government.

In addition to political forces, there is a second and crucial reason for the persistence of the material and capital growth process. That is, money has assumed a role as a production factor, a profound extension of its original use as a means of trade only. The historical development from traditional self-sufficient economies to modern economies, using capital as an important production factor, illustrates the dynamics of this system.

The advancement from the original hunting society to agrarian economies made possible the storage of harvests for times of need. Further developments in productivity of agricultural labor released a part of the labor forces to produce other items such as tools and clothing. These products could then be traded for surplus food from the agricultural sector. The process of division of labor had begun, but under conditions much unlike those of today. Surplus products from one sector were traded through a "natural," not a monetary market. However, the convenience of a universal, symbolic trading medium was soon recognized; money was introduced in the form of coins. But still the crucial threshold had not yet been passed. Money still functioned as a universal means of trade for all other products. It was not yet used as a production factor. Interest on capital did not yet exist.

This next step was introduced in the fifteenth century by the development of the trade between distant locations, for example between Europe and the Far East via sea. This necessitated a substantial time lag between buying and reselling a product such as linen or tea. As a result, someone had to pay for a product long before it could be productive or used. This time lag is a crucial factor in the whole analysis [3]; it was the origin of interest on money, and thus of the productive function of money. Currency no longer was saved merely for the purpose of trading it at later times for needed natural products. Instead capital was saved and accumulated as a production factor to secure more capital in the future. It was used for the financing of new capital facilities for the production of goods and services. This marked the origin of banking institutions and greatly facilitated the process of capital generation. Now, investments are no longer financed solely with savings, but they are prefinanced with credits, accelerating the open-ended process of capital generation, investment, and production.

Here we must point out the intimate relationship of this crucial threshold—that is, money itself becoming a productive factor—to the development of science and technology, the process of industrialization, continued division of labor, urbanization, and the concentration of capital and economic power. We do not mean to deny the social justification of the original objectives of this change in the role of money—namely, the liberation of man from the physical hardships of illness, hunger, and natural disasters—and by no means do we propose a "return to the middle ages." However, the very success of this development has blinded society; people do not realize that the process has begun to generate its own dynamics and has replaced goals with means. Technological, industrial, and economic development, the concomitant of material growth, have grown away from social objectives and control. From a societal standpoint, the process has proceeded into a state of overdevelopment; it no longer serves true human values and needs, but economic means. Therefore "progress" can no longer be considered progress.

Micro-level. The coercive forces to maintain growth in the microsystems are visible at the level of the individual enterprise, private and public. At least two major interrelated sources for these forces can be identified. First, there are external pressures; an enterprise must sell enough to cover its fixed and variable costs. Sociopolitical mechanisms continually increase labor costs, forcing the company to increase its sales. Because individual enterprises may realize substantial economies of scale, greater sales are in most cases sought by an increase in the volume of production as well as by an increase in productivity of labor. Because stockholders expect a maximum profit on their investments, they also exert a pressure to increase productivity and production volumes. The mechanisms of fixed-cost overhead and economies of scale foster the process of concentration of economic power through the fusion of enterprises.

Second, there are internal pressures; the management of large firms develops forces for material growth for reasons of career advancement and social status. Of course, the growth-seeking behavior and career selection criteria of organizations perpetuate each other. As a result, many firms actually are expanding at a higher than optimal rate. Their profits would thus be higher if their growth rates were lower [4, 5]. These firms are unwittingly substituting maximum growth rates for maximum profits.

Dynamics of the Sociocultural Subsystems

As shown in Figure 12–1, the original, interdependent societal system has gradually evolved into three decoupled subsystems—economic, sociocultural, and political-administrative. Their functional separation and the resulting necessity of their reintegration through new institutions, laws, and regulations are important factors in explaining the dynamics of the system and the generation of its problems. Previously, when the system functioned as a whole, the sociocultural domain had been able to perform its function of specifying and developing societal objectives. Its ability to fulfill human needs was a direct result of the proper functioning of an integrated system. Through the development of decoupled subsystems, the capacity to fulfill real human needs has been destroyed. Human fulfillment depends on a subtle balancing of disparate needs. But, it is essentially impossible to obtain an appropriate dynamic balance among the products of the three decoupled systems.

For example, the economic system has taken over more and more domains of human activity, but it satisfies socioeconomic demands based only on a purely economic rationale. This incomplete fulfillment creates new, surrogate desires, which, in time, develop into needs. Such artificial needs bring with them additional social costs and secondary problems that did not exist before. For example, specialization and division of labor has eliminated to a large extent well-balanced jobs, which combine physical labor, meaningful work, and a role in community functions. Specialized jobs often provide none of these desired characteristics. They induce new needs for recreational facilities, hobbies, clubs, as well as new transportation needs. Generally speaking, however, the threshold of each need is lower when all needs can be met simultaneously.

The uncoordinated fulfillment of the various needs fosters the attempt to compensate, but an unfulfilled need cannot really be balanced by the "overfulfillment" of another need. No amount of food or drink can really compensate for personal dissatisfaction; no salary can really make up for the dehumanizing effects of an assembly line job. Each compensation thus attempts to respond to a synthetic need or problem, but, at the same time, generates new problems and new needs. Specialization of labor and centralization of production have not only created problems and imbalanced the fulfillment for those working, but they have destroyed the cultural integration of older members of society. This is partially due to the type of work required of laborers today, and partially due to the increased mobility of the younger members. One symptom is the elimination of three-generation families. The older members, who as a result are no longer part of family or community structures, as well as the chronically ill or psychologically disturbed, who also cannot produce in the economic system, require social security, professional care, and institutionalization.

An alternative to such a solution is being proposed by a group of trained social workers in Switzerland. These workers, most of whom are unwilling to work in large automated institutions for disturbed children, would prefer to take two or three children into their own homes in order to provide them with the needed individual attention and continuing affection. In addition to providing real benefits to all concerned, their expenses per child are only one-fifth of the institutional costs, helping eliminate the need for such institutions.

At this time, such a solution seems unacceptable to Swiss authorities. In contrast, Sweden and Germany already officially support such a human solution.

The above-mentioned examples demonstrate various characteristic weaknesses of the societal mechanisms of problem solution; the existence of a problem is *a priori* accepted, and means and ways are then developed to abate or counteract the negative effects of the problem. Control mechanisms are devised to master the problem. Little consideration is given to the possibility that the problem should not exist in the first place. This altogether represents a positive feedback loop between solution rate and problem generation rate.

It can be empirically shown that strategies that aim at increasing the problem solution rates are prone to accelerating the whole process without decreasing the problem or crisis level. In addition, they follow a path of increased technocratic and professionalized, rather than democratic, societal decision-making. Individuals and social groups are less and less able to influence their own course of development. As a result, they become politically passive. They feel, subconsciously, that decisions affecting them are made at the top of large and complex technocratic, administrative, and international economic systems, and that their own influence steadily diminishes. Their understandable reaction is complacency, assuming that "the system" will cope with the problems around. As a result, small problems which would normally be handled at the local level remain unsolved, spreading into larger circles. With a certain time lag they reach enough proportions that they are "recognized" as problems, and measures for solving them are enacted. These measures, however, due to the inherent time lags, may no longer be effective enough in ameliorating the situation. The result is an increasing demand on technocratic decision-making, stemming from the artificially created problems, which would not even have arisen in a system allowing for participation and feedback at the level of problem initiation.

For example, the industrialization and centralization of agricultural production has eliminated the normally existing feedbacks between producer and consumer, and simultaneously subjected this sector to the dynamics of the economic sector. When farmers produced for the needs or wants of the community, the quantity and quality were to a large extent determined by this direct feedback. Even though the variety of products offered the consumer has increased, one must still question if he can obtain what he really wants. The situation is rather that he is convinced through large-scale advertising that what is available is what he wants, regardless of nutritional value, toxicity, or price.

In Switzerland, where veal is a prized specialty, the fashion has been toward producing a meat very light in color. The desired lightness is obtained by feeding the calves a diet deficient in iron. The calves, in a state of advanced anemia, are very susceptible to diseases, and must be fed large amounts of vitamins and antibiotics. Such chemical manipulation of livestock has led to the current situation in which 80 percent of the vitamin production is used by meat and egg producers. This regime is cruel to the animals and expensive to the farmers, but the consumer has been conditioned to want light meat. The farmers have attempted to alter the trend by informing the public of the animals' unhealthy state and of the chemicals fed them, of which residuals remain for human consumption. The farmers themselves, however, are coerced by the economic pressures. If they produce a rosy meat, they are paid less by the butchers' associations. As a result, they continue to produce only white meat. Those consumers aware of the situation cannot buy what they want. The others think they want what they buy.

Industrialization of the food industry is a self-perpetuating process. The increasingly mechanized treatment of food products has decreased their nutritional value, creating the "need" for vitamins and mineral supplements and therefore the "need" for the manufacture of such goods. The increased consumption of refined carbohydrates, which are essentially "empty calories" (calories without the vitamins or minerals required for their metabolism), places stress on the human body and is considered a major factor in the ever-increasing incidence of the diseases of civilization.

As previously mentioned, the decoupling of subsystems has complicated the information flow. Furthermore, the sectors of society and the economy no longer cooperate with each other for the overall welfare, but are in competition to the detriment of each part. Manipulation of information is one of the main weapons in this competition. Presentation of selected partial information often suffices for the creation of an advantageous position. This practice is acknowledged and accepted in advertising and in the presentation of political information. A financially strong interest group, such as industry or real estate, can win a vote on income tax or land tax reform with a campaign budget twenty times larger than the budget of the opposition. Penetrating advertising subtly convinces a majority of people to vote against their own interests.

A similar information problem exists in the educational system. Here, behind the myth of value neutrality of the official educational system, present social-value systems are perpetuated and the groundwork is often laid for uncritical acceptance of official information and values. Furthermore, the school system often serves as a forum for the presentation of selective information coming directly or indirectly from industry and presented as "educational material." For example, sugar, psychologically loaded in its role as a reward for positive behavior, is praised as an energy giver, but tooth decay, development of diabetes, and increased cardiovascular problems are not mentioned. The "Green Revolution" is praised for its success in increasing grain production, but there is no comment made on the short-lived efficacy of the endeavor. Pharmaceuticals are praised for their effectiveness, albeit very often over the short term, but no mention is made of side effects, of bacterial resistance, of mutagenic and teratological effects. Much less is any question raised whether the causes for drug "need" could be substantially eliminated.

Dynamics of the Political-Administrative Subsystem

The political-administrative subsystem of Switzerland has evolved in constant interaction with the economic and sociocultural system, as indicated in Figure 12–1. During this process, it has acquired the same basic characteristics as the other subsystems—specialization of functions and concentration of power in higher-level government agencies. These agencies have acquired a reactive philosophy of problem-solution by developing new technical control systems to counteract the effects of existing problems, rather than by eliminating the sources of problems. For example, reacting to the environmental pollution symptoms, the Swiss government has invested some twelve billion francs in waste water treatment systems, and probably less than 5 percent of this amount in reducing or eliminating the residuals generation at the sources [6]. The nationwide water treatment strategy is based on large central treatment plants. The problem of each citizen's and each industry's waste water is delegated to a new branch of specialists. They are paid indirectly by government taxes. Another feedback between a problem and the individuals causing it is thus eliminated by a new technical large-scale compensating system. It even goes so far that relatively new home sludge tanks must be eliminated when the central sewage plant goes into operation. The official reason is "otherwise the plant does not receive enough waste load. And besides no one can be expected to reliably empty his own tank on a regular basis, even out in the country!" [7]. No wonder, if the individual's sense of responsibility continues to be systematically undermined by technological "progress."

Figure 12–1 shows how the political subsystem receives inputs from and produces outputs to the economic, sociocultural, and environmental subsystems. Through this interdependence, it is subject to the same coercive forces toward material growth as well as toward methods of centralized problem-solution. The preponderances of expenditures over the last twenty years for the highway system as opposed, for example, to education are good examples. Further, the relative priorities within the education and research sectors support this thesis even more strongly: technical science and medicine receive more than 80 percent of funds. Human sciences, arts, tradework, and handicrafts receive negligible amounts. Technical universities produce, in accordance with the objectives of the economy, top quality specialists: chemists, physicists, engineers, and doctors. Why is medicine, for example, considered so important? Today, it represents another prime example of an artificial scientific-technological subsystem designed to correct the side effects of a problem existing somewhere else: to treat some 30,000 victims of car accidents per year, to cure cancers due to smoking, to get heart attack victims back to their managerial jobs as quickly as possible, to take care of alcoholics and drug addicts, or to undo psychological damages. To top it all off, international statistics measure the number of doctors and hospital beds each nation has, implying the more of them, the higher developed it is! And all these services, which essentially are designed to undo socioeconomic ills created elsewhere in the system, add to the GNP per capita!

Conclusions About the Societal Systems

At the present stage, we can summarize our findings as follows: first, a strategy of technological breakthroughs to mitigate growth in industrialized countries would be technologically possible for one or possibly even a few generations without degrading the natural environment further. Experience and empirical data show, however, that in reality there is always a time lag between occurrence, sociopolitical recognition of the deterioration, and the implementation of the necessary corrective measures. This undermines the success of this strategy. As for the longer-term future, nobody today can prove or disprove the feasibility of unlimited technological growth. Yet, it is already evident that ecological risks, unprecedented in kind and magnitude, are inherent in the present course of technological-economic development. Therefore, the decision whether or not to follow the strategies of technological breakthrough is a moral and ethical one, involving the assessment of these risks. This question cannot be resolved on a scientific basis only.

Next, the economic systems of all industrialized countries are subject to systematic forces which coerce them toward continued material growth. The fundamental driving functions are the separation of the producer from the consumer, and the role of capital as a production factor. These lead to a positive feedback between production, the need for new investments, and new material production. The resulting economic system cannot show self-saturation.

Finally, the fundamental dynamics of the societal system in industrialized countries is the result of an historical process. Originally the three subsystems—economic, political-administrative and sociocultural—formed one integrated whole, whereby the sociocultural domain clearly could perform its function of specifying and developing societal objectives. At present, the three subsystems are far along their development into separate systems. The objectives of science and technology have been directed toward material and economic growth. This has led to the substitution of labor by capital and energy (explored in detail by Hannon in Chapter 4) and thereby has driven the process of industrialization and division of labor. The latter in turn has led to the creation of more and more special services. Increasingly, the economic system has expanded into domains of the sociocultural system. The latter has lost in importance and stability. Human activities are governed increasingly by the rationales of economic and intellectual thinking, and decreasingly by the more subjective and effective mechanisms intrinsic to the sociocultural system, such as ethics, tradition, or religion.

The economic system, which should only provide the means for attaining social goals, has thus become itself goal-setting, dominating the sociocultural system. This must be recognized as a crucial point in a complex set of driving mechanisms which has produced the systematic coercions to material growth. By no means should this imply that the original objective of this process, namely the liberation of man from material hardships, was not socially desirable. However, it does imply that the process has acquired its own dynamics largely beyond the control of the sociocultural system, and has led to a state of overdevelopment which now perpetuates itself.

STRATEGIES FOR SOCIETAL DEVELOPMENT

We have found that one encounters the problem complex of growth, environment, and society at three distinct levels of cause and effect. At the first level, we perceive the problem as one of environmental quality and technological solutions to it. Soon we recognize, however, that this process is governed by the dynamics of the economic system. At this second level, it seems that constraining or rationing strategies, forcing the economic system to produce only within the ecologically feasible limits, would be necessary and sufficient to produce a system in equilibrium. However, such a constrained economic system would be incompatible with the evolved and existing societal value structures. This conflict leads us to the third and ultimate level—the social, political, and psychological issues.

What are ultimately necessary are strategies that eliminate the roots of coercion to material growth in the social, political, and economic systems, such that goal-seeking mechanisms compatible with long-term stability evolve from within. Thus, society faces the problem of reforming from the inside a closed system of which mankind itself is a part. The momentum inherent in aspects of the current system constitutes the major constraint in devising practical new strategies for system redesign.

Corresponding to the three distinct levels of the problem, the overall strategy would comprise measures at three different levels. At the first level, a balanced package of environmental control strategies would be designed to create immediate buffer room by extending the material limits to growth: technological and organizational pollution abatement procedures, recycling programs, supply-oriented energy strategies, and increased government efficiency in solving existing and new environmental problems are examples of possible schemes. To a large extent, most of these procedures are more or less like pain relief for a patient; they alleviate the symptoms of an illness without eliminating the causes. Therefore, these immediate buffers should only be supplementary to the more fundamental strategies within the economic and sociocultural system. At the second level, a set of constraining strategies would be developed, which could, if necessary, perform the function of an emergency barricade. Essentially, these are rationing-type strategies which would prevent the economic system from expanding beyond the ecological limits. For the most part they are intended to be applied only if the buffers should be exhausted before the fundamental strategies at the third level become effective. This final group of strategies is intended to eliminate gradually the forces that coerce growth and to develop new social objectives which are intrinsically compatible with physical limits and true human needs. Only from this level can a solution to the overall problem of material growth, environment, and society evolve. In the long run, evolution in this direction should essentially make the buffering and constraining strategies superfluous. The most basic and indispensible element in this strategy would be to redirect more social and economic responsibility to smaller, decentralized units, which operate on a basis of self-determination and cooperation with other units. Fewer functions would be delegated to large, centrally-controlled technical and administrative systems.

Buffering Strategies

There is no need in this paper to describe these strategies in detail because the existing system is equipped to develop them. For example, the Swiss government is preparing a fairly comprehensive Environmental Protection Act which foresees expanding and improving the existing programs for waste water treatment, for controlling traffic noise and air pollution, and for constructing waste incineration plants and sanitary landfills. This plan is necessary, but we have some reservations. First, the programs place too much emphasis on so-called end-of-pipe-measures—that is, treating and transforming generated residuals. As Daly also points out in Chapter 8, it would be more economical, though politically more difficult, to reduce residuals generation at the source. Too little use is made of the "polluter pays" principle. This principle is hailed in political campaigns, but all-too-seldom implemented after elections.

Second, we see a danger in the fact that the large-scale application of buffering strategies, by yielding temporary visible improvements in water and air, will mislead society into believing that the real solution has already been found. This could boomerang within a few decades. The rate of resource consumption, including energy, can also be markedly reduced by designing motor vehicles and equipment to be longer lasting, easily repaired, and readily recycled. However, without a basic change in attitudes toward the wasteful consumption of these products, the impending exhaustion of resources would be staved off by only some years. A similar point can be made about food production. One can make many suggestions leading to a marked and rapid reduction of the wasteful consumption of food, and energy for food production—decreases in meat consumption in the "overdeveloped" countries, or substitution of whole grain flours for refined flours, thus allowing more people to be fed more healthfully from the same amount of land. Again, this saving, without additional sociological changes, would yield basically only short-term benefits.

Third, the technological and administrative structure of the buffering strategies should help to open, not close, the options and potentials for the development of the basic therapeutic strategies for human and social development. For example, both the advancement of intermediate energy technology in small units in the 10- to 100-kilowatt range, as well as the construction of 500-megawatt nuclear parks, can be looked at as buffering strategies. Yet there are far-reaching differences in their long-range social impacts. From our point of view, the official Swiss policy, which calls for ten large nuclear plants by 1990 or 2000 and looks at solar energy as nice but without significance, must be considered counterproductive to reaching those social objectives which even the proponents of such an energy policy say they consider desirable. On the other hand, we have found a number of experiments in the right direction. Some industrial firms have developed concepts for energy and water savings, with savings in the 30 percent range. In at least one case, these conservation programs were not merely computed by experts and decreed by the board, but were developed in a mutual information and learning process with the employees. It was recognized how important the active participation of all concerned was, and that this participation could not be achieved by decrees.

Economic Constraining Strategies

Probably the single most important goal of the constraining strategies is to redirect the existing instrument of capital investment policy from growth-oriented objectives toward the basic human objectives we have presented here. Capital investment control is exercised today by the Swiss national bank and by the federal government. Traditionally, their financial policies benefited mainly those growth-oriented sectors: for example, highway construction and energy production facilities. The exceptions to growth policies were the urgent federal bills of 1973 designed to stabilize inflation. They placed limits on total capital investments financed by the banks, and decreed almost total construction bans for many regions. In the future it will be necessary to apply such capital investment policies to other areas: for example, energy, transportation, and land-use policy. Industry, in addition to its usual financial accounting, should be required to keep an ecological and resources-accounting system which can be used as a basis for environmental violation charges [8].

An energy policy should be adapted which concentrates on energy conservation measures and domestic renewable energy sources. Within a period of ten to fifteen years from now, total energy consumption should be stabilized at a level not higher than 15 to 20 percent more than today's. This would allow for the decrease in oil imports from 80 percent of total energy today to about 50 percent within fifteen years. An energy tax should be introduced. This would be differentiated by the degree of scarcity of the particular resources and the energy content of the consumed fuels. This tax would increase the prices of high value energy by 2 to 3 percent per year over the next twenty years. To minimize adverse social impacts due to this price increase, the basic energy needs of households—90 percent of today's consumption—would be guaranteed at normal prices on a per capita basis. This is administratively feasible. A larger share of the federal budget would go into conservation measures and technologies; into domestic renewable energy sources, especially solar; into daily and seasonal energy storage systems; and into public information campaigns for energy conservation. The fraction of GNP for energy investment should not be increased over the next ten to twenty years. These investments should be structured so that a technologically more decentralized system evolves, stressing solar energy, heat pumps, and combined heat and electricity generation.

This strategy would not necessarily, as has often been proposed, lead to unemployment. On the contrary, it would change the input factor prices of capital, energy, and labor in favor of the latter. The precondition is, however, that no abrupt and unplanned changes would be provoked, as was the case during the energy crisis of 1973–1974. Instead, the basis for a smooth and well-coordinated transition is created, first by eliminating the energy slacks in the economy, and then by steadily shifting the product output mix as well as slowing down or reversing the trend of substituting energy for labor. Our own work, as well as that of others, shows that this policy tends to increase, and not decrease, employment without affecting the material standard of living [9].

In the transportation sector, total expenditures, today some 20 percent of GNP, should increase at a rate no higher than half that of GNP. In addition, the ratio of investments between individual and collective transportation systems, today six to one, should be changed to four to one within five years and to three to one or two to one within fifteen years. A part of these investments should be used to maintain and improve the network of hiking trails, and to establish a network of bikeways in and between urban centers. It should be a national policy to decrease the number of working hours inside the economic system, at least to the extent that productivity increases, and to increase the number of hours each member of society devotes to social and civic tasks. Environmental impacts of transportation noise and pollution should be reduced to acceptable levels, and all social costs of the remaining effects should be internalized. This will lead to a 40 percent increase in the cost of truck transport, relative to rail for example.

The Swiss federal act on spatial and land-use planning should be passed. The act would have two important effects: first, it would define restricted zones for the stepwise realization of settlements, thus hindering their uncoordinated proliferation; and second, it would tax away a portion of unwarranted capital gains on zoned land. In addition, national policies dealing with land use, housing, and capital investment should redistribute investments from the large urban centers, especially Zurich, to surrounding smaller centers. Another desirable strategy would devise regulatory and incentive structures to foster renovation and reconstruction of existing buildings, rather than claiming farmlands for construction, and to foster methods of housing construction which allow for adaptation to changes in requirements for use. This would contribute substantially to reducing resource consumption. Most important, the total volume of building permits should be limited, such that in each ten-year interval, no more than 30 to 50 percent of the remaining reserves of zoned land may be used up.

A final constraining step would replace GNP per capita, currently misused internationally as a single indicator for economic and—who would believe it?—social progress, with a set of genuine social indicators. The GNP calculation should be revised; services that can be identified as being necessary to correct economic ills must be subtracted from, and not added to, the GNP. For example, end-of-pipe pollution abatement, many categories of transportation services, socioeconomic costs of traffic accidents, and health costs for heart attacks and other diseases of civilization all belong in this category. An immediate possibility to improve our information on how much true progress is made would be for the Swiss federal statistical agencies to develop and apply this concept unofficially and publish the results along with traditional GNP numbers.

Fundamental Social Strategies

These strategies are designed to foster the evolution of a harmonious societal system by dissolving intrinsic coercive forces for material growth from within the psychological, sociocultural, and economic systems. The principles on which this class of strategy is based are the following: first, restore a higher degree of self-determination, and thereby of social responsibility, to smaller, decentralized units working together on a cooperative basis, rather than being externally controlled by large economic and administrative systems; and second, restore the proper functioning of the sociocultural system as the goal-setting system. To this end, certain domains of human activity which are now governed by the rationale of the economic system must be reintegrated stepwise into the sociocultural systems: for example, care of the old and the disabled. A portion of the working potential of every adult should be withdrawn from the economic system and should be used to increase the strength of the family and other communities. This measure will help to restore the feedbacks among the now decoupled subsystems, and thereby increase the stability of the societal system as a whole.

What means are available to begin doing this? We view as an important beginning stepwise establishment of community networks in various forms, overlapping in function and membership. They constitute the vehicle by which members of a family, a commune, or a neighborhood can organize themselves to solve the usual problems of the group, such as taking care of the children of working women or men during the day, establishing a food market where local farmers sell their products directly to the consumer, establishing local hobby and repair centers, or taking on older or disabled members rather than sending them to a regional institution.

We recognize, however, the major difficulty. The present economic system will make it difficult for many a father to cut back his paid working hours, or for a wife and a husband each to have half a professional career so that each can devote part of his/her time to family and community life. First steps are possible, however. The individual firms could convert the benefits won by increased productivity into lowering the working hours required from the employee, rather than increasing salaries, especially for those in the higher brackets. Also, a smooth transition from full-time employment to retirement could replace the abrupt severance which is often a tragic event.

Some experiments in the right direction are working in Switzerland in food supply. In more communities, a square in the middle of town is again used for selling fresh produce from the local farms. Besides reestablishing direct contact between the producer and consumer, this practice eliminates a part of the energy-, transportation-, and capital-intensive infrastructure to truck the food to centers, store and refrigerate it, pack it, and then redistribute it with other trucks to automated, air-conditioned, anonymous supermarkets. Even though local markets may decrease the GNP, they contribute to the quality of life.

A more comprehensive experience in direct community participation has long produced financial and social benefits to the small mountain community of Fanas, Switzerland. Many collective responsibilities, normally performed by paid employees, such as painting of public buildings and cleaning streets, are divided among the residents in turn. As a result, local income taxes, upkeep, and repair are kept to a minimum. The direct participation develops a feeling of responsibility and respect toward community property. Experiments similar to this are also possible in urban communities in adapted forms.

In addition to these forms of grass roots community networks, community and civic services on a larger scale are also possible. In

Switzerland, every male citizen serves some three weeks per year in the military service. This principle can be generalized; every member of the community could devote a certain time of his life to civic services. Examples would be maintenance of hiking trails, maintenance of forests, collection of local waste, provision of social and health services, development work in maintaining communities, or emergency relief work in storm, flood, or earthquake areas. The practice of helping on farms should be revived. This would provide the farmer with needed extra help during harvest times and give children or students a chance to learn about the functioning of nature and the production of food.

The official social policies in health and old age care can, and must, be changed toward socially more intact and less expensive solutions. Government must encourage qualified families to take in socially damaged children, and must abandon its breakthrough strategy, based only on professionalized institutions. The latter eliminates the chance for the socially superior and economically less expensive solutions.

All these fundamental strategies must not only look for points of leverage at the macro levels—institutions or other social and political mechanisms—but also at the micro levels of the sociological-psychological situation of the individuals. Rather than trying to alter his external socioeconomic boundary conditions, the individual can gradually develop an awareness of what is really necessary and important. He then has an internal basis for his own standards, independent of trends, fashions, or what his neighbors do.

He thus liberates himself from external systematic coercions, which thereby become for him irrelevant and superfluous. We do not believe that there is only one single philosophy, spiritual or psychoanalytical theory, or religion which should be sold as a general theory for finding this satisfaction and happiness. The individual's own basic goals, plus his desire and initiative to follow them, are essential.

The process of making these fundamental strategies effective is necessarily a long one. The problems discussed here have been created as much by high rates of change as by the factors which have caused these changes. Thus, strategies aiming at the reconstruction of one harmonious, integrated societal system must proceed gradually if further instabilities are to be avoided. Their full effects might be apparent not within a few years, but only over decades or generations. Nevertheless, only working at this level of awareness is it possible to establish the fundamental conditions leading to a course of development consistent with human values and dignity. These values are the necessary and sufficient precondition as our economy becomes compatible with the physical limits to growth.

 *Chapter 13*

International Migration and World Stability

John Tanton

> The history of manking is strewn with habits, creeds, and dogmas that were essential in one age and disastrous in another—
> *James Reston* [1]

Continued population growth is now widely recognized as a major component of the social, economic, and environmental problems facing mankind, and there are mounting efforts to reduce the birth rates in many areas of the world. But population growth within any region depends not only on the difference between births and deaths; it is influenced by migration as well. Unfortunately, the causes and consequences of migration have been largely ignored by those interested in speeding the transition from growth-dominated systems to ones that may be indefinitely sustained. This omission is due in part to oversight. The emphasis on fertility reduction has crowded out concern for migration. The complexity of issues related to migratory rights is another impediment. Extensive federal law, legal precedence, administrative rulings, cultural traditions, and economic incentives govern the movement of people across national boundaries. Fear of criticism may well be another factor suppressing the discussion of international migration in many circles [2]. Immigration questions are often avoided as too sensitive or controversial. Though these constraints may be based on misconceptions or on factors that are no longer relevant, their effects linger on.

However, obstacles to discussing international migration must be overcome. The effects of migration are long run and cumulative, becoming apparent only after decades have passed. Davis and Mauch, for example, trace in Chapter 12 the delayed consequences of the Swiss policy decision to recruit foreign workers during times of economic boom. By the time such problems become severe enough to command general public recognition, the opportunity for preventative action has often long been lost.

The principal countries receiving immigrants—the United States, Canada, and Australia—are approaching their population limits. In time they will move to curtail immigration. Indeed, this process is already under way in Canada [3] and Australia [4]. In early 1976, New Zealand followed suit. If change is to come, it should be based upon thorough understanding of the causes and consequences of population movements. It is important to determine:

—the original purposes of international migration and the current validity of migration's original goals;

—the effects of emigration on the source and recipient nations;

—the degree to which migration affects world stability and order;

—the desirability of a rapid end to significant, international population movement.

In this paper I will discuss these issues, for those concerned with population and environmental problems must now begin to deal with them. Otherwise, a whole new set of problems will arise, and the achievement of population and material equilibrium will be significantly delayed.

HISTORICAL BACKGROUND AND DEMOGRAPHY

Man has been a migratory species as far back as human history can be traced [5]. In the earliest years men were hunters, and migration was often forced by depletion of the local resource base of game animals. With the development of agriculture, exhaustion of cultivated fields forced people to move in search of virgin land. As civilization advanced and cities were built, the dominant pattern of migration up through the 1700s was from less-developed to more-developed areas, and from the rural to the urban. Nor was all of this migration voluntary, for slavery was a common source of energy for developing civilizations.

These patterns persisted until the 1800s, when populations in Europe began to press hard upon the resource base and environment. Timber resources had been depleted. In Ireland, blight severely damaged the monoculture of potatoes upon which increasing populations had come to depend. Disaster was avoided or reduced as the less-developed world of that day—North and South America and Australia—opened to comparatively easy migration about 1850. Steamships came into use, increasing the speed of transoceanic voyages while reducing their difficulty and danger [6]. Excess people went abroad while food and other necessary resources were imported, lessening pressures in Europe.

The twin factors of "push" to leave home and "pull" of opportunity abroad served to reverse historic migration trends. People began migrating in massive numbers from the developed to the less-developed world. Between 1840 and 1930 at least 50 million persons emigrated from Europe. This trend of migration continued in pulses of varying strength through 1950, with recipient countries developing and in many cases surpassing countries of origin in their stage of development. In the past one hundred years, 25 million persons emigrated from Italy alone, a huge movement considering its present day population of 55 million.

Since the end of World War II, the flow of emigrants from the developed countries of northern Europe has gradually slowed. Between 1951 and 1955 about 2.8 million people migrated from Europe to Australia, New Zealand, Canada, the United States, South Africa, and Latin America. In the period from 1966 to 1970, that flow declined to 2.3 million people. The historic pattern of migration from less-developed to more-developed regions has returned. The poorer countries around the Mediterranean Sea and those of Latin America, Africa, and Asia are now supplying increasing numbers of migrants to the developed countries. From 1951 to 1955, 0.4 million people from these four areas migrated to Australia, Canada, and the United States. In the period from 1966 to 1970, the corresponding figure was 1.4 million [7]. Times have changed, however. This present-day migration must be viewed in the context of the massive populations and overpopulation of many sending and receiving countries. There are no remaining virgin continents waiting to be peopled or to have their resources exploited.

Since the end of World War II, there have been large intracontinental movements of people in Europe. More than 10 million "guest workers" have migrated from southern Europe and the Mediterranean area into northern Europe to participate in and facilitate the economic recovery that followed World War II [8, 9]. This influx has been most marked in Switzerland, where migrants currently make up about 30 percent of the work force [10].

In North America, the United States and Canada together received more than 7.5 million migrants between 1951 and 1970. The rate of migration to both countries has increased since 1970. The United States in 1975 had a population growth from natural increase, the excess of births over deaths, of about 1.2 million, supplemented by about 400,000 legal immigrants [11]. (Emigration is estimated at 37,000 yearly by the Bureau of the Census. No accurate data are available on numbers of people leaving the United States.) Legal immigration thus increased the United States population growth in 1975 about one-third over what it would otherwise have been.

In addition, a new phenomenon of the last decade—large-scale illegal immigration—adds an inaccurately known, though apparently large, number. Estimates range from 800,000 to 1 million or more persons yearly, most of whom come from a wide variety of less-developed countries [12]. Combining the net legal immigrants figure of about 400,000 with the lower estimate of 800,000 for illegal immigrants (about twice the number of legal immigrants), immigration currently about equals natural increase as a source of the United States' population growth. If these rates continue in a parallel trend to the turn of the century, immigrants plus their children born here will account for the addition of about 15 million for legal [13] and 30 million for illegal United States residents [14]. There is no way to calculate the latter figure accurately, as data are lacking on age and sex ratios and other parameters of the illegal alien population. According to the best estimates, however, this combined increase of 45 million people from immigration compares with a natural increase of 38 million by the year 2000 [15]. (All these projections assume families limited to an average of two children.)

International migration also played an important role between 1950 and 1970 in the population growth of countries and regions within Europe, North America, and Oceania. It has perpetuated population growth in the more developed countries, as the less developed countries export surplus people. The ratio of net migration to natural increase between 1950 and 1970 was +51 percent in Western Europe, −29 percent in Southern Europe, −21 percent in Eastern Europe, +2 percent in Scandinavia, −101 percent in Ireland, −5 percent in the United Kingdom, +19 percent in New Zealand, +65 percent in Australia, and +31 percent in Canada [16].

The United States' situation may be contrasted with that of its developing neighbor to the south. Mexico has about 59 million people and an annual growth rate of about 3.2 percent, which dictates a doubling time of twenty-two years. Forty-six percent of its population is under fifteen years of age [17], poised to enter a labor market in which unemployment and underemployment may be as high as 40 percent [18, 19]. Mexico's natural increase is 1.8 million persons per year—50 percent larger than that of the United States, which has nearly four times as large a population! Differentials in per capita gross national product across the border are perhaps seven to one [20]. This ratio of averages understates the comparison, for it fails to take into account that income distribution is generally more unequal in less-developed than in more-developed countries [21].

Mexico is a major source of illegal immigrants for the United States. The driving force behind the migration northward is the great disparity in employment opportunity and income between the two nations. This differential promises to increase with time, not so much from economic growth on the American side, as from a lack of economic growth on the Mexican side relative to its high rate of population growth.

Conditions similar to those in Mexico exist throughout the rest of Latin America, which as a whole had a 1975 population of about 324 million, a 2.7 percent annual growth rate, a doubling time of twenty-six years [22], and generally high unemployment and underemployment rates. Asia and Africa have similar situations. Obviously, a great storm is brewing. Any scenario for the future should take into account these massive pressures to migrate from less-developed to more-developed countries, whether legally or illegally. In the United States, extensive programs have been undertaken in an attempt to learn the numbers and characteristics of illegal aliens. But in setting policy and looking to the future, an understanding of the causes and trends of illegal migration is far more important than precisely enumerating illegal aliens at any one time. Studies of illegal migration should focus on causes as well as quantities.

Further data could be cited, but the discussion above adequately conveys the historical setting of the immigration dilemma and the numbers of people involved. The phenomenon of international migration touches many other aspects of life, and significantly affects prospects for achieving material equilibrium. How should these additional factors influence immigration policy?

EFFECTS ON COUNTRIES OF EMIGRATION

The sociological and economic analysis of international migration has focused heavily on the effects of immigration on the recipient country, and on the immigrant as a person. Effects on the country of origin and on the populace left behind have largely been ignored. The damaging effects of the "brain drain" have long been argued. The term originally applied to migration of highly skilled persons from the war-torn yet developed countries of Europe to North America. Despite the fact that an increasing proportion of migrants is coming from less-developed nations in Asia, Latin America, and Africa, the transfer of highly skilled persons has continued and even increased. Among immigrant workers coming to the United States, the percentage of professional and technical workers has steadily increased in recent years. It was 19.8 percent during 1961 to 1965, 24.6 percent for the period 1966 to 1968, and 29.6 percent between 1969 and 1972 [23]. The toll of this outflow on the economies of the source countries is exacerbated by the fact that the professional and technical worker immigrants to the United States come disproportionately from the less-developed countries. Of the 35,000 such workers admitted to the United States in the year ending June 30, 1974, 22,000 came from Asia, 1,400 came from Africa, and 1,400 from South America. All of Europe contributed only 6,400 [24].

This new form of the brain drain has a more profound effect. It is now developing nations that are losing not only some of their most talented citizens, but also scarce capital that has gone into their rearing and training. They also lose the very persons on whom campaigns of social and economic development must be based: those with highest expectations, greatest initiative, and most intelligence, and those most dissatisfied with conditions at home [25].

In particular, loss of physicians and nurses retards development of birth control programs in some less-developed countries. This conclusion was reached by a staff survey team of the United States House Foreign Affairs Committee. The team studied United States aid to population and family planning in Asia, and concluded that physicians and nurses are an essential ingredient in the development of effective national family planning programs. In Korea, the Philippines, and Thailand, a serious doctor shortage was found to be related, in part, to migration of physicians to the United States.

Data for fiscal year 1972 show the extent of the medical brain drain. In that year, American medical schools graduated 9,551 new doctors [26], and 7,143 physicians immigrated to this country. Of these, 1,513 came from India—a country with a population problem of some magnitude—and 782 came from the Philippines. During the period from 1966 to 1970, nearly 3,000 doctors immigrated to the United States from the Philippines, and another 525 came from Korea. The survey team observed:

> Rather than encouraging the increased immigration of doctors from the less-developed countries, the United States—if it is truly committed to

> limiting world population growth—should be working with less-developed countries to encourage their physicians to stay home and fulfill a crucial role in providing contraceptive services and information [27].

In the absence of such health workers, population growth continues, and development programs have an even more difficult time raising per capita incomes.

The educational systems in many less-developed countries date to colonial times. These systems were frequently patterned on Western models and were designed to meet the needs of the colonizing power. Natural inertia of human affairs has tended to keep such educational systems set in their traditional patterns, despite changes wrought by new nationhood and decades of population growth. In many cases, what less-developed nations lack is public health workers and dispensers of birth control, not physicians trained in esoteric Western medical specialties. The need is for agricultural engineers, not nuclear engineers.

Among other reasons, outmoded patterns of education have persisted because graduates could emigrate. If, however, the inappropriately-educated had been unable to find employment abroad, it seems likely their agitation at home for jobs would soon have produced educational reforms. The changes would be aimed at providing training in fields offering a prospect of employment, in skills that would necessarily be more appropriate to the country's level of development.

There is widespread discussion about the effect on the less-developed countries of exploitation of their material resources. Little concern is evidenced, however, about the exploitation of human resources—except in the less-developed countries themselves. Human resources are perhaps the scarcest and most valuable of all. The dollar value of the brain drain from some less-developed nations to the United States has exceeded American foreign aid to the same countries [28, 29]. This economic relationship has been dubbed "reverse" foreign aid. One United Nations publication termed it "a gift from the needy" [30]. One of the most effective forms of aid that developed nations could give to less-developed ones is simply to stop appropriating the latter's human resources.

The antithesis of the brain drain can be seen in the Selective Migration Programme of the Intergovernmental Committee for European Migration (ICEM). Established in 1951 to facilitate migration and resettlement of European refugees from World War II, the committee has since expanded its horizons. ICEM recognized the need to encourage migration of skilled persons from developed to less-developed countries, to help promote the recipient's growth and development. The program is centered on Latin America. In its first ten years, ICEM recruited, moved, and placed 12,811 migrants, including 514 university professors, and 3,628 teachers of other grades and instructors. ICEM calculates the capital investment required for training a middle-level technician at an average of some U.S. $20,000, and the dollar value of human resources transferred to Latin America during the life of this project at $260 million [31]. For contrast, note that during 1974 alone the United States bled Latin America of 4,689 professional and technical workers (ignoring the other three less-skilled categories) [32].

ICEM's migration policy is one which developed countries such as the United States could well emulate, supplanting current policies for transferring skilled persons to their own countries. It would do considerable international good, and at the same time would help find useful jobs for the oversupply of skilled persons found in some developed nations.

The policies of the developed nations which perpetuate the brain drain, whether so intended or not, serve to perpetuate the economic relationships of colonial times. The brain drain retards the development efforts of less-developed nations. Lack of development consigns them to their traditional roles as suppliers of raw materials and purchasers of manufactured goods. To the extent that less-developed nations are able to make economic progress, they will become the competitors of developed nations for raw materials and markets for manufactured goods. Pertinent to note here is that many of the top ministers of the Organization of Petroleum Exporting Countries were Western educated before returning home to work in highly effective ways for their own country's advantage. What if they had remained in the West?

Emigration also tends to remove persons of productive age, leaving behind the children and old people, further increasing the already high ratios of dependent to productive persons in less-developed countries [33]. This also tends to slow development efforts.

Traditional analysis holds that deleterious effects of the brain drain and worker migration are in part balanced by remittances from workers in developed nations. These remittances are viewed by some as a fairly effective form of foreign aid, since such money is instilled throughout the social structure. This view holds that foreign aid given to governments seldom finds its way down to the people.

However, developing nations dependent on remittances are doubly vulnerable to conditions in the developed countries. If, in the latter, growth declines and employment falls, foreign workers are often discharged. Less-developed countries lose not only remittances, but often get unemployed workers back home as well. Countries of southern Europe experienced just such a sequence of events from 1974 to 1976 with the economic turndown in northern Europe. The dynamics are similar whether the decline in the developed nations is unintended, as in Europe today, or planned, as in transition to a stationary state. Stationary state planners in countries with large foreign-worker populations will have to pay particular attention to such problems.

The value of remittances has been questioned by Jonathan Power in an excellent analysis of the costs of emigration to the country of origin [34]. Power contends that such monies are spent mainly on consumer goods, often imported, and not on financing development. In the end, trade deficits are increased, native agricultural systems are undermined, and the more enterprising families are lost to the economy of the less-developed country as they are attracted by emigration.

EFFECTS ON COUNTRIES OF IMMIGRATION

The brain drain and related migration phenomena also affect the recipient developed countries, and their prospects for attaining a stationary economic state.

Brain Drain Effects

Since World War II, the countries of immigration—the Statue of Liberty's pronouncement notwithstanding—have actively sought out skilled persons across the world as immigrants. The clear and continuing purpose has been to stimulate and facilitate their own economic growth and development. The basic United States immigration law gives an example of this intent. The 1952 McCarran-Walter Immigration Act set aside 50 percent of all visas for those in professions who would "substantially benefit prospectively the national economy, cultural interests, or welfare of the U.S." [35]. The Act makes no mention of concern for effects on the country of origin. Without question the infusion of highly-skilled persons has been an effective economic stimulant [36, 37], just as a ready supply of inexpensive labor provided by earlier immigrations was an essential factor in industrial growth.

I have already mentioned that international migration raises the ratio of dependent to productive persons in sending nations. In recipient nations, the converse holds: dependency ratios fall. The recipient country gains highly motivated, ambitious, and hard-working persons whose goal is personal economic growth. These factors all encourage further national economic growth.

On the pathway to stabilized world material consumption, developed nations must not only restrain their demands on world resources, but also make some provision for reducing income disparities between countries. In part this means improving living conditions of the world's poor. The international migration of skilled persons has tended to widen the gap between the less-developed and more-developed countries. Ending this transfer of skills would move us toward a more stable and less disparate world, a goal that should take precedence over short-term economic objectives.

A flow of highly trained immigrants can mask a need to develop and encourage domestic talents—for example, in the medical field. Although medical schools have been steadily expanding enrollments, nearly 50 percent of the Unites States' demand for doctors in recent years has been met by immigrants trained abroad. It appears that without the availability of these foreign doctors, medical schools would have been under greater pressure to increase enrollments and provide more educational opportunities for all Americans, particularly minorities and women. In the early 1970s, there were more Filipino than black doctors practicing in the United States, showing the inequities that can arise [38].

Developed countries have encouraged the immigration of skilled persons because of a misconception about where their interests lie. They have asked what is good for themselves as a recipient country, ignoring effects on the country of origin and on the world as a whole. Further, the analysis has been short range. Should an evaluation of purse snatching end with determination of advantages for the thief, ignoring effects of the victim? There must be a new, broader, and worldwide view of what is good for the developed countries. It is necessary to look not only at short-term advantages, but also at the long-term price that will be exacted for further increases in economic disparity between countries: greater world instability. Immigration policy should be integrated into this new world view.

Illegal Immigration

Illegal immigration is partially a by-product of the brain drain. Increasing economic disparity between nations is a chief impetus to illegal immigration, and the brain drain contributes to this disparity. A measure of retribution is in prospect, however. Several of the steps that may be needed to control illegal migration promise to affect very directly some of the developed countries' most cherished liberties and freedoms. These steps may well include such Orwellian measures as increased restrictions on movements across international borders, more vigorous efforts to detect illegal aliens once in the country, and requirements that everyone carry an identity card to establish his right to social benefits, a job, and residence. In this way, inhabitants of developed countries will be directly affected by the rampant population growth and the dire economic straits of many less-developed nations.

Resource Effects

Immigration helps to perpetuate population and economic growth in the developed nations, which, in turn, will increase their draw on world resources. The opposite trend is needed. Additional population growth in food-exporting countries—whether from natural increase or immigration—will likely result in more urbanization of agricultural land, decreasing the capacity to produce food. Concurrently, the exporter's own food requirements will increase. Taken together these changes will decrease food available for export. Here it is interesting to note how closely a list of major food-exporting nations coincides with those still receiving immigrants: the United States, Canada, Argentina, Australia, New Zealand. What will happen if populations in these fortunate nations grow until their food-exporting capacity is overtaken by domestic needs? Whose interests would such a turn of events serve? The whole cannot exceed the sum of its parts. If certain regions of the world are overpopulated and food-deficient, others must remain "underpopulated" (a relative term) and have a food surplus for export, or the whole world will be food-deficient. For reasons already stated, the massive movement of persons from food-deficient to food-sufficient regions is not a solution, as some have proposed.

The Demographic Implications

The demographic implications of continued immigration for developed nations were outlined in the historical section above, using the United States as an example. The estimates I presented for population increase from immigration are probably understated, for the results I cited assumed replacement levels of fertility for all groups. But more than half of America's legal immigrants now come from less-developed countries [39], as do nearly all illegal immigrants, and migrants from less-developed countries may well bring traditionally high fertility patterns with them. If they do, they will account for an even greater proportion of United States population growth than projected above. To the extent that averted births are replaced by immigrants, developed countries lose the benefits of their citizens' declining fertility. Those Americans who have consciously decided not to have children will find their decision nullified by this country's immigration policies.

Socioeconomic Problems

In the United States, the bulk of post-World War II "baby boom" children are entering their twenties and the job market; the peak year for births was 1957. To accommodate this influx of potential workers, the United States must create two million additional jobs each year between 1975 and 1980, and 1.5 million yearly after that date [40]. Whether the economic system can meet so severe a test remains to be seen, especially given the depressed conditions and unemployment at the outset. Legal immigration aggravates these employment problems, since the average immigrant is in his early twenties [41] and is likely to be economically active within two years of entry [42].

Careful economic analysis would be needed to quantify the value to a developed country of inputs of cheap foreign labor. In the United States, if estimates of several million illegal workers out of a labor force of about 80 million are correct, the effect may be significant. In countries of northern and western Europe, where foreign workers make up as much as 30 percent of the work force [43], effects are clearly substantial. In Europe, most of these "guest workers" are legally in the host country, but are usually not allowed to become citizens. Commonly, they must return home after a period of work, a move enforced by host countries to help prevent guest workers from becoming too established. The effect of foreign workers on the economy of a developed country depends somewhat on their legal status, for illegal aliens are more subject to exploitation than are legal residents.

Illegal immigrants tend to take jobs at the bottom of the socioeconomic scale in restaurants and hotels, in agricultural labor, or as domestic employees. Without this input of inexpensive labor, developed countries would have to choose between improving pay and working conditions of such jobs to attract domestic workers, or going without. The former course would tend to level incomes; the latter would decrease consumption. Either course, or both, would be desirable en route to a stationary state. As Herman Daly has pointed out, "The rich only ride their horses—they do not clean, comb, curry, saddle, and feed them, nor do they clean the stables" [44]. Without someone to carry out such servile tasks, consumption is perforce limited by lack of time, for individuals must do their own maintenance work.

Preferences doubtless vary, but I opt for a society in which individuals do at least some of their own maintenance work and accept resultant lower levels of consumption. I view such a society as ethically, and physically, more healthy than one which relies on poorly paid service workers, whether domestic or foreign, to maintain its standard of living.

As a result of their taking jobs at the bottom of the socioeconomic scale, illegal migrants compete for jobs with the most disadvantaged and underemployed sectors of American society: minorities and teenagers, and minority teenagers in particular. This competition dims chances for improving the lot of these hard-pressed segments of society.

Immigrants tend to concentrate in urban areas, where their jobs and relatives are found. For the United States, assuming replacement levels of fertility for both the population resident in 1970 and immigrants arriving after that date, the Commission on Population Growth and the American Future projected that legal immigrants and their descendants would account for about 23 percent of all urban population growth between 1970 and 2000. Any illegal immigrants must be added to this. Hence immigration adds to already massive urban problems, affecting in particular those states and cities on the borders and seacoasts where immigrants are most apt to congregate. Two-thirds of recent immigrants intended to settle in six states: New York, California, New Jersey, Illinois, Texas, and Massachusetts [45].

In developed countries, achievement of material equilibrium and many of the emerging goals for environmental quality will require a great unanimity of values and purposes. Such agreement is just now showing signs of emerging. Will immigrants who migrate looking for personal economic growth share these new values and purposes? Any language barriers will increase difficulties engendered by cultural and economic differences. As in developed countries in their early stages and developing countries today, the ethic of environmental quality and the pursuit of a stable state will doubtless place a poor second to economic growth.

THE WORLDWIDE PERSPECTIVE AND SOME ETHICAL DILEMMAS

Kingsley Davis argues that countries that export a large proportion of their excess populations postpone inevitable changes in birth or death rates which would make such emigration unnecessary [46]. He cites comparative data to show that European countries with the highest rates of emigration postponed longest the reduction of their birth rates. If Ireland had experienced no emigration, and had still exhibited the birth and death rates it actually attained, its population today would be nearly 12 million, not 3 million. For Europe as a whole, the comparable figure without emigration would be 1.08 billion in 1970, rather than 650 million. Hence emigration appears to allow continued world population growth which might otherwise be avoided.

In the special case of Italy, it is interesting to speculate on whether Roman Catholic attitudes on birth control would have changed if emigration had not relieved its population pressures. In Mexico and the Philippines, to name two countries hard pressed by population problems, Roman Catholic bishops have changed their stance and now support birth control. If Italian population pressures, unrelieved by emigration, had brought about such changes in general Catholic doctrine several decades ago, it could have appreciably lessened opposition in countries such as the United States to fertility research and programs providing birth control, both domestically and through foreign aid programs. An earlier start on contraceptive programs could well have ameliorated population problems confronting many nations today.

International migration contributes to increasing world consumption by transferring people from less to more consumptive life-styles, the major impetus to migration being hope for an improved economic situation. But what today's world needs is a reduction of excessive and wasteful life-styles, not the opposite. Resources required to support the migrant in his new, more affluent life-style could support many more of his former countrymen in their less-materially intensive way of life [47].

As society approaches the stationary state, turnover for people as well as material goods should be minimized. For material goods, consumption can be reduced as durability is improved. For people, the goal is also durability: long life expectancy and low mortality rates. This in turn requires low levels of births equal to deaths, on the average. I believe stability also implies minimal turnover in a population from migration, with low levels of immigration approximating levels of emigration.

The world population problem is too large for solution by mass international migration. Kingsley Davis points out that if developed nations took in the annual growth of the less-developed nations, they would have to accommodate 53 million persons yearly. Then, the developed nations would have an annual growth rate of 6.3 percent, and a doubling time of eleven years [48], clearly an impossible situation. The main avenue open for developed nations to help their less-developed brethren is to restrain their own resource consumption by controlling domestic population and economic growth, and to help apply some of the resources so conserved to solution of problems facing less-developed nations.

Refugees

Refugees make up a very small part of world migratory movements, despite the prominent role they play in the lore of migration. For example, only 2.5 percent of United States immigrant visas go to refugees, though special programs have admitted additional refugees, such as those from Hungary, Cuba, and Vietnam. The refugee problem is simply too large for solution by international migration. Worldwide, there are more than 14 million refugees and orphans, according to the U.S. Committee on Refugees [49]. Admitting refugees may even be counterproductive to finding solutions to refugee problems. Receiving a token number of refugees may well assuage consciences and blunt the search by recipient nations for solutions to those problems that cause refugee movements. There is also the problem of definition. Should refugees be defined only as victims of racial, religious or ideological persecution? (The United States Immigration and Nationality Act even more narrowly defines political refugees as persons fleeing from: (1) any Communist-dominated country or area; or (2) any country within the general area of the Middle East [50].) Or should victims of natural disaster and those seeking a higher standard of living also be included? If the latter, their number would swell to billions.

Among all immigrants, refugees are most in need of a new start in life. Admission of victims of persecution is the one truly humanitarian portion of United States immigration policy. This practice should be continued on its present scale, and could even be increased both in absolute numbers and as a proportion of all immigration, while overall immigration is pared by dropping less-deserving categories. In my opinion, admission of refugees should become the cornerstone of American immigration policy and should be emphasized in issuing whatever visas are available.

Control

Who has responsibility to regulate migration? As holders of the "trump cards" of jobs, money, and prestige, developed nations obviously have *de facto* control. The United Nations Universal Declaration on Human Rights clearly sets forth emigration as a basic human right, not to be abridged by any signatory nation, stating in Article

13, Section 2: "Everyone has the right to leave any country, including his own, and to return to his country." There is no right of immigration stated in the United Nations Declaration, nor in international law. The admission of immigrants is at the option of each country. Ethically, the onus for controlling migration seems to fall squarely on receiving nations. For skilled persons in particular if developed nations will not restrict flows, less-developed nations will of necessity resort to restricted emigration, surely less to be preferred than controlling immigration. Pakistan has already done so [51]. One can ethically and logically favor policies of open emigration and limited immigration, just as one can argue for freedom to leave one's own or another's home, while recognizing limited rights to enter another's domicile. Note that this position is compatible with the United Nations' Declaration cited above.

The Fortress Nation Concept

The objection has been raised that restriction of immigration is a retreat from internationalism, to a "fortress" concept where each nation attempts to fortify itself against external problems. An alternative view recognizes that no nation can address its problems if it cannot circumscribe them. In the absence of world government, a unified and peaceful world will more likely flow from individual people and nations making necessary changes until the process has spread throughout the world, rather than from waiting until all are prepared to change simultaneously. If individual nations cannot delimit and solve their own problems, then there is little hope that solutions to world problems can be found.

Nepotism

The United States, Canada, and Australia strongly emphasize family ties in their immigration systems. Prospective immigrants who are related to persons already admitted receive special consideration. The United States assigns 74 percent of its preference system visas to relatives of past immigrants. In addition, many other relatives enter outside of ceilings.

Put yourself in the place of two similarly qualified applicants for a United States immigration visa, the first with relatives already in this country, the second without such connections. The first applicant gets a visa because of the family ties; the second either must wait longer for a visa or fails to obtain one at all. The message: it is not what you know, but who you know—or more damaging yet, who you're related to—that makes the difference. Anyone can attempt to widen the scope of his knowledge, or expand his circle of acquaintances. But it is no more possible to change one's relatives than the color of one's skin. People should not be judged by their birthmarks.

In other areas of human activity, such as college admissions or appointments to government posts, nepotism is clearly unacceptable. Is such favoritism a legitimate framework for an immigration policy? I think not. In my opinion, special preferences for relatives should not extend beyond the immediate family unit of the immigrant: the spouse, parents, minor sons and daughters, and dependent minor brothers and sisters of the immigrant. One concerned group, Zero Population Growth, offers suggestion about such changes in United States immigration laws, policies, and practices [52].

The Melting Pot

In a word, the melting pot is a myth. The phrase comes from an otherwise forgotten play of the early 1900s [53]. It was once thought to describe a process by which a new homogeneous American race was being forged out of its varied peoples. While there has been mixing of some ethnic groups, many have maintained separate identities. A resurgence of ethnicity in the 1970s indicates this separatism will continue awhile longer, and may even increase. Much has been written recently on the breakdown of the melting pot concept [54].

Arbitrary Ceilings

The present ceilings on United States immigration numbers are the result of historical accident and legislative compromise. Limits on Eastern Hemisphere migration were set in 1924 at 164,667 [55]. This highly specific number resulted from legislative compromise over the percentage by which various ethnic population groups were to be multiplied to give the quota. There was further compromise over whether to use the ethnic count of the census of 1890, 1910 or 1920, each of which was employed at various times [56, 57]. Later compromise rounded the number off to 170,000. Western Hemisphere ceilings were first set in 1965, largely at the insistence of Senator Sam Irvin. He felt "that everybody from the Western Hemisphere might suddenly decide to move to the United States, and thus flood our country with immigrants which we could not assimilate for many generations. This was what prompted me to offer my amendment [to establish a Western Hemisphere ceiling.]" [58]. Western Hemisphere immigration in 1965 was running at about 112,000 yearly without numeric controls; a ceiling of 120,000 yearly was simply picked as an easy, round, and somewhat large number.

Neither hemispheric ceiling was set with any view of its population, resource, or environmental implications. Since the Eastern Hemisphere ceiling was chosen, the United States has increased its population by 100 million, consumed many of its resources, and seen other vast changes. Surely the suitability of limits set in such an arbitrary fashion should be reexamined from time to time in light of new understandings and changing conditions.

The Statue of Liberty

The United States has long promoted itself as a nation of immigrants. As the representation of this immigrant heritage, the Statue of Liberty has become one (if not *the*) predominant symbol of the country. The question goes: how could such a nation now consider further limits on immigration? Upon reflection, one realizes that the United States differs from many other nations only in the recency of its immigration phase. England was composed from the stock of many invading tribes. Germany and other European nations have similarly variegated backgrounds. At the height of Italy's power some two millennia ago, Caesar observed that "all roads lead to Rome." Those roads carried immigrants, both slave and free, from all corners of the ancient world. Through the generations they have become the Italians of today. So immigrant origins do not distinguish the United States from other nations. Rather, the challenge would be to find a nation anywhere that does not have immigrant roots. Even the native American Indians are immigrants, though from a considerably earlier era than most Americans.

Upon further reflection, one notices that many nations entered a period of emigration following their immigration phase. The three countries mentioned above are prime examples. One could even postulate a sequence in the development of nations running generally from a phase of immigration and population growth accompanied by resource exploitation and economic growth, to a period of overpopulation, resource depletion, and economic stagnation, followed by a stage of emigration, resource dependency, and economic decline. It seems most unlikely that the United States will ever experience large-scale emigration, for there are simply no virgin continents awaiting immigrants. Rather, a new pattern in the evolution of nations seems likely to develop, in which the emigration and resource dependency stage must of necessity be replaced by one in which population and resource consumption stabilize, and economic systems adapt to these new and challenging conditions.

If the United States brings to a close its immigration phase, the country will not be turning its back on its history or the proud traditions symbolized by the Statue of Liberty. Rather, it will simply be following many other nations in a development pattern which passes beyond the immigration phase. A significant question is: how far into overpopulation and resource depletion must the country go before appreciating her plight and making the inevitable transitions?

The Statue of Liberty is such a powerful symbol of opportunity and freedom that its mere mention tends (and is often used) to close off discussion of immigration limits. Such a short-sighted response is unproductive and unworthy of American traditions, and should not be allowed to stand in the way of a full consideration of the implications of immigration.

Diversity

In the past the continued infusion of new people has added variety and diversity to American society. Few would argue against these two healthy characteristics of social and biological systems. It is a paradox, but it is nonetheless true, that while legal immigration today is a major factor in United States population growth, it can no longer have much influence on the ethnic composition of its populace. This is due to the already massive size of the United States population, about 215 million in 1975. Admission of 400,000 legal immigrants per year is a drop in this huge ethnic bucket—less than 0.2 percent of the total population yearly. It would take a truly massive immigration to have significant effect on the racial composition of this fourth most populous nation of the world. For better or worse, our past immigrations have largely set our character. Further, the American system of issuing visas based on family relationship helps assure that new immigrants are generally of the same stock as those already here. In any event, the United States need not feel compromised on the question of diversity, for its people are already among the most varied on earth.

If diversity has advantages, it has limits as well, particularly in the area of communication. One of the blessings history bestowed on the United States was fairly easy communication through a common language, although there have always been many Americans with a second tongue at their disposal. As part of the resurgence of ethnicity in the 1970s, a strong movement sprang up to provide in minority languages many of life's communication necessities such as voting ballots, government publications, court proceedings, and education. I judge this a just and socially useful movement, but only as long as part of the goal is to develop a working knowledge of English along with the second language. Care must be taken that the goal of bilingual programs does not evolve into one of making people competent in some language instead of English. Such a change could create new or expand existing enclaves where English is not understood, and in which people cannot communicate readily with other Americans. This would be diversity of a damaging sort, for if people cannot communicate directly with one another, difficulty in solving problems will increase by several orders of magnitude.

Anyone who sees a straw man in this argument should acquaint himself with bilingualism in Canada, where both French and English were recently declared official languages. Most federal employees, both new and current, must now become bilingual to a prescribed level in order to keep their jobs. Those deficient in either tongue may take up to a year away from their work to reach the required language proficiency, while the government pays their salary and training expenses. Debates in the House of Commons may be in either language, though simultaneous translation is provided. Debates are translated and then published in both languages. All government documents for public distribution are printed in both languages. One can imagine the confusion and expense that would ensue if those United States congressmen with a second language began to use it on the floor of the House of Representatives, and if demands were made for routine translations of the *Congressional Record* and many other government documents into a variety of minority languages.

Accidents of history, the separatist movement in Quebec, and other factors that need not concern us here made bilingualism politically unavoidable in Canada. Canadians have no Equal Protection Clause in their equivalent of our Constitution. This is fortunate, for, to use one example, the country's 800,000 Italians, 4 percent of the population, cannot demand equal treatment for their language. The mind boggles at the chaos that would result if additional languages were to receive official status.

The 1975 extension of the United States Voting Rights Act of 1965 required that ballots be provided in any language used by more than 5 percent of the voters in any district. The city of San Francisco will now have to print ballots, voter pamphlets, and other election materials in English, Spanish, Chinese, Korean, and Tagalog (Filipino), and possibly Japanese as well [59].

The point is twofold. First, I believe that the United States has unwisely allowed its varied linguistic background to lead towards the adoption of multiple official languages. This political error should be promptly corrected, and English should be formally declared the official language. (We should at the same time, however, reaffirm our commitment to the encouragement of second language teaching.) A knowledge of English should continue to be required for naturalized citizenship, at least to a proficiency that will allow voting. Whether this is possible under the Equal Protection Clause of the United States Constitution is an open question. Second, most language problems facing the United States can be traced almost entirely to continued high levels of immigration, both legal and illegal, among non-English-speaking people, and to the concentration of these immigrants in ethnic neighborhoods. While further restriction of immigration is justified for other reasons, the communication problem itself is a strong reason to consider such a policy.

CONCLUSIONS

The time has come to take a fresh look at international migration in light of new needs to slow, rather than stimulate, population and economic growth in developed nations, and a continuing need to assist efforts of less-developed countries to raise their standard of living. Current migration policy hinders the achievement of both goals and stimulates overall world population growth as well.

Portions of the globe that deal most effectively with their population and environmental problems will stabilize sooner than other regions. The attractiveness of stabilizing regions will increase relative to jurisdictions that are making less progress, or are even slipping backwards. Increasing disparity in attractiveness will generate pressures for international migration which, if allowed, will tend to destabilize regions otherwise approaching equilibrium conditions. Consequently, international migration will need to be stringently controlled, or no region will be able to stabilize. If no region can stabilize until all do so together, then there is little prospect that the world will ever achieve stability in an orderly and humane fashion, or at a level above subsistence. The lowest common denominator will prevail. Given existing population and economic contrasts between more- and less-developed countries, control of international migration will be among the chief problems confronting all nations during the transition to equilibrium conditions.

Immigration doubtless remains good for the vast majority of the migrants themselves. They find new economic opportunities and, in the special case of refugees, new freedoms. In the main, however, international migration now runs counter to the long-range interests of countries of origin, recipient countries, and the world as a whole. This generalization remains true whether analysis is conducted by those pursuing economic growth or by those interested in a stable state. What first appears as a new conflict between individual freedoms and the interests of society is in reality a conflict between the interests of individuals who migrate and those who do not. I believe precedence should now go to the larger and longer-range interests of the mass of people who will never be able to migrate, rather than to a select few who can. More weight must be given to the plight of unseen countrymen the emigrant leaves behind to live with conditions the emigrant might have helped to change. Future historians may well record that such a broadened examination of the effects of international migration was a major factor which led to the close of the era of large-scale movements of people between countries.

The question now faced is not whether immigration should be restricted. It has been restricted for decades in all countries. Nor is there any serious proposal to end immigration altogether. Rather, the question is: what restrictions are appropriate in today's world? Further, can present arbitrary limits be replaced by rational ones sensitive to population, resource, environmental, and other factors seldom considered before in setting immigration policy?

Fortunately, this essay can end on an encouraging note. One can envision a world in which international migration could become free and unfettered. Appropriately, it is the world of a stable state, one in which people of different nations and regions are in equilibrium with their resources and have, as a result, a reasonable chance for self-fulfillment and social equity in their home area. Under such conditions, international migration could be unfettered, for there would be little incentive to move. Contentment with conditions at home, coupled with man's strong attachment to things familiar, would provide all the control necessary. While freedom to migrate at will is incompatible with the realities of today's world, such freedom can one day be realized if man achieves a balance with his environment.

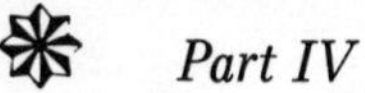

Life-styles and Social Norms for a Sustainable State

Introduction to Part IV

Dennis L. Meadows

> Those who question mindless growth wish to choose new strains from today's seedbed of future images. They wish to explore ways to nurture certain seeds so that they will capture the minds of the late twentieth century and produce behavioral sequences that will lead society into a twenty-first century existence that expands human capacities and respects physical constraints.
>
> *Elise Boulding*—Chapter 15

The human nervous and muscular systems provide the potential for an infinite variety of personal sensations, conceptions, and actions. But if this entire array were ever manifested in one social setting, it would bring instant chaos. Technological advance, economic activity, interpersonal communication, and justice are among many essential aspects of society that can be attained only when individuals can be depended upon to follow a very narrow set of actions under specific circumstances. Becoming civilized is thus importantly a process of simplifying the range of human perceptions, interpretations, and acts to a small set that will be shared by all members of a society and that will facilitate satisfaction of their basic physical and psychological needs.

The process of simplification is built in at many levels. The nervous system itself contains filters that prevent most sensations from ever reaching the brain. Every language structures the process of conceptualization to emphasize some interpretations and to make others impossible. Even the repertory of thoughts and acts possible within one language is limited by adoption of conceptual structures, or paradigms, that aid in interrelating information, assist in identifying problems, help in assigning priorities among conflicting calls to action, and facilitate the identification of appropriate responses. Social norms further limit possible responses by creating mutual expectations regarding interpersonal behavior. Religion with its ethical precepts and the law with its formal sanctions both provide constraints by identifying appropriate goals and acceptable behavior.

Each of these psycho-physical and social factors is essential in fashioning an effective, internally-consistent, mutually beneficial set of relationships among the members of a society. Of course, the precise design of a useful norm can and does differ very widely among societies. Headhunting was part of a sustainable society for millenia in some regions; it would precipitate substantial disruption if pursued by a significant minority in any Western culture. It is only necessary that in each semi-distinct society the set of goals, norms, institutions, and human capacities be internally consistent and produce social and economic activities which can be sustained by the environment over the long term.

When mankind was divided into small groups whose members were in close touch with each other and with their natural environment, there was a rich web of feedback relationships that could reinforce the members' beneficial perceptions and actions and discriminate against those that did not foster long-term survival. This feedback permitted the perceptual and behavioral repertory of each social system to evolve and develop while remaining in balance with its slowly changing environment. Now, however, social units are so large that most members are emotionally isolated from each other; technological advance has separated people economically and physically from each other and from the natural world. The result is a loss of feedback and decreased learning potential. Perceptions and behaviors evolve in isolation from one another according to their own, short-term, internal logic. They become mutually inconsistent. Norms such as those favoring high human fertility or the violent resolution of conflict persist in an environment that can no longer accommodate their consequences without producing disaster. The adaptive capacity of society is reduced. In a period of rapid environmental and technological change, social collapse is inevitable.

In this section, four authors analyze the determinants, the nature, and the implications of current paradigms, norms, laws, and religion. Their common goal is to identify a set of new social images, new educational programs, and new communal patterns that will reestablish the long-term stability of human relationships with each other and with the natural environment.

Jean Houston traces the deteriorating effects of technological advance on human cognitive and physical capacities. She suggests that a fundamental Western religious distinction between God and the earth has encouraged in modern societies both the exploitation of nature and the separation of people from their environment. Inherent in this trend has been a deterioration in the scope and the quality of human psychological and spiritual processes. Rapid technological "progress" has distorted the natural world and the human capacity to cope with it. Increased mobility, stress produced by overcrowding, preoccupation with internal realities, the warping of the natural sensual world by the media—these are both the symptoms and the causes of the technological malaise. If this spiral perpetuates itself, societal breakdown cannot be avoided.

But Houston seeks an alternative outcome. Convinced that people currently use only a small fraction of their potential mental and physical abilities, she sketches out ways in which improved nutrition and psycho-physical reeducation could create a new mind set, a more effective and powerful way of knowing and dealing with reality. The result could be a holistic perspective and an ecological ethic in which people act in concert with nature, amplify their inherent capacities, and achieve the reintegration of individual, organization, and culture.

In her paper, Elise Boulding elaborates on Houston's proposals to educate people to extend the use of their sensations and imaginations in order to design a nonthreatening and sustainable future. Like Houston, her aim is to create awareness that technological growth and the social organization it implies actually stand in the way of developing higher human potentials. She hopes to spur efforts to create new visions of the future and new social norms.

Growth in the scale of human communities and in the influence of technology has impoverished the network of sensations and feedback that once interrelated individuals with each other and with their natural environment. One result is a loss of social stability; another is society's inability to imagine a future devoid of continuous expansion. Boulding explores what it would mean to devote the educational resources of society to recreating these connections and to fostering the futures-creating potential of the entire population. She suggests procedures for reestablishing an individual's contact with his own body rhythms and with natural cycles. She talks of ways to extend the time frame within which one's perceptions and thoughts are assessed and to reacquire a sense of coupling with the natural environment. If her ideas are accepted, formal schools appear quite inadequate to the real job of teaching, and Boulding describes how the entire community might take over the role of educating its members.

In his Mitchell Prize-winning paper, Robert Allen describes the detrimental effects of technologism for the society as a whole. He describes how luxuries have progressively become necessities, so that society is forced to seek perpetual growth as compensation for the nonmaterial amenities increasingly lost through the process of industrialization. The costs are ecosystem deterioration, social disruption, and inflation. New laws are not alone sufficient to arrest this headlong plunge or to ameliorate its consequences. Laws are at best unworkable, at worst counterproductive, unless accompanied by supporting norms, or social expectations that define acceptable modes of behavior. These serve to maximize satisfaction of social wants within a given environment. What is required today are norms that help to stabilize the population and reduce growth in material consumption. Norms cannot be unilaterally defined and imposed by the government. They must evolve in concert with goals, technologies, laws, and institutions.

There are some signs that new norms are emerging, but it is important not to wait passively for their development. Instead, Allen advocates the identification of the circumstances likely to stimulate their appearance and does this himself by analyzing several equilibrium societies. He describes the procedures by which these societies hold their populations in balance with the carrying capacity of the environment. He then derives a description of the attributes that most predispose a society to adopt norms leading to a sustainable state—explicit ideals of smallness and widespread valuation and sharing of a luxury whose availability is sensitive to fluctuations in the environmental support capacity.

In a world that still pursues material growth and industrialization, the initiation of alternative norm systems will have to remain the responsibility of relatively small communities. But Allen does spell out two policy recommendations that could be pursued nationally to facilitate innovation at the local level. Nations should deliberately seek a polytopic society, one in which a diverse array of communities is free to pursue its own values and goals. Federal governments should work to avoid the concentration of populations in large urban cores. As that is done, those interested in experimenting with new ways of life can work to develop primary life-styles, living arrangements within small communities which are relatively self-sufficient, intimately connected to their environment, and self-governing. The effort to develop sustainable life-styles is an experiment, since the knowledge base is small. But from primitive communities Allen has gleaned some guidelines that can increase the chance for success.

Edward Goldsmith explores in more depth the idea of new communities. He suggests that the development of concentrated urban areas is part of a continuous process that has reduced the stability of social systems. It would probably be possible for the current, counterproductive policies to be pursued indefinitely, for they are economically and politically expedient. But their costs are becoming unsupportable, and Goldsmith forecasts the bankruptcy of all large cities. He suggests it is time to search for community patterns that offer more stability and more comprehensive satisfaction of human needs.

In pursuing this alternative, he analyzes the characteristics of hunter-gatherer encampments and the small settlements of traditional societies. Recognizing that a modern society of four billion people cannot return to nomadism, he nevertheless believes that contemporary society could reacquire many of the most important attributes of the earlier and more humane living patterns. He discusses the concept of social stability, then describes how it could be enhanced through decentralization, and new attitudes toward work, education, religion, and land ownership. By slowly evolving communities consistent with the requirements for social stability and designed to exploit the renewable resources of the natural world, he holds out the hope that mankind might find more durable and satisfying substitutes for the material benefits of the industrialized world.

I consider this section to be the most important of the book. Yet it contains proposals which are most difficult to link to concrete actions. The four authors deal with innate attributes of the mind and culture that have evolved over millenia. It would be naive to imagine these attributes could be changed quickly, even if there were consensus about the direction in which they should develop. But it is at the level of abstraction adopted by these four papers that many keys to a sustainable state must be found. There is no alternative to persistent probing at the fringe of human consciousness to rediscover and adapt to current realities the homeostatic mechanisms that ensured survival of the species during its first several hundred thousand years on earth. It is essential to test the sometimes sweeping generalizations put forward here and to search for greater understanding of the relation between inner and outer worlds.

The small number of sustainable societies, like the Brüderhof in New York State, that have emerged from the nineteenth and twentieth century Western world indicate that a new ideal can spark pursuit of radical alternatives, at least within small groups. We need many more such groups, experimenting with alternative theories of the relation between man and nature and offering alternative models to the rest of society as it continues to debate the direction of its future. Mankind may need the challenge of a new frontier. Let it look not to outer space but instead to the depths of the human mind and interpersonal relationships.

 *Chapter 14*

Prometheus Rebound: An Inquiry into Technological Growth and Psychological Change

Jean Houston

THE ANCIENT ROOTS OF THE PROBLEM

The origins of the awesome dangers and critical distortions which unchecked technological growth seems to bring to the human condition lie deep in the Western psyche, and, specifically, in its religious roots. In the first chapter of Genesis, God is not consonant with His creation. It is a "handiwork" which He declares "good." In many non-Christian myths and scriptures of the beginning times, the god is implicit in, and often indistinguishable from, the creation. He or She is the sky or the earth, the primal water or a shooting star. In the Judeo-Christian story, there is an immediate distancing between Creator and creation, an I–it objectification of reality. The world and all that lies within is manufactured from without, and so it is "other." Man, the being created in the image of God, is similarly authorized to dominate and be removed from the subhuman world.

Lynn White and other social historians argue that these scriptural attitudes provide the basis for an aberrant technology, one that exploits and manipulates the world and leads inevitably to ecological disaster. They suggest that Genesis may already contain the seeds of the current Western fixation on GNP and the excesses of the multinational corporation. This trans-historical whimsy is not as exotic as it first appears, but instead has a continuous tradition in the history of Western production. White notes, for example, that Frankish calenders "show men coercing the world around them—plowing, harvesting, chopping trees and butchering pigs. Man and nature are two things, and man is master" [1].

At a time when Western Europe was a small primitive outpost of the great centers of civilization, Western peasants and artisans were technologically precocious. By the year 1000 A.D., they were applying water power to industrial processes other than the milling of grain, and shortly thereafter, by means of such inventions as the stirrup and the horse plow, were gaining a sense of manipulative power over nature virtually unique in the history of human cultures [2]. "By the mid-thirteenth century," according to White, "a considerable group of active minds, stimulated not only by the technological successes of recent generations but also led on by the will-o'-the-wisp of perpetual motion, were beginning to generalize the concept of mechanical power. They were coming to think of the cosmos as a vast reservoir of energies to be tapped and used according to human intentions. They were power conscious to the point of fantasy" [3]. By the middle of the fourteenth century these fantasies prompted the invention of all kinds of mechanical contraptions and laid the groundwork for the galaxy of technological aftereffects that followed in the wake of Gutenberg. The pace so accelerated that in 1444 a visitor to Italy from another culture (one could almost say another planet), a highly cultured Greek ecclesiastic, Bessarion, suffered from an early version of future shock. He encountered a vast display of ingenious mechanical devices; witnessed the superiority of Italian ships, arms, textiles, and glass; and was astonished by the vision of waterwheels sawing timbers and pumping the bellows of blast furnaces.

Succeeding centuries saw a steady acceleration in the extension of "the empire of man over things." The genius of Bacon, Galileo, Newton, and Descartes served to deepen the estrangement of man and nature—nature now seen as a measurable, mechanistic function, to be "interrogated with power." Bacon, perhaps, was the principal architect of this process. He gave to the Western mind-set the most thorough justification for the principle of domination by affirming that "the command over things natural—over bodies, medicine, mechanical powers, and infinite others of this kind—is the one proper and ultimate end of true natural philosophy." It was Bacon also who, through his own curious experiments and speculative essays, joined his New Philosophy to technology and mechanical innovation, assuring us that men would go on to create "a line and race of inventions that may in some degree subdue and overcome the necessities and miseries of humanity" [4].

The ecological critique was announced by the poet John Donne.

A contemporary of Bacon, he sounded an alarm that was to become prophetic for the events of the twentieth century:

> And new Philosophy calls all in doubt,
> The Element of fire is quite put out;
> The Sun is lost, and th'earth, and no mans wit
> Can well direct him where to looke for it.
> And freely men confesse that this world's spent . . .
> 'Tis all in peeces, all cohaerence gone;
> All just supply, and all Relation . . . [5].

The spending of the world's substance and the loss of supply and relation were not perceived by the technological heirs of Francis Bacon. They insisted on maintaining Bacon's illusion of unlimited power and unlimited progress, which in turn helped to prolong the dualistic agony of man separate from nature. If power, the dictum went, then the world outside of one can continue to be mastered; and if unlimited power, then unlimited mastery. Now that many are suspecting for either ecological or political reasons that the power is no longer so readily at hand, the trauma of technological man is deepening and plunging many into a too hasty retreat to simplistic solutions, withdrawal psychologies, and a tendency to polarize technology as "the enemy" or "the friend."

The Nineteenth Century As Pandora's Box

Prometheus, so the legend goes, had a brother, Epimetheus, a fey, benighted fellow whose name means "Afterthought." Zeus, furious over Prometheus' giving of fire to mankind (and thereby some measure of control over the powers of nature), sent Pandora to be Epimetheus' bride, complete with a dowry of the famous box. Interestingly, late-Renaissance thinkers identified strongly with the figure of Prometheus, but only insofar as he was the agent of new knowledge and new power, not in the fact that he was ultimately responsible for the unleashing of unimagined woes.

Pandora's box, given to Western man in the seventeenth century, was not really fully opened until the nineteenth century with its radical acceleration and extension of industrial and technological change into all avenues of life. The Industrial Revolution compelled the destruction and transformation of all the traditional ways of being, knowing, having, and living. It was perhaps the most intense assault the world has ever seen on the traditional image of man and the notion of what it means to be human [6]. Cumulatively, the number of changes resulting from the growth of population, expansion of industrialization, the birth of many new sciences and modes of investigation, and the revolution in social, familial, and value structure constituted a quantum jump in the whole fabric of human existence, as well as in the psychological dynamics of human experience. Family, land, Church, profession, way of life—the traditions and expectations of millennia were overthrown in a few short years. Especially in the arena of economic change, human self-understanding encountered the most drastic effects:

> The social effects of the Industrial Revolution markedly transformed the lives and actions of individuals in Europe, especially by the mid-nineteenth century. For example, the emergence of the concept of "factors of production" (land, labor, and capital) had revolutionary implications for the Western image of humankind. Humans (the labor component) were no longer a part of the organic whole of society; rather, the person, the laborer, became an objectified and standardized component of the production process. The tendency to see people as mere units in the production process, bought in an impersonal market place and forced to submit to the dictates of the factory in order to survive, was reinforced by the post-mercantilist socioeconomic ideology of laissez-faire, which discouraged government intervention in economic activities. The image inherent in this setting could reasonably be described as "economic man": rationalistic (able to calculate what was in his own self-interest), mechanistic (a factor of production), individualistic (with great responsibility to take care of himself), and materialistic (with economic forces acting as primary if not exclusive reward and control mechanisms) [7].

Such an objectification of human personality and needs in terms of factors of production served to discourage the search for a subtler and more organic guiding process for the industrial era. Again, the larger sensibility of the poet and novelist detected the greater ills to come. For example, in a passage from *The Duke's Children*, written in 1880, novelist Anthony Trollope described a group of aristocratic fox hunters discussing the perils of hunting "in these modern days:"

> not the perils of broken necks and crushed ribs . . . but the perils from outsiders, the perils from new-fangled prejudices, the perils from more modern sports, the perils from over-cultivation, the perils from extended population, the perils from increasing railroads, the perils from indifferent magnates . . . and that peril of perils, the peril of decrease of funds and increase of expenditures! [8].

This late Victorian scenario proved predictive of the kinds of problems that were soon to plague the twentieth century. A telling realization of these is found in the table of selected successes and associated problems of the present technological era prepared by the Stanford Research Institute's Center for the Study of Social Policy

[9]. Table 14–1 is a remarkable statement; it shows a compounding of the fears of the nineteenth century social critics.

The Syndrome of the Sorcerer's Apprentice

Table 14–1 shows the dreadful fruition of the ancient but constant effort of objectifying and dominating nature. Rooted in scrip-

Table 14–1. Stanford Research Institute Table of Selected Successes and Associated Problems of the Technological/Industrial Era

The number of changes resulting from the growth of population expansion of industrialization, the birth of many new sciences and modes of investigation, and the revolution in social, familial, and value structure constituted a quantum jump in the whole fabric of human existence, as well as in the psychological dynamics of human experience. Family, land, Church, profession, way of life—the traditions and expectations of millenia were overthrown in a few short years.

Benefits of "Success"	*Detriments of "Success"*
Reduced infant and adult mortality rates.	Regional overpopulation; problems of the aged.
Highly developed science and technology.	Hazard of mass destruction through nuclear and biological weapons; vulnerability of specialization; threats to privacy and freedoms, (for example, surveillance technology, bioengineering).
Machine replacement of manual and routine labor.	Exacerbated unemployment.
Advances in communication and transportation.	Increasing air, noise, and land pollution; "information overload;" vulnerability of a complex society to breakdown; disruption of human biological rhythms.
Efficient production systems.	Dehumanization of ordinary work.
Affluence; material growth.	Increased per capita consumption of energy and goods, leading to pollution and depletion of the earth's resources.
Satisfaction of basic needs.	Worldwide revolutions of "rising expectations;" rebellion against non-meaningful work.
Expanded power of human choice.	Unanticipated consequences of technological applications; management breakdown as regards control of these.
Expanded wealth of developed nations; pockets of affluence.	Increasing gap between "have" and "have-not" nations, frustration of the revolutions of rising expectations; exploitation; pockets of poverty.

ture, reinforced by medieval fantasies of power, given philosophical and mechanical force by the Promethean men of the late-Renaissance and early modern period, proliferating everywhere in the nineteenth century, the effort at mastery is now, finally, laden with the near-apocalyptic results of excessive success. It is an enactment on the field of history of the story of the Sorcerer's Apprentice. The Apprentice, understanding almost nothing of the subtle dynamics of the powers he is dealing with, and of himself in relation to these powers, is overwhelmed by his evocation of the animated brooms. He is nearly done in by the sheer excess of his success.

Lacking in the story of the Sorcerer's Apprentice, and in the history of Western technological success, was a sense of the vital ecology that links inner and outer worlds. The dominant social paradigm of reality perceived largely in economic and technological terms is deficient in that it is bound only by the objective, "outer" dimension of things, and consequently contains no internal limiting factor. But the outer environment is itself strictly limited in its resources, and so each technical solution yields ten new problems.

Lacking the full complement of nature in all its parts, technology and its stepchild, materialism, are frankly unworldly—in fact, almost unworlding. Today's singular drama of ecological, social, political, and psychological breakdown, much of which is due to the doings of the technological apprentice, is as powerful a drama of the unworlding of a world as one could ever see.

Why are people unworlding themselves at such a catastrophic rate? Why are society's successes such failures? A great deal of blame lies with psychological inadequacy and abuse of success. The natural continuum of man and nature, as well as the richness of human psychological and spiritual processes, has been ignored and derided during the reign of quantity. The archaic premises of technology, based as they were on nineteenth century attitudes and principles, are psychologically naive, linear, insular, and exploitative, and have been harmful to the human personality. As E.F. Schumacher notes, "The economics of giantism and automation is a left-over of nineteenth century conditions and nineteenth century thinking and it is totally incapable of solving any of the real problems of today" [10]. Then, too, the glorification of "demonstrable proof" led to the structuring of more humanistic disciplines, such as psychology and social science, in terms of the operational mechanisms of nineteenth century science.

Shaped and manipulated by the technological environment, modified by education, social plans, and therapies still based for the most part on obsolete mechanistic models, many people have come to think of themselves as prosthetic extensions of the technological process, instead of considering technology a prosthesis of the human process. Hence, Ernst Junger's powerful statement that technology is the real metaphysics of the twentieth century [11].

TECHNOLOGY AND THE PATHOLOGY OF SPACE AND TIME

Much has been written about the effect on man of the technological environment. To research this literature is to wrestle with darkness; it is to review a literature filled largely with futile visions, negative scenarios, and the death of hope. The scholarly reflections of a Mumford [12] or an Ellul [13] and the printouts of the well-programed computer all share a consensus of despair and depletion. However, much of what has been written may be misleading in that it is ideologically determined by one or another economic, political, or psychological position, which may itself be determined by the dogmatics implicit in technological method. Almost no one has attempted a holistic examination of the impact of the new modern environments on consciousness and the human nervous system, or on the bodymind generally.

Modern environments exhibit many unique factors for which the human race is unprepared. Stripped of his bio-rhythmic roots in nature and surrounded instead by a new vibratory pollution of noise, frequencies, amps, ergs, volts, and accelerating change, man has lost the physiological sureties of his ancestral tempo and ancestral space. As Jacques Ellul writes:

> Technique has penetrated the deepest recesses of the human being. The machine tends not only to create a new human environment, but also to modify man's very essence. The milieu in which he lives is no longer his. He must adapt himself, as though the world were new, to a universe for which he was not created. He was made to go six kilometers an hour, and he goes a thousand. He was made to eat when he was hungry and to sleep when he was sleepy; instead, he obeys a clock. He was made to have contact with living things, and he lives in a world of stone. He was created with a certain essential unity, and he is fragmented by all the forces of the modern world [14].

I will review some of the psychological effects occasioned by the interaction of technology with space and time.

Abstraction

To begin with, technology joined to space interrupts the critical succession of events necessary to the process of symbiosis. The natural ecology of life demands an adaptive and nurturing interchange between man and environment. The ancestral way was largely one of affinity to the symbiotic process. Only with the technological transformation of the environment has symbiosis in many of its forms become a casualty of modern civilization. Under the technological rubric, for example, skill becomes equated with technique and with the technological mastery of machines, losing thereby its ancient meaning rooted in the symbiosis with other living material processes.

The "switch" becomes the dominant mode of interacting with the environment, the dominant form of making a decision. To throw the switch is to modify and operate radically upon the world. The existential implications of the switch are profound. The world is no longer weather, wind, and trees, but *mundus machina*, a macro-artifact set into motion by an arbitrary throwing of a switch. A gap of ignorance lies wide between the operated switch and the operating world. One is not only ignorant of the process contained in the gap, one is also removed several times from the environment upon which the machine operates. One becomes observer with little or no social or spatial responsibility, and little if any contact with wood or iron or wool. Again, one is unworldly—the ignorant slave of abstraction, blind to process, a mechanic with little knowledge of his material.

The abstraction process is stepped up in the world of the technologically-based white-collar worker, where there is a tendency to diffuse and confuse the power base. Bosses give way to managers. Decision-making becomes an arcane method of identifying the proper response in a programed situation that is forever changing its program. A quality reminiscent of the novels of Kafka and the Theatre of the Absurd is frequently pervasive as a sense of contact is lost with the decisions and deciders governing everyday life.

The abstraction mode also allows people to project into the process all of the negatives of their lives. Something as unknown as technology is, by so many on so many levels, becomes a convenient receptacle for devils. The assumption of mythic proportions of the technology of defense and offense since World War II has furthered the demonizing tendency, leading to the frequent penchant for regarding oneself while in the technological mode—that is, when using powerful machines and automobiles—as semi-satanic, full of libidinous power drives and energized naughtiness. As a result, the powerful machine becomes a convenient compensatory device, a way of acting out repression and pathology without ever having to come to terms with them until they take a serious psychological toll.

In these ways, technological abstraction has served to distance people more thoroughly from themselves.

In the Western world the abstraction process reaches its most ominous level. Abstraction has helped to create a huge, vacant space between the government and corporation, which control and maintain production, and the isolated consumer, who increases his rate and quantity of consumption in proportion to his isolation. As one thoughtful critic puts it:

> Western society is on the brink of collapse—not into crime, violence, madness or redeeming revolution, as many would believe, but into withdrawal. Withdrawal from the whole system of values and obligations that has historically been the basis of public, community, and family life. Western societies are collapsing not from an assault on their most cherished values, but from a voluntary, almost enthusiastic abandonment of them by people who are learning to live private lives of an unprecedented completeness with the aid of the momentum of a technology which is evolving more and more into a pattern of socially atomizing appliances [15].

Demands by ecologists and others that growth be limited and consumption be curbed run afoul of the deep psychological pattern of consumer life-style in the technological age. Consumption and affluence, and their maintenance, are virtually inevitable results of the distancing and isolation of man from nature, man from government and the processes of production, and most importantly, man from himself. To set limits to growth successfully is to effect first a critical growth process in the human use of human beings. I will further discuss this premise in the concluding pages of this paper.

Mobility

Technology wedded to problems of spatial distance has created the mobility phenomenon. Radical mobility has outmoded the nature of boundaries—whether political, environmental, or conceptual. Consider that, for thousands of years in Western consciousness, "the journey," especially "the journey to the East" and back, was one of the major symbolic themes of growth and self-discovery. From the Mediterranean wanderings of Ulysses, to the travels of the Crusaders, through *Pilgrim's Progress*, even to Hermann Hesse's metaphysical jaunts, the journey—difficult, profound, and immensely enriching—was the way of knowledge as Western man moved from one loaded spatial constellation to another. Now owing to mobile technology, the journey has been replaced by footlooseness, a state of being "on the road" for no particular reason.

The consequent lack of rootedness has produced wandering dropouts who pick up and truck on whenever their minimal efforts to find a place for themselves fail. In poor countries, mobility has stimulated mass migration into cities from the rural areas, thereby fueling catastrophic famine. In both rich and poor areas, mobility has contributed greatly to crime, alienation, and the diminishment of personal and family support of larger social structures. Lately, however, the ancient motivations may be reasserting themselves. Among these travelers, many persons are again on the journey, looking for "truth" or "meaning" or a place, a style, a person who will make it all make sense again.

The fluidity of spatial life abrogates the traditional form of roots, but this apparent rootlessness may also be hiding a more pervasive unity of humankind and a new and deeper rooting. The new mobility, after all, allows for the rapid gathering together of people who share similar loyalties and moral concerns. Witness the thousands who came from everywhere to join the peace marches, or groups petitioning for civil rights. Mobility has produced the global village and a larger sense of the union of the human community. With this larger sense may also come a broader scale of moral concern, and a responsive resonance to the needs of peoples and countries wherever they may be.

Stress

In the context of the stressful, overcrowded urban environments, technology has generated a spatial milieu which undoubtedly has had the most profound effects upon the human nervous system. The nature of urban and technological stress, as Hans Selye has shown, is pan-systemic and not limited to the booming buzzing confusion of our problem cities [16]. Provoked by chronic environmental conditions of a deleterious nature, stress induces prolonged changes in body and mind. Selye designates stress as the general syndrome of bodily adaptations designed to terminate or overcome evocative stimuli called stressors. The cumulative effects of these adaptations brings about major changes in the neuroendocrine systems. The stress syndrome follows a characteristic adaptive pattern which Selye calls the General–Adaptation Syndrome. There are three stages in the syndrome: (1) an alarm reaction, including the initial shock phase and a countershock phase, in which the body's defense system begins to work; (2) a stage of resistance, in which the organism offers the most optimal adaptive response and defense; and (3) a stage of exhaustion, marking the loss of acquired adaptation [17]. These adaptive stress reactions have always been characteristic of the human being. What is unique in the modern situation is that masses of people live in a state of chronic adaptation to the stress syndrome, with potentially more or less permanent damage to the body-mind.

Our cities in particular manifest the results of the maintenance and exhaustion of such adaptation. The senses react by reducing the perceptual field on the one hand, but demanding ever more intense forms of stimulation on the other. Eventually, the city-dweller must protect himself by perceiving less and less of the sounds, smells, and sights actually present in his environment. Here we have some explanation of the reduction of sensory acuity in "civilized" man, relative to the exercise of the same capacities in so called "primitive" groups. Furthermore, the numbed senses demand stronger stimulation—louder sounds, more vivid colors, brighter lights, more intense sexual expressions—in order that the organism feel alive, and the person feel himself and his world to be real. The stress syndrome of everyday life both demands withdrawal and creates the demand for artificial extremes.

Since changes in the nervous systems of younger people are naturally the more pronounced, their alienation from the everyday world is more complete and the stimulations demanded by their senses are more extreme. What is pleasurable or evocative of a "tang" of reality for many of the young is actually unbearable for many older people, and to an extent probably not seen before in history. The technological environment spawns a new nervous system which in turn generates still further changes in the environment and in the technology required to satisfy the latest needs.

Moreover, many young people are coming very early to a state of being overwhelmed by the intensity of the sensations they have sought and experienced. The experience of young users of psychedelic drugs in the 1960s and 1970s is a case in point. Their personal odysseys lead to a rejection of the source of stimulation and a flight away from it back to the land, or even a strange nostalgia for a past that belongs not to their experience but to that of their parents and grandparents, a past that is only imagined and which corresponds more or less with what was the actuality. The success of such television programs as "The Waltons" points to the nostalgia for a sterner, simpler ethic and way of life, as well as a longing for the less ambiguous demands of a frontier. Such programs serve as a stress adaptation.

Sensory and existential overload primes the exhaustion phase of the syndrome until the brain, overburdened with ideas and images and inundations of data, sooner or later loses its capacity to cope. A good many of these brains simply give up, rejecting knowledge and the society that inflicts such overabundance. In the aftermath of rejection may come rage, bewilderment, loss of ability to distinguish adequately between what is real and unreal, apathy, and a sense of impotence. When the macrocosm of society becomes too much for people to handle, the microcosms begin to form—people trying to find and create special interest groups, subcultures, communes. Overwhelmed by the "too-muchness" of modern life, many people have moved into little worlds that they share with others, but which are largely incomprehensible to members in good standing of the macrocosm. In any event, the move toward subcultures is a move toward creating a manageable consensus reality, albeit with the consequent cutting of lines of communication to the outside world and to other subgroups. Their behavior is an ironic demonstration of the principle that the more technology "enriches" the society, the more impossible is the kind of unity that the society needs to survive.

The overstressful environment also generates a turning inward, a preoccupation with interior states of consciousness, and with traditional Eastern and Western disciplines of self-knowledge. Certainly, too, the widespread use of psychedelics has been for many a use of modern chemistry to escape the outer world while leaping into an equally kaleidoscopic subjective reality [18]. The current widespread interest in altered states of consciousness in both scientific and experiential circles is indicative of a sensibility that arises in times of ontological breakdown—whether pre-Alexandrian Greece, second and third century Rome, post-World War I Germany, or even today. When many of the structural and formal underpinnings of society break down, then psychological energy which had been bound to these social structures moves inwards, breaching the unconscious, activating archaic and symbolic, as well as irrational, psychic contents.

During these eras, and today is no exception, consciousness escapes inward. An extensive fascination with the arcane, the occult, and interior states of consciousness arises. A belief emerges that eternal verities lie in internal states, and that the tapping of some mystical or psychological process can give a new consensus on reality and bring order out of chaos. In these times, hope is born that in the return to subjective realities—to the green world within that belies the wasteland without—there will come a remythologizing, a revisioning of the world so as to make sense again [19].

Time

Technology joined to time is equally bizarre in that it tends to involve us in the peculiar time zone of the radical "now." The tyranny of clock-time and the rule of the machine over the rhythms of daily life have served to fragment and dissociate the flow of living time and natural rhythms. "Abstract time became a new milieu, a new framework of existence" [20]. The new framework aids efficiency, but brings an accompanying loss of a sense of past and future. With abstraction of space and time and with the loss of a sense of the stages in any operational process, comes, inevitably, a loss of a sense of duration. When the rule of life is "no sooner said than done," then the whole temporal fabric of existence becomes warped.

Warped, too, becomes the necessary lag in duration between wants and the satisfaction of those wants. Recent studies indicate that between 1950 and 1970 many people, especially adolescents, became less future-oriented, less able to defer gratification of their wants, indicating a loss of the sense of duration and of the time flow necessary to make critical choices [21]. A diminishment in attention span may also be attributed to this trend. The ultimate negative form of the phenomenon may lie in depriving language of meaning and value, since so much of grammatical experience and the logic of language is grounded in the interrelationship of grammar, logic, and duration [22].

Radio and TV

Alice said it, of course: things keep on getting curiouser and curiouser. The most curious effects of technology on human personality come from radio and television. Radio offers an adaptive mechanism for stress in that, by providing an aural environment, it affords an exaggerated response to the high threshold of noise in our lives. Radio serves up, in regular doses, quasi-sacraments: music that does not amuse but mythologizes, and a liturgy of patter which is just that—noises from space, a torrent of sounds that have strangely changed their content. Witness the post-verbal fervor of a Detroit disc jockey: "Hey baby! This is me! Rockin Robbie D! I'm so bad I make flowers die I make babies cry I take candy from babies and give dogs rabies and if that ain't bad the rain don't fall and that ain't all—biscuits ain't bread."

The effects of this on the constant listener may be the decline of speech, the inhibition of words with sound, and the triumph of stream of consciousness over considered language. One apologist for this phenomenon suggests that "words, in an age of immediate electronic communications, may not be able to hold their own; they may become increasingly part of larger patterns, expressions which are predominantly non-verbal—in a word, synergetic. Whereas the power of words once lay in precision, the power of the new synergetic expression will be a uniting of subjectivities, a communion of spirit and sensibilities" [23]. This is a fascinating idea and provides another example of the interiorization tendency, but does nothing to explain the use of radio in the twentieth century to achieve an extraordinarily successful "communion of spirit and sensibilities" with dictators and vocally-charismatic totalitarian types.

Television is yet another conundrum unique in human experience. So far, no one has been able to ascertain the effects of prolonged television viewing on children who have been exposed from very early ages. But surely, watching the thousands of pulsing strobes that make up the television picture cannot fail to have some effect on the neurological system. Television is a completely novel situation for the nervous system and especially for the formative stages of psycho-physical development.

Then there is the problem of content. After 2000 years, people wag their heads disapprovingly about the brutish and violent public entertainments of the Roman Empire and speak virtuously about the decline and fall. Yet equally vicious and brutish events are simulated every day in the living rooms of millions. Bread and circuses were never like this.

Apart from these obvious follies, television may be affecting human perceptual and psychological structures in subtler and more far-reaching ways, causing us to learn to transcend the usual boundaries of space and time, inner and outer. In both television and motion pictures, perspective becomes relative. There can be an almost instantaneous change of perspective on an event: up close, far away, sky-view, ground-view, and even point-of-view. This constellation of perspectives cannot help but provide a richer environmental sense, a deepening awareness of all that the environment contains. It may be no exaggeration to suggest that the global sensibility, the deepening moral concern for people half a world away, as well as the growing ecological concern, is in part a response to the multiple perspective which television encourages and to the breadth of information which it affords.

Television also renders diaphanous the division between objective and subjective realities. The switch gives you at one moment "hard" news of earthquakes, murders, and assassination attempts, and, at the next, the doings of federal agents on other star systems. The blend and flow of fantasy and fact is so swift that consciousness loses its capacity to determine absolutely what is real and what is imagined, and whether the difference makes any difference. The video environment may be making people more susceptible to entering altered states of consciousness, while giving them more fluid notions of the nature of reality. If so, then the psychopathology of one generation could become the extended reality of the next. Or, as one eminent social scientist remarked recently: "I am quite prepared to accept that there are twenty separate realities going on in this room right now."

WHAT, IF ANYTHING, DOES IT ALL MEAN?

Technology is an environment, and as such plays a critical role in shaping the human condition. Of itself, technology is neither good nor evil, neither beneficial nor harmful. Technology is what human beings make of it. Technology is an extension and reflection of man. Its aberrations are in part the aberrations of man's philosophy of domination over nature, and his psychology, which sees the world as object. A different philosophy, a different attitude toward world and environment, might well have produced a different kind of technology. But, as presently developed, technology is among the most potent of man's prosthetic extensions. The uses made of technology can alter man himself and, as I have tried to show, is doing just that. The alteration is probably producing neither grotesque nor angel; it may, however, be the source of some alternative life-styles.

The balance of this paper will investigate briefly several possible scenarios, including both negative and positive features, that are emerging or have already emerged today as a result of changes in the human being wrought by technology.

Some Negative Scenarios

Although many negative features have already been discussed in this paper, several of the more insidious possibilities deserve further exploration. First, the technological environment may be functioning to diminish several critical human mental and physical capacities. Whether one talks with teachers or publishers, or for that matter with anyone concerned with human communication, there is considerable unanimity about the growing breakdown in the communications process itself. The breakdown extends into thinking and focusing attention, learning, and the general capacity for expression. The evidence for such a decline in all classes of people indicates a pervasive problem that is no respecter of persons and which evidently does not respond well to panaceas defined by doles of money and social services.

Whether the apparent decline of communicative capacities stems from the technological factors mentioned previously, from the toxic stress of pollution, or from bad nutrition, it is a specter worth every effort to avoid. As an illustration of this latter example, we have found that in recent years a growing number of children with hyperactivity symptoms have become a serious problem for the schools. Treated with daily doses of ritalin, many of these children grow into adolescence without ever knowing what their nondrug personalities are like. Now it has been discovered that many of these children were hyperactive because they were being poisoned by various chemical preservatives and artificial colorings found in their daily diets. In many cases, according to Dr. Ben Feingold of the Kaiser Medical Center, the symptoms of hyperactivity cease when the children stop eating these foods and then return when they go back on their old diets.

In some of our studies of human capacities at The Foundation for Mind Research, we are beginning to gather data that suggest the man-machine interface may presently be detrimental to thinking and communication. The body-mind needs a certain sensuous as well as conceptual involvement with the unfolding process of any operation for the healthy development of language and logic, for the sustaining of thought processes and the attention span, and for adequate communication in general. The "switch" phenomenon may interfere significantly during the formative years with the evolution of neural connections and the growth of body learning.

A study of the early years of highly intelligent people indicates that many had a sensory involvement with materials and a sequential learning of the methods of transforming materials [24]. One of the most intelligent and realized people that I have ever known or studied is Margaret Mead. The chronicle of her childhood indicates that she was encouraged to understand and participate in the beginning, middle, and end of all processes—whether weaving, putting together mechanical devices, or using building materials. This participation may well have been a major determinant in the development of her remarkable intellect, her keen use of senses, and her adeptness with analogy in relating and explaining things. It would also explain the thoroughness of much of her work and the lucidity of her communications [25]. Mead's example suggests that educational environments should allow young children a vital participation in learning how things work and how materials are transformed. Such an education might go far to offset the effects of abstraction, as well as setting a basis in brain and behavior for better communication skills. Educational technology should be directed toward creating inexpensive learning environments that surround the child with engaging opportunities to immerse himself in process.

Another negative feature is one that looms in times when society undergoes a profound crisis in consciousness, as well as an ontological breakdown. Characteristic of such times today there is an overwhelming multiplicity of choice, a confusion of values, and an exacerbation of these symptoms by the technological environment. Historically, this kind of crisis has often led to chaos, bloody conflict, and the disintegration of the society. Frequently, order has been reinstituted through the coming of a dictator who promises to bring reality into manageable proportions. After the excesses of an age of crisis, there are many who are only too ready to fall into the totalitarian embrace. When people are so confused and bewildered, patriarchical dictates come initially as a great relief. Like having Daddy back, one has a chance to regress and start all over again, with values and schedules all laid out and most answers given. Technology is brought under control, limited, and adapted to the goals of the leadership, and superfluities are eliminated.

But then comes the awful dénouement. The reinstitution of order by a dictator is accomplished by psychological ploys which serve to contract the mass consciousness, imposing more limited norms of what is permissible to consciousness than the norms preceding the crisis—a consensus on an ever narrower reality, a constricted reality unable or unwilling to tolerate any deviation [26]. Such a narrowing consensus is maintained by limiting and monotonizing stimuli of all sorts. The press is controlled. Only permissible ideas are allowed dissemination. Works of art are rigorously censored. Architecture becomes monolithic (witness modern Peking or Speer's plan for Germania). Modes of dress are restricted. Color, form, esthetic modalities—the entire spectrum of sensory and ideational input—are severely limited. Dictatorship amounts to the politicization of brain function. Brain function is restricted, stabilized, and maintained by a complex array of devices, drastically limiting both inputs and outputs. Technology becomes a principal channel of control and limitation of human experience.

There is actually not much likelihood in the foreseeable future of Western societies falling into this kind of political totalitarianism. We of the twentieth century are too close to horrendous examples of the police state to repeat the syndrome. Hopefully, we have been inoculated against this political "disease," although we still must maintain constant vigilance that it does not happen again. What might befall us instead is a variation of totalitarianism based on a form of techno-psychological imperialism (compared to which, most historical imperialisms would probably pale by contrast).

The groundwork for such an imperialism is already laid in the growing phenomenon of privitization. As described by Martin Pawley, the private citizen of the West is beginning to be enmeshed in a "willfully sustained system of therapeutic deceptions" [27]. Technology and media simulate personal fantasies and provide constant divertissements away from present and future crises. There is a growing primacy of secondary realities. Styles of clothes and fashions offer fantasy identities. Media and advertising flood the mind with dreams. The technology of secondary reality has become central to marketing, production, and economic health itself.

Production-line workers seem to spend much of their time in fantasy. (How could it be otherwise, since so many of their leisure hours are spent being bombarded by fantasy?) Here is the self-description of one line worker:

> There are nine men all told who work on our line, and each one is a character, an individual in his own right. My work comes to me in a completely automatic way, in the gestures of automation. With a rag wrapped around my eyes I could still do it, and could do dozens before I realized that I had done any at all. But underneath all this my mind never stops working. It lives by itself. Some call it dreaming, and if so, I am dreaming all day long, five days a week. The whole bench dreams like this. It is a galley of automatons locked in dreams [28].

It is not difficult to imagine how a dictatorship of psycho-technology could orchestrate a society of blissful ninnies. By giving sanction to the great divorce between sensation and action, by governing dreams and images, and by offering frequent rewards of taped delight, the psycho-technologist could quite literally run the show. Western man's removal from nature would become complete in the epiphany of the happy cyborg.

Some Positive Scenarios

I do not accept the inevitability of the psycho-technological scenario, although the prophets of science fiction and the doom-sayers of social critique say it could be so. Instead, I believe that the sheer intensity of present reality has caused society to turn a corner. I suspect this is a time when the convergence of complexity with crisis is creating a *tertium quid*, a whole new mind-set on how to know and deal with reality. Times in which the dominant paradigm or way of understanding begins to shift have been called times of "transvaluation of values" (Nietzsche); "hierarchical re-structuring" (Platt);

"conceptual mutations" (Bois and White); and "new-system functions" (Korzybski) [29]. Humans may now be in the early stages of a qualitative and quantitative departure from the dominant technological paradigms. There are signs that people are finally moving out of the objectifying, manipulating philosophy of power which has reigned for too long.

The ecological crisis alone is doing what no other crisis in history has ever done: it is challenging people to a realization of a new humanity and a new way of dealing and working with our world. A holistic perspective is emerging as well as an ecological ethic in which the human acts in concert with nature to bring about more symbiotic ecological relationships and to establish needed recycling processes. The new ecological ethic also tends to further the achievement of synergy between individual and organization micro-decisions, thereby providing a healthier basis for the ensuing macro-decision.

The ethic also provides an organic basis for interdisciplinary and intercultural coordination; a good example is the program of intermediate technology recommended by Schumacher and others [30]. This technology with a human face is "vastly superior to the primitive technology of bygone ages but at the same time is much simpler, cheaper, and freer than the super-technology" [31]. Small-scale and energy-sparing, it puts hands and brains back into the production process, restores man's relationship with nature, and generally corrects the pathologizing of space and time that characterizes typical modern technology. Although developed chiefly for the Third World, intermediate technology will undoubtedly find more extensive use in Western countries, if only out of psychological necessity.

It is enormously significant that the current crisis in consciousness—the loss of a sense of reality by so many, the rising tides of alienation—occurs concomitantly with the ecological destruction of the planet by technological means. Man is no encapsulated bag of skin; man is organism-environment. Understanding this difference should bring people to the realization that society has reached the momentous point in human history where, to survive, it must reverse the ecological plunder. Such a reversal will mean discovering new forms of consciousness and fulfillment apart from the traditional ones of consumption, control, aggrandizement, and manipulation. The time has come to take off the psychological shelf all the dormant potentials that were not immediately necessary to man in his role as Promethean Man-Over-Nature.

Based on many kinds of evidence and sixteen years of research in the field, I believe that human beings can definitely acquire the capacity to use much more of their potentials than all but a few people presently use. This could be achieved both by preventing active psycho-physical damage and by eliciting and developing potentials that now remain latent in most persons. Today mankind uses but a fraction of his capacities, perhaps 10 percent of the possible physical capacity, and 5 percent of available mental potential. But what would happen if human beings could learn to use 12 or 15 percent? Surely that would permit a very different existence—a different human being, a different technology, a different society, and so on. Hopefully, the difference would also mean improvement, both in the humane use of human beings and in society's modes of problem solving.

First examine some of the active damage to be remedied if the human being is finally to come into his own. One very basic area urgently in need of correction is human nutrition. Surprisingly little support is available for research in nutrition and there are few real authorities. Seeking advice from physicians is often not very hopeful, since they receive no adequate training in this area so fundamental to human health. In light of our ignorance, some degree of malnutrition is probably almost universal. In recognized cases, undernourishment or improper nourishment during the first two years of life causes some form of brain damage. The manifest effect is impairment of all intellectual functions, and also emotional impairment extending into interpersonal relationships. Later in life, dietary deficiencies appear to be factors in many varieties of mental illness. Only recently has the new orthomolecular psychiatry, a psychiatric approach that works with nutritional elements to improve brain functioning, begun to come to terms with this condition [32]. But again, the recognized cases tend to be the ones where disturbance is severe. There must be many other cases, doubtless millions, where the functioning is significantly affected, but the condition is not recognized.

Equally basic are such matters as posture and movement. A study conducted for the World Health Organization determined that, in Europe, Britain, the United States, and Australia, neither physicians nor physical educators were able to recognize faulty posture or many other physical defects, except for gross distortions [33]. Yet the known effects of faulty posture and movement include impaired mental and emotional functioning, various diseases, premature aging, and doubtless premature death [34]. In movement is included breathing, a vital function that becomes impaired in the great majority of persons. When posture and movement improve significantly, there is an accompanying improvement in sensory acuity, thinking and feeling functions, and overall awareness [35]. Again, much more research and dissemination of knowledge are urgently needed.

In making possible a greater use of human capacities and a more complete human experience, one tool of the greatest importance is relatively unknown by the general public: the method of neural reeducation created in its most sophisticated from by an Israeli physicist, Moshe Feldenkrais, with antecedents in the work of the late F. Matthias Alexander [36]. Alexander's work has been carried on principally by Dr. and Mrs. Wilfred Barlow at the Alexander Institute in London, and was the subject recently of a Nobel Prize acceptance speech by Nikolaas Tinbergen [37]. From these researchers comes the knowledge that sensing, thinking, feeling, and movement are functions so interrelated in the human being that all can be drastically affected by interference with or treatment of any one of them. As I have already illustrated, when technology affects one of these functions, the impairment readily leads to deterioration of the other functions.

On the therapeutic side, Feldenkrais, with an unrivaled knowledge of body mechanics, developed an elaborate series of exercises by means of which the human frame may be virtually rebuilt. But more, his method reeducates the kinesthetic sense, the awareness of the body—particularly in movement—producing thereby a much expanded body awareness which acts on the nervous system so as to improve thinking and feeling, and to alleviate many symptoms of physical, mental, and emotional disorders [38]. Our Foundation's research, based on first-hand observation and study of the Feldenkrais and Barlow work, has confirmed these findings, a claim which some will find extravagant. However, one might note that the late John Dewey was of the opinion, expressed in many books, that Alexander's discoveries were perhaps the most important in the history of twentieth century science [39].

The Work of the Foundation for Mind Research

Our work attempts to join these psychophysical reeducation methods to an investigation of the capacities of consciousness and perception. We explore experimentally with our research subjects the immediate experiential, therapeutic, and creative values of altered and extended states of consciousness, alternative cognitive modes, acceleration of mental process, the creative and problem-solving process—fertilized by a variety of experimental techniques and devices, the programing and use of dreams, the physiological control of involuntary states, and many other varieties of human capacity that tend to be inhibited in the ordinary person. Some of the devices and procedures used in this research include biofeedback, sensory deprivation chambers, sensory overload environments, varieties of trance and hypnotic induction, hyper-alerting inductions, guided imagery techniques, and many others [40].

One of the most interesting of our studies has to do with the experimental investigation of imagistic thinking. Almost all children have some capacity to think with visual images as well as with words, but because they receive no encouragement in the dominant educational system with its emphasis on verbal linear thinking, the capacity for this potential is lost. It typically reemerges only in the dream life, or when consciousness is altered by hypnosis or drugs, or in some pathological cases when illness changes brain chemistry. It is significant, however, that the access to visual and sometimes other sensory imageries (auditory, kinesthetic) is retained by a statistically large number of persons deemed unusually intelligent or creative [41]. This is plausible, for evidence indicates that thinking in images permits the expression of ideas and the conception of solutions that are inconsistent with purely verbal reasoning. Thinking in images is more given to patterns, to symbolic processes, and to synthetic constructs. Consequently, more information is likely to be condensed and contained in the matrices of the symbolic image. Our studies indicate that during the creative process, a kind of interior visual dialogue and orchestration frequently occurs between these larger patterns of information which are part of the imaginal, symbolic process. What would happen if this natural capacity were cultivated and applied in the schools?

At Marburg, Germany, before World War II, just such an experiment was undertaken under the direction of the brothers Walther and E.R. Jaensch [42]. Different groups of children were encouraged throughout their school years to apply visual imagery to learning, thinking, and creative expression. The results were most encouraging. By the time they reached their teens, children taught the image-based thought process were more creative, retained the capacity to paint and draw, and scored higher on intelligence tests than the control group of children whose imagery was inhibited by an education too oriented to verbal processes. There also occurred a more complete personality development since the children suffered no attempts to prevent or limit the use of this potent natural capacity. To the researcher in human potentials, the result is not surprising.

Through educational techniques it is possible to facilitate thinking in images as well as in words, so as to sustain both verbal and imagistic faculties in children. As our research indicates, it is not difficult to evoke this inhibited capacity also in adults. People then gain access to both verbal and visual thought processes. They are able to extend their perspective on issues, to consider more alternatives and solutions, and in general to think more effectively and creatively. In this era of pluralities of choice, this kind of multileveled thinking should come as a considerable boon.

Our work with adults also suggests that gaining access to various internal imageries tends to increase the acuity of the corresponding senses related to perception of the external world. Thus, internal visual imagery often acts to improve vision in general and internal auditory imagery seems to facilitate normal hearing. Many subjects also report increased energy, less stress and tension, and a sense of being better able to deal with problems. A large proportion of these subjects have been urbanites living with the conditions of stress described earlier. The programs of reeducation in the extended use of body and mind seem to make them less vulnerable and more prepared to receive, contain, and deal with the overloads of this technological era.

As a general principle, the more one uses one's physical and mental capacities, in an intelligent manner, the more one tends to grow; a rich unfolding of the self becomes manifest. The capacities contributing to unblocking and growth include not only use of the sensory imageries, but also the uses of subjective time and the acceleration of thought processes—for example, experiencing several minutes of clock time as some hours of internal experience; cross-sensing, such as hearing color and seeing sound; self-regulating pleasure and pain; and establishing voluntary control over some of the autonomic functions by means of biofeedback and autogenic training. Individuals are enabled in these programs to experience states of consciousness not ordinarily accessible to them, and are encouraged to find creative and productive applications of these states in everyday life. Some of these applications include better self-knowledge, learning to work with dreams, better concentration and memory, the control of mood and perception, the heightening of both sensory and cognitive awareness. Research subjects can also learn to tap the organic flow of the innate creative process, and can experience levels of the psyche where the images are archetypal, mythological, and possibly transpersonal.

CONCLUSIONS

To develop these capacities could be to restore the ecological balance of inner and outer worlds and to gain a wider use of the self and a larger measure of self-knowing; to move beyond present conditionings, cul-de-sacs, and diminishments that the technological environment imposes; to extend the frontier of inner space, which, unlike outer space, has inexhaustible resources.

From this kind of research emerges the conviction that most people, given the necessary opportunity and education, can realize more of their potentials in varying degrees. They can learn to think, feel, and know in new or unaccustomed ways; to have wider horizons; and to aspire within realistic limits to a multidimensional awareness. Our research with many hundreds of subjects shows that it is not especially hard to effect such changes if there is a willingness to be emancipated from the anxieties and inhibitions associated with new kinds of experience—experience which would not seem to move towards the goals typically regarded as the only ones possible or worthwhile. With understanding of the limits self-imposed through a myriad of false concepts, shrunken aspirations, and taboos comes ability to achieve a larger freedom to think, to dream, to aspire, and to experience. Possibilities for authentically new ways of being are opened up. Now that survival is at stake, psychological capacity will grow and the uses of technological power will change.

 *Chapter 15*

Education for Inventing the Future

Elise Boulding

NEW IMAGES OF THE FUTURE

There is a kind of existential terror associated with the concept of "limits to growth" for the Western person in the late twentieth century. The reason for the terror is evident enough. The type of growth associated with expansion in population and economic productivity has somehow come to be synonymous with growth in personhood and growth in the body social. This produces the equation in people's minds: limits to growth equals death.

It is easy enough to point out that growth can be redefined, so that even drastic cutbacks in physical resources can take place in a context of continuing social growth. But the redirection of the social will involved in such a redefinition is no small matter. How does a society that has been brought up on "bigger is better" come to believe that "small is beautiful," not just as a truth for Third World folk, but for themselves? How does a society that equates self-worth with the degree of technological mastery over physical systems come to believe that this very know-how, and the technology of social organization associated with it, stand in the way of the development of higher human potential, potential that could be carefully fostered to lead humanity in new directions? I believe the current understanding of cognitive and social processes permits useful answers to these questions. In this analysis I will suggest several ways in which educational programs could be extended and revised to achieve the new social norms required for the invention of better futures.

History indicates that the social will has from time to time been redirected. As Fred Polak has shown in his macrohistorical survey of images of the future [1], at any point in time each society is a veritable seedbed of potential futures. Every image projected by the writers, artists, saints, scholars, and public figures of a society is a seed of the future. Most of them never sprout, but some do germinate and guide society down a path different from the one it might have taken. Through a process that is not understood very well, certain images capture the social imagination of a people and acquire social resonance. They become time bombs with a double charge, exploding in the now and in the then, as people act on what have become believable possibilities and thereby create the imaged future.

Those who question mindless growth wish to choose new strains from today's seedbed of future images. They wish to explore ways to nurture certain seeds so that they will capture the minds of the late twentieth century and produce behavioral sequences that will lead society into a twenty-first century existence that expands human capacities and respects physical constraints. Not everyone holds the same images of a desired future or gives the same weight to the cognitive, moral, and spiritual dimensions of that future. Physical systems are visualized differently too. Some see a high-energy society of the future based on technological breakthroughs that make possible a "safe" nuclear technology. Others visualize a solar-powered society not very different from today's fossil fuel-powered society, except that power need no longer be centralized, so that every household can be a self-sufficient unit. In this image, explored by John Todd in Chapter 2, bioengineering would provide the same household servicing as mechanical systems but at lower energy levels.

Utopian Images

Given present planetary habits, global society may be close to a critical systems break. There is consequently a certain compulsion to act to unleash the futures-creating process even in the midst of great debate about what the future should be. It is useful to consider how societies in the past have handled the threat of systems breaks. There is historical evidence that system breaks have always been anticipated by utopia-writing. The utopian tradition of designing alternative futures is a very old one. In the written record, utopia design goes back to the era of the founding of the universal religions, stretching roughly from 500 B.C. to 500 A.D., from Buddha to Mohammed.

In the past, however, utopia design has been the province of a very small elite. Would it be possible to take what we have learned from 2000 years of utopia design and apply it to the educational process so that entire populations can learn to reconceptualize the human possibility, and engage in participatory futures creation? This is an important question, because utopian planning and the ideal of the participatory society have historically stood at opposite poles.

Since any feasible image of the future forecloses important options, the process of designing the future must be broadly representative of social needs; it should therefore involve a wide spectrum of society. The dilemma posed by Friedrich von Hayek in *The Road to Serfdom* [2], the dilemma recognized by H.G. Wells when he confessed that he could not live in any utopia he could design, the dilemma faced by New Town planners to close off certain life-style choice options for the future populations of the town they are designing by the very act of making initial units operational—this dilemma must be confronted creatively in the educational process if we are to create a widely accepted future for the planet. Only if an image of the future has broad appeal can it generate the consensus required to initiate and sustain constructive action.

Fostering the Future

In the rest of this paper I will explore what it would mean to devote the educational enterprises of society to a fostering of the future-creating capacities of the entire population. I will focus specifically on the content of the educational process and the structure of educational institutions. My conclusions derive from several assumptions about existing levels of human adaptation to life in the solar system. First, I believe that human potential in every subsystem of the individual, including the physical, cognitive, empathic, and spiritual-intuitive, remains largely undeveloped after 10,000 years of experience with urban population concentrations and the accompanying cultural elaborations in successive civilizations.

I also believe that as long as human collectivities remained small, in units of two to five hundred people, and the environments familiar, feedback systems were operative among humans and between humans and their environment. These feedbacks enabled people to engage in the finely-tuned adaptations that produced steady-state societies. When hunting and gathering bands destroyed environmental resources, as described in Peter Farb [3], it was in situations where they were exposed to unfamiliar environments through climatic changes and migrations. Under stable conditions they carefully preserved environmental resources, as can be seen in the behavior of surviving hunting and gathering bands in marginal areas of the planet today.

The complex forms of social organization and resource control that accompanied urbanization created a scale of existence in which the feedback systems operative in the band could no longer function. Instead, a series of specialized feedback loops giving partial information about the total system developed along with specialized mastery of various aspects of the environment. The specialized masteries involved use of water, wind, sun, soil, and minerals, plus controlled animal and human energy to construct new environments.

This increasing technological ingenuity in the mastery of certain parts of the environment created a set of screens preventing perception of the environment as a total system. The resulting segmentary type of knowledge has until recently been adaptive in protecting humans from overload due to complexities of the emerging physicosocial system. But people must understand the total ecosystem at all levels, from local communities to the planetary ecosystem, if society is to survive; perturbations at one level increasingly affect environments at other levels. It therefore becomes imperative not only to create more feedback loops giving more information about the total ecosystem, but to work with the human capacities to comprehend system complexity and anticipate future consequences of present system interactions. Thus new modes for perceiving reality will be essential in developing the capacity of humans to cope with ecological complexity. In the absence of enhanced capacities to deal with complexity, the survival instincts of humans will drive them to misdirected efforts to cut off necessary information and rely on the type of technological manipulations of parts of systems that have served them in the past.

NEW INFORMATION PROCESSING TECHNIQUES

Taking these assumptions into account, I will suggest some ways to enhance human capacities to absorb information about the world and utilize it in the evolutionary process of futures creation. I will touch on:

—ways of experiencing micro-time and macro-time, both in their cyclic and noncyclic aspects;

—procedures for experiencing micro-environments and macro-environments;

—approaches for reconstructing learning environments that break down age, sex, ethnic, and other types of societal segregation that hamper the adequate modeling of total systems;

—ways of building up mental models of reality through different kinds of mapping of environments, and through use of nonlinear as well as linear thinking;

—techniques for shifting the evolution of culture away from higher levels of aggression toward paths that lead to higher levels of nurturance.

Learning to Experience Time

Does it sound ridiculous to suggest that people must learn to experience time? Fred Polak says that twentieth century people are moment-ridden, perceiving only micro-time [4]. The ability to think of futures requires familiarity with many different characteristics of time. One set of characteristics relates to cycles. As in all the suggestions to be made here, I propose to begin with an in-depth exploration of cycles that can be experienced with our own bodies, and then move to an examination of personal surroundings. No one knows how many subcycles exist within the human body, but a few of them can be discovered.

Individual Cycles. The preschooler is already interested in body cycles. Awareness of breathing is perhaps the child's first experience of a cycle. This soon expands to an interest in the sleeping-waking and fueling-excretion cycles. These quickly become battlegrounds for parent and child from the earliest months of a child's life, as each party attempts to assert the prerogative of control. Suppose the educational system were geared to a progressive understanding of more and more of the hundreds of cyclic processes and rhythms of the human body? Gay Luce suggests that this would transform care of infants, children, and the aging, to say nothing of people in the middle years of life, because if people learned to hear and understand messages about the functioning of their body systems, they could develop adaptive behavior in resting, eating, sleeping, exercising, and other functions that would produce levels of health and well-being unavailable through common sense and medication [5].

At the moment biofeedback is somewhat cultic, and associated with social attitudes that involve preoccupation with personal body states. It could, however, be taught as social hygiene. Also, it could provide an early experience with computer-assisted interactive learning that would be a valuable tool for later learning about more complex systems. In the context of the present discussion, biofeedback is not only inherently valuable in tuning individuals in to their body's primary feedback systems with which they will be living all their lives: it also provides a reality base from which to expand the understanding of cycles. From a body cycle to an individual life cycle is a small yet profound step. Learning mentally to move around in the total life space of three score and ten years is the basic future-imaging exercise open to participation by anyone of any age.

From some years of asking parents, college students, and children to image their personal futures in ten-year intervals, I can testify that people are generally unaware of their life space beyond the coming year. Plans for the future tend to be mechanistic and career-focused and to ignore the potentials for holistic development of self-in-society. Since people are generally punished rather than rewarded for fantasizing and daydreaming, the one available source of future imaging in the average young person is nipped in the bud rather early. Yet it is but a step from personal daydreaming to social daydreaming.

Some children grow up with their fantasy capacity intact, especially if they have been allowed enough solitude as children. Edward Bellamy was such a person, and his *Looking Backward* is a good example of constructive social daydreaming that really caught the imagination of his own age [6]. Edward Bellamy clubs were formed all over the United States in the 1880s and 1890s. I examined the relationship between solitude and creativity in children in my paper "Children and Solitude" [7].

The problem inherent in familiarizing oneself with the total life space is that the individualistic achievement ethic of American society often makes such fantasizing too narrow and self-oriented. A real challenge is to develop imaging exercises that will help children and adults to broaden the concept of their total life space.

Universal Cycles. In addition to the personal body cycles, there are two other sets of cycles that every person experiences in a primary way and that can be utilized from the very beginning of the educational process: the family life cycle and the cycles determined by earth's place in the solar system. There is good reason to believe that the interaction of three sets of cycles—of the individual human being, the family, and the day-week-month-season-year—provided the basic starting point for the kind of time-binding and storying of human experience that launched the adventures of Homosapiens in civilization after millenia of wanderings [8, 9].

Today's passion for astrology is an understandable, if pathological, analogue of ancient human experience in taking significant cues from seasonal changes for the patterning of life. For the Neanderthals such cues were a matter of life and death. They related to the spawning of fish, the birthing of animals, and the fruiting of grasses, bushes, and trees. The customary position today is that such knowledge is superfluous for all but farmers and hunters. Yet how much richer society's perceptions of reality would be if those seasonal changes could be seen as part of a pattern that includes life and death both for the individual and for families, as they form households and move through successive configurations of age-youth relationships until the old die and the young re-form households.

It has been the historic function of religion to articulate and synchronize these various environmental and human life-cycle rhythms. Special feast days in all religious traditions celebrate key intersection points for the human and environmental rhythms. The irony of secularization is that it creates feasting without celebration, since the feasters are no longer in touch with the cycles that the festivals punctuate.

If children can again be given an awareness of the many intersecting cycles they can touch with their own lives, by the age of ten they can gain an empathy with the cycle of civilizations. The most vivid memory of my own tenth year was living through the flowering and decline of Greek civilization with a gifted fourth grade teacher. However partially and incompletely, this teacher taught me to pattern social understandings. The historic rhythms of war and peace, arms and disarmament, economic depression and prosperity, should be discussed cautiously and nondogmatically as exercises in examples of social patterns that have infinite variations. Cycle patterning should be taught first because it is the most easily identified. But such rhythms must not be taught as mechanical regularities; it must be clear that cycles are only one of many possible patterns.

Skills of pattern identification are important for the futurist, since they elucidate the character of time flows. Part of the present crisis is caused by the several generations of social scientists, planners, and administrators who have been trained only to perceive certain segments of patterns and to do simple projections of those segments in forecasting futures.

For the young to learn to critique as well as to identify patterning is crucial, since an excessive intellectual attachment to certain types of patterning, particularly cycles, can also lead to entrapment. An education that puts everything in terms of cycles, for example, could lead to its own peculiar rigidities. This is why nonrecurrent sequences must be discovered along with the cyclic. To feel at home in time requires the ability to differentiate between circularity and openendness. All the great universal religions make this distinction, although variant sects that emphasize the cyclic nature of history are found in every universal religion including Christianity. This aberrant tendency towards total closure is correctly noted as a source of social apathy. The understanding of body cycles and body limits serves as a corrective to mechanistic cyclic thinking. Personal feedback about the constraints imposed by body cycles enhances the capacity to function by giving signals about when one can be maximally effective and about the open-ended moment for an individual, as well as about when we personally have reached our limits. At the simplest level one should not try to accomplish major tasks on "off days" if it can be avoided.

Extended Present. In addition to feeling at home in the multi-patterned, multilevel complexity of social processes at the micro-level and the macro-level by a gradual extension of personal, primary feedback experiences through the reading of history, the futures-creating individual must learn to live in an extended present. The present as defined by the year, the decade, or even the quarter century is too small for an adequate grasp of significant social processes. I propose that all our teaching be based on the concept of a two hundred-year present. This interval is an organic temporal unit; it reaches back to the year of birth of the centenarians in our midst and forward to the year of death of the future centenarians being born today. Two centuries is the time spanned by current members of the race. During the student antiwar movement of the late 1960s, many students swore off social activism because they had not stopped the war with two or three months' effort. To overcome their discouragement I developed the concept of an extended present to convey to young people the length of the time spans required for changing and assessing social processes.

What does taking this time span as our familiar present do for futurists? It makes accessible the beginnings of global thinking in the nineteenth century world fairs of London, Paris, and Chicago, and in the transnational associations for humanitarian, cultural, and economic purposes that arose in large numbers at the beginning of the twentieth century. It emphasizes the Eurocentric character of globalism and provides a better perspective on the Third World's aspirations. Goals of the poor in the South and East will increasingly reshape thinking with differentiated concepts of a multicultural globalism in the next hundred years of the current extended present. Two hundred-year profiles of fossil fuel use and population growth are becoming common, but the image of cultural evolution still encompasses a short time span.

Warren Ziegler and his associates at Syracuse University developed a technique for describing an achieved social goal in 1990 and then wrote a year-by-year scenario from 1990 back to the present. To discover how a social goal was attained helps the student conceive of the extended present. Children who begin learning about this extended present in elementary school will have a lot less to unlearn as they grow older, because their curriculum will not have been so disproportionately focused on an international system, the traumas of war, and diplomatic failure in the first three-quarters of the twentieth century. They will be familiar with a United States in which the defense budget has been less than 1 percent of the GNP instead of over 7 percent, and they will also know its imperialist habits better.

Experiencing Feedback Systems

I have focused so far on identification of patterns in time. Starting from an initial recognition of body and seasonal rhythms, I have suggested ways a child may acquire greater capacity to read time-patterned signals about process in the present, past, and future. Now I will turn to the matter of identifying signals from environments about conditions in the present. The problem is to overcome the handicaps of the chronological screening that protects individuals from feedback about larger environments, and particularly to overcome the ideology that assigns a positive value to escaping the need for information about that environment. A handy example of that ideology is Bellamy's umbrella for cities, so their inhabitants would never know when it rained [10]. The problem divides into two parts: how to teach children and adults to absorb feedback at even the simplest level, and how to cope with multiple feedback about macroenvironments.

Since I chose the body as the source for primary experience of cycles, I will use the simplest imaginable habitat as the generator of primary experience of environments. A simple program would involve twenty-four hours spent on a small square of ground with no shelter and no equipment with instructions to monitor every happening and change of state. Simple variants for older young people could be underground shelters with oxygen and moisture content varied from outside, and with computer equipment provided for monitoring and adjustment. More elaborate efforts could involve replication of a complete life-support system as designed for space, with life-support components varied. The goal is to enhance the individual's capacity for absorbing feedback from the environment. An increasingly finer tuning of that feedback capacity could be developed with further, more controlled conditions.

What would such experiences of environments do for an individual? When presented in the proper context, they could become a metaphor for planetary ecosystems, just as the body becomes a metaphor for time. By introducing this metaphoric approach to complex environmental systems, the individual can grasp complex wholes in ways that do not involve tracing out untraceable linear sequences. Systematic training in nonlinear representation of successively more complex ecosystems, accompanied of course by all the analytic training that ecology can provide, will enable students to cope with complexity in the face of incomplete understanding, rather than to retreat from it, or to simplify it. I require students to provide metaphoric and nonlinear representations of community ecosystems and social change processes so that they begin to see dimensions of the phenomenon they would not otherwise uncover. This alternative thinking appears to enrich their analytic capacities. The danger of reductionism is always present, but a careful paralleling of linear and nonlinear modes of thinking, and an occasional switch to simpler systems for a concrete reference point, expands the capacity to take feedback from complexity.

My discussion has been couched in terms of physical environments. The same exercises can be conducted within social environments, using the family as the primary social experience. But the program can be carried out so that it first articulates all the feedback systems created by familial interaction, and then moves to secondary associations, complex national institutions, transnational networks, and finally the sociosphere. Use of metaphor, introduction of computer interactive equipment, and regrounding in simple primary systems when excessive confusion sets in, apply equally to exercises in processing feedback from social systems.

Reconstructing the Learning Sites of Society

Until now I have been discussing ways to help individuals regain the capacity and the self-confidence to take feedback from physical and social systems and to deal with that feedback. The focus has been on learning situations, with learning sites a secondary consideration. It is time now to turn to the issue of where people learn. On the whole, classrooms are unlikely sites for the kind of learning just described. In fact, they are important parts of the set of screens preventing perception of the environment as a total system. Not only do they filter out information, but they also reinforce a pattern of hypersegregation that divides society into a series of noncommunicating sectors and creates high levels of social autism and mistrust. The school system is the kingpin of the age-segregation system that takes children out of meaningful involvement with the productive processes of society and carries them lockstep through life in their own age sets from toddler groups to golden-age retirement clubs.

Since the school system also to a considerable extent reinforces sex segregation through differential expectations of achievement and reinforces neighborhood-based ethnic and racial segregation, it seems a poor instrument for teaching anyone how to employ feedback about complex social systems.

Apprenticeships. I propose that the entire community be conceptualized as a complex of learning sites, full of teachers and learners of all ages, engaged in all kinds of occupations and avocations representing various skill levels. Much of the learning will be done through apprenticeship, and no one is too old to be an apprentice, or too young to be a teacher. This is not a wild notion; both Illich and Freire have expounded similar ideas [11, 12]. Archibald Shaw put forth a practical proposal for such an educational system in 1956. His idea was to turn

> the school into a headquarters, and the entire community into a complex of learning sites. This would involve a substantial redeployment of personnel and resources in our public schools, as well as a substantial redefinition of the relationship between school and community, teachers and community persons, adults and children. The school headquarters provides classroom teaching for very specific skills, and the rest of the learning takes place in a variety of apprenticeship situations which are arranged between pupils and every adult in the community at his place of work. . . . A substantial part of the school personnel, now engaged in classroom teaching or in-house administrative work, would be developing and coordinating the numerous linkages which would be needed to ensure that every adult in the community spent some time in a teaching relationship with pupils at his place of work [13].

In 1971, I wrote about this scheme:

> This of course could produce a horrendous new bureaucracy, unless the linkage persons themselves were also involved in community-based productive work. Previous experiments have broken down largely because linkage persons have remained outsiders, resented by the community. They have appeared as advocates of second-class education for minority children, as a force to deprive the already deprived of chances to enter the success system the outside innovator remains cosily esconced in. Part-time employment at various apprenticeship sites in the community for all persons associated with the educational system may be part of the answer here. This breaks down the specialist role of both the teacher and the administrator. There would naturally be enormous resistance to this. Think of the resistances, and also the potentials, in a project of turning all labor union headquarters, including teacher's unions, into learning sites for children [14].

Imagine every church having to take on apprentices to teach the skills involved in maintaining a church, every community club taking on apprentices to teach the skills involved in being a community organization with a civic purpose, every father and mother taking on young girls and boys who are not their own children to teach home-craft, cooking, or infant care. The amount of reflection that adults would have to go through in order to identify what they do and why they do it would be enough to cause a social revolution in itself. This learning model involves acquiring competence in what you do in the process of training others to do it. It is also a model for meaningful integration of community members from all sectors into the total life of the community.

Mapping. This approach to acquiring a complex of vocational and avocational skills, combined with a judicious use of school buildings as special skill centers, lays the groundwork for developing mental models of the community as a complex social system that fits nicely into the discussions of temporal and situational feedback systems. The focus is no longer on children alone, since everyone is part of this system. The best efforts of the school centers would go into helping people of all ages make various kinds of maps of the community in terms of different kinds of community resources, and into building up a model of the total community that can become the basis for futures thinking at the community level. I have watched a neighborhood in the town of Boulder, Colorado, go through this model-building process. College students in architecture and in sociology were apprenticed to a neighborhood association over a period of several years, and the area became a learning site. The next steps will bring in the neighborhood elementary and high school. The emergent model of the neighborhood in the city, in the state, and in the nation is new to everyone. Feedback loops are being identified that were previously unrecognized. The general competence level of the neighborhood is being uncovered and appreciated. Small-scale experiments with this type of use of school as headquarters and the community as the learning setting already exist in some other communities across the country, notably in Philadelphia, Minneapolis, Cincinnati, and Berkeley.

Chadwick Alger's City-in-theWorld/World-in-the-City project initiated several years ago in Columbus, Ohio [15], takes the same type of community mapping to the global level, and makes it possible for any community to discover its interconnectedness with the world. Replications of this project both inside and outside the United States are demonstrating that this approach to understanding the world as a total system has great potential.

There is a whole complex of processes involved in identifying sociophysical systems in their two hundred-year present, in mapping them, and in tuning in on the feedback loops. The free play of the imagination with this information reconceptualizes the future. The reconceptualization, however, must be grounded in the primary experience of microenvironments. Some global mappers seem to have learned in this way by accident, not by design of any school system. (I would suggest Jonas Salk and Donella Meadows as examples.) They have a strong feeling for the human ingredients in the systems in which they work. Why not redesign the educational system so everyone can learn to link primary experience with complex systems? The humanistic world modelers are the exception in our society, not the rule.

Most of our student population, from kindergarten on, is trained for the ultimate tasks of administering or designing systems of human services in settings removed from all possibility of reality feedback. It is people so trained who are having to struggle with the administration of bankrupt cities, with unworkable welfare or health care delivery systems, with a totally unwieldly and largely uncontrollable military defense system. There are few futurists among them. They are mainly harried redesigners who often make systems worse by attempted modification of obvious ills. An example of such a failure is the recent collapse of nursing home care in some areas of the United States, through new centrally-administered specifications.

The Futurist as Lover

Nothing has been said about energy crises or the need for changing life-styles in the face of world poverty and hunger in this paper. So far I have dealt with the development of perceptions of system wholes and system limitations in ways anchored to primary experience and drawn from both analytic and intuitive capacities. I have looked at a way of organizing the schooling of society that breaks down existing barriers to perception of and participation in social processes at the community level. While the analysis has focused more on the community than the globe, all the approaches proposed can be translated to the global level. I have not said anything about behavioral responses to the new perception of total systems, whether locally or internationally. Whatever people find out, will they care when they find out? Will they want to do anything? Will they become creative futurists? Or will they perhaps become demonic manipulators of time and society? People educated in the ways I have described are highly unlikely to become manipulative futurists. A continual emphasis on grounding in primary experience would develop their capacity for social empathy, as feedback is taken in from higher level systems. This type of grounding would also develop competence to act on empathic perceptions. The metaphoric mode should carry empathy upwards. Nevertheless, such developments should not be taken for granted. The accidents of social drift, a term used in sociobiology to describe trends in animal society that may be triggered accidentally but once started gain their own momentum, have led to an overdevelopment of the genetically programed predisposition to aggress. It is not a uniquely significant programing because it exists along with a number of other programed predispositions, including the one to nurture. Environments and situations can selectively reinforce one set of predispositions over and against the other.

At this moment in history very high levels of violence are taken for granted in many societies. Thus it is important to go as far as possible in fostering the predisposition to nurture and in creating alternatives to the dynamics of violence. A detailed analysis of the dynamics of altruism and nurturance is not possible here [16], but it may be said briefly that the capacity for such behavior in agents of social change depends on feelings of competence developed through past success in problem-solving, a behavioral repertoire accumulated over a fairly wide range of social settings, some experience of being alienated and set apart from society, and a reintegrating perception of the possibility of a caring society triggered by exposure at some point in life to caring people.

To the curriculum suggestions presented here, then, must be added the plus of people who can communicate caring and joyfulness to others out of their own inner abundance. It is difficult to develop an analytic model of love processes, but easy to identify human role models. They are the Epoch B people described by Jonas Salk in *The Survival of the Wisest* [17]. A celebration of the capacities for loving and joy wherever they are found, and a new focus in history books and the mass media on the conflict resolvers and peacemakers, are countertrends that must be initiated soon. The dynamics of violence will not be reversed as long as all communication channels reward aggression.

The true futurist is a lover, one who loves the whole turbulent mass of humanity and sees flashes of beauty where others see only confusion. The ancient impulse to construct imagined utopias is triggered by the perception of the flashes of beauty, and the desire to expand these flashes into holistic conceptions of what society could be like. Every utopia harnesses certain technologies to its vision. During the next one hundred years of our extended present, more technologies will be explored as more sectors of the world society enter upon futures invention. Not homogeneity, but increasing heterogeneity lies ahead, particularly as the next generations develop a feel for complexity without the crutches of hierarchy and centralization. Who knows how many ways there are to live humanly on a finite planet?

Chapter 16

Towards a Primary Life-style

Robert Allen

CURRENT PROSPECT: THE GRIP OF DISEQUILIBRIUM

Nowadays, most human societies, industrial and non-industrial, are gripped by disequilibrium. That is to say, they are collapsing. Collapse is a process whereby a society grows progressively less capable of realizing its objectives. The onset of collapse is obscured by humanity's apparent capacity for lowering its sights and aiming for less ambitious objectives step by step with a growing incapacity for achieving the higher ones. Diminishing aspiration masks diminishing ability to fulfill. Since it is axiomatic, at least in industrial and industrializing countries, that progress cannot be stopped, at the merest hint of its coming to a halt it must be redefined.

The citizens of industrial countries apparently regard spiritual and emotional fulfillment—and even good health—as sufficiently nebulous goals for them to be abandoned without much ado as long as material wealth increases. If and when the increase of material wealth becomes more difficult, its quality is sacrificed seemingly without qualm so long as the quantity is maintained. Should quantity be threatened, then at once the range of moral concern is reduced; first other countries are excluded, then "different" communities within

Editor's Note: This chapter has been substantially revised by the editor from the longer original Mitchell Prize-winning paper. Many of the anthropological data supporting Allen's arguments have been removed in order to focus the discussion on the alternatives to growth theme. The full version of the paper with supporting data is available from the author or the editor.

the nation are excluded, and finally all but families and crucial individuals are excluded.

This unhappy process is occurring because technologism, the driving force of the industrial way of life, is an unusually expensive way of satisfying human needs. Its propellant is consumerism, a form of economic addiction whereby luxuries are turned into essentials. For example, when the automobile first came on the market, it was merely an amusing novelty, and for as long as it was owned by only a few people the pleasure it gave was harmless. Now, however, society has been thoroughly transformed by it, and a great many people could not survive without the car.

The growth and maintenance of an industrial economy demands that luxuries become essentials, but each transformation of a luxury into an essential requires the commitment of that much more energy, capital, and effort for essentially the same return (in terms of the satisfaction of human needs). Thus, the members of an industrial (or industrializing) society are caught on a treadmill. A nation with a GNP of x will aspire to a GNP of $x + 1$ in order to acquire that luxury that will compensate, it is hoped, for the losses—of perhaps health, or peace, or other nonmaterial goods—incurred through achieving the GNP of x. However, on achieving $x + 1$, it will find that unless $x + 1$ is maintained, the standard of living will drop. By virtue of the fact that luxuries become essentials and "needs" proliferate, all that is achieved by the growth of GNP is the provision of progressively inferior compensations for progressively more serious deprivations.

These deprivations are mounting. They are only beginning to become obvious because in many cases industrial society has managed to defer them to future generations or displace them to other countries. This policy of deferment, while understandable, is ultimately self-defeating, partly because willy-nilly the long-term becomes the short-term, and partly because if the industrial economy is at all successful it must inevitably reduce the number of countries willing to accept a disproportionate amount of deprivation. Industrial countries depend in large measure on the availability of poor nonindustrial ones to supply them with low-cost materials. However, to persuade such countries to participate in this venture rich countries must dangle a carrot in front of them, the carrot in question being the benefits of industrial development. When at last some of these countries do begin to develop, two things happen. First, the number of low-cost supplier countries diminishes; second, the number of countries demanding the compensations of affluence increases. So "traditional" industrial countries find that, because they have fewer cheap suppliers, their costs go up and their competitive trading advantage narrows and eventually disappears. At the same time, they find it much more difficult to satisfy the demands of their vociferous peoples for luxuries and, indeed, essentials at prices they can afford, because competition for them has become so great.

The deferred costs of technologism include the disruption of ecosystems on which man depends for high-quality, economical food production, thus making it more expensive to grow food; the depletion of high-grade mineral ores, thus making manufacturing more costly; and social disruption—for example, anomie, neuroses, and violence—thus making it more expensive to maintain even the fiction of social harmony. These costs, which at first merely contribute to inflation, will eventually become unpayable. The biological and social systems on which people depend for survival and well-being are not resources in the currently accepted economic sense. Yet depend on these systems they do, whether or not they have sufficient grasp of the functions of these systems to "demand" them. If people fail to put the appropriate value on them until they are so reduced that the law of supply and demand forces their accurate valuation, it will be too late.

Even assuming that this analysis is widely perceived, it is unlikely that governments are in a position to act on it. For too long they have promoted as the only possible solutions to whatever problems that beset them, those that will inevitably deepen disequilibrium. To a significant extent, this is due to their inability to win enough of the trust of their peoples for them to be confident that any appeal they might make for economic restraint would be responded to by all of the more powerful sections of society. Hence the concentration of their appeal on the lowest common social and economic denominators—not a promising position from which to direct a nation from disequilibrium to equilibrium.

The large-scale, quasi-centralized societies of Europe and America have not yet developed satisfactory systems for justly and harmoniously determining their objectives, for which reason there remains a general absence of clearly stated and accepted goals. Normally, this would not matter, because most societies are, or used to be, sufficiently homogeneous for their goals to be understood. Now, however, especially in industrial countries, they are agglomerations of minorities, some ethnic, some religious, some class, some occupational. Often the majority is an artificial one, emerging only at elections, the product of an illusory consensus. Hence the dangerous uncertainty to which many Western nations are prey. They no longer consist of functioning communities but are rag-bags of competing interest groups; in Chapter 11 LaMontagne labels this characteristic factionalism. By whatever name, these groups impel themselves along the line of least resistance, and there is a new concept in political mobility: headlong drift.

A NEW PROSPECT FOR EQUILIBRIUM: THE DEVELOPMENT OF NORMS

Yet out of this unprecedented combination of chaos and impotence could emerge equilibrium societies. Encouraging signs include:

—the growing demand for social and environmental services that divert capital and labor from industry, thus slowing economic growth, whether intentionally or not;

—the growing interest in the concept of equilibrium, and the increasing number of well-argued appeals that equilibrium should be a prime policy goal;

—the formation of small communities, generally at the tiny "commune" level, with the object of developing a life-style consistent with and promoting equilibrium;

—the continued, and somewhat miraculous, survival of societies of hunter-gatherers, hunter-gardeners, and other modest rural economies, that have lived in equilibrium for many generations.

The first three of these signs may be interpreted as societies' early, tentative steps towards the development of norms, without which the more general achievement and maintenance of equilibrium is impossible. Needs, wants, and norms may be distinguished as follows. Needs are requirements established phylogenetically, during the evolution of the human species, and thus are experienced by all mankind. Wants are personal preferences established ontogenetically, during the development of the individual, and thus may be experienced by only a few individuals. However, individuals do not perceive needs as such but only as wants. Norms are cultural devices by which a society assures the satisfaction of the needs of all its members through the satisfaction of their wants.

For example, some form of dwelling is a biological necessity in order to protect the body from too much heat, cold, or wet, and to help give the individual a sense of security. However, individual preferences as to the form of dwelling are likely to vary markedly and could provoke destructive competition if they required the disproportionate use of scarce resources. Different societies have therefore developed different ideas common to their members alone of what a dwelling should consist. The climates of Italy and California are very similar, so that the considerable differences between the traditional house-forms of Italians and Californian Indians for the most part express differences of culture rather than of physical conditions. The important function of this cultural adaptation is the collective satisfaction of individual wants. Any further variation from the norm is thus more likely to be modest, unassertive, and harmless.

Norms ensure the satisfaction of the needs of a community's members through the optimization of their competing wants. Norms are a name for internal controls. The advantages to a community of internal over external controls are the same as for any system. If a person's body temperature, blood pressure, fluid release, and so on, were not controlled by self-regulating internal devices, but were regulated externally by him in response to readings from a set of dials, he would find his attention fully occupied for every second of his life. It would be impossible for him to account for the competing requirements of every physiological process, every response to the changing external environment, every interaction among all these, and the subtle tradeoffs between them.

Similarly, a society whose controls are internalized will balance the competing desires of its component individuals better than would a judge, a policeman, or a taxman. To put it crudely, laws enshrine the possibility of disobedience. Norms make it virtually inconceivable. This is not to say that laws are unnecessary, but to suggest that, in the absence of norms, they are at best unworkable and at worst counter-productive.

RETROSPECT: AN ANALYSIS OF PAST EQUILIBRIUM

Accordingly, the dominant trend that will accompany equilibrium, indeed the indispensable condition of an equilibrium society, must be the emergence of such norms—specifically, norms that lead to a stable population in which births do not exceed deaths, and a stable consumption rate by which both the needs and wants of people are met with the minimum disruption of the environment.

By definition, such norms will not be articulated as a declaration of rights, a set of laws, or a memorandum of agreed objectives. They will evolve step by step with the evolution of well-integrated, homogeneous societies. This does not mean, however, that people should sit on their hands and wait for deliverance. Much can be done to facilitate the development of equilibrium communities.

A major goal should be the discovery of the norms that operated in recent equilibrium societies and may operate still in the few that survive. This is *not* because it is necessary or desirable to imitate, still less duplicate, past societies. Rather, it is because by discovering these norms we may discover the principles or general rules whereby norms governing the regulation of human numbers and human acquisitiveness might operate. The study of past and surviving equilibrium societies is not a backward step, nor an invitation to one, but a way of avoiding the fatuous utopianism of inventing a future without a meaningful link to human experience.

Population Control in Equilibrium Societies

Equilibrium societies have always determined family size by social convention assisted by mechanisms to inhibit, or mitigate, the effects of fertility. The evidence that many hunter-gatherers and other similar peoples achieved and maintained equilibrium is now widely accepted [1, 2]. The mechanisms by which they have achieved equilibrium vary: for example, the Sharanahua practice abortion [3], the Desana use oral plant contraceptives [4], and the Tapirape resort to infanticide [5]. Combinations of some or all of these are common, generally reinforced by various sexual taboos.

By definition, those populations that have intuitively recognized their optimum size do not grow. Those that are growing, however, are not necessarily below optimum size. These populations have often exceeded their optima, but because they have lost the intuitive recognition of the optimum, they have also lost any semblance of control. Such is the case globally, and socioeconomic measures should be developed to encourage consistently smaller families so that communities, instead of growing, simply replace themselves. The search for an equilibrium society would be facilitated if it were possible to find out what feedbacks operated among equilibrium societies to encourage their members to have small families. The development of internal controls in this society would be aided if it were clear what internal controls operated on others. The mechanisms—contraception, abortion, and so on—are of secondary importance, since if people are strongly enough driven to limit family size they will do so irrespective of the means available to them. Whatever the mechanisms, some form of feedback whereby a population intuitively recognizes and adjusts to its optimum, is essential—and it must be powerful enough to overcome the great attachment almost all people have for children.

For the purposes of discovering these feedbacks, I have explored the norms of those societies for which there is good evidence that they are, or have been until recently, in equilibrium. The analysis was restricted to certain hunter-gatherers, such as the San of Botswana and the Australian Aborigines, and obviously stable hunter-gardeners (agriculturalists for whom hunting and/or fishing is an important source of protein) in the Americas and various islands of the Pacific. Those of other areas were not included, because of the probable role of epidemics in periodically suppressing their populations. The Americans are unusual in that they seem to have been completely isolated from major epidemics like smallpox and probably malaria until the arrival of Europeans [6], and therefore epidemics cannot be invoked as a factor enabling precontact American populations to achieve equilibrium.

Also omitted are unusually warlike peoples like the Jivaro of Ecuador and the Yanomamo of Venezuela, to exclude the possibility of warfare regulating numbers. Perhaps this is an unnecessary precaution as the losses incurred through tribal hostilities are rarely high enough to be decisive for population control and the Yanomamo have to resort to abortion, infanticide, intercourse taboos, and prolonged lactation to reduce the average effective live birth rate to about one child every four or five years [7]. Nevertheless, since I do not wish to promote normative principles that might arguably depend for their effectiveness on epidemics or warfare, my conclusions derive from study of a selection of populations regulated relatively peacefully and of their own volition.

Various hypotheses have been suggested as to what the principal internal controls might be that enable such peoples to maintain equilibrium. For hunter-gatherers, Lee [8] and Howell [9] have proposed a nomadic burden hypothesis, perhaps supplemented by the effects of diet, and this has been developed by Dumond [10] to incorporate his interpretation of hunter-gatherer economic relationships. I have discussed the influence of meat availability [11], and Siskind the influence of the availability of women [12]. For certain agriculturalists, Douglas has proposed that the availability of much sought-after luxuries provides the control [13]. These hypotheses can be unified into one that has relevance to the contemporary predicament.

Nomadic Burden Hypothesis. Dumond points out that the need by a nomadic mother to space her children so that they would not impede her performance as a mother and the provider of plant foods would strongly motivate her to resort to such mechanisms as infanticide or abortion, if only as emergency measures when the presumed effects of long lactation failed to function [14]. He argues that this motivation is reinforced by the direct economic responsibility placed on hunter-gatherer parents by their organization in nuclear families; and he goes on to derive comfort from this in relation to our own circumstances as industrialization reduces the extended family to the nuclear. Unfortunately, this oversimplifies the hunter-gatherer economic order, in which the food-sharing ethic is so strong that it crosses the boundaries of nuclear families, such as they exist, and overrides any "irresponsibility" by a mother.

Meat Availability Hypothesis. Indeed, food-sharing probably plays an important part in the operation of another likely control, that of meat availability, in cultures where meat is an "essential luxury"—in other words, something that is necessary for well-being and is highly valued, but is not critical to survival. The limiting factor in the growth of a population may be food or water or, in the cases of industrial societies, oil or some other commodity. Whatever it is, an effective control must operate well before the limiting factor comes under pressure, and the longer the time-lag required for response to the control, the earlier the control must come into play.

Men hunt, women gather. The plants that are gathered are the principal support of the community; the meat that is hunted helps control the community's population dynamic. There remains, however, the problem of how the individual is persuaded to act in a way that is beneficial to the community but is hurtful to himself. I believe the answer lies in the pattern of food sharing. When food is shared, there is a close identity of interest between individual and community. Significantly, the sharing of plant foods, small game, insects, and the like is normally confined to the family, and it is the meat (specifically from large game) that is shared throughout the entire community.

Meat availability provides an important cultural control enabling hunter-gatherer populations to stabilize within the carrying capacity of the land. It is of unquestioned nutritional importance, yet its periodic scarcity or absence would not provoke demographic catastrophe, while that of a plant staple would. Its cultural importance is attested by the fact that even though gathering is the main subsistence activity, men concentrate on hunting. Also, the shortage of meat stimulates band fission in some populations and probably contributes to the interpersonal tensions that have the same effect in others. Finally, the fact that meat is shared throughout the community means that every individual feels the need for it. Thus the influence of meat availability is both powerful and pervasive enough to be an effective control.

It would be a mistake to suppose, however, that meat availability provides the only cultural control. Controls that depend on a single variable are highly vulnerable, and there is reason to believe that those affecting hunter-gatherer population dynamics are rather complex. The nomadic burden hypothesis, for example, complements that of meat availability, the former operating through the women, the latter through the men. However, the nomadic burden hypothesis is obviously not applicable to hunter-gardeners and other agricultural and more settled peoples. For them, it is more profitable to pursue the theme of essential luxuries.

Essential Luxury Hypothesis. This idea has been advanced most persuasively by Douglas who suggests that the controls regulating most equilibrium societies operate through the demand for luxuries within well-established prestige structures [15]. She illustrates her theory with the Polynesian Island of Tikopia, which in 1929 with 1,300 inhabitants was believed by its inhabitants to be densely populated. "Strong social disapproval was felt for couples who reared families of more than two, or at most three children. Their population policy was aimed at steady replacement. It was exerted by contraception, abortion, infanticide . . ." [16]. Yet there was no evidence of pressure on the land, and the people were very free and easy about borrowing and lending the garden land on which they grew their staples, taro and yams. However, they were strict about orchard land, where the coconuts are grown. A difference over orchard land would make men fight. Then in 1952 and 1953, typhoons brought famine. Few people died of starvation, but the orchards were destroyed. Fear of such famines, which occurred every twenty years or so, kept the population down, not because people feared starvation, but because there would not be enough coconuts. Coconuts were highly valued for their cream: they made food much more palatable. Without coconuts, the Tikopians did not like to hold feasts; without feasts they could have no religious ceremonies; and without ceremonies the entire social life would collapse.

Here, as always, an indispensible condition is a shared value system, so that the entire population perceives the luxury as an essential without which life becomes intolerable. Once they come to believe that their religious ceremonies are humbug or that Coca Cola is better than coconuts, then the controls vanish. This emerges very clearly in certain South American hunter-gardeners, like the Desana of Colombia, the Sharanahua of Peru, the Tapirape of Brazil, the Waiwai of Guyana, and the Yaruro of Venezuela.

Identification with Nature. Because the cultural focus of the Desana, as of the other American hunter-gardeners, is not the garden but the hunt, their dependence on the natural environment, rather than their capacity to manipulate it, is emphasized. It strengthens their belief in the close identity and interchangeability of humans and other creatures. This conviction is found in many equilibrium societies. The Desana, for example, believe that the hunter may kill only certain game animals and only on specified occasions; if he violates this principle he will fall victim to dangerous animals and diseases, justice will be done by his death, and equilibrium restored when the latent energy in his spirit is returned to the animals. The Waiwai have a spirit category of animals created from the souls of the dead which include some of their more important game animals like the tapir and the deer.

This intimate identification with the rest of nature is at the center of the complex of norms that has enabled South American hunter-gardeners to so restrain their numbers that they have succeeded in living well for generation after generation in one of the most difficult environments in the world—the interfluvial zone of the Amazon basin. Meggers sums up their achievement thus: "With the exception of the Siriono, the *terra firme* [interfluvial] tribes appear to have enjoyed abundant subsistence resources and a generally easy life. In fact, they illustrate very well the idyllic existence that has led temperate zone observers to regard Amazonia as a paradise not fully exploited by the indigenous inhabitants [although it] . . . is a counterfeit paradise rather than a land of unrealized promise" [17]. What Fock has said of the Waiwai may be generalized to most such equilibrium societies: "It is not Nature herself, but the Waiwai appreciation of it, that is to say their religious ideas, that limit or shape their cultural development" [18].

Essentials for Modern Equilibrium

Hunter-gardener societies are so far removed from industrial societies that the adoption of the formers' population control mechanisms might seem inherently impossible today. Some of these mechanisms, like meat availability, are impossible to reestablish; a few others, like infanticide, are undesirable. Of course, it cannot be denied that there is an enormous gulf between an equilibrium society and one of disequilibrium. It is the contention of this essay that contemporary societies are unlikely to achieve equilibrium without adopting the essential elements of these controls, and that these elements are, under certain conditions, within the grasp of many of them.

It is perhaps necessary to point out, in passing, that the only alternative theory of population equilibrium, that of the demographic transition, is now being sharply challenged; its interpretation of post-industrial equilibrium has been found to be much oversimplified [19], and that of pre-industrial (paleolithic) equilibrium to be doubtful if not false. For example, demographic transition theory holds that paleolithic equilibrium was the result of high birth rates offset by high death rates, when it seems more likely to have been the result of relatively low death rates matched by control of birth rates. As Teitelbaum observes, "Close examination of transition theory in both historical and modern perspective shows that policy-makers would be ill-advised to adopt such a simplistic and deterministic view [that in all circumstances industrial development will 'take care of' population matters]" [20].

The essential elements of the controls needed for equilibrium may be summarized as follows:

An Explicit Ideal of Smallness. The individual members of most of the societies I have described share the conviction that the ideal family is a small one, consisting of no more than three children. One example, that of the Desana, has already been noted; another is provided by the Tapirape, who believe that a woman should not have more than three children, and that no more than two of them should be of the same sex [21]. Many of these societies are conscious of the dangers of overpopulation, and some have an explicit awareness of an optimum size. The Yaruro, for example, apparently have an ideal of one person per square mile (though it is not articulated as such) [22], and one of their myths refers to overpopulation [23]. This essential is not beyond industrial society. However, it is not sufficient for equilibrium, and must be reinforced by a complex of norms with the following basic features.

Essential Luxuries. To be effective, a control must operate well before any limiting factor is reached. The scarcity of an essential luxury persuades people to regulate their numbers at levels that protect them from environmental fluctuation. For the hunter-gatherers and most of the hunter-gardeners I have discussed, the essential luxury was meat, but for the Tikopians it was coconuts. For future equilibrium societies, it is impossible to specify what the essential luxuries will be, but it is clear that they must meet both of two conditions. The essential luxury must be much more sensitive to environmental fluctuation than any of the limiting factors (such as the staples on which the community depends for survival). The essential luxury must be highly valued by all the members of the community, and, whenever it is available, must be shared evenly among them, so that any scarcity is felt by all.

I have already noted at the outset that the consumerism of industrial societies converts luxuries into essentials, so this feature is still available to contemporary society—albeit in a highly attenuated form and one that is most unsatisfactory for the purpose of achieving equilibrium. This is true for three reasons: (1) few current essential luxuries are sufficiently responsive to ecological variables; (2) luxuries tend to become genuine essentials (for example, Los Angeles would have difficulty surviving without the automobile); (3) trends change so rapidly that such luxuries rarely, if ever, meet the condition of universality, and, in any case, communities are generally not homogeneous enough for the same luxury to be valued as an essential by all members. This brings me to consider the need for cultural homogeneity.

Cultural Homogeneity. Although industrialization tends to homogenize communities, the result is not necessarily an association of similar and mutually-supportive communities, because many of the communities disintegrate as industrialization removes their functions. However, without the redevelopment and continued support of well integrated, fully-functioning communities, shared value systems cannot reemerge. These are indispensible if luxuries that act as controls are to be perceived as essential.

There is no hard-and-fast rule about the ideal structure of these communities; indeed there is room for great variation. It is doubtful that it matters, for example, if the family is nuclear or extended. In the hunter-gardener equilibrium societies of South America, it is extended. However, it is likely that each community should function to achieve reciprocity, secure basic autonomy, and attain proximity to nature.

I have already suggested that the essential luxury should be shared if it is to exert the desired effect on the entire community. This sharing is important as a means of binding the community together, as is the sharing of other goods on a reciprocal basis. Indeed, a person's community could be defined as all those individuals with whom he exchanges some or all food items and/or certain other goods, in contrast with those outside the community with whom he trades.

It is not necessary that a community be entirely self-sufficient in food and other goods; in fact, not only is self-sufficiency impracticable for most potential communities, it is probably undesirable, since trade provides important links with other communities and reduces the likelihood of inter-community hostility. However, self-sufficiency in major foods is essential in order to reinforce both the feeling of community and a sense of dependence on, and identity with, the natural environment. Similarly, it is unnecessary and impracticable for a community to be absolutely independent politically. There can be, and probably should be, strong political links with other communities. However, a shared value system is more likely to develop with a significant degree of autonomy. A community should be able to make all major decisions concerning food production, education, welfare, and, of course, its optimum size. This particular question is worth a book in itself. Here it is necessary only to reiterate that each community needs a degree of autonomy sufficient for the development and maintenance of shared values.

Communities should be small enough, or if large, dispersed enough, to establish and retain close links with the rest of nature. This is essential for the development of cultural norms that will create and reinforce a strong awareness of humanity's interdependence with other organisms. This will be achieved partly by people growing most of their own food, which in any case is possible for families only in small or dispersed communities; but there needs also to be a close relationship with elements of the natural environment that the community cannot manipulate.

Cognitive Complexity. Cognitive complexity is a pompous phrase to describe a striking and important feature of equilibrium societies: the complex nature of their associations of customs, beliefs, symbols, and artistic practices, all of which are mutually reinforcing, are shared by every member of the community, and are important to the stability and continuity of the social system. Unfortunately, it will take many generations for a contemporary community to achieve this complexity. As with all systems, complexity is a matter of time.

NEW PROSPECT: PRIMARY LIFE-STYLES IN A POLYTOPIA

In referring to potential equilibrium communities, I have taken care not to state an optimum size for them and to equivocate about the level or organization concerned—that is, whether "commune," village, county, or other regional structure. This is because I am unable to state even a maximum, and in any case do not wish to rule out any attempt at creating the appropriate conditions for equilibrium that might be made by fairly large groupings of people. On the evidence of those communities that have maintained equilibrium for long periods of time, I believe that as long as the essential elements, or the opportunities for their development, are there, then it would be possible for equilibrium societies, or associations of equilibrium communities, to develop at the regional level. However, this is increasingly unlikely as one proceeds towards the national level, especially in large pluralistic nations—although with them one can visualize (albeit faintly, on the horizon of possibility) that they could perhaps develop as alliances of equilibrium societies.

For the time being, however, such developments are clearly out of the question. The majority of people are apparently intent on industrializing or on staying industrialized. Those people desirous of participating in what is necessarily (because our notions of how to move from disequilibrium to equilibrium are still rather crude) an experiment in, or a quest for, equilibrium, will be people already living in, or intending to live in, relatively small communities. Accordingly, it is to them that the guidelines at the end of this essay are addressed, and only two proposals concerning national policy are here put forward.

A Polytopian Strategy

The first is that nations adopt what I have called elsewhere a polytopian strategy [24]. As Utopia means "no place" (from the Greek *ou*, not; *topos*, place), so Polytopia means "many places." A polytopian nation would be a many-placed nation—a more democratic, less centralized one than those being built today. It would permit greater cultural diversity by allowing a multitude of niches in which communities could develop, if they wished, in ways of their own. Clearly, large numbers of people will remain persuaded that the industrial way of life offers them more than any alternative could, but their pursuit of the industrial should not, and does not have to, prevent others from following different courses. In a polytopia, technologism might continue to be the value system of the dominant culture, but other cultures would be free to adopt other value systems.

The strategy is especially appropriate for nonindustrial countries that wish to develop a modern society, but not some pastiche of the United States, the Soviet Union, or China. The polytopian approach provides them with an opportunity to create a purpose and identity of their own out of the knowledge and values of their constituent peoples, and to develop from there.

No one has the plans for Utopia or for anywhere remotely resembling it. No one can be dogmatic about what is the best or the only way of life available to society, and no individual, or group of individuals, has the right to impose a particular pattern of development on others. Yet large-scale technological development is being imposed on communities as a single, everybody-swim-or-sink-with-it, strategy. People are being imprisoned in a nightmarish, mirror-image Utopia in two complementary and mutually justifying ways. First they cherish a faith in technology that is utopian not only in its visionary form, with its promise of a future of mechanized perfection, but also in its most practical form; the claim that the continued growth of technology and productivity will cure the numerous ills that beset humanity is based on the assumption that throughout the world mankind will achieve social conditions ideal for technological development. That this is utopian has already been demonstrated by the failure of a technologically-based strategy to feed the growing populations of the tropics, and its replacement by a strategy more responsive to local cultural and ecological requirements. Then all other social options, actual or potential, in which technology is subordinated to other cultural attributes are condemned as utopian and therefore not meriting consideration. The chief virtue of a polytopia is that, by conserving a diversity of social options, it is a means of commuting the life sentence of every one of us to the particular "utopia" of technologism without putting us behind the bars of another.

A Primary Life-style

My second proposal is not at all novel, but is crucial to the development of polytopian social structures: that projected rates of urbanization be prevented from becoming self-fulfilling prophecies. Between now and the end of the century the human population is expected to almost double, from 3.8 billion to 6.5 billion. This increase can hardly be prevented, but a still more threatening phenomenon—that of a flight from the country to the cities twice as fast as the rate of population growth—can. By the year 2000 some 3.5 billion people will be in settlements of more than 20,000 inhabitants and, for the first time in human history, more people will be urban than rural [25]. Urbanization of this intensity is likely to so thoroughly erode cultural differences that the only ones left will be those settled by violence. Furthermore, by depriving so many people of any but the most attenuated relationship with the innumerable animals and plants on which they depend, urbanization threatens to erase all prospect of the eventual stabilization of numbers at a sustainable level.

Polytopias are still feasible, but they or any other social structure offering any hope of well-being for large numbers of people will rapidly assume the distant aspect of Utopia if ways of revitalizing rural and semi-rural economies and patterns of living cannot be found. In particular, I advocate promoting, or at least allowing people to adopt, primary life-styles.

A primary life-style is one in which people live intimately with their environment and are to a significant extent both self-sufficient and self-governing. It contrasts sharply with a secondary life-style, such as that of an industrial society, in which the practitioners live at various removes from the environment on which ultimately they depend, and participate only marginally in the everyday business of growing their own food and governing their own affairs.

It would be easy to dismiss primary life-styles as arcadian because they emphasize proximity to nature and because they subordinate technology to other cultural attributes. However, they are not incompatible with technological development; rather, they require that it be responsive to cultural demands instead of culture responding to technology. One of the elements necessary for equilibrium, for example, is the sharing of certain goods—and this communalization of material goods ensures also that innovation is beneficial to the community, so that the innovative spirit of humanity will not be thwarted but directed along lines that are socially constructive.

In fact, primary life-styles, far from requiring the abandonment of technology, demand the development of many new tools and techniques. A dispersed society is in an ideal position to take advantage of renewable energy resources like the sun, wind, and water, which themselves are dispersed; but special technologies are required to do so. Moreover, the requirement that each family grow much of its own food need not bar it from participating in other economic activities. The members of most of the hunter-gardener communities I have mentioned in this essay spend no more than four hours a day on subsistence activities, and there is no reason why the time spent on food-growing by each member of modern equilibrium societies should be longer. Even in areas of quite high unemployment, provided that land were made available for family-scale food production, it would be possible to establish primary life-styles. Indeed, it would be logical, since more people could be employed half-time, spending the rest of each day on growing food.

An important feature of primary life-styles is that they provide an environment consistent not only with population equilibrium but also with reduction of individual consumption. There is no space to go into this point, except to observe that in communities where the sharing ethnic is strong and where prestige is won in other ways than the accumulation of possessions, there is no incentive for individual ownership of goods such as freezers or washing machines when community ownership would do just as well. In addition, wherever primary life-styles were adopted, the compensation process I described —in which technologism transforms the biological and social systems to which man has adapted and then provides compensations in their stead—would be reversed and hence consumption reduced.

The compensation process is closely linked to the proliferation of material goods. As I have shown, among hunting peoples when an animal is killed the meat is shared. There is no need for an individual to keep any meat since there is an abundance of game, and each member of the community can be confident that whoever kills an animal will share it equitably. By contrast, a modern industrial community cannot assure its members a regular abundance of meat at prices they can afford: its population is too great, its impact on the environment creates oscillations with unpredictable effects on supply and demand, and the feedstuffs vital for production come from another continent. In addition, community bonds have so deteriorated that the idea of families sharing meat, or any food, has become rather quaint. Accordingly, the industrial family has to buy a refrigerator and/or freezer; compensation for inability to share food comes in the form of material possessions. Clearly, however, it is less expensive—in money, natural resources, and energy—to have a friend instead of a freezer.

Finally, primary life-styles in a polytopia could conserve the diversity and resilience of the human species. A great deal is claimed for the adaptability of the human species, with the wide range of his cultural adaptations—from the Arctic ice to the equatorial rain forests—cited in support. Humanity should take care, however, lest it conclude that it can adapt to whatever insults it thrusts upon itself by the urbanization and synthetic chemicalization of its environment, for people are now more vulnerable than ever before. Increasing numbers are incapable of surviving even in the most favorable environments without the support of an intricate high-energy technology.

"Alternative" communities, adopting primary life-styles, are often accused of escapism, and are sometimes too ready to confess to it. In fact, they would not be vainglorious to look upon themselves as helping to safeguard a greater number of social options than those offered by the industrial way of life—and hence of participating in the mainstream of our evolution. Many of these communities may fail; some will succeed. They are a growing undercurrent of variety, optimism, and enterprise against the tide of uniformity, despair, and destruction.

Chapter 17

Settlements and Social Stability

Edward Goldsmith

MODERN INSTABILITY

It is clear that the world is moving in the direction of urbanization. If this trend were to continue, by the end of the century over half of the world's population would be living in cities of more than one hundred thousand people, with most concentrated into one hundred or so massive conurbations of between one and sixty million people [1]. This is a particularly frightening prospect, since it is in the existing conurbations that the ills from which industrialized society is suffering are to be found in their most concentrated forms. It seems unnecessary to list these ills, or to demonstrate that the measures undertaken to combat them are increasingly ineffective. However, it is crucial to understand why urbanization and industrialization have created these problems, if real solutions are to be found.

The tendency, of course, is to blame past failures to solve the problems on mere technicalities—errors in implementation of policies rather than in the policies themselves. These policies are the only ones consistent with an industrialized world view; hence they are the only ones society is capable of proposing.

Let us consider the main features of this world view. Implicit in it is the notion that the world is imperfect. In the Middle Ages, the Cathars and other heretical sects also regarded the world as imperfect [2]. Their reaction, however, was to cut themselves off from it, and live instead in a spiritual world of their own. Contemporary society, on the other hand, has set out systematically to "improve" the earth. By means of science, technology, and industry, modern man has persuaded himself that it can be transformed into a paradise a la Herman Kahn, in which everyone will have at his disposal an extraordinary array of consumer products and ingenious technological devices, and in which vast specialized institutions will deal so "scientifically" with all such problems as unemployment, homelessness, ignorance, crime and delinquency, famine and disease—which are supposed to have afflicted mankind since the beginning of time—that they will be eliminated once and for all.

Subjective Definition of Problems

This transformation is referred to misleadingly as "development," and the direction in which it points as "progress." It is therefore not surprising that any problems that arise are ascribed to "underdevelopment" and that, to solve them, more scientific research, more technological innovation, and more industrial expansion—that is, more development—are invested in order to maintain society on the course to which it is ideologically and materially committed. In other words, rather than interpret the problems objectively (which is what science is supposed to enable him to do), contemporary man has interpreted them subjectively. He has made them appear amenable to the solutions he has decided in advance will apply, the only ones that are compatible with his world view, as well as the only ones that society is organized to provide.

Thus, for instance, "poverty" is defined as a shortage of material goods, which justifies the production of more. Although it might be more realistic to regard poverty as an aberrant situation in which more material goods are required than can actually be produced, the solution would then be to create a situation in which fewer material goods were needed, and this could not be done without changing the very direction in which society is moving. Or again, the housing problem is interpreted as a shortage of houses, which justifies the building of more. It might be more realistic to regard it as an aberrant situation largely caused by the disintegration of the family, as a result of which, where once there were eight or ten people per house, there are now only two or three. This interpretation would be inconvenient since society already knows how to build houses, but it has not provided the technique for restoring the integrity of the family unit [3].

In the same way, the high crime rate is seen as a sign that the police force is inadequate or insufficiently equipped, but not as a symptom of the aberrance of society. Although society knows how to engage more policemen, build prisons, and manufacture more armored cars and burglar alarms (the United States already spends about $20 billion a year in this way), there is no available mechanism for creating a sounder society without compromising the achievement of other high priority goals.

Although the ineffectiveness of the measures undertaken so far would never be likely to deter urban society from applying them, unanticipated logistical problems are beginning to appear. The cost of applying these measures is rapidly becoming insupportable, especially in the cities, where, as already noted, the problems exist in their most acute form. If one attempts to calculate the costs in terms of the necessary services—such as power, sewage works, schools, highways, police protection, public housing, daycare services, old people's homes, and unemployment benefits—required to keep cities functioning in the next decades, it will become apparent that these costs cannot conceivably be met. New York may be the first to go bankrupt, but it will not be the last. Every city in the industrial world is heading in precisely the same direction. In the nonindustrialized world, major cities have long ago given up the idea of providing the basic amenities of urban living to their ant-like populations. Yet urban populations are still increasing—in South Asia alone, at the rate of three hundred thousand a week [4]. If urbanization continues in both the industrial and the nonindustrial world, social chaos, epidemics, and famine are imminent on an unprecedented scale, as cities simply break down and cannot provide the basic necessities of life for their inhabitants.

There are two ways of looking at this situation. The pessimist simply feels that all is lost. The optimist—in fact, the realist—feels quite differently. Only the urban industrial way of life is lost, and this is not a disaster but a deliverance; the solutions it has offered to human problems have not worked, and the world it has created is not a paradise but a nightmare. Here, then, is the opportunity to build up a better one. But first I will examine why industrialization has been such a failure.

First, consider this process of "development" or more precisely "industrialization," its latest phase. First, it is not autonomous. It does not occur in a vacuum as is implied by modern economics. If the world were a lifeless waste as is the moon, there could be no industrialization. Over the past few thousand million years, the primaeval dust has slowly been organized into an increasingly complex organization of matter—the biosphere, or world of living things, or the real world—which provides the resources entering into this process. Industrialization is something that is happening to the biosphere. It is the biosphere, the real world, that is being industrialized.

Because of this process, a new organization of matter is building up—the technosphere, or world of material goods and technological devices, or the surrogate world. What is important is that the surrogate world is in direct competition with the real one; it can be built up only by making use of resources extracted from the real world, and by consigning to the real world the waste products it must inevitably generate.

Man is part of the real world, not the surrogate one. In fact, he has been designed phylogenetically (and at one time, as I shall show, culturally) to fulfill specific differentiated real-world functions. It would be very naive to suppose that the systematic destruction of this real world would not affect man in some way. To demonstrate exactly how, I will consider the basic features of the real world. The most basic principle of the behavior of the biosphere is that it is goal-directed or directive [5], as can be shown to be true of all the behavioral systems which comprise it. Its goal is stability, the steady state.

Stability in the Natural World

Stability is usually defined as the ability of a system to return to a ground position after a disturbance—like a thermostat when the water temperature rises above a predetermined point. As is more apparent among living things, however, changes are, strictly speaking, irreversible. Experiences cannot be annulled. An action taken to correct a disequilibrium must give rise to a new situation, rather than assure a return to the old one. If the system is stable, however, the divergence from the original will be as small as possible. It is for this reason that Waddington suggests that the term "homeostasis" (same position) be replaced by "homeorhesos" (same flow) [6]. It is thereby more realistic to regard a stable system as one characterized by small rather than large oscillations, one that is capable of maintaining its basic structure in the face of change.

It follows, of course, that stability does not mean immobility. An immobile system would not be stable, because it would not be adapting to predictable environmental changes. It also follows that stability is not a position in space-time, or a goal in the conventional sense of the term, but a course or trajectory along which a system must proceed if it is to preserve its basic structure. Waddington suggests that it be referred to as the "creode" or necessary course [7].

When proceeding along this course, a system will not just be moving to successive positions of short-term equilibrium, but to successive positions from which, as it can predict on the basis of its previous experience, diversions will be minimized. This explains the occurrence of positive feedback processes such as ontogeny, all of which are contained within appropriate negative feedback loops.

Clearly then, stability is not just a quality on its own, but a relationship between a system and its environment. Adaptation means increasing the stability of this relationship, and as it occurs (via phylogeny and ontogeny) a system becomes correspondingly committed to this, its optimum environment. Again, this environment is not immobile. It will always be changing. Heraclitus said, "You cannot step into the same river twice." However, there is a limit to the rate at which such change can occur, and I shall examine this more closely further on. Suffice it to say at this point that, if the environment changes too radically, adaptive responses to it can no longer be mediated. The system is then out of control. Oscillations increase and eventually the system must collapse.

It is a feature of a stable system that, in the face of change, it seeks to preserve not only its own structure, but also that of the environment to which it is committed. Otherwise it could not remain stable. Behavior at all levels of organization proceeds by differentiation, so that functions once fulfilled in a general way become fulfilled, by means of increasingly specialized mechanisms, in an increasingly differentiated way. In other words, systems are developed by the evolutionary process to fulfill specialized functions within their particular environments. It stands to reason that by fulfilling these functions in such an environment, their needs, also the product of the evolutionary process, are best satisfied. This is obvious among nonhuman animals. The needs of a tiger, most people will concede, are likely to be best satisfied by allowing it to hunt, as it has always done, in the jungle. A trout meets its needs by swimming in the sort of streams in which it has evolved.

Unfortunately, people refuse to face the evident fact that this principle must apply equally well to man [8]. To do so would force the realization of the futility of the "development" process to which man is so committed, a process which consists of systematically transforming his environment so that it ever less resembles that to which he has adapted by his evolution. This change can only result in less adaptive behavior in the social system, behavior characterized by ever larger oscillations and greater instability which must eventually lead to collapse.

Cultural Maladjustment to the Surrogate World

It is realistic to regard many of the problems that face man today as but the symptoms of societal instability. Thus Boyden regards such diseases as heart disease, many if not all forms of cancer, diabetes, appendicitis, peptic ulcers, varicose veins, diverticulitis, and even tooth cavities as but the biological symptoms of man's "phylogenetic maladjustment" to the industrial environment in which he is made to live [9]. This hypothesis is consistent with the fact that the incidence of these diseases increases almost in direct proportion to per capita GNP [10].

One can equally well regard the increasing social problems which society faces—such as crime, delinquency, drug addiction, vandalism, illegitimacy, suicide—as the social symptoms of phylogenetic maladjustment to structureless mass society. The fact that the incidence of these social aberrations increases with evolution from the tribe to the rural village to the country town to the city, and is at its highest in the large industrial conurbations of the West, lends substance to this thesis [11]. What is more, the increases in the incidence and severity of infectious diseases among men, nonhuman animals, and plants associated with population explosions of microorganisms, and the diseases with which man is afflicting the biosphere itself as a result of his own population explosion, can similarly be regarded as the ecological symptoms of phylogenetic maladjustment [12].

The question is, how can he deal with this host of maladjustments occurring at every level of organization? The answer has been presumed to be by material, technological, and institutional means—that is, by indulging in further "development," which must cause his body, his society, and his environment to diverge still further from the optimum, creating still more serious maladjustments. Man is thus caught up on a positive feedback course towards ever-increasing instability from which it will be extremely difficult to extricate himself without transforming his world view and the way his society is organized.

The world view that must be developed would lead him to see the host of material goods, technological devices, and institutional services provided for him as but poor compensations for benefits that were previously provided by the normal functioning of the biological, social, and ecological systems that make up the biosphere. Thus domestic appliances are necessary today only because the family has disintegrated. People now live two or three to a house instead of eight or ten as was previously the case, and there is consequently no one available to do the household chores. The present elaborate welfare system is required for a similar reason. The extended family of old provided its members with all the security they needed, and far more effectively than the anonymous civil servant in some distant capital does today.

Since technospheric benefits not only give rise to increasing and ever less tolerable biological, social, and ecological instability, and since, in any case, society cannot afford them, there is no choice but to restore the proper functioning of the natural systems that make up the biosphere, so as to exploit fully the corresponding biospheric benefits. These, as it happens, not only favor social and ecological stability; they are available absolutely free. In other words, for the technospheric paradise a la Herman Kahn, man must in fact substitute a biospheric one a la Jean-Jacques Rousseau.

If the large modern conurbation is the ideal type of settlement for the purpose of maximizing the benefits of the surrogate world—and hence reflects the goal our society has set itself—what then is the ideal type of settlement for a society which has set itself the opposite goal, that of maximizing the benefits of the real world?

LESSONS IN STABILITY FROM OUR FOREBEARERS

The answer, however absurd it may sound to anyone brought up with the values of our industrial society, is the temporary encampment settlements of our hunter-gatherer forebearers. Indeed, their mode of life and settlement patterns appear to have been advantageous from any objective viewpoint. In terms of health, their small populations would probably not have provided a sufficient niche for viable populations of the microorganisms transmitting contagious diseases [13]. It is unlikely that they suffered from measles, influenza, smallpox, and mumps [14]. It has been estimated that measles requires a population of at least half a million people in order to maintain itself [15]. Boyden considers that "the existence of a large number of viruses (150 to 200) at present circulating in human populations must be a new biological development—a consequence of the creation, through the great increase in the human population, of a situation which is permitting a sort of explosive radiation among viruses capable of multiplying in the tissue of man" [16].

The fact that hunter gatherers were nomadic with a defined territory also meant that they did not have to live close to their own excreta, or other wastes. This too must have contributed to reducing infectious diseases, along with their ready access to fresh food and clean water, both increasingly unavailable in the modern world. Their resistance would also have been increased by their healthy outdoor life, and likewise by their varied diet, which included plenty of proteins and structured fats [17]. A relatively high level of infant mortality would have assured the elimination of the less resistant individuals before they reached reproductive age.

The absence of mobility between the areas within which the hunter-gatherers were nomadic would have favored the best possible adaptation to those pathogens for which there might have been a niche. This means that the diseases they communicated would have had time to become endemic, killing off mainly the unadaptive (as was the case with malaria until the World Health Organization declared war against its vector and lost). In general, by leading that life to which our species has been adapted by its evolution [18], they would have been largely exempt from degenerative diseases [19].

Their impact on their physical environment was also minimal. They made very little use of nonrenewable resources, since they had no need for material possessions [20]. As a result, they generated no wastes that could not be readily absorbed into normal life processes, and a few weeks after they abandoned a camping site, there was practically no trace of their passage. Nor, when they lived in their natural environment, did they adversely affect the populations of wild animals on which they lived, since they mainly killed the old and the weak as do other predators. It is said that, in general, they consumed no more than 30 percent of the available food resources at any given time, very much as insect populations appear to do [21].

Their way of life also favored social stability. The small size of groupings permitted a high degree of social cohesion, while aggression within the group was readily settled by fission into separate groups [22]. At the same time, the causes of war were reduced to a minimum; since each group lived off a relatively small proportion of available food supplies and other resources, there was no need to try to acquire other people's. Aggression, when it occurred, was highly ritualized and provided an excellent outlet for instinctive aggressivity, while giving rise to the minimum physical damage [23].

Empirically, the stability of hunter-gatherer groups speaks for itself. Their life-style did not change for very long periods. Flint-chipping techniques, for instance, were relatively unchanged over two hundred thousand years. Particularly important is the fact that their life-style and settlement patterns were compatible with the survival of climax-ecosystems. This must be the supreme test of stability. It is only in such conditions that the real (as opposed to the monetary) costs of our activities are reduced to zero, and it is in this way that the free benefits of the biosphere or real world are maximized.

Urban man cannot go back to being a hunter-gatherer. First of all, his environment has been so seriously degraded that there is very little left to hunt or to gather; second, there are nearly four billion people in the world, and the hunting and gathering way of life could probably only sustain twenty or thirty million. Man is, as Ferrari says, too poor to be a hunter-gatherer [24]. He does not have anything like the per capita requirements of real resources such as land, forests, clean rivers, and wild animals to be able to adopt the life-style.

It is not clear, however, that man has scored a victory over nature by adopting any other life-style. The hunter-gatherer way of life could have supported twenty or thirty million people indefinitely, until such time as geophysical changes made the earth uninhabitable. Agriculture and industry have provided the means to sustain four billion people, but for a very limited period only. Other life-styles are thereby possible, but only at the cost of reduced stability and hence longevity. It must follow that a hunter-gatherer society is, in a sense, a climax social system. It is the most "progressive" possible, if the term is to have any real meaning.

Benefits of Decentralization

Man must face his situation as it is. The earth's population must be taken as given (though it is almost certain to be reduced very considerably in the next decade or so). The problem is how to deploy it so as to ensure its maximum stability and hence to permit its survival for as long as possible. Lessons can be drawn from the experience of hunter-gatherer societies and other tribal peoples.

The first lesson is that of decentralization. If today's massive population were deployed in small villages instead of large cities, people would then be in the closest possible contact with the real world and would have maximum access to its benefits (instead of being totally immersed in the artificial environment of a city, in which only the benefits of the all-encompassing surrogate world are available). Because the inhabitants of a large city are so isolated from the biosphere, wastes are concentrated in such massive quantities that their disposal becomes a considerable problem. The number of cities in the world that can afford tertiary sewage treatment plants is negligible, so much so that the only effective tertiary treatment is still that provided by the normal self-regulating mechanisms of the real world [25].

The isolation of the inhabitants of a large city from food-producing areas radically increases the price and precariousness of food distribution and necessitates a great deal of expensive processing, which is unnecessary in a small village. Furthermore, in a village the costs of social disintegration are reduced to a minimum because the village provides a more suitable physical infrastructure for a healthy human community than does a city. For these and similar reasons, the quantity of material goods, technological devices, and institutional services required in a decentralized society is very much lower than in an urbanized society [26]. Decentralizing a society reduces its impact on the natural systems that make up the real world, and, as a result, maximizes that society's benefits.

Decentralization, however, is not sufficient if social benefits are to be maximized. To find out what other measures are required, I will look a little more closely at the functioning of stable societies in the nonindustrial world.

The Community as an Extension of the Family

A society is not just made up of random people who happen to inhabit the same area and are thereby governed by the same institutions. It is a system capable of self-regulation without the aid of formal institutions, which only become necessary as it disintegrates [27]. Any system has an identity of its own. It is a unit of behavior. For this to be possible, its parts must be able to cooperate in such a way as to subordinate any possible divergent interests to those of the system as a whole. This, as I have shown, requires that the system provide its members with the environment that satisfies their needs. A common satisfaction of needs provides the bonds which hold the system together [28].

What, then, are these bonds? Contrary to the ideas of Freud and Trotter, who regarded man as originally living in horde-like groups like baboons, the basic social unit of man is the family. Tinbergen has shown that the human brain does not possess centers for specifically social behavior [29]. Social behavior is only an extension of family behavior, just as the community is but an extension of the family. This is undoubtedly the most important fact of social organization, and one of the most generally ignored. It means that, whereas the information and corresponding instructions that will make man a family animal are transmitted genetically from one generation to the next, those that will make of him a social animal must be developed during the socialization process. That is what education is about, a fact of which our educationalists have long ago lost sight [30].

The family is held together by a set of asymmetrical bonds, in such a way that the relationships between its various members are all different [31]. These family bonds are the only ones available for holding together the different members of a community [32]. The building up of the community, in fact, consists in extending these family bonds to hold together more people. This is reflected in the elaborate kinship terminology in use among tribal societies, which identifies all the members of the community, whether or not they are in fact related, in terms of the basic family classifications. This device greatly facilitates the extension of the corresponding bonds, permitting the establishment of "wide range systems of kinship" [33]. What is important is that the use of each kinship term reflects a different pattern of social relationships [34]. In this way, a society is socially, not just economically, a differentiated system.

Family bonds, like all other bonds, however, have limited extendability [35]. They cannot be made to hold together effectively more than a limited number of people; this is why an effective community must be small, and why attempts to develop bigger communities have failed. Among tribal peoples, the maximum size of a community appears to be about one thousand people [36]. The family bonds can be used to organize the family into larger lineages and also to create all sorts of specialized intermediary associations. Thus tribesmen often are divided into age grades, military associations, secret societies, and so on, and, within each of these, members will refer to each other by kinship terms, indicating that close bonds have been established. Thus the community has what Ortega y Gasset calls "social elasticity" [37]. Everybody is in contact with everybody else —by being closely associated with them in at least one such grouping [38]. An individual thereby requires a very precise status as a member of a large number of such groupings, instead of being an anonymous member of a crowd as in modern mass society [39].

Communities need not be totally isolated from each other. If necessary, they can be associated with others to form larger ones. They can be built up by exploiting laws of intermarriage and associated laws of residence such as matrilocality. The clan, a consanguineal grouping that is more often present than absent among tribal peoples, usually transcends local groupings which are consanguineal and affinal, and helps create the bonds that give rise to larger social groups [40]. By exploiting the family bonds in this way, rather than by subordinating different communities to the same asystematic institutional control, a larger social unit can be created, however diffuse. This point was quite clear to Durkheim, who regarded the instability of the modern nation state as being due to the absence of intermediary associations [41].

As we move from the local community to larger social groupings, however, the bonds become weaker and the society correspondingly more diffuse. Usually the society is still capable of acting as an effective political unit when subjected to a challenge that requires cooperation among its members, such as an enemy invasion. For the business of everyday living, however, there is usually little need to establish a community of more than one thousand people (save as an endogamous cultural unit which acts as a culturally determined population or gene-pool, a unit for long-term evolutionary and cultural adaptation).

However, even the presence of intermediary crisscrossing associations is not sufficient to assure the cohesion of a community. For it to display real order, all activities occurring within it must contribute to, rather than detract from, its stability, the latter being the case in modern industrial society.

Economics

There is no specifically economic behavior within tribal societies [42]. People do not make or distribute things so as to maximize return on capital, labor, or any other factor of production. Rather they produce in order to satisfy kinship obligations and religious and ritualistic requirements, and to acquire prestige, which is the basic goal of human behavior [43]. As I shall show, it is by exploiting this general desire for prestige that human communities can become self-regulating. To do so, of course, means accepting the principle of inequality of prestige, which many people, ignorant of the situation, are loath to do.

It was only with the development of the market economy that a separate sphere of activity emerged that could really be called "economic" [44]. The activities involved ceased to be subordinated to the requirements of social stability and became subordinated instead to those of the market, which is unrelated to the needs of the community. So that economic activity serves social ends, the units of economic activity in a tribal society coincide with those into which people are organized for all other social requirements. There is thus no need for the surrogate social environment of "companies," whose existence we take for granted. In many industrialized nations, a man's social position is to a large extent determined by his economic position. In a tribal society, it is the other way round. "He tends to hold his economic position by virtue of his social position. Hence to displace him economically means a social disturbance" [45].

If, in a stable society, there is strictly speaking no economic behavior, there is also strictly speaking no work or labor—that is, as distinct from other day-to-day activities. There is no word for work in the language of tribal peoples. Hence, there is no need for labor-saving devices. What modern technologists call work in tribal societies and set about eliminating by introducing modern labor-saving devices, is often a set of pleasurable and socially necessary functions. Thus, the introduction of piped water in a North African village was strongly opposed by local women; the daily expedition to the village well, which Western technologists interpreted as work, was the only opportunity they had for gossip and general social intercourse.

If there is no work, it must follow that there is no need for financial remuneration and hence for corresponding energy-and resource-intensive financial goods and services. In a self-regulating social system, people fulfill their necessary functions because they obtain the maximum satisfaction from so doing.

That this is so within the traditional family unit should be evident. A mother requires neither coercion nor financial remuneration to look after her children, nor does a father to assure their sustenance. They were designed by their biological and social evolution to fulfill these functions and to do so satisfies very basic social needs. It is not generally recognized that the same is true of the functions fulfilled by the members of a cohesive and stable social system, which like a family generates its own incentives and rewards.

For instance, welfare in a stable society, over and above that dispensed within the family, is assured by what Polanyi refers to as "redistribution" [46]. The chief, or Big Man as he is referred to in Melanesia, accumulates a food surplus which he redistributes, mainly during communal feasts. Since this is the principal means by which he acquires prestige, it is built into the society. Its operation is not dependent on any external inducement. This system may not appeal to everyone brought up on the egalitarian ethic. However, total equality is not a realistic option, and inequality of prestige, as long as it is acquired by fulfilling necessary social functions, may well be the most effective alternative to the great material inequality that characterizes industrial society.

To subordinate economic activity to social requirements means, above all, drastically reducing the size of markets and hence the scale of economic activities. This way the family and community would slowly regain their economic functions. This would also permit a reduction in mobility, which in the modern world effectively prevents the development of those bonds required to hold together human communities.

Education

In a stable society, education must also be a tool of social stability. The very object of education is to communicate to the young the information that will enable them to become differentiated members of their family and community. Education is, in fact, but another word for socialization. And, in a disintegrated society, socialization cannot occur. First, there is no society into which people can be socialized. Second, the socialization process is but a specialized instance of a developmental process within the biosphere. As such, it is a programed sequence of interrelationships between an organism and its environment, which means that the information received must be derived from the appropriate source and in the order that will give rise to the appropriate sequence of responses [47].

This means that random information from the mass media and from a misguided educational system that reflects the values of a disintegrated society must seriously interfere with socialization. What is more, the role played by institutions in the educational process has been seriously overrated. In a stable society, a child is educated simply by being subjected to the appropriate influences at the correct time—which occurs by simply living and fulfilling his normal functions within his family and community. Institutions usually imply centralization at a national or, worse still, international level. This effectively prevents the socialization of young people into their local social groups, to which process the information imparted institutionally tends to be only randomly related [48]. For this reason, a centralized and institutionalized educational system is incompatible with the survival of stable, and hence small and diverse, social groupings. Educational decentralization and deinstitutionalization is thus a prerequisite of social stability.

Religion

Religion too must contribute to social stability. This is the case in tribal groups among whom the very concept of religion as something separate from their traditional culture is unknown; there is no word in their vocabulary to correspond to it [49]. Their gods, insofar as the term is appropriate, consist largely of their ancestors. Rather than gravitate at their deaths to some distant paradise, tribal members remain members of their families, their clans, and their tribes. They are regarded simply as having graduated to a higher and more prestigious age grade. It is said, in fact, that a primitive tribe is made up of the living, the dead, and the yet to be born, which is but another way of saying that the tribe is continuous and stable [50].

This also means that a tribe's pantheon must reflect its social structure, for the relationships obtaining among the ancestor-gods are the same as those which obtained among them during their lifetimes [51]. This has the effect of sanctifying the social structure, which no individual would dare modify for fear of incurring the wrath of the ancestor-gods. For a tribal society, all the important physical constituents of the environment are also associated with some spirit, which means, in effect, that the physical environment is also sanctified. It is thereby protected in the same manner from any possible human predations.

It is undoubtedly true that for the social structures to have disintegrated into the present mass society, man had at the same time to reject the social religion of his tribal ancestors in favor of a largely asocial one, in which duties to men were largely replaced by duties toward God. In other words, it was necessary to desanctify his social structure, just as he had to desanctify his physical environment in order to devastate it. Also, in order to have developed today's rootless society, geared as it is to improvising ever more desperate short-term expedients to accommodate ever less tolerable changes, he had, at the same time, to separate religion from the rest of culture, in order to desanctify its underlying principles and, in this way, transform them to suit his nefarious purposes.

In a stable society, the sanctification of these principles, which tend to be regarded in some way as divinely inspired, means that they can be transmitted unchanged from one generation to the next via the socialization process. Cultural information thereby reflects the experience of the cultural group as a whole from the time it first developed its own cultural identity, and not just the experience of the last one or two generations. In this way, cultural information is transmitted from one generation to the next in very much the same way as is genetic information.

This is very important, for a stable behavior pattern must be based on stable and hence continuous information (the Continuity of Information Principle) [52]. If this pattern changed to satisfy the apparent requirements of each new generation, a society could "adapt" to freak conditions—precisely what science, with which man has sought systematically to replace traditional cultural information, is doing to the industrialized society. What is more, such a rapid adaptation would be self-defeating, since the very object of behavior is to preserve continuity or stability. Rapid adaptation could only occur at the cost of disrupting a social structure and its environment and thereby putting long-term adaptive processes into reverse. That is the basic reason why science cannot conceivably replace religio-culture as the control mechanism of a stable society [53].

Land Tenure

Within a stable society, the distribution of land among the cultivators is not determined by the operation of a random mechanism such as that of the market. The determining factors are purely social. A man has a right to a specific piece of land because of his specific position within the social group. In ideal conditions, the pattern of land tenure reflects a society's social structure. Thus among the Tiv, the position of a man's farm "varies from one crop rotation to the next, but neither his juxtaposition with his agnatic kinsman, nor his rights change in the least" [54]. In all cases, as Maine points out, "the land is an aspect of the group but not the basis of grouping" [55]. A man does not derive his status from the ownership of a piece of land, but rather obtains his ownership of a piece of land by virtue of his status.

A stable system of land tenure is clearly essential to a stable society. If land is bought and sold, the community's necessary structure cannot be maintained. Also, people will be tempted to exploit the land for short-term ends rather than to apply proved methods of husbandry, assuring that their descendants will inherit it in as good condition as they found it themselves. In a program of social stabilization, land would be removed from the market. It would theoretically belong to the community, although individual families would occupy it perpetually, as long as they fulfilled their communal obligations. This is the basis of the "Gramdan" system which Vinobe Bhave and J.P. Narayan, Mahatma Gandhi's successors, have sought to introduce in India.

Settlements

Similarly, a stable society's settlement pattern is determined not by economic but by social forces. The arrangement of the houses in a traditional village reflects its social structure and behavior pattern and hence its social stability [56]. This is pointed out by Levi-Strauss with reference to the Bororo of Brazil [57], and also by Jaulin with reference to the Motilone Indians of British Guiana [58]. Missionaries forced the Motilone to abandon their traditional dwellings and live in modern cement houses arranged in rows to favor efficiency. In the words of Jaulin, "the imposition of this modified habitat has led to a marked deterioration in physical well-being and has very seriously disturbed their social life, the intimacy of the family, and a division of responsibility notable for its grace and stability" [59].

For a modern settlement to contribute to the stability of the family and the small community, it would have to be much smaller. The buildings, too, would have to be on the right scale. For a house to provide the optimum infrastructure for a human family, it must be capable of lodging all its members (not just the amputated nuclear family of today) but still remain on a human scale. The high-rise block is clearly on the wrong scale. People have difficulty in regarding it as a permanent home. The family also needs a certain privacy if it is to act as a self-regulating system, and the same is true of the community. The houses must be arranged in such a way as to confer on the settlement a feeling of wholeness and oneness. In southwestern France two neighboring towns, Marmande and Villeneuve-sur-Lot, are said to exert very different influences on their inhabitants. The former is stretched out along the main road, while the latter, an ancient "bastide," is built around a central square. The former is much less of a community than the latter [60].

This central square is very important as a place where the citizens can gather to run their affairs. It is probable that no self-regulating social system can do without one. The Greeks, as it is known, could not conceive of a city without its "agora" [61]. In the Arab city, which was not geared to social stability as much as to common worship—and which tended as a result to be run by an autocrat—the Mosque effectively replaced the agora [62]. Significantly in the industrial cities of the United Kingdom, it is now the shopping precinct and the multi-storied car park that have taken over.

Siena is possibly the ideal city, by virtue of being effectively divided into seventeen separate social groups, or contrades, medieval territorially-based associations which have preserved their traditions and hence their identity. Twice a year the contrades wage ritual battle with each other in the form of a horse race—the Palio [63]. Each contrade is intergenerational in membership and transcends social classes. Because of the close links between members of a contrade and the effective ritual channel for aggression, social problems such as crime and delinquency are reduced to a minimum. This is an interesting instance of dividing up a city, for certain purposes at least, into village-like units. In this way society is catering to the needs of "natural man" as, according to Valerius Geist [64], town planners should do, rather than to what appear superficially to be the needs of modern domesticated man. It is certain that the same principles could be applied in a more comprehensively decentralized society set up within a program of social stabilization.

An equally important stabilizing influence is a society's architecture. Like its rituals, and language, buildings provide a society with an identity of which people can be proud and which distinguishes it from its neighbors. No one can feel proud of belonging to a society whose physical infrastructure is a wilderness of shoddy, faceless blocks, perched on the edge of congested highways and interspersed with factories, gas containers, garbage dumps, and power stations. Nor can such an environment help to distinguish those who live in it from others living in equally depressing circumstances elsewhere.

Hildyard tells how a group of young men in Walsall, a suburb of Birmingham, told him sadly, almost tragically, how ashamed they were of their city. This could not be in starker contrast to the pride taken by Siennese youth in the extraordinary beauty of their city.

A society's monuments also provide a link with its past and thereby contribute to its stability and continuity. Very recently, the inhabitants of a small island in Melanesia were persuaded by the leader of a nativistic cult to reject Westernization and return to their old ways. One of the first steps was to build a museum to house the artifacts of their pre-colonial past. Since most of these had been removed as souvenirs, the people were obliged to reconstruct them as best they could, on the basis of the vague indications of a few old men who still remembered them. The museum, called the House of Memories, provided the islanders with a link with their semi-forgotten past. Its role was to help restore their society's continuity, which the colonial powers had so irresponsibly destroyed.

Only a most degenerate society, well on the road to collapse, can treat its traditional artifacts and monuments with the indifference that industrial society shows. The degeneration of this society is nowhere more evident than in its readiness to mutilate its historic buildings beyond redemption so as to accommodate a motorway or a shopping center. This attitude is explicable in terms of the utilitarian ethic, which leads its supporters to value only those things that provide them with material benefits. It also draws strength from the fact that esthetics cannot be measured in "controlled laboratory conditions," or its function formulated in scientific propositions.

To conclude, an ecological approach to the design of human settlements would seek to assure that they accommodate, as satisfactorily as possible, all those activities that contribute to social stability—the *sine qua non* of overall ecological stability—and inhibit those activities that, on the contrary, might compromise it. Thus, economic activities would be on a small scale so as not to interfere with more important social processes, and, if possible, the units of economic activity would correspond to basic social units such as the family, the lineage, and the village.

Education would consist of socialization within the village community, with the minimum dependence on centralized institutions. Religion would be merged with the rest of the society's culture so as to render that culture's generalities as nonplastic as possible; in this way, the continuity of the information on which the society's social behavior pattern is based would be assured. To this end, religion would also be decentralized and deinstitutionalized.

The essential continuity of land-tenure would be assured by removing land from the market economy and vesting its guardianship in the village community, its occupancy by the same families being assured from one generation to the next.

The type of settlement that would best accommodate all these requirements would be a village community, or a small town subdivided into village-like units. The physical infrastructure of the settlement would reflect its social structure so as to reinforce it. The architecture would be as aesthetically pleasing as possible, and would contribute significantly to the society's individuality and sense of continuity.

Once these conditions are satisfied, such communities would be likely to develop, however slowly, those divergent religio-cultures required to control their relationship with their specific environments, thereby gradually increasing their stability and assuring their long-term survival.

Notes

NOTES TO THE PREFACE

1. Herman Daly (ed.), *Towards a Steady-State Economy* (San Francisco: W.H. Freeman and Co., 1973), p. vii.

NOTES TO THE INTRODUCTION

1. John Stuart Mill, *Principles of Political Economy* (London: John W. Parket and Son, 1957), p. 326.
2. Ibid.
3. Harrison Brown, *The Challenge of Man's Future* (New York: Viking Press, 1954).
4. *The Ecologist*, "Blueprint for Survival," vol. 2, no. 1 (January 1972).
5. Donella H. Meadows et al., *The Limits to Growth* (New York: Universe Books, 1974).
6. Dennis C. Pirages and Paul R. Ehrlich, *Ark II: Social Response to Environmental Imperatives* (New York: Viking Press, 1974).
7. Herman E. Daly (ed.), *Toward a Steady State Economy* (San Francisco: W.H. Freeman and Co., 1973).
8. Ibid., p. 14.
9. Edwin O. Reischauer, *Japan Past and Present* (New York: Alfred A. Knopf, 1953).

NOTES TO INTRODUCTION TO PART I

1. Ernst F. Schumacher, *Small Is Beautiful* (New York: Harper and Row, 1973).

NOTES TO CHAPTER 1
THE WORLD FOOD PROBLEM: GROWTH MODELS AND NONGROWTH SOLUTIONS

1. *1975 World Population Data Sheet*, Population Reference Bureau, 1754 N Street, N.W., Washington, D.C. 20036.

2. Alexander M. Carr-Saunders, *World Population: Past Growth and Present Trends* (Oxford: Clarendon Press, 1936), p. 42; and Department of Economic and Social Affairs, *Statistical Yearbook* (New York: United Nations, 1960–1975).

3. Food and Agriculture Organization, *Provisional Indicative World Plan for Agricultural Development*, vol. 2 (Rome: United Nations, 1970), p. 491. To express dietary intake in vegetable-equivalent kilocalories, the kilocalories consumed as animal matter are multiplied by the number of vegetable kilocalories required to produce one kilocalorie of animal product. This number varies from 3 to 10. Thus a person eating 1000 kilocalories of meat per day may be consuming as many as 10,000 vegetable-equivalent kilocalories per day from that source alone.

4. Lester Brown, *By Bread Alone* (New York: Praeger, 1974), p. 43.

5. Georg Borgstrom, *Focal Points: A Global Food Strategy* (New York: MacMillan Publishing Co., 1974), p. 178.

6. Study of Critical Environmental Problems, *Man's Impact on the Global Environment* (Cambridge, Mass.: The M.I.T. Press, 1970), p. 118. Fertilizer use from Georg Borgstrom, *Too Many* (New York: MacMillan Publishing Co., 1969), p. 27.

7. Brown, *By Bread Alone*, p. 36.

8. Ibid., pp. 37–38.

9. Earl Butz, statement before the U.S. House Committee on Agriculture, Subcommittee on Department Operations, July 23, 1974, printed in *World Population and Food Supply and Demand Situation* (Washington, D.C.: U.S. Government Printing Office, 1974), pp. 27–29.

10. For an extended discussion of this phenomenon, see Dennis L. Meadows, *The Dynamics of Commodity Production Cycles* (Cambridge, Mass.: Wright-Allen Press, 1970).

11. For examples of this argument, see Fred H. Sanderson, "The Great Food Fumble," *Science* 188 (May 9, 1975) :502–509; Thomas T. Poleman, "World Food: A Perspective," *Science* 188 (May 9, 1975) :510–18; and Don Paarlberg, statement before the U.S. House Committee on Agriculture, *World Population and Food Supply and Demand Situation*, p. 16.

12. Garrett Hardin, "Lifeboat Ethics—The Case Against Helping the Poor," *Psychology Today* 8 (September, 1974) :38.

13. Bernard Berelson, "Beyond Family Planning," *Science* 163, 533 (1969).

14. Lenni W. Kangas, "Integrated Incentives for Fertility Control," *Science* 169, 1278 (1970).

15. Garrett Hardin, "The Tragedy of the Commons," *Science* 162, 1243 (1968).

16. Hardin, "Lifeboat Ethics," and William and Paul Paddock, *Famine—1975!* (Boston: Little, Brown and Co., 1967).

17. Cliff Conner, "Hunger," *International Socialist Review* (September, 1974), p. 20.

18. See Ernst F. Schumacher, *Small Is Beautiful* (New York: Harper and Row, 1973).

19. Roger Revelle, interview with William L. Oltmans in *On Growth* (New York: G.P. Putman and Sons, 1974), p. 185.

20. Ansley J. Coale, in *Proceedings of the IUSSP International Population Conference* (Leige, Belgium: International Union for the Scientific Study of Population, 1973), pp. 53–77.

21. See Maaza Bekele, "False Prophets of Doom," *UNESCO Courier* (July–August 1974), p. 42; interview with Mercedes Concepcion in *Ceres* (New York: UN Food and Agriculture Organization, November–December, 1973), p. 58; and Varendra T. Vittachi, "No Future Without a Present," *Newsweek* (September 2, 1974), p. 12.

22. Similar criticisms of the general applicability of the Demographic Transition Model can be found in Ansley J. Coale and Edgar M. Hoover, *Population Growth and Economic Development in Low Income Countries* (Princeton, N.J.: Princeton University Press, 1958), pp. 13–17; and in Michael S. Teitelbaum, "Relevance of Demographic Transition Theory for Developing Countries," *Science* 188 (May 9, 1975) : 420–25.

23. Thomas Frejka, *The Future of Population Growth* (New York: John Wiley and Sons, 1973).

24. P. Buringh, H.D.J. vanHeemst, and G.J. Staring, "Computation of the Absolute Maximum Food Production of the World" (Wageningen, The Netherlands: Agricultural University, 1975), p. 47.

25. Dennis L. Meadows, William W. Behrens, Donella H. Meadows, Roger F. Naill, Jørgen Randers, and Erich K.O. Zahn, *The Dynamics of Growth in a Finite World* (Cambridge, Mass.: Wright-Allen Press, 1974).

26. *The Universal Declaration of Human Rights*, 15th Anniversary Edition (New York: United Nations, 1963).

27. United Nations, "Studies in Family Planning," *The World Planning Plan of Action* 5, 12 (New York: United Nations, December 1974), p. 383.

28. See, for example, Willard A. Hanna, "The Republic of Singapore: Population Review 1970," *American Universities Field Staff Reports* 19, 5 (1971) and "China's Experience in Population Control," U.S. House Committee on Foreign Affairs (Washington, D.C.: U.S. Government Printing Office, September 1974).

29. George F. Kennan, "Realities of American Foreign Policy" (Princeton, N.J.: Princeton University Press, 1974), quoted in *The New Yorker* (April 21, 1975), p. 29.

30. Commission on Population Growth and the American Future, *Population and the American Future* (New York: Signet, 1972).

31. Richard A. Easterlin, "On the Relation of Economic Factors to Recent and Projected Fertility Changes," *Demography* 3, 131 (1966).

32. Bernard Berelson (ed.), *Population Policy in Developed Countries* (New York: McGraw-Hill, 1974).

33. Richard Barnet and Ronald Müller, *Global Reach: The Power of Multinational Corporations* (New York: Simon and Schuster, 1974).

34. Hans Linnemann, *Fourth Report to the Club of Rome* (Amsterdam, The Netherlands: in press).

35. For examples see such publications as *Appropriate Technology* (quarterly from Intermediate Technology Publications, Ltd., 9 King Street, London WC2E8HN) and *Coevolution Quarterly* (Box 428, Sausalito, Calif. 94965).

36. For examples from developing countries see Keith Griffin, *The Political Economy of Agrarian Change* (Cambridge, Mass.: Harvard University Press, 1974), pp. 38, 42, 59. For data from the United States, Japan, and India see Kusum Nair, *The Lonely Furrow* (Ann Arbor: University of Michigan Press, 1969).

37. Schumacher, *Small Is Beautiful*, p. 186.

38. Ibid., p. 57.

39. For examples of "how-to" publications with circulations in the millions, see *Organic Gardening and Farming* (Organic Park, Emmaus, Pa. 18049); *Mother Earth News* (P.O. Box 70, Hendersonville, N.C. 28739); and Frances Moore Lappe, *Diet for a Small Planet* (New York: Ballantine, 1971).

NOTES TO CHAPTER 2
TECHNOLOGIES FOR A NEW LIFE-STYLE

1. See particularly Joseph Needham's writings on the Taoists and the Chin and Thang Taoists in his *Science and Civilization in China*, vol. 2, "History of Scientific Thought" (Cambridge: University Press, 1956), pp. 33–164.

2. For a critical but excellent overview of the hermetic tradition, see Francis A. Yates' *Giordano Bruno and the Hermetic Tradition* (New York: Random House, Vintage Books, 1969).

3. How alchemical philosophy meshed with a scientific and a sacred world view is described by Joseph Needham in his *Science and Civilization in China*, vol. 5, "Chemistry and Chemical Technology," Pt. II (Cambridge: University Press, 1974).

4. John E. Bardach, John H. Ryther, and William O. McLarney, *Aquaculture: The Farming and Husbandry of Freshwater and Marine Organisms* (New York: Wiley Interscience, 1972), p. 67.

5. Rezneat M. Darnell, "Tropic Spectrum of an Estuarine Community Based on Studies of Lake Pontchartrain, Louisiana, an Estuarine Community," *Ecology* 42 (1961) : 553–568.

6. William O. McLarney and John Todd, "Walton Two: A Compleat Guide to Backyard Fish Farming," *Journal of the New Alchemists* 2 (1974) : 79–117.

7. John Todd, "An Ark for Prince Edward Island," *Journal of the New Alchemists* 3 (1976).

NOTES TO CHAPTER 3
LIMITS TO ENERGY CONVERSION

1. Amory B. Lovins, "Long-Term Constraints on Human Activity," *Environmental Conservation* 1, 1 (Geneva, Switzerland, 1976) : 3–14.

2. Amory B. Lovins, *World Energy Strategies: Facts, Issues, and Options* (Cambridge, Mass.: Friends of the Earth/Ballinger Publishing Company, 1975).

3. Amory B. Lovins and John H. Price, *Non-Nuclear Futures: The Case for an Ethical Energy Strategy* (Cambridge, Mass.: Friends of the Earth/Ballinger Publishing Company, 1975).

4. Amory B. Lovins, "Energy Strategy: The Road Not Taken?" , *Foreign Affairs* 55, 1 (October 1976) : 65–96.

5. Amory B. Lovins, "Scale, Centralization, and Electrification in Energy Systems," Oak Ridge Associated Universities Symposium "Future Strategies for Energy Development," Oak Ridge, Tenn. (October 1976); revised version reprinted as topical appendixes in Amory B. Lovins (ed.), *Soft Energy Paths: Toward a Durable Peace*, Pt. I (Cambridge, Mass.: Friends of the Earth/Ballinger Publishing Company, 1977).

6. Lovins, "Energy Strategy."

7. Lovins, "Scale."

8. Harold P. Green, "The Risk-Benefit Calculus in Safety Determinations," *George Washington Law Review* 43 (March 1975) : 791–807.

9. Hannes Alfvén, *Bulletin of Atomic Scientists* 25, 5 (May 1972) : 5.

10. Robert Heilbroner, *An Inquiry into the Human Prospect* (New York: Norton, 1974).

11. Russel Ayres, "Policing Plutonium: The Civil Liberties Fallout," *Harvard Civil Rights—Civil Liberties Law Review* 10 (Spring 1975) :369–443; J.H. Barton, "Intensified Nuclear Safeguards and Civil Liberties," report to U.S. Regulatory Commission, Stanford Law School, October 21, 1975.

12. Hannes Alfvén, *Bulletin of Atomic Scientists* 30, 1 (1974) :4.

13. Allen V. Kneese, "The Faustian Bargain," *Resources* 44 (Washington, D.C.: Resources for the Future, September 1975), p. 1.

14. Green, "Risk-Benefit Calculus."

15. Lovins and Price, *Non-Nuclear Futures.*

NOTES TO CHAPTER 4
ECONOMIC GROWTH, ENERGY USE, AND ALTRUISM

1. Michael Rieber and Ronald Halcrow, "Nuclear Power to 1985: Possible versus Optimistic Estimates," Document 137P, Center for Advanced Computation, University of Illinois, Urbana, Ill. 61801 (1974).

2. Michael Rieber, "Low Sulfur Coal: A Revision of Resource and Supply Estimates," Document 88, Center for Advanced Computation, University of Illinois (1973).

3. U.S. Geological Survey, "Geological Estimates of Undiscovered Recover-

able Oil and Gas Reserves in the U.S.," Circular 275, USGS National Center, Reston, Va. 22092 (1975).

4. George Löf, "Solar Energy: An Infinite Source of Clean Energy," *The Annals of the American Academy of Political and Social Science* 410 (November 1973) : 52–64.

5. Robert Herendeen and Clark W. Bullard," U.S. Energy Balance of Trade, 1963–1973," Technical Memo 60, Center for Advanced Computation, University of Illinois (1975).

6. Clark W. Bullard and Bruce Hannon, "The Causes of Energy Growth, 1963–1967," Document 172, Center for Advanced Computation, University of Illinois (1975).

7. Clark W. Bullard and Robert Herendeen, "Energy Impact of Consumption Decisions," *Proceedings of the Institute of Electrical and Electronics Engineers* 63, 3 (1975) : 484.

8. Robert Herendeen, "Energy Impact of Final Demand Expenditures, 1963 and 1967," Technical Memo 62, Center for Advanced Computation, University of Illinois (1975).

9. Bruce Hannon, "Energy Conservation and the Consumer," *Science* 189 (July 11, 1975) : 95–102.

10. Ibid.

11. Robert Herendeen and Jerry Tanaka, "Energy Cost of Living," Document 171, Center for Advanced Computation, University of Illinois (1975).

12. Robert Herendeen, "Affluence and Energy Demand," *Mechanical Engineering* 26 (October 1974) : 18–22.

13. "Patterns of Energy Consumption in the Greater New York City Area," Resources for the Future, Washington, D.C. (July 1973).

14. Roger Bezdek and Bruce Hannon, "Energy, Manpower, and the Highway Trust Fund," *Science* 185 (August 23, 1974) : 669–675.

15. Ernst Berndt and David Wood, "An Economic Interpretation of the Energy–GNP Ratio," in Michael S. Macrakis (ed.), *Energy* (Cambridge, Mass.: M.I.T. Press, 1973).

16. Clark W. Bullard and Arye L. Hillman, "Energy Separability and Production: A Taxonomic Note," Document 167, Center for Advanced Computation, University of Illinois (1975).

17. John Moyers, "The Value of Insulation in Residential Construction," Document ORN NSF EP9, Oak Ridge National Laboratory, Oak Ridge, TN (1971).

18. Hannon, "Energy Conservation."

19. Bruce Hannon, "An Energy Standard of Value," *The Annals of the American Academy of Political and Social Science* 410 (November 1973) : 139–153.

20. Bruce Hannon, "Bottles, Cans, Energy," *Environment* 14 (March 1972) : 14–19.

21. Hugh Folk, "Two Papers on the Employment Effects of Mandatory Deposits on Beverage Containers," Document 73, Center for Advanced Computation, University of Illinois (1972).

22. Hannon, "Energy Conservation."

23. Norman Wengert, "The Ideological Basis of Conservation and Natural-Resource Policies and Programs," *The Annals of the American Academy of Political and Social Science* 344 (1962) : 65–76.

24. William Nordhaus, "The Allocation of Energy Resources," Brookings Papers on Economic Activity, No. 3, Brookings Institute, Washington, D.C. (1973), pp. 529–576.

25. Garrett Hardin, "The Tragedy of the Commons," *Science* 162 (June 28, 1968) : 1234–1248.

26. Herman Daly, "Steady-State Economics versus Growthmania: A Critique of Orthodox Conceptions of Growth, Wants, Scarcity, and Efficiency," *Policy Sciences*, vol. 5 (Amsterdam: Elsevier Scientific Publishing Co., 1974), pp. 149–167.

NOTES TO CHAPTER 5
NEW PERSPECTIVES ON ECONOMIC GROWTH

1. Donella H. Meadows et al., *The Limits to Growth* (New York: Universe Books, 1972).

2. Mihajlo Mesarovic and Eduard Pestel, *Mankind at the Turning Point* (New York: E.P. Dutton and Company, Inc., The Reader's Digest Press, 1974).

3. Jay W. Forrester, *World Dynamics* (Cambridge, Mass.: Wright-Allen Press, Inc., 1971).

4. Ibid.

5. Dennis L. Meadows and Donella H. Meadows (eds.), *Toward Global Equilibrium: Collected Papers* (Cambridge, Mass.: Wright-Allen Press, Inc., 1973).

6. Dennis L. Meadows et al., *Dynamics of Growth in a Finite World* (Cambridge, Mass.: Wright-Allen Press, Inc., 1974).

7. Jay W. Forrester, *Collected Papers of Jay W. Forrester* (Cambridge, Mass.: Wright-Allen Press, Inc., 1975).

8. Nathan B. Forrester, *The Life Cycle of Economic Development* (Cambridge, Mass.: Wright-Allen Press, Inc., 1972).

9. Nathaniel J. Mass, *Economic Cycles: An Analysis of Underlying Causes* (Cambridge, Mass.: Wright-Allen Press, Inc., 1975).

10. Jay W. Forrester, *Industrial Dynamics* (Cambridge, Mass.: M.I.T. Press, 1961).

11. Jay W. Forrester, *Principles of Systems* (Cambridge, Mass.: Wright-Allen Press, 1968).

12. Jay W. Forrester, "Business Structure, Economic Cycles, and National Policy," System Dynamics Group Memorandum D–2245–2, Alfred P. Sloan School of Management, M.I.T. (from a speech given at the National Association of Business Economists 17th Annual Meeting, Boca Raton, Fla., on October 7, 1975). In a somewhat shorter form, available in *Business Economics* 11, 1 (January 1976).

13. Moses Abramovitz, "The Nature and Significance of Kuznets Cycles," *Economic Development and Cultural Change* 9 (April 1961) : 225–248.

14. Robert A. Gordon, *Business Fluctuations* (New York: Harper and Row, 1951).

15. Nikolai D. Kondratieff, "The Long Waves in Economic Life," *Review of Economic Statistics* 17, 6 (November 1935) : 105–115.

16. George Garvy, "Kondratieff's Theory of Long Cycles," *Review of Economic Statistics* 25, 4 (November 1943) : 203–220.

17. Forrester, "Business Structure."

NOTES TO CHAPTER 6
THE COMING ECONOMIC TRANSITION

1. See, however, the work on energy modeling which has been more explanatory of the phenomenon of "slumpflation"—that is, the work of Howard T. Odum, Nicholas Georgescu-Roegen, and Malcolm Slesser.

2. Hazel Henderson, "The Entropy State," *Planning Review* (April/May 1974).

3. Francois Meyer and Jacques Vallee, "The Dynamics of Long Term Growth," *Technological Forecasting and Social Change* 7, 3 (1975) : 285–300.

4. *New York Times*, September 23, 1974, Op-Ed page.

5. See, for example, Howard T. Odum, *Environment, Power, and Society* (New York: Wiley Interscience, 1972).

6. Alfred Eggers, U.S. Senate Conference on Economic Planning sponsored by Senator John Culver of Iowa, May 22, 1975. Transcript available from Senator Culver's Office, Senate Office Building, Washington, D.C.

7. Council on Environmental Quality Review, requested by Senator Muskie and Representative John Dingell (April 1975). Copies available from CEQ, 722 Jackson Place, Washington, D.C.

8. For several of these proposals and insights into efficient factor-mixing, the author is indebted to: Dr. Mason Gaffney, Director, British Columbia Institute for Economic Analysis, Victoria, B.C., Canada; also Louis O. Kelso, author, San Francisco; Dr. Robert Edmonds, economic analyst, San Francisco; Dr. Richard Pollack in an unpublished paper; and Professor Herman Daly, Department of Economics, Louisiana State University.

9. *Environmentalists for Full Employment Newsletter*, 1785 Massachusetts Avenue, Washington, D.C. 20036 (Fall 1976) : 5.

10. Louis O. Kelso, *Two Factor Theory: The Economics of Reality* (New York: Vintage Books, 1967).

11. See, for example, Hazel Henderson, "The Decline of Jonesism," *The Futurist* (October 1974).

12. "A National Public Works Investment Policy," U.S. House Committee of Public Works, 93rd Congress, 2nd session (November 1974).

13. From a statement of the Ad Hoc Committee for Full Economic Representation, press release of October 15, 1971. A copy may be obtained from the Public Interest Economic Center, 1714 Massachusetts Avenue, N.W., Washington, D.C.

NOTES TO CHAPTER 7
EQUITY, THE FREE MARKET AND THE SUSTAINABLE STATE

1. Donella H. Meadows, Dennis L. Meadows, William W. Behrens, III, and Jørgen Randers, *The Limits to Growth* (New York: Universe Books, 1972).

2. Kenneth E. Boulding, "Equity and Conflict," *Annals of the American Academy of Political and Social Science* (September 1973) : 7.

3. Ibid.

4. Mahbub ul Haq, "The Limits to Growth: A Critique," reprinted in *Growth and its Implications for the Future*, Part I, U.S. House Committee on Merchant Marine and Fisheries, Subcommittee on Fisheries and Wildlife, 93rd Congress, Doc. No. 93–7 (Washington, D.C.: U.S. Government Printing Office, 1973), p. 210.

5. Zbigniew Brzezinski, "The Politics of Zero Growth," *Newsweek* 79 (March 27, 1972) : 54.

6. "Provisional Indicative World Plan for Agricultural Development," vol. 2 (Rome: United Nations Food and Agriculture Organization, 1970), p. 490.

7. For a precise model of the effect of response delays on commodity price fluctuations, see Dennis L. Meadows, *The Dynamics of Commodity Production Cycles* (Cambridge, Mass.: Wright-Allen Press, 1970).

8. Philip M. Budzik, "The Future of Vermont Dairy Farming," Master's Thesis, Thayer School of Engineering, Dartmouth College, 1975. All information about Vermont cited in this paper is taken from this thesis unless otherwise noted.

9. "Vermonters on Vermont," (Montpelier: Vermont Natural Resources Council, January 1972).

10. Data from District Ludhiana in the Punjab are from John B. Wyon and John E. Gordon, *The Khanna Study* (Cambridge, Mass.: Harvard University Press, 1971), pp. 304–307.

11. Land distribution statistics from the Punjab are cited in Keith Griffin, *The Political Economy of Agrarian Change* (Cambridge, Mass.: Harvard University Press, 1974), p. 77 and p. 215.

12. Based on *ELFAC, Dairy Farm Business Analysis*, Northeastern States Cooperative Extension Service, 1973 data. For copies contact Mr. Raymond Tremblay, Resource Economics, 178 South Prospect, University of Vermont, Burlington, Vt. 05401.

13. Griffin, *Political Economy of Agrarian Change*, pp. 39, 44, 59, 94, 99. See also William Rich, "Smaller Families through Social and Economic Progress," monography #7 (Washington, D.C.: Overseas Development Council, January 1973).

14. Alex F. McCalla and Harold O. Carter, "Alternative Agricultural and Food Policy Directions for the U.S. with Emphasis on a Market-Oriented Approach," *Special Publication* 43, Agriculture Experiment Station, College of Agriculture, University of Illinois (August 1976).

15. John Kenneth Galbraith, *Economics and the Public Purpose* (New York: Signet, 1973).

16. The biologists seem to be most aware of the self-destruction of competitive systems. In ecology it is called the "competitive exclusion principle." See Garrett Hardin, "The Cybernetics of Competition," *Perspectives in Biology and Medicine* 7, 58 (1963); and Bertram G. Murray, Jr., "What the Ecologists Can Teach the Economists," *New York Times Magazine* (December 10, 1972) :38.

17. Joan Robinson, *Exercises in Economic Analysis* (London: Macmillan & Co., 1961), p. 239.

18. Budzik, "Future of Vermont Dairy Farming," p. 174.

19. Herman E. Daly, *Toward a Steady-State Economy* (San Francisco: W.H. Freeman and Company, 1973), p. 168.

NOTES TO CHAPTER 8 ON LIMITING ECONOMIC GROWTH

1. *Wall Street Journal*, September 17, 1975, p. 16.

2. Herman E. Daly (ed.), *Toward a Steady-State Economy* (San Francisco: Freeman Co., 1973). See especially the seventh essay.

3. Ibid.

4. Henry George, *Progress and Poverty* (New York: Robert Schalkenbach Foundation, 1951). Originally published in 1879.

5. John Ise, "The Theory of Value as Applied to Natural Resources," *American Economic Review* (June 1925) : 284.

6. Jahangir Amuzegar, "The North-South Dialogue: From Conflict to Compromise," *Foreign Affairs* 54, 3 (April 1976) : 547.

7. For a defense of transferrable birth licences, see Daly, *Toward a Steady-State Economy*, pp. 158–60.

8. David M. Heer, "Marketable Licenses for Babies: Boulding's Proposal Revisted," *Social Biology* (Spring 1975) : 1–16.

9. The original statement of the plan is found in Kenneth E. Boulding, *The Meaning of the Twentieth Century* (New York: Harper and Row, 1964), p. 136.

NOTES TO CHAPTER 9 LESSONS IN EQUITY FROM LOCAL COMMUNITIES

1. See Earl Finkler and David L. Peterson, *Nongrowth Planning Strategies: The Developing Power of Towns, Cities, and Regions* (New York: Praeger, 1974) for a more detailed definition and description of the local nongrowth movement in the United States. Also, Earl Finkler, William J. Toner, and Frank J. Popper, *Urban Nongrowth—City Planning for People* (New York: Praeger, 1976).

2. See, for example, William Alonso, "Urban Zero Population Growth," *Daedalus* 102, 4 (Fall 1973) : 193.

3. See Herman E. Daly, "The Steady-State Economy: Toward a Political Economy of Biophysical Equilibrium and Moral Growth," in Herman E. Daly (ed.), *Toward a Steady-State Economy* (San Francisco: W.H. Freeman and Company, 1973), p. 151; and Carl Pope, "Growth and the Poor," *Sierra Club Bulletin* (April 1975) : 3; and William J. Toner, "Introduction to Nongrowth Economics," in Finkler and Peterson, *Nongrowth Planning*, p. xviii.

4. "The Wealth of Cities," *Municipal Performance Report*, Council on Municipal Performance, 84 Fifth Ave., New York, N.Y. (April 1, 1974), p. 9.

5. Daniel J. Alesch and Robert A. Levine, *Growth in San Jose: A Summary Policy Statement* (Santa Monica, Calif.: The Rand Corporation, May 1973), pp. 16–21.

6. Elting E. Morison, *From Know-How to Nowhere* (New York: Basic Books, 1974).

7. Randall W. Scott (ed.), *Management and Control of Growth*, vol. 1 (Washington, D.C.: The Urban Land Institute, 1975), p. 2.

8. "List of Areas with Growth Constraints," Urban Land Institute, 1200 18th Street, N.W., Washington, D.C. (March 1973).

9. "Managing the Environment at the Local Level," *Urban Data Service Report*, International City Management Association, 1140 Connecticut Ave., N.W., Washington, D.C. (February 1974), p. 8.

10. "Constitutional Issues of Growth Management," National Science Foundation research grant to the University of North Carolina for Urban and Regional Studies, Chapel Hill, N.C. Project deadline: May 1976.

11. Telephone conversation with David Brower, University of North Carolina, August 8, 1975.

12. The Rockefeller Brothers Fund, William Reilly (ed.), *The Use of Land: A Citizen's Policy Guide to Urban Growth* (New York: Thomas Y. Crowell Company, 1973), p. 33.

13. George Gallup, Jr., "What do Americans Think About Limiting Growth?", mimeographed paper presented at the National Conference on Managed Growth (September 16, 1973), p. 2. Contact the Urban Research Corporation, 5645 S. Woodlawn Ave., Chicago, Ill. 60637, for more information on the Gallup paper and the conference.

14. Gallup survey conducted for the National Wildlife Federation, as reported in ibid., p. 8.

15. William Watts and Lloyd A. Free (eds.), *The State of the Nation, 1974* (Washington, D.C.: Potomac Associates, 1974), pp. 174–175.

16. Ibid.

17. Ibid., p. 75.

18. Louis Harris, "Sinking Confidence—Still Time for Change," *Western City* (August 1975), p. 13.

19. Watts and Free, *State of the Nation*, p. 277.

20. Ibid., p. 285.

21. Ibid.

22. Ibid., pp. 280–281.

23. Ibid., pp. 281–282.

24. Arizona Institute for Research, *Community Attitude Survey: A Report to the Comprehensive Planning Process*, City of Tucson Planning Department, City Hall, Tucson, Ariz. (July 1974).

25. Orange County Citizens Direction Finding Commission, *Citizens' Responses to Orange County's Population Growth*, Orange County Planning Department, Santa Ana, Calif. (February 1974), p. 8.

26. Phyllis Myers, *Slow Start in Paradise* (Washington, D.C.: The Conservation Foundation, 1974), p. 11.
27. The Rockefeller Brothers Fund, pp. 38–39.
28. Ibid., p. 52.
29. Ibid.
30. Saul Baldenegro, verbal testimony at a Dow rezoning public hearing held by the Pima County, Arizona, Board of Supervisors on July 7, 1975, in Tucson, Arizona. Transcript of the Dow hearings available from Southwest Environment Services, 115 W. Washington, Tucson, Ariz.
31. The Rockefeller Brothers Fund, p. 54.
32. "Court Backs Right of Cities to Curb Growth," *Los Angeles Times*, August 14, 1975.
33. See, for example, Fred P. Bosselman, "Can the Town of Ramapo Pass a Law to Bind the Rights of the Whole World?", *Florida State University Law Review*, no. 1 (1973) : 234–235.
34. Herbert M. Franklin, *Controlling Urban Growth—But for Whom?* (Washington, D.C.: The Potomac Institute, 1973), p. 13.
35. See Finkler, Toner, and Popper, *Urban Nongrowth*, pp. 46–81.
36. Bosselman, "Can the Town of Ramapo," p. 248.
37. See, for example, Sylvan Kamm, "Inflation: Curbing Inflation in Residential Land Prices," *Urban Land* (September 1971), p. 5.
38. Jay Forrester, *Urban Dynamics* (Cambridge, Mass.: The M.I.T. Press, 1969).
39. Anthony J. Yudis, "City Work Park the Next Trend in Development," *Boston Globe*, July 21, 1974.
40. Ibid.

NOTES TO CHAPTER 10 IN DEFENSE OF LONG-RANGE FEDERAL PLANNING

1. U.S. Senate, Balanced Growth and Economic Planning Act, SB 1795, 94th Congress, 1st session, May 21, 1975.
2. James Donnelly, testimony before the U.S. Senate Subcommittee of the Committee on Banking and Currency, Hearings on SB 380, 79th Congress, 1st session, 1946, p. 667.
3. Nathan S. Sachs, testimony before the U.S. Senate Subcommittee of the Committee on Banking and Currency, Hearings on SB 380, 79th Congress, 1st session, 1946.
4. Robert Wagner, testimony before the U.S. Senate Subcommittee of the Committee on Banking and Currency, Hearings on SB 380, 79th Congress, 1st session, 1946.
5. Jacob Javits, "The Need for National Planning," *Wall Street Journal*, July 8, 1975.

NOTES TO CHAPTER 11
THE PITFALLS OF NATIONAL PLANNING

1. Robert Gilpin, *France in the Age of the Scientific State* (Princeton: Princeton University Press, 1968), Chapter 8.

2. Mihajlo Mesarovic and Eduard Pestel, *Mankind at the Turning Point* (New York: E.P. Dutton & Co., Inc., 1974).

3. Glenn T. Seaborg, "The Recycle Society of Tomorrow," *The Futurist* 8, 3 (June 1974).

4. U.S. Senate, Balanced Growth and Economic Planning Act, SB 1795, 94th Congress, 1st session, May 21, 1975.

5. Maurice LaMontagne, House of Commons Debates, July 11, 1963, p. 2087.

6. Lester B. Pearson, House of Commons Debates, June 7, 1963, p. 793.

7. Economic Council of Canada, "The Economic Council at Work," Annual Report, Fiscal Year 1970–1971 (Ottawa: Information Canada, 1971), p. 47.

8. H. Bert Waslander, "Candide Model: Project Papers," series available at the Economic Council of Canada, Ottawa, Canada (1972–1975).

9. Economic Council of Canada, "Economic Targets and Social Indicators," Eleventh Annual Review (Ottawa, 1974), p. 68.

10. Ibid., p. 68.

11. Economic Council of Canada, "Economic Goals for Canada to 1970," First Annual Review (Ottawa, 1974), p. 4.

12. Wassily Leontieff, "Theoretical Assumptions and Non-Observed Facts," *American Economic Review* (March 1971) : 4.

13. Economic Council of Canada, "Performance and Potential, Mid-1950's to Mid-1970's" (Ottawa, 1970), p. 55.

14. Donald A. Schon, *Beyond the Stable State* (London: Temple Smith, 1971), Chapter 2.

15. Quoted by Alvin Toffler in *Future Shock* (New York: Random House, 1970), p. 421.

16. Quoted by Jack Frieman in "A Planned Economy in the U.S.," *New York Times*, May 18, 1975.

17. Toffler, *Future Shock*, p. 422.

18. Geoffrey Vickers, *Making Institutions Work* (London: Associated Business Programmes, 1973), p. 30.

19. Claude Gruson, "Replique aux Objecteurs de Broissance," *Expansion* (July-August 1972).

20. For a description of this process, see John Platt, *The Step to Man* (New York: John Wiley and Sons, Inc., 1970). See chapter entitled "Seed Operations."

NOTES TO CHAPTER 12
STRATEGIES FOR SOCIETAL DEVELOPMENT

1. Samuel Mauch, "Wie objektiv sind die Grenzen des Wachstums?", ETH-Symposium, "Technik für oder gegen den Menschen" (November 1973).

2. Alvin Weinberg, "Social Institutions and Nuclear Energy," *Science* 177 (July 7, 1972) : 27–34.

3. Hans Christoph Binswanger, "Analyse der Wachstumszwänge und des Wachstumsverlaufs im Wirtschaftssystem," Internal Project Report II–A–44 NAWU (November 1974).

4. Arich Ullman, "Wirtschaftswachstum und Umweltgerfährdung: für ein umweltgerechtes Verhalten," Internal Project Report II–B–41 NAWU (October 1974).

5. Rudolph Müller-Wenk, "Kritik der Sättigungsthese aus der Sicht der Erkenntnisse über menschliches Verhalten," Internal Project Report II–B–49 NAWU (May 1975).

6. "Preliminary Study of the Federal Institute for Water Resources," Gewässerschutz 2000, available from EAWAG, 8600 Dübendorf, Switzerland.

7. *Freiaemter Tagblatt*, August 26, 1975.

8. Rudolph Müller-Wenk and Arich Ullman, "Oekologische Buchhaltung," Internal Project Report II–B–40 NAWU (September 1974). Available from NAWU Sekretariat, Gloriastr. 35, 8006 Zürich, Switzerland.

9. Elmar Ledergerber and Theodore Ginsburg, "Gesamtenergiekonzeption für die Schweiz: Stabilisierungsvarianten," Internal Project to the Swiss Federal Committee for Energy Policy, 1975.

NOTES TO CHAPTER 13 INTERNATIONAL MIGRATION AND WORLD STABILITY

1. "Declaration of U.S. Policy of Population Stabilization by Voluntary Means, 1971," U.S. Senate Committee on Labor and Public Welfare, Special Subcommittee on Human Resources, Hearings on S.J. Res. 108, 92nd Congress, 1st session, document no. 68–976, p. 13.

2. John Higham, *Strangers in the Land* (New York: Atheneum, 1963).

3. *Immigration Policy Perspectives: A Report of the Canadian Immigration and Population Study*, Information Canada, 171 Slater Street, Ottawa, Ontario, Canada (1974).

4. *Population and Australia, A Demographic Analysis and Projection*, 2 vols. (Canberra, Australia: Australian Government Publishing Service, 1975). Available from the National Population Enquiry, P.O. Box 1921, Canberra City, A.C.T., Australia 2601.

5. This section generally follows Kingsley Davis, "The Migrations of Human Populations," *Scientific American* 231, 3 (September 1974) : 93–105.

6. See in general Marcus L. Hansen, *The Atlantic Migration, 1607–1860* (New York: Harper-Row Torchbooks, 1961).

7. *International Migration Trends, 1950–1970*, U.N. Secretariat Background Paper for the Bucharest World Population Conference, Document E/Conf. 60/CBP/18, May 22, 1974.

8. Ibid.

9. Ian M. Hume, "Migrant Workers in Europe," *Finance and Development* 10, 1 (March 1973) : 2–6.

10. Jonathan Power, "The New Proleteriat," *Encounter* 43, 3 (September 1974).

11. *Annual Report, Immigration and Naturalization Service* (Washington, D.C.: U.S. Government Printing Office, 1974). Available from the Superintendent of Documents.

12. "How Millions of Illegal Aliens Sneak into U.S.," *U.S. News and World Reports* (July 22, 1974) : 27–30.

13. *Population and the American Future*, Report of the Commission on Population Growth and the American Future (Washington, D.C.: U.S. Government Printing Office, 1972). See Chapter 13.

14. Andrew C. McLellend and Michael D. Boggs, "Illegal Aliens: A Story of Human Misery," *AFL–CIO Federationist*, 815 Sixteenth Street, N.W., Washington, D.C. 20006 (August 1974) : 17–23.

15. *Current Population Reports, Population Estimates and Projections*, series P–25, no. 493, U.S. Department of Commerce, Bureau of the Census (December 1972). See series X, p. 26.

16. *International Migration Trends.*

17. *1975 World Population Data Sheet*, Population Reference Bureau, 1754 N Street, N.W., Washington, D.C. 20036.

18. Hume, "Migrant Workers in Europe."

19. Harvey Ardman, "Our Illegal Alien Problem," *American Legion Magazine*, P.O. Box 1055, Indianapolis, In. 46206 (December 1974). Hard data on rates of unemployment and underemployment in the developing countries are difficult to find.

10. *1975 World Population Data Sheet.*

21. Overseas Development Council, *The U.S. and World Development* (New York: Praeger, 1975).

22. *1975 World Population Data Sheet.*

23. Charles B. Keely, "Immigration Composition and Population Policy," *Science* 185, 4151 (August 16, 1974) : 587–93. See also the correspondence on this article in *Science* 187, 4178 (February 28, 1975) : 700.

24. *Annual Report, Immigration.*

25. *Brain Drain: A Study of the Persistent Issue of International Scientific Mobility*, U.S. House Committee on Foreign Affairs, Subcommittee on National Security Policy and Scientific Developments, Doc. No. 35–962 (September 1974). Available from the Superintendent of Documents.

26. "Undergraduate Medical Education," *Journal of the American Medical Association* 234, 13 (December 29, 1975) : 1336–44. (No author is listed for this staff report.)

27. *U.S. Aid to Population/Family Planning in Asia*, report to U.S. House of Representatives, Committee on Foreign Affairs, February 25, 1973, Doc. No. 89–939, p. 9.

28. *Brain Drain.*

29. Judith Fortney, "Immigrant Professionals: A Brief Historical Survey," *International Migration Review* 6, 1 (Spring 1972) : 50–62.

30. "A Gift from the Needy," The Inter-Dependent (New York: United Nations Association, May 1974) : 7.

31. *Review of Achievements, 1973*, Intergovernmental Committee for European Migration, 1346 Connecticut Avenue, N.W., Suite 711, Washington, D.C. 20036, p. 18.

32. *Annual Report*, Immigration.

33. Davis, "Migrations of Human Populations."

34. Power, "The New Proleteriat."

35. *Immigration and Nationality Act*, Sec. 302 (a) (3), 82nd Congress, 2nd session, passed June 27, 1952 (Washington, D.C.: U.S. Government Printing Office).

36. Power, "The New Proleteriat."

37. Fortney, "Immigrant Professionals."

38. *Population and the American Future.*

39. *Annual Report, Immigration.*

40. "U.S. Goal: Jobs for 2 Million People a Year," *The Christian Science Monitor*, September 16, 1975.

41. *Annual Report, Immigration.*

42. Personal communication to the author from David North, a specialist on the labor effects of immigration.

43. Power, "The New Proleteriat."

44. Herman Daly, "Toward a New Economics: Questioning Growth," *Yale Alumni Magazine* (May 1970).

45. "How Millions of Illegal Aliens Sneak into U.S."

46. Davis, "Migrations of Human Populations."

47. John Tanton, "Immigration: An Illiberal Concern?" *Zero Population Growth National Reporter* 7, 3 (April 1975) : 4.

48. Davis, "Migrations of Human Populations."

49. *Annual World Refugee Report*, U.S. Committee for Refugees, 20 West 40th Street, New York, N.Y. 10018 (1974).

50. *Immigration and Nationality Act*, Sec. 203 (a) (7), 82nd Congress, 2nd session, passed June 27, 1952 (Washington, D.C.: U.S. Government Printing Office.)

51. "Pakistan Is Acting to Stem Emigration," *New York Times*, February 8, 1976.

52. *Recommendations for a New Immigration Policy for the United States*, Zero Population Growth, 1346 Connecticut Ave., N.W., Washington, D.C. 20036 (1975).

53. Nathan Glazer and Daniel Moynihan, *Beyond the Melting Pot*, 2nd edition (Cambridge, Mass.: The M.I.T. Press, 1970), p. 289

54. Michael Novak, *The Rise of the Unmeltable Ethnics* (New York: MacMillan Publishing Company, 1971).

55. *Our Immigration*, U.S. Department of Justice, Immigration and Naturalization Service, Document M–85 (Washington, D.C.: U.S. Government Printing Office), revision of 1967, pp. 8–9.

56. Higham, *Strangers in the Land.*

57. Novak, *Rise of Unmeltable Ethnics.*

58. Personal communication to the author from former senator Irvin.

59. "Five-Language Exercise for Next S.F. Election," *San Francisco Chronicle*, July 31, 1975, p. 1.

NOTES TO CHAPTER 14
PROMETHEUS REBOUND

1. Lynn White, Jr., "The Historical Roots of our Ecological Crisis," *Science* 155 (March 10, 1967) : 1203–1207.
2. Lynn White, Jr., "St. Francis and the Ecologic Backlash," *Horizon* (summer 1967) : 42–47.
3. Lynn White, Jr., *Medieval Technology and Social Change* (London: Oxford University Press, 1967), pp. 133–34.
4. Francis Bacon, "Sphinx, or Science," in *The Works of Francis Bacon*, vol. VI (London: Longmans, 1870), p. 40.
5. John Donne, "An Anatomie of the World: The First Anniversary," in Charles M. Coffin (ed.), *The Complete Poetry and Selected Prose of John Donne* (New York: Modern Library, 1952), p. 191.
6. A discerning discussion of this especially as it affected human values is found in Jerome B. Schneewind, "Looking Backward: Technology, Ways of Living, and Values in 19th Century England," in Kurt Baier and Nicholas Rescher (eds.), *Values and the Future* (New York: The Free Press, 1971), pp. 110–32.
7. *Changing Images of Man*, a report of the Center for the Study of Social Policy, O.W. Markley, project director, Stanford Research Institute, Menlo Park, Calif. (1973), p. 54.
8. Quoted in Schneewind, "Looking Backward," p. 110.
9. *Changing Images of Man*, p. 7.
10. Ernst F. Schumacher, *Small Is Beautiful: Economics As If People Mattered* (New York: Harper and Row, 1975), p. 70.
11. Cited in Jacques Ellul, *The Technological Society* (New York: Vintage Books, 1964), p. ix.
12. Lewis Mumford, *Technics and Civilization* (New York: Harcourt, Brace and Company, 1934). See also Lewis Mumford, *The Myth of the Machine: The Pentagon of Power* (New York: Harcourt, Brace and Jovanovich, Inc., 1970).
13. In addition to Ellul's seminal work *The Technological Society* cited above, see also his *Propaganda: The Formation of Men's Attitudes* (New York: Alfred Knopf, 1965).
14. Ellul, *The Technological Society*, p. 325.
15. Martin Pawley, *The Private Future* (New York: Random House, 1974), p. 8.
16. Hans Selye, *The Stress of Life* (New York: McGraw-Hill, 1956).
17. Ibid., pp. 4–124 passim.
18. Robert Masters and Jean Houston, *The Varieties of Psychedelic Experience* (New York: Holt, Rinehart and Winston, 1966).
19. I discuss this phenomenon at some length in my article "Myth, Consciousness, and Psychic Research," in Edgar D. Mitchell and John White (eds.), *Psychic Exploration: A Challenge for Science* (New York: G.P. Putnam and Sons, 1974), pp. 578–96.

20. Ellul, *The Technological Society*, p. 329.

21. A remarkable long-term experiment of describing changes over a fifteen-year period in delinquent teenagers' attitudes toward time and gratification is found in a study by Anthony Davids and Bradley Falkoff entitled "Juvenile Delinquents Then and Now: Comparison of Findings from 1959 and 1974" in the *Journal of Abnormal Psychology* 84, 2 (1975) : 161–64.

22. For a profound discussion of the effects of technology on the sense of duration, see Enrico Castelli's study, *Il Tempo Esaurito* (Rome: Bussola, 1947).

23. This statement is found in a curious but brilliant little volume by William Kuhns, *Environmental Man* (New York: Harper and Row, 1969), p. 94.

24. This study will be found in Robert Masters and Jean Houston, *New Ways of Being* (New York: The Viking Press). Manuscript in preparation.

25. See for example Margaret Mead's autobiographical work, *Blackberry Winter: My Earlier Years* (New York: William Morrow, 1972). As an example of Dr. Mead's ability to communicate issues of great complexity in a lucid and decisive manner, see her book *Continuities in Cultural Evolution* (New Haven: Yale University Press, 1968).

26. Jean Houston, "Myth Consciousness and Psychic Research," pp. 586–89.

27. Pawley, *The Private Future*, p. 185.

28. Quoted in Pawley, p. 190.

29. A discussion and example of this kind of radical paradigm shift is found in John Platt, "Hierarchical Restructuring," *Bulletin of Atomic Scientists* (November 1970).

30. Schumacher, *Small Is Beautiful.* The literature in this area is growing constantly as evidenced, for example, by the proliferation of books, ideas, theories, and how-to articles in such publications as *The Whole Earth Catalog*, *The Mother Earth News*, and *The Coevolution Quarterly*. Two recent examples of the combining of an ecological ethic to intermediate technology principles would be Daniel Kozlovsky, *An Ecological and Evolutionary Ethic* (Englewood Cliffs: Prentice-Hall, 1974) and Paul Shepard and Daniel McKinley (eds.), *The Subversive Science: Essays Toward an Ecology of Man* (Boston: Houghton Mifflin Co., 1969).

31. Schumacher, *Small Is Beautiful*, p. 145.

32. See, for example, David Hawkins and Linus Pauling (eds.), *Orthomolecular Psychiatry* (San Francisco: W.H. Freeman, 1973).

33. This report is discussed in Wilfred Barlow, *The Alexander Technique* (New York: Alfred A. Knopf, 1973), p. 73.

34. These defects and their causes are discussed at length in the Barlow book cited above, note 33.

35. Robert Masters, "Psychophysical Education: Recovering the Body," *The International Journal of Psychoenergetic Systems* 2, 1 (1976).

36. Moshe Feldenkrais, *Awareness Through Movement* (New York: Harper and Row, 1972). Alexander's work is found in *The Resurrection of The Body: The Work of F. Matthias Alexander*, selected and introduced by Edward Maisel (New York: University Books, 1969).

37. Tinbergen's Nobel Prize speech is found in Nikolaas Tinbergen, "Ethology and Stress Diseases," *Science* 185 (July 5, 1974) : 20–27.

38. See Feldenkrais, *Awareness Through Movement.*

39. Three of John Dewey's introductions to books by Alexander are contained in *The Resurrection of The Body*, pp. 169–84.

40. For a fuller discussion of some of our work, see Jean Houston, "The Psychenaut Program: An Exploration into Some Human Potentials," in *Journal of Creative Behavior* 7, 4 (1973) : 253–78. Some of these techniques are presented in Robert Masters and Jean Houston, *Mind Games* (New York: Delta, 1973).

41. This is discussed by me in both of the above references. See also Jacques Hadamard, *The Psychology of Invention in the Mathematical Field* (Princeton: Princeton University Press, 1945). For a self-description by many different creative people of the use of imageries during the creative process, see Brewster Chiselin (ed.), *The Creative Process* (New York: New American Library, 1952).

42. Erich R. Jaensch, *Eidetic Imagery and Typological Methods of Investigation* (London: Routledge & Kegan Paul, Ltd., 1930).

NOTES TO CHAPTER 15
EDUCATION FOR INVENTING THE FUTURE

1. Fred Polak, *The Image of the Future*, translated and abridged by Elise Boulding (San Francisco: Jossy Bass/Elsivier, 1973).

2. Friedrich A. von Hayek, *The Road to Serfdom* (Chicago: University of Chicago Press, 1944).

3. Peter Farb, *Man's Rise to Civilization* (New York: E.P. Dutton and Co., Inc., 1968).

4. Polak, *Image of the Future.*

5. Gay Luce, *Body Time: Psychological Rhythms and Social Stress* (New York: Pantheon, 1971).

6. Edward Bellamy, *Looking Backward: 2000–1887*, reprint (New York: Random House, 1887).

7. Elise Boulding, "Children and Solitude" (Wallingford, Pa.: Pendle Hill Pamphlet, 1962).

8. Elise Boulding, "The Underside of History: A View of Women Through Time" (in preparation), Ch. 3.

9. Alexander Marshack, *The Roots of Civilization* (New York: McGraw-Hill, 1972).

10. Bellamy, *Looking Backward.*

11. Ivan Illich, *De-Schooling Society* (New York: Harper and Row, 1971).

12. Paulo Freire, *Pedagogy of the Oppressed* (New York: Seabury Press, 1971).

13. Elise Boulding, "New Approaches to Learning—Alternative Education and Open Schools," a paper prepared for the Science Education Commission of the American Association for the Advancement of Science (April 1971).

14. Ibid.

15. Chadwick Alger, "Your City in the World, the World in Your City" (Columbus, Ohio: Ohio State University, Mershon Center, November, 1974). Mimeographed.

16. Elise Boulding, "The Child and Nonviolent Social Change," in Christoph Wulf (ed.), *Handbook on Peace Education* (Oslo: International Peace Research Association, 1974).

17. Jonas Salk, *The Survival of the Wisest* (New York: Harper and Row, 1973).

NOTES TO CHAPTER 16
TOWARDS A PRIMARY LIFE-STYLE

1. James V. Neel, "Lessons from a 'Primitive' People," *Science* 170 (November 20, 1970) : 815–22.

2. Don E. Dumond, "The Limitations of Human Population: A Natural History," *Science* 187 (February 28, 1975) : 713–21.

3. Janet Siskind, "Tropical Forest Hunters and the Economy of Sex," in Daniel R. Gross (ed.), *Peoples and Cultures of Native South America* (Garden City, N.Y.: Doubleday, National History Press, 1973).

4. Gerardo Reichel-Dolmatoff, *Amazonian Cosmos* (Chicago: University of Chicago Press, 1971).

5. Charles Wagley, "Cultural Influences on Population: A Comparison of Two Tupi Tribes," *Revista do Museu Paulista* 5 (1951) : 95–104.

6. Peter Kunstadter, "Demography, Ecology, Social Structure, and Settlement Patterns," in Geoffrey A. Harrison and Anthony J. Boyce (eds.), *The Structure of Human Populations* (Oxford: Clarendon Press, 1972).

7. Neel, "Lessons."

8. Richard B. Lee, "Population Growth and the Beginnings of Sedentary Life Among the !Kung Bushmen," and "The Intensification of Social Life Among the !Kung Bushmen," in Brian Spooner (ed.), *Population Growth: Anthropological Implications* (Cambridge, Mass.: The M.I.T. Press, 1972).

9. Nancy Howell, "The Population of the Dobe Area !Kung," in Richard B. Lee and Irvin DeVore (eds.), *Kalahari Hunter-Gatherers* (Cambridge, Mass.: Harvard University Press, 1976).

10. Dumond, op. cit.

11. Robert Allen, *The Paradise Paradox*, in press.

12. Siskind, op. cit.

13. Mary Douglas, "Population Control in Primitive Groups," *British Journal of Sociology* 17 (1966) : 263–73.

14. Dumond, op. cit.

15. Douglas, op. cit.

16. Ibid.

17. Betty Jane Meggers, *Amazonia: Man and Culture in a Counter-Paradise* (Chicago: Aldine, 1971).

18. Niels Fock, "Waiwai: Religion and Society of an Amazonian Tribe," National Museets Skrifter, *Etnografish Raekke* 8 (1963).

19. Michael S. Teitelbaum, "Relevance of Demographic Transition Theory for Developing Countries," *Science* 188 (May 2, 1975) : 420–25.

20. Ibid.

21. Wagley, op. cit.

22. Anthony Leeds, "Yaruro Incipient Tropical Forest Horticulture: Possibilities and Limits," in Johannes Wilbert (ed.), *The Evolution of Horticultural Systems in Native South America*, Anthropologica Supplement Publication no. 2 (Caracas: Sociedad de Ciencias Naturales La Salle, 1961).

23. Vincenzo Petrullo, "The Yaruros of the Capanaparo River, Venezuela," *Smithsonian Institution Bureau of American Ethnology*, Bulletin 123, 1939.

24. Allen, op. cit.

25. HABITAT, UN Conference of Human Settlements, preparatory information from United Nations Environment Program, Vancouver, 1976.

NOTES TO CHAPTER 17 SETTLEMENTS AND SOCIAL STABILITY

1. "The World's Million-Cities," Population Division, Department of Economic and Social Affairs of the United Nations Secretariat, no. 72–06207 (New York: United Nations, 1972).

2. Stephen Runciman, *The Medieval Manichee* (Cambridge: University Press, 1947).

3. Edward Goldsmith, "Does Building Houses Cause More Homelessness?", *The Ecologist* 5, 12 (December 1975).

4. Eduard Pestel and Mihajlo Mesarovic, *Mankind at the Turning Point* (New York: E.P. Dutton and Co., Inc., Readers Digest Press, 1975).

5. Edward S. Russell, *The Behavior of Animals* (London: E. Arnold and Co., 1938).

6. Conrad H. Waddington, *The Strategy of the Genes* (London: Allen and Unwin, 1957).

7. Ibid.

8. Stephen Boyden, "Health and Evolution," *The Ecologist* 3, 8 (August 1973).

9. Ibid.

10. Robert Waller, "The Diseases of Civilisation," *The Ecologist* 1, 2 (August 1970).

11. See Marshall B. Clinard, *Anomie and Deviant Behavior* (New York: The Free Press, 1964), in particular, the annotated bibliography of theoretical studies, pp. 290–311.

12. Charles C. Hughes and John M. Hunter, "Development and Disease in Africa," *The Ecologist* 2, 9–10 (September-October 1972).

13. George Armelagos and Alan McArdle, "Population, Disease and Environment," *The Ecologist* 6, 5 (June 1976).

14. Steven Polgar, "Evolution and the Ills of Mankind," in Sol Tax (ed.), *Horizons of Anthropology* (Chicago: Aldine, 1974).

15. Armelagos and McArdle, "Population, Disease and Environment."

16. Boyden, "Health and Evolution."

17. Michael Crawford, *What We Eat Today* (New York: Stein and Day, 1972).

18. Boyden, "Health and Evolution."

19. Thomas L. Cleave et al., *Diabetes, Coronary Thrombosis and the Saccharine Disease*, 2nd ed. (Bristol: John Wright, 1969); and Virgil J. Vogel, *American Indian Medicine* (Norman, Okla.: University of Oklahoma Press, 1970).

20. Marshall Sahline, "The Original Affluent Society," *The Ecologist* 4, 5 (June 1974).

21. Richard B. Lee and Irwin Devore (eds.), *Man the Hunter* (Chicago: Aldine, 1968).

22. Irenaus Eibl-Eibesfeldt, "The Fighting Behavior of Animals," *Scientific American* 205 (December 1961) : 34.

23. Robert Lowie, *Primitive Society* (London: Routledge and Kegan Paul, 1963); and John C. Ewers, "Blackfoot Raiding for Horse and Scalps," in Paul Bohannon (ed.), *Law and Welfare* (New York: American Museum of Natural History, 1967).

24. Mario Ferrari, personal communication.

25. Eugene Odum, personal communication.

26. Kenneth Watt, *The Titanic Effect* (Stamford, Conn.: Sinauer Associates, 1974).

27. Lowie, *Primitive Society*; and Lucy Mair, *Primitive Government* (London: Penguin, 1963).

28. Edward Goldsmith, "The Family Basis of Social Structure," *The Ecologist* 6, 2 (February 1976).

29. Niko Tinbergen, *Social Behavior in Animals* (London: Methuen, 1953). See also: R.W. Gerrard, "A Biologist's View of Society," *General Systems Yearbook* 1, 1 (1956).

30. Bronislaw Malinowski, *Sex and Repression in Savage Society* (London: Routledge and Kegan Paul, 1961).

31. George Peter Murdock, *Social Structure* (New York: The Free Press, 1965).

32. Malinowski, *Sex and Repression.*

33. Henry Maine, *Ancient Law* (London: J. Murray, 1861).

34. Alfred R. Radcliffe-Brown, *Structure and Function in Primitive Society* (London: Cohen and West, 1965).

35. Edward Goldsmith, "The Family Basis."

36. Ralph Linton, *The Study of Man* (London: Peter Owen, 1965).

37. Jose Ortega y Gasset, *Espana Invertebrada* (Madrid: Calpe, 1921).

38. Lowie, *Primitive Society.*

39. Linton, *Study of Man.*

40. Lowie, *Primitive Society.*

41. Emile Durkheim, "The Solidarity of Occupational Groups," in Talcott Parsons (ed.), *Theories of Society* (New York: The Free Press, 1970).

42. Karl Polanyi, *Primitive, Archaic and Modern Economics* (New York: Doubleday, 1968).

43. Lowie, *Primitive Society.*

44. Polanyi, *Primitive, Archaic and Modern Economics.*

45. Raymond Firth, *The Elements of Social Organisation* (London: C.A. Watts and Co., 1951).

46. Polanyi, *Primitive, Archaic and Modern Economics.*

47. Edward Goldsmith, "The Family Basis."

48. Edward Goldsmith, "Education: What For?", *The Ecologist* 4, 1 (January 1974).

49. Fustel de Coulanges, *La Citė Antique* (Paris: Hachette, 1927).

50. Linton, *Study of Man.*

51. Francis L.K. Hsu, *Under the Ancestor's Shadow* (London: Routledge and Kegan Paul, 1949); Edwin Driver, *Indians of North America* (Chicago: University of Chicago Press, 1961); Cora Dubois, *The People of Alor* (New York: Harpers, 1960); William J. Goode, *Religion Among the Primitives* (New York: The Free Press, 1964); Hilda Kuper, *The Swazi: A South African Kingdom* (New York: Holt, Rinehart and Winston, 1963); Melville Jean Herskovits, *Dahomey* (New York: Augustin, 1938).

52. Edward Goldsmith, "The Religion of a Stable Society," *The Ecologist* 5, 11 (November 1975).

53. Edward Goldsmith, "Is Science a Religion?", *The Ecologist* 5, 2 (February 1975).

54. Paul Bohannon, "Africa's Land," *The Centennial Review* 55 (1960).

55. Maine, *Ancient Law.*

56. Amos Rappaport, "The Ecology of Housing," *The Ecologist* 3, 1 (January 1973).

57. Claude Levi-Strauss, *Tristes Tropiques* (Paris: Plon, 1955).

58. Robert Jaulin, "Ethnocide," *The Ecologist* 1, 18 (December 1971).

59. Ibid.

60. Albin Peyron, personal communication.

61. Gustave Glotz, *The Greek City and Its Institutions* (New York: Alfred A. Knopf, 1930).

62. Gustave Edmund von Grunebaum, *Islam: Essays on the Nature and Growth of a Cultural Tradition* (London: Routledge and Kegan Paul, 1955).

63. Edward Goldsmith, "The Ecology of War," *The Ecologist* 4, 4 (May 1974).

64. Valerius Geist, "About Natural Man and Environment Design," *Proceedings of the Third International Conference on the Unity of the Sciences* (Tokyo: International Cultural Foundation, 1975).

Index

About the Editor

Dennis L. Meadows, Associate Professor of Engineering at Dartmouth, holds a B.A. degree from Carleton College and a doctorate from M.I.T. He was director of the Club of Rome Project on the Predicament of Mankind at M.I.T. from 1970 to 1972. He has been a Research Fellow at the East-West Population Institute in Honolulu and the International Institute for Applied Systems Analysis in Austria. His research and teaching focus on population-resource interactions within a finite world. He currently directs a graduate program at Dartmouth on public systems analysis and design, and consults for a number of government agencies on system analysis techniques and resource policy. His books include *The Limits to Growth*, *Dynamics of Growth in a Finite World*, and *Dynamics of Commodity Production Cycles.*

About the Contributors

Robert Allen is a professional journalist and a free-lance writer on ecology and anthropology who heads Membership and External Affairs for the International Union for Conservation of Nature and Natural Resources (IUCN) in Morges, Switzerland. Born in Dorset, England, he co-founded the *Ecologist* with Edward Goldsmith in 1970 and jointly edited that journal until 1973. In 1972 he received a Winston Churchill Fellowship to study the environmental attitudes of the Majangir, an Ethiopian tribe of hunter-gardeners. He has written for the *London Times*, the *New York Times*, and *Development Forum*, among other publications, and his books include *A Blueprint for Survival* (1972), *Natural Man* (1974), and *The Paradise Paradox* (in press).

Elise Boulding. I have kept Elise Boulding's biography short, for no paragraph can do justice to her many careers. She was born in Oslo and grew up in the United States where she studied, married and raised five children. Throughout her life she has been an active member of the Religious Society of Friends. She completed her doctorate at the University of Michigan in 1969 on the relation of industrialization to the social participation of women. Now she is a professor of sociology at the University of Colorado in Boulder. She has traveled and lectured widely. Her books and articles number nearly 100, including two volumes she translated from Dutch and one paper translated from Swedish. She is simultaneously one of the nation's leading futurists, feminists, and peace researchers. In short, she personally exemplifies the title of a lecture she delivered in Colorado in 1968, "101 Ways to be a Woman."

Herman Daly is a unique economist; he combines a solid foundation in the history and theory of modern economic practice with an appreciation for the laws of thermodynamics and ecology. Educated at Rice and Vanderbilt Universities, he completed his thesis under Georgescu-Rogen. His interest in the economics of Latin American countries led him first to a concern for population growth, then to more general interest in the determinants and implications of sustained physical growth. He is currently on the faculty of Louisiana State University, where he teaches a variety of basic economics courses and searches for the keys to a steady-state economy within current institutions and values. His research tools are a typewriter, a sharp wit, a healthy scepticism about the perfection of current economic and social science, and a collection of the classic contributions to earlier branches of economic thought, formulated before the power of technology gave man the illusion that he had been set free from the constraints of a finite planet.

Joan Davis received her Ph.D. in Biochemistry from Ohio State University. Since 1970 she has been on the research staff of the Swiss Federal Institute for Water Resources and Pollution Control. She has been active in the design and promotion of national energy strategies for Switzerland based primarily on solar energy, water power, and conservation.

Earl Finkler is a planning consultant and free-lance writer based in Tucson, Arizona. He has worked for the American Society of Planning Officials in Chicago and has planning experience in Alaska, Canada, and Milwaukee, as well as in Tucson. He has published articles on nongrowth in *Landscape Architecture*, the Chicago *Tribune*, *Planning*, and *Equilibrium*, and has coauthored *Nongrowth Planning Strategies*, with David Peterson, and *Urban Nongrowth: City Planning for People*, with William J. Toner and Frank J. Popper. He has taught planning part time at the University of Arizona, and has formal degrees in urban affairs and journalism.

Jay Forrester is Germeshausen Professor at the Massachusetts Institute of Technology, where he directs the System Dynamics Group within the Alfred P. Sloan School of Management. His early work was in the field of electrical engineering and included invention of the memory device which helped facilitate the development of modern digital computers. His work at the Sloan School since 1956 has produced a distinct field of systems analysis and applied it to basic problems in industry, urban planning, global dynamics, and macro-economics. His work has catalyzed the development of activity in social systems analysis around the world; his books and inventions have brought him numerous national and international awards.

Edward Goldsmith was born in Paris, France, and educated at Magdalen College at Oxford University. Since leaving that institution in 1950, he has had no connection with any formal seat of learning, except for a brief appointment as Adjunct Associate Professor at the University of Michigan in 1975. He has nevertheless devoted most of his time to intellectual pursuits, his principal interests lying in the fields of general systems, anthropology, and ecology. In 1969, he founded the *Ecologist*, a journal which he still publishes and edits. He is a founding member of the British Ecology Party and of the Cornwall Ecology Party, and is ecological consultant to *L'Express* in Paris.

Bruce Hannon was educated in engineering mechanics. While on the faculty of the University of Illinois, he shifted his interests from the study of physical structures to analysis of energy flows within the United States economy. Using the computer facilities of the University's Center for Advanced Computation, where he now teaches, he and his associates have developed a detailed input-output model that provides new insights into the role of energy in providing goods and services. He has consulted for a variety of corporate and public organizations on energy policy.

Hazel Henderson was born in Great Britain and educated there before coming to the United States, where she now works and lives. She is co-director, with Carter Henderson, of the Princeton Center for Alternative Futures, a think-tank and conference center that promotes exploration of alternatives for the industrialized world in an age of increasing planetary interdependence. Hazel Henderson does not fit neatly into any disciplinary pigeonhole; her professional role is that of gadfly to the establishment and organizer of new agencies designed to influence federal policy at the interface of economics, environment, and social policy. She sits on the advisory boards of at least ten organizations, many of which she helped found—for example, the National Council for Public Assessment of Technology and Environmentalists for Full Employment. She consults, writes, and lectures in a great variety of geographic and topical areas.

Jean Houston, Ph.D., is a pioneer in the exploration and development of human potentials and in the study of human consciousness. As Director of the Foundation for Mind Research, she has pursued extensive non-drug studies of altered states of consciousness, accelerated mental processes, time distortion, bio-feedback training, the psychology of creative processes, and the laboratory study of religious and peak experiences. She has co-authored several books, including *Mind Games*, and has taught religion, psychology, and philosophy at Columbia, Hunter, The New School for Social Research, and Marymount College.

Jacob K. Javits, senior United States Senator from New York, is now in his fourth Senate term and his thirtieth consecutive year in elective office. Educated in New York City's public schools, Javits attended night classes at Columbia and graduated from NYU Law School in 1926. Some of his major legislative interests in his twenty-one years in the Senate have included foreign economic policy, public service programs, retirement plans, and community daycare. His advocacy of national planning led to his coauthorship with Senator Hubert Humphrey of the Balanced Growth and Economic Planning Act in 1975.

Maurice LaMontagne was a professor of economics at Ottawa University when, in 1958, he became Economic Advisor to Canadian Prime Minister Lester Pearson. Elected a Member of Parliament in 1963, he also became a Cabinet Minister in the Pearson government and President of the Queen's Privy Council for Canada. In 1964 he was appointed Secretary of State, and, in 1967, he was named a Senator. He holds an M.A. in Economics from Harvard as well as several honorary degrees, and is a member of the Club of Rome in Canada.

Amory Lovins studied physics at Harvard and Oxford before becoming the British representative of Friends of the Earth. He travels extensively to "pollinate the international energy grapevine," to stay abreast of technical and political developments influencing energy development, and to debate the proponents of nuclear-powered or large-scale energy systems. He has testified before numerous legislative assemblies and consulted for more than a dozen corporate, federal, and international organizations. His numerous books and articles deal with land use controls, mining regulation, global limits to growth, nuclear power, and alternative energy strategies. He spends each summer in New England hiking and photographing the various moods of the region's many mountains.

Dr. Samuel Mauch, a citizen of Switzerland, received his Ph.D. from the Massachusetts Institute of Technology in civil engineering. A year spent at M.I.T. as a visiting faculty member in 1970–1971 brought him into contact with the team engaged in the early phases of the Club of Rome's project on limits to growth. That gave him an interest in the distant future, and he returned to Switzerland to head up an industrial long-range planning group. He worked with Dr. Joan Davis for four years as coordinator of an interuniversity research project on socioeconomic development, technology, and the environment in Switzerland.

Donella Meadows was a biophysicist at Harvard in 1970 when the opportunity to work on the first Club of Rome project at M.I.T. led her away from basic research. She developed the population sector of the project's global simulation model and was the principal author of *The Limits to Growth*. Now she is on the faculty of Dartmouth's Environmental Studies Program where she teaches policy analysis and conducts research on modeling methodologies and population-resource interactions. Her paper, "The World Food Problem: Growth Models and Non-Growth Solutions," was originally prepared in response to the United States Department of State's request for a study of the foreign policy concerns likely to command attention over the next five years.

John Tanton is an ophthalmologist in the north Michigan town of Petoskey. His involvement in a variety of natural history groups in his state finally led him to a strong interest in population growth. He worked initially with regional family-planning groups and then became associated with a prominent United States organization called Zero Population Growth, assuming its national presidency in 1975. He chaired the ZPG Immigration Study Committee from 1973 to 1975. His research in that capacity led to the paper printed here.

John Todd was a marine biologist at the Woods Hole Oceanographic Institution when, in 1969, he became interested in the prospects of combining ecology with engineering and psychology with management science to design habitations that integrate productive systems for food, shelter, and energy. He helped found and now directs the New Alchemy Institute. Todd is a dreamer who dares conceive of a society in which individuals decrease their material wants and increase their responsibility for the vital services needed to ensure a humane and secure life. But he follows up his dreams with experimentation, sophisticated engineering, and a canny sense of what is economically and socially viable in today's world. New Alchemy structures are already operating at several locations in the United States and abroad.

Contributions to the Conference

LIMITS TO GROWTH '75:

First Biennial Assessment of Alternatives to Growth

The Woodlands, Texas October 19–21, 1975

October 19

Philip G. Hoffman—President, University of Houston
Welcome Address

Sicco Mansholt—Former President, European Common Market
"Limits to Growth '75, an International Perspective"

Dennis L. Meadows—Director, Research Program on Technology and Public Policy, Dartmouth College
Conference Overview

October 20

Jay W. Forrester—Germeshausen Professor, Massachusetts Institute of Technology
"New Relationships Shaping Economic Growth for the Next 30 Years"

Gordon J. MacDonald—Chairman, National Academy of Sciences Commission on Natural Resources, former member of the President's Council on Environmental Quality
"The Failure of Technology to Overcome the Limits to Growth—A Case Study"

Yujiro Hayashi—Director, Institute for Future Technology, Tokyo, Japan
"The Conditions for Shaping the Mature Society in Japan"

Lester Brown—President, World Watch Institute
"Gaining Ground"

Hans Linnemann—Economist and Director, Club of Rome Project on Feeding the World's Population
"A Plan to Feed the Next Population Doubling"

Jahangir Amuzegar—Ambassador-at-large and Chief of the Iranian Economic Mission
"The Role of the Middle East"

Amory Lovins—Consultant, United Nations Environmental Program and Friends of the Earth
"The Technical and Ethical Case for Concern Over Growth in Energy Production"

Alvin F. Hildebrandt—Director, Solar Energy Laboratory, University of Houston
"The Solar Role in Energy Production"

William Olphuls—Author, political commentator
"The Political Implications of Sustained Growth"

Donald N. Michaels—Professor of Organization Behavior, University of Michigan
"Planning to Learn and Learning to Plan"

Carl H. Madden—Chief Economist, Chamber of Commerce of the U.S.
"Management in an Era of Changing Values"

Donella Meadows—Professor of Environmental Studies, Dartmouth College
"The Trade-Off Between Agricultural Growth and Equity in the Third World"

Mabub el Haq—Former Pakistani Minister for Planning and Development
"Economic Growth and the Needs of the Third World"

Jean Houston—Director, Foundation for Mind Research
"Growth, Change, and Psychological Alienation"

Robert Theobald—Author, lecturer, consultant
"We Can Choose the Future We Desire"

Herman Kahn—Founding Director, The Hudson Institute

"Growth is Good for You"

<u>*October 21*</u>

Fletcher L. Byrom—Chairman of the Board and Chief Executive Officer, The Koppers Company, Pittsburgh, Pennsylvania

"Corporate Policy in a Finite World"

E.F. Schumacher—British Economist and author

"Small Is Beautiful"

John Todd—Director, New Alchemy Institute

"Personalized Agriculture"

James G. Horsfall—Principal author, 1967 Report to the President on global food problems and the 1975 National Academy of Sciences' report on agriculture

"Perspective on Agriculture's Future—Rising Costs, Rising Doubts"

Elise Boulding—Professor of Sociology, University of Colorado

"Education for Life in the Steady State"

Lewis J. Perelman—Consultant

"The Implications of Limits to Growth for Education"

James Steven Turner—Consumer advocate

"The Consumer's Role in Limits to Growth"

Jacob K. Javits—United States Senator from New York

"Growth and the Importance of Long-Range Federal Planning"

Maurice LaMontagne—Canadian Senator

"The Conflict Between Frequent Elections and Distant Goals"

Philippe Deseynes—Senior Special Fellow, United Nations Institute for Training and Research

"Implications of Limits to Growth for the U.N."

Bruno Fritsch—Director, Institute for Economics Research, Swiss Federation of Institutes of Technology

"International Consequences of Restricting Growth"

Herman E. Daly—Professor of Economics, Louisiana State University
"Institutions for a Steady State Economy"

Hazel Henderson—Co-Director, The Princeton Center for Alternative Futures, Inc.
"Beyond Economics: Energetics and the Conceptual Limits to Quantitative Methodology"

Ian McHarg—Chairman, Department of Landscape Architecture, University of Pennsylvania
"Ecological Inventory and Invention"

Edward Goldsmith—Editor, *The Ecologist*
"Decentralization of Processes and Settlements"

Related Publications

Robert Allen

The Paradise Paradox (London: Penguin Books, in press).

Elise Boulding

"The Child and Nonviolent Social Change," in Christoph Wulf (ed.) *Handbook on Peace Education* (Oslo: International Peace Research Association, 1974), pp. 101–32.

"Alternative Capabilities for World Problem Solving," *International Studies Notes* 2, 3 (Spring 1976).

The Underside of History: A View of Women Through Time (Boulder, CO: Westview Press, 1976).

"Disarmed World: Problems in Imaging the Future," *Journal of Sociology*, in press.

Herman Daly

Toward a Steady-State Economy (ed.) (San Francisco: W.H. Freeman, 1973).

"The Developing Economies and the Steady-State," *The Developing Economies* (Tokyo: April 1976).

Joan Davis

"Energy Limits to Technical Recycling," *CRE* 1 (Montreux, Switzerland: 1975).

Earl Finkler

Nongrowth Planning Strategies, with David Peterson (New York: Praeger, 1974).

Urban Nongrowth: City Planning for People, with William J. Toner and Frank J. Popper (New York: Praeger, 1976).

Jay W. Forrester

Urban Dynamics (Cambridge, Mass.: M.I.T. Press, 1969).

World Dynamics (Cambridge, Mass.: M.I.T. Press, 1971).

Collected Papers (Cambridge, Mass.: M.I.T. Press, 1975).

Edward Goldsmith

A Blueprint for Survival (London: Tom Stacey Ltd., 1972).

"The Future of an Affluent Society: The Case of Canada," *The Ecologist* 7 (1977).

"De-industrialising Society," *The Ecologist* 7 (1977).

Bruce Hannon

"An Energy Standard of Value," *The Annals of the American Academy of Political and Social Science* 410 (November 1973), pp. 139–53.

"Options for Energy Conservation," *Technology Review* 76, 4 (February 1974) : 24–31.

"An Employment, Pollution, and Energy Model," with Hugh Folk, *Energy* (Cambridge, Mass.: M.I.T. Press, 1974), pp. 159–74.

Hazel Henderson

"The Limits of Traditional Economics: New Models for Managing a Steady State Economy," *Financial Analysts Journal* (May/June 1973).

"Ecologists Versus Economists," *Harvard Business Review* (July/August 1973).

"Organizational Future Shock," *Management Review* (July 1976).

"Inflation: The View From Beyond Economics," *Planning Review* (December 1976).

Jean Houston

The Varieties of Psychedelic Experience, with Robert Masters (New York: Holt, Rinehart, and Winston, 1966).

Mind Games, with Robert Masters (New York: Delta, 1973).

Psychophysical Education, with Robert Masters (New York: Holt, Rinehart, and Winston, 1977).

New Ways of Being, with Robert Masters (New York: The Viking Press, in preparation).

Jacob Javits

Order of Battle: A Republican's Call to Reason (New York: Atheneum Publishers, 1964).

Maurice LaMontagne

"Government and Research" (Canadian Political Science Association, June 4, 1970).

"La société d'abondance et de technostructure," *Caisses Populaires Desjardins* (1970).

Amory Lovins

World Energy Strategies: Facts, Issues, and Options (Cambridge, Mass.: Ballinger Books/Friends of the Earth, 1975).

Non-Nuclear Futures: The Case for an Ethical Energy Strategy (Cambridge, Mass.: Ballinger Books/Friends of the Earth, 1975).

Soft Energy Paths: Toward a Durable Peace (Cambridge, Mass.: Ballinger Books/Friends of the Earth, 1977).

Samuel Mauch

"On a hierarchical model of the planning process," *Town Planning Review* (January 1973).

"Regional Residuals Environmental Quality Management Modeling RREQMM): Criteria for an Optimal Planning Effort in the Real World," *Journal of Environmental Management* 4 (July 1976).

Donella H. Meadows

The Limits to Growth, with Dennis L. Meadows, Jørgen Randers, and William W. Behrens III (New York: Universe Books, 1972).

Toward Global Equilibrium, with Dennis L. Meadows (eds.) (Cambridge, Mass.: Wright-Allen Press, 1973).

The Dynamics of Growth in a Finite World, with Dennis L. Meadows, William W. Behrens, Roger Naill, Jørgen Randers, and Eric K.O. Zahn (eds.) (Cambridge, Mass.: Wright-Allen Press, 1973).

John Tanton

"Immigration: An Illiberal Concern?" *Zero Population Growth National Reporter* 7, 3 (April 1975) : 4.

Recommendations for a New Immigration Policy for the U.S., Zero Population Growth, 1346 Connecticut Avenue, Washington, D.C. 20036 (1975).

John Todd

"An Ark for Prince Edward Island," *The Journal of the New Alchemists* 3 (1976).

"A Modest Proposal," in Robin Clarke (ed.), *Notes for the Future* (New York: Universe Books, 1976).

"The Dilemma Beyond Tomorrow," *The Journal of the New Alchemists* 2 (1976).